CENTERING
ANISHINAABEG
STUDIES

AMERICAN INDIAN STUDIES SERIES

Gordon Henry, Series Editor

Editorial Board

Kimberly Blaeser

Joseph Bruchac

Heid Erdrich

Matthew Fletcher

P. Jane Hafen

Winona LaDuke

Patrick Lebeau

Michael Wilson

CENTERING ANISHINAABEG STUDIES

Understanding the World through Stories

Edited by Jill Doerfler,
Niigaanwewidam James Sinclair,
and Heidi Kiiwetinepinesiik Stark

Michigan State University Press   &   University of Manitoba Press
East Lansing   Winnipeg

∞ The paper used in this publication meets the minimum requirements of
ANSI/NISO Z39.48-1992 (R 1997) (Permanence of Paper).

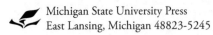 Michigan State University Press
East Lansing, Michigan 48823-5245

Printed and bound in the United States of America.

19 18 17 16 15 14 13   1 2 3 4 5 6 7 8 9 10

LIBRARY OF CONGRESS CATALOGING-IN-PUBLICATION DATA

Centering Anishinaabeg studies: understanding the world through stories / edited by
Jill Doerfler, Niigaanwewidam James Sinclair, and Heidi Kiiwetinepinesiik Stark.
    p. cm. — (American Indian studies series)

    ISBN 978-1-60917-353-1 (ebook) — ISBN 978-1-61186-067-2 (print : alk. paper)

1. American literature—Indian authors. 2. Ojibwa Indians—Literary collections. 3.
Ojibwa Indians—History. 4. Ojibwa Indians—Conduct of life. 5. Ojibwa Indians—Social
life and customs. I. Doerfler, Jill. II. Sinclair, Niigaanwewidam James. III. Stark, Heidi
Kiiwetinepinesiik.

    PS508.I5C46 2013
    810.8'08973—dc23   2012028340

LIBRARY AND ARCHIVES CANADA CATALOGUING IN PUBLICATION

Centering Anishinaabeg studies : understanding the world through stories / edited by
Jill Doerfler, Niigaanwewidam James Sinclair, and Heidi Kiiwetinepinesiik Stark.
Includes bibliographical references and index.
Co-published by: Michigan State University Press.

    ISBN 978-0-88755-761-3

1. American literature—Indian authors. 2. Ojibwa Indians—Literary collections. 3.
Ojibwa Indians—History. 4. Ojibwa Indians—Conduct of life. 5. Ojibwa Indians—Social
life and customs. I. Doerfler, Jill II. Sinclair, Niigaanwewidam James III. Stark, Heidi
Kiiwetinepinesiik

    PS508.I5C45 2013
    810.8'08973   C2012-905002-4

Book design by Scribe Inc. (www.scribenet.com)
Cover design by David Drummond, Salamander Design, www.salamanderhill.com
Cover art is *Sacred Otters with Children* © by the Estate of Norval Morrisseau, photo credit
Bockley Gallery. Used with permission. All rights reserved.

g green press INITIATIVE Michigan State University Press is a member of the Green Press Initiative and
is committed to developing and encouraging ecologically responsible publishing
practices. For more information about the Green Press Initiative and the use of recycled
paper in book publishing, please visit www.greenpressinitiative.org.

Visit Michigan State University Press at www.msupress.org

Contents

Maajitaadaa
Nanaboozhoo and the Flood, Part 2

JOHN BORROWS

Mewinzha Nanaboozhoo bimose noopiming.[1] This is how he got there. As usual he was very hungry. He also had a deadline, another writing assignment, but it was hard for him to concentrate. Hunger usually won out over work, and hunger was winning again. He wasn't making much progress on his preface. Despite all his good intentions, his computer screen was empty. Nanaboozhoo scolded his laptop for being so lame. He wanted it to write beautiful sentences and overwhelm people with his profound thoughts. In short, he wanted to show off. Unfortunately, not only was his computer being uncooperative, but his stomach kept distracting him too. He thought to himself, "*Nimbakade;* I'm hungry. I have to eat. Maybe I can find some food that will make me a great writer." Nanaboozhoo left his work in search of food.

As he was walking through the forest, Nanaboozhoo came upon a clearing. In the middle of a wide field was a building he had never before seen. It was made of wood, and was approximately eight feet tall and four feet wide. It had a new moon, *oshki-agoojin,* etched on the door.

Nanaboozhoo immediately hit the dirt. He crawled on his belly back into the woods. When he felt safe, at some distance beyond the field, he cautiously peered through the trees. He studied the new structure from different vantage points. He slowly made his way around the clearing, within the woods, examining the building from every angle. When he felt confident that no one was hiding behind the structure, Nanaboozhoo stood up and walked into the clearing. He called out: *Awiya na ayaa? Indaa-minwendaan igo miijim.* I'd like some food. *Awegonen dino wiyaas eyaaman?* What kind of meat do you have?

There was no answer. Nanaboozhoo listened for a long time. He grew more curious. He circled the clearing once again—this time in plain view of the tall, yet tiny house. When he finished circumnavigating the field, he again called out the same questions. As before, there was no answer.

He was now intrigued by the mysterious building. Nanaboozhoo circled the field a third time, walking halfway between the tree line and the small house. Upon completing this third round, Nanaboozhoo's calls once again met with no reply.

Nanaboozhoo grew bold. He walked right up to the front door of the house. He knocked. There was no answer. He pulled firmly at the handle and the door easily swung open, almost knocking him over. He stepped back and hid behind the door, warily peering inside. As his eyes adjusted to the inner darkness, Nanaboozhoo spied a bench within the structure, raised about two feet off the floor, taking up most of the space. His eyes were soon drawn to a dark hole in the center of the bench. It looked promising. But Nanaboozhoo knew from experience that he often lived to regret his curiosity, so he grew suspicious. He shut the door and walked back into the woods. He went searching for help in his quest for food.

He was quickly rewarded. Just within the edge of the forest, Nanaboozhoo encountered a lynx, fish, and bear, sitting around some papers, shuffling and rustling their leaves. They were eagerly passing them back and forth. The three didn't notice their new visitor, they were so intent on their work. Clearing his throat, Nanaboozhoo briefly interrupted their trance-like focus: "*Boozhyou*," he said. The three young ones barely looked up from their work. They said, almost as if speaking to the air, "We're writing a book and we need help. Do you know who might help?"

Nanaboozhoo thought for a moment as the three continued their work. They didn't seem to recognize him. Seeing their intensity, a thought occurred to him. He replied, "I think I *can* help. I know just the place to look." Nanaboozhoo was thinking that these three might help him discover whether any food was inside the building back in the field. He said, "*Ambe.* Come on. You really need to see something."

With eagerness, the three gathered their papers and followed in Nanaboozhoo's shadow, making their way towards the field. Emboldened by his earlier explorations, Nanaboozhoo walked straight towards the tiny new house. He opened the door and pointed to the center. "Help is right in here," he said, pointing towards the hole in the middle of the bench. "I think I overheard you talking about centering Anishinaabeg Studies. This is the center."

The four of them crowded into the building and peered down the hole. Just at that moment, a large wind blew across the clearing. The door slammed shut behind them and Nanaboozhoo lost his balance. He tried to steady himself, but in grabbing onto his companions, he only managed to destabilize them too. They lurched forward, tipped suddenly, and found themselves falling headlong down the hole.

They fell for a long time.

Below them was the deepest darkness.

Above them was the ever-decreasing-in-size hole, through which a small amount of light poured. It was like a hole in the sky, *bagone-ghezhisk*.

They fell so long that the four of them eventually fell asleep: *giikiiban-gooshi*. They dreamed the dream of life. They only woke when Nanabush called out from his sleep, "*Wiidookawishin*," at which point a giant turtle rose out of the sludge just below them.

Slamming down onto the turtle's back, the four immediately stirred. They seemed to be floating on a vast, sludge-like sea.

"I think I've been here before," said Nanaboozhoo.

"What's that smell?" said the lynx.

"It's awful," said the bear.

The four stood up and huddled on the middle of the turtle's back. Light poured down on them from the hole in the sky, but it was hard to see anything beyond the turtle and the brown, lumpy surface of the sea.

The fish said, "I don't think that's water."

Nanaboozhoo looked around him. "Hmmmnnn, this is all vaguely familiar, but something's different too." Poring through the recesses of his mind, he thought aloud, "There might be something below all this mess. Does anyone here want to volunteer for a dive, to see if you can find something solid beneath us?"

Lynx looked at fish, who then looked at bear, who shrugged her shoulders.

Nanaboozhoo continued, "I'm sure you'll find what you're looking for down there. You'll probably find many categories of stories that begin with the letter 'R.' It's all very clever. There will be all sorts of stories as roots, relationships, revelations, resiliency, resistance, reclamation and reflection. I'm sure they'll be lying there in seven layers, just like I listed them, because that's our way, you know?"

Nanaboozhoo's three companions looked at Nanaboozhoo, and again looked at the sludge surrounding them. They clung even more tightly to one another.

The turtle, with his nose barely above the water-like line said, "Don't take all day up there. I can't tread this stuff forever you know."

Sensing his companions' hesitancy to explore the world below, and taking the turtle's warning to heart, Nanaboozhoo looked up, searching for other alternatives to deal with their predicament.

Just at that moment the sky darkened, and a great thunder rolled across the upper world.

Lynx, fish, and bear also cast their eyes aloft and saw the hole in the sky close.

"Whew! *Chi-boogidit*," came a distant voice from above.

As the hole in the day eventually became visible once again, the four companions saw some papers floating towards them, also falling through the sky.

After what seemed like an eternity, the leaves eventually settled around them.

They stooped and gathered those closest to them. They struggled in the dim light to read what was etched on them.

Bear intoned, "I think this says, 'Anishinaabeg stories are roots; they are both the origins and the imaginings of what it means to be a participant in an ever-changing and vibrant culture in humanity. In the same vein, stories can serve as a foundation and framework for the field of Anishinaabeg Studies, providing both a methodological and theoretical approach to our scholarship. They embody ideas and systems that form the basis for law, values, and community. Stories are rich and complex creations that allow for the growth and vitality of diverse and disparate ways of understanding the world.'"

"That's profound," Lynx said. "We could use that for our book."

"I'm not sure," said Fish. "It's kinda wordy—don't you think."

"No, it has tenure written all over it," said Bear.

As Bear finished her thought, the sky once again darkened. Glancing upward she saw what looked like the end of the world. This time a storm of tremendous fury was unleashed. Blasts of light and darkness spewed from the hole in the day, flooding their world in sound. With each grand reverberation, flashes of paper streamed through the sky. Each volley sent sheets of white rushing and surging through the aperture above. Papers again began to fall, cascading through the upper reaches of their realm. With great force, the papers soon settled in layers around them, as deep as the thickest of winter snows.

After what seemed like an eternity, with the forces of air and sound competing for supremacy, the storm eventually subsided. Nanaboozhoo, Lynx, Fish, and Bear, who had taken shelter beneath the drifts of white, slowly began digging themselves out.

When they emerged, the world seemed pristine and clear. White, crisp, and clean lines stretched from horizon to horizon, as far as the eye could see. The papers reflected the light from the now-clear hole in the day above, giving the ground beneath them a bright, shimmering glow. It was as if the world was new once again, reclaimed from its toxic state.

The animal trio began reading the words on the pages around them. As they did so, Lynx began chronicling the titles they encountered on each folio: "Is That All There Is?," "*Name*," "Comets of Knowledge," "Companionship with Stories in Anishinaabeg Studies," "Storying Ourselves into Life," "Teaching as Story," "Every Dream Is a Prophecy," "A Conversation with Gerald Vizenor," "And the Easter Bunny Dies," "A Philosophy for Living," "Indian Culture and Tribal Law," "Will Mishipizhu Survive Climate Change, or Is He Creating It?," "Wild Rice Rights," "Transforming the Trickster," "Theorizing Resurgence from within Nishnaabeg Thought," "Story as Process and Principle in Twenty-first Century Anishinaabeg Painting," "Stories as *Mshkiki*," "The Visual/Performative Storytelling of Three Anishinaabeg Artists," "Anishinaabeg Studies: Creative, Critical, Ethical, and Reflexive," "Reorienting the Legal and Political Events of the Anishinaabeg," "Stories and Reflections from Neyaashiinigiming."

Listening to these titles, Nanaboozhoo sat down in the midst of the papers surrounding him. His stomach growled in hunger. He looked at Lynx, Fish, and Bear, once again huddled together, just as they had been earlier when he met them in the forest above. The three excitedly conferred with one another about each chapter, and what they were learning as they read. Naboozhoo heard Bear say, "Now this is what it means to center Anishinaabeg Studies. When the world is covered with our knowledge, we will again find our roots, build healthy relationships, receive new revelations, meet our tests with resilience, effectively resist those who seek to oppress us, reclaim our presence within creation, and reflect our dynamic cultures with all humanity."

Listening to them speak, Nanaboozhoo had to admit he was more than a little impressed too. As a practitioner of Indigenous law, he had long known that what flowed from the bench above created fertile ground. Nanaboozhoo only hoped others would see how deep this work could take them.

Centering Anishinaabeg Studies was an excellent book. He wanted everyone to read it. This book contained the best collection of articles on Anishinaabeg Studies he had ever encountered. It showcases the thoughts of some of the most interesting Anishinaabeg writers living today. The editors of the book have done an excellent job of soliciting and organizing the material to provide maximum clarity and insight. As a result, readers of this book will learn why Anishinaabeg stories have the potential to transform how we relate to the world; they will more clearly understand our place within our Anishinaabe-akiing. The work is brimming with creativity and overflowing with ideas. It opens up a great space for critique and learning: *michi-daawadanaa*. Contemplating these thoughts made Nanaboozhoo happy. Even though he was still hungry, at least he now had some ideas about how to finish his preface.

NOTE

1. In addition to the excellent articles and stories in this book, further inspiration for this preface is drawn from Basil Johnston, *Ojibway Heritage* (Toronto: McClelland and Stewart, 1976), 14–16; Basil Johnston, *Honour Mother Earth: Mino-audiaduah Mizzu-Kummik-Quae* (Cape Croker, ON: Kegedonce Press, 2003), 4–9; "Our Ancestry Is of the Sky," in Basil Johnston, *Think Indian: Languages Are Beyond Price* (Cape Croker, ON: Kegedonce Press, 2011), 6–14; "Moowis," in *Schoolcraft's Ojibwe Lodge Stories*, ed. Philip P. Mason (East Lansing: Michigan State University Press, 1997), 56–57; Anna C. Gibbs, "Gaag Miiniwaa Wiikehn," in *Oshkaabewis Native Journal* 7 (2010): 24–27.

Bagijige
Making an Offering

JILL DOERFLER,
NIIGAANWEWIDAM JAMES SINCLAIR,
AND HEIDI KIIWETINEPINESIIK STARK

In Anishinaabe tradition, an offering is a gift. It's a gesture of relationship between people, animals, spirits, and other entities in the universe, given in the interests of creating ties, honoring them, or asking for assistance and direction. Offerings are acts of responsibility. Making one includes acknowledging value, promising respect, and affirming the presence of another being. They carry duties matched only by the acceptance of the offer, forming what is hoped to be a mutually beneficial partnership, not only for participants, but for the universe around them.

For most Anishinaabeg, offerings are the currency of life; they constitute ties that form a network of Creation. They can take many forms, from *asemaa* (tobacco) to *nagamowin* (songs) to *zhooniyaa* (money). Food is an offering. A story can be an offering. Knowledge can be an offering. One can witness hundreds of examples of offerings in ceremony—ceremonies are indeed offerings unto themselves—but there are many other places these can be given too. Offerings can be made a single time, over a set amount of time, or consist of multiple components over a long period of time, even in perpetuity. Offerings can be given by individuals, a family, a clan, or an entire community—depending on the demands and constant changes in any relationship. In Anishinaabemowin, the word for an offering is *bagijigan* (plural: *bagijiganan*), and the act of making an offering is *bagijige*. This collection, and the many words and ideas that constitute it, is an offering. It is a gift that hopes to engage, affirm, and inspire relationships with all who read it. It is also a gesture towards future offerings.

The idea to create *Centering Anishinaabeg Studies: Understanding the World through Stories* came about at the American Indian and Indigenous Studies conference in 2008 at the University of Georgia (the organization is now known as the Native American and Indigenous Studies Association, or NAISA). This should come as little surprise as what are conferences if not a collection of people coming together to share stories? NAISA embodies the notion of offerings: bringing scholars together to explore our relationships to one another and to share our stories. In Georgia, the three of us discussed how we often felt that many conferences we'd attended had primarily focused on history, anthropology, literature, or another epistemological divide—with not a lot of engagement across the disciplines. NAISA broke down this barrier and allowed us the opportunity to become aware that there were many scholars working on related issues, using similar methodological approaches. Both during formal presentations and in informal conversations, we observed that many of our colleagues were using stories as a kind of methodology or center point. We noticed that stories—in their broadest sense—were being used as theoretical frameworks guiding questions in law, history, anthropology, environmental studies, and other fields. This was particularly evident among scholars working in Anishinaabeg Studies, many of whom were exploring issues and interests of their own communities. Then, when we reflected upon the traditional and contemporary practices of our home communities and cultures, and those of our relations, it occurred to us that stories were operating as different entryways, foundations, beginning points—as centers—to Anishinaabeg Studies. We explored the notion further and came up with the idea for this collection.

We were also inspired by how vast our storied community of Anishinaabeg scholars had grown, from our critical and creative ancestors from ancient times to the vast body of new work produced over the past few decades. Much scholarship produced by Anishinaabeg (and cited within this collection) could be argued as different embodiments of the idea that Anishinaabeg Studies resides in and through Anishinaabeg stories—past, present, and future. As before, Anishinaabeg are examining our community's offerings, adding perspectives and ideas, and making new stories in the interests of carrying forward an intellectual and collective future. While a tribally centered field—but not altogether different and separate from studies privileging theories of pan-Indianism, hybridity, and transnationalism—Anishinaabeg-centered scholarship emerging from an examination of Anishinaabeg stories represents some of the most innovative and exciting work being produced today. Most often locally focused and interested in specific issues surrounding Anishinaabeg expressions, lands, resources, cultures, and communities, Anishinaabeg scholars offer a different way of viewing the world that does not narrow intellectual approaches but open them up, constituting a sort of global studies. It is in these interests that we hope this collection offers a perspective of what Anishinaabeg Studies has been, what it is, what it can be, while at the same time encouraging others in their own conclusions about its possibilities. In the end, that's the power of the Anishinaabeg stories—and we and our colleagues hope that this book is an inspiration for others. As our colleague Gerald Vizenor once remarked in an interview: "You can't understand the world without telling a story. There isn't any center to the world but story."

The Anishinaabe span a vast geographic region from the Great Lakes to the Plains and also reside in other urban and rural communities throughout North America. Historically and today, the Anishinaabe are a people who share many beliefs and practices, yet individual bands are influenced by their particular histories, geographic locations, political relationships, and internal conflicts. There are therefore many ways Anishinaabeg speakers and thinkers use the term "Anishinaabe." For example, it's a word that also exists as Anishnawbe, Anishinape, Anicinape, Neshnabé, Nishnaabe, Nishnawbe, Anishinaubae, and Nishinabe—just to name a few. Each lives in a locality, history, and context that can open up entire discourses. What brings these terms together, however, are the similarities, connections, and overwhelming number of ties that emerge when they are considered in relationship. Like strands and points of an interconnected web, these specific and shared names are what communities known now as Ojibwa, Ojibwe, Chippewa, Ojibway, Saulteaux, Mississauga, Nipissing, Potawatomi, and Odawa (and others) use to describe *themselves.* Each different incarnation of Anishinaabe shapes a connection, defines a relationship, and is an offering to a multiply defined whole. There are, of course, lots of definitions and interpretations of these names, but we like Basil Johnston's description in "Is That All There Is? Tribal Literature," when he describes "Anishinaubae" as both a noun and a verb—something that *we are* and *we do* at the same time. Complexity is the tenet perhaps most evident and unifying in Anishinaabeg life, culture, and nationhood. Just as there are many distinct definitions of Anishinaabeg, we are still connected. What connects us, as we see it, are stories.

In Anishinaabemowin, two words are predominantly used to describe, and sometimes classify, narrative. While there are many ways these terms are explained and defined, *Aadizookaanag* are generally considered "traditional" or "sacred" narratives that embody values, philosophies, and laws important to life. They are also *manidoog* (manitous), living beings who work with Anishinaabeg in the interests of demonstrating principles necessary for *mino-bimaadiziwin*, that good and beautiful life. These stories are most often classified as animate in Anishinaabemowin. *Dibaajimowinan*, another word used to describe narratives, is generally translated to mean "histories" and "news." They range in time from long ago to today, and often tell of family genealogies, geographies, and historical experiences. They are often classified as inanimate in Anishinaabemowin. There are, of course, exceptions in both cases and many blurry lines in these groupings. In this collection, Leanne Simpson refers to these two types of stories as interrelated forces, echoes, and parts of a greater whole—a wonderful way to conceive of both.

To illustrate this for a moment, take the Anishinaabeg Creation Story, which tells of our creation, time on Turtle Island, migration from the east, and path into the future. It is made up of a vast collection of stories that embody history, law, and many experiences and perspectives. These live, change, and grow through continuous retellings, constituting a dynamic narrative practice and process by a people. It is often said that there are as many versions of the Creation Story as there are storytellers—all contribute to understandings of who we are. The Creation Story therefore is both *aadizookaanag* and *dibaajimowin*. Both concepts are necessary parts of Anishinaabeg narrative tradition. Together they are like maps, or perhaps instructions, that teach us how to navigate the past, present, and future. They tell about the past, but at the same time inform our present and guide our future. *Aadizookaanag* and *dibaajimowinan* are ultimately about creation and re-creation. We believe that all of our stories include and encompass senses of *aadizookaanag* and *dibaajimowinan* and together form a great Anishinaabeg storytelling tradition.

INITIATING A DIALOGUE

Centering Anishinaabeg Studies is a collection of offerings. We seek to engage in an open dialogue about the multifarious and vast opportunities that stories afford us in the ongoing development of the field of Anishinaabeg Studies. In this spirit, the next segment of our introduction emerges out of a conversation we recorded on Friday, November 10, 2010, in Duluth, Minnesota. Edited for conciseness and focus, it best expresses the inspiration, influences, and goals for the collection.

Heidi Kiiwetinepinesiik Stark (HKS): This book emerges out of interests to honor and contribute to our diverse and complex collectivity. We want this book to be thought of not as an authoritative guide defining Anishinaabeg Studies, but a vision, *a community of voices*, about our field. This collection not only comes out of a long Anishinaabe tradition of storytelling, but it is also part of a larger conversation across Anishinaabeg geographies, histories, and communities. *Centering Anishinaabeg Studies* is one step along a long, intellectual, and storied path of our people. We look forward to, and want to encourage, the development of more voices, more ideas, more discussion.

Jill Doerfler (JD): Indeed. So many Anishinaabeg have thought deeply about stories, and we have lots of different perspectives. For example, Basil Johnston argues in *Ojibway Heritage* that "It's through story, fable, legend, and myth that fundamental understandings, insights, and attitudes toward life and human conduct and quality and their diverse life forms are embodied and passed on." Gordon Henry Jr., on the other hand, writes in the introduction to *Stories through Theories, Theories through Stories* that "Stories seem to transcend jurisdictions of nation, culture, time, and text irrespective of whether they are spoken, written, heard, smelled, filmed, or performed." I envision an Anishinaabeg understanding of story that includes diverse points of view.

Niigaanwewidam James Sinclair (NJS): So do I. I think of the contrast between David Treuer, who in *Native American Fiction: A User's Guide* argues that looking for culture within stories ossifies that culture, and Patronella Johnston, who in *Tales of Nokomis* documents stories she heard in her community because she wanted to maintain culturally specific teachings and values that she saw threatened by colonialism. Stories imagine, construct, and unify communities, but they can also deconstruct, destroy, and divide them. Stories have abilities to do all sorts of things, sometimes all at the same time. Thinking of all of these as part of a whole was the challenge set before us as we created our call for papers.

JD: I'd also like to acknowledge that this book emerges out of a long intellectual history. Anishinaabe writers produced and published one of the largest bodies of American Indian narratives during the first half of the nineteenth century. I am so proud of the work done by George Copway, Jane Johnston Schoolcraft, and William Warren. Learning about these early writers helped me to understand that writing is very much a part of Anishinaabe tradition.

NJS: Contemporary collections like Gerald Vizenor's *Touchwood* and Kimberly Blaeser's *Stories Migrating Home* remind us that our work emerges from some pretty significant footprints. We have a lot of intellectual ancestors, predecessors, and contemporaries.

HKS: We've already mentioned a few, and there are too many for us to list, but I have to mention the important work that has been done by Maude Kegg, Michael Witgen, Jim Northrup, Dale Turner, Kateri Akiwenzie-Damm,

Brenda Child, Rebecca Kugel, and Anton Treuer. I also want to acknowledge our ancestors who told our stories to anthropologists and others to record, which led to a large collection of published work. For example, *Ojibwa Texts*, recorded by William Jones at the beginning of the nineteenth century. I believe that our ancestors shared these stories in the hope that future generations would look to these rich sources for guidance and direction.

NJS: Anishinaabeg Studies has really been operating since time immemorial. Our communities have always been intellectual and philosophical, with stories and storytelling practices at the center of this endeavor. It doesn't seem to matter what activity—whether ceremonies, hunting trips, history sharing, medicine gathering, constitution writing, or cooking—there is a body of Anishinaabeg knowledge involving stories about it. If you look at anthropological and ethnographic studies, even from people whose conclusions are certainly debatable, stories come up time and time again as primary vessels of knowledge. For millennia our storytellers have assured our existences as speaking, thinking, creating, and struggling beings in this landscape. They've done this so we could be here now, doing this work.

HKS: Many theories have emerged from Anishinaabeg stories.

JD: And we could argue that stories are theories, to reference Gordon Henry Jr.'s title. Gerald Vizenor has been a real leader in this direction. There's a vast body of important work by Jace Weaver, A. LaVonne Ruoff, Deborah Madsen, and others that expound on Vizenor's stories/theories. So much of Vizenor's work has focused on challenging the idea of the *indian* and asserts that Natives are *postindians* who hold the power to create a new world. What I love most about Vizenor's writing is the way in which it creates openings and allows for imagination—it also has a focus on action, which is very empowering. It upsets and challenges in positive and productive ways; it's never fixed or static. Words carry the power of creation—we create ourselves with stories.

NJS: I've always been inspired by Louise Erdrich's work, which we all know also has wide popular appeal. She has been able to introduce many readers to the diversity and complexity of Anishinaabe life while embodying interesting themes and struggles, and doing it with a rich sense of humor. I really like the intricate connections and relationships between characters, families, and history in her texts. Her work reminds me of the multiple layering and changes many Anishinaabeg experience in our own families and lives.

HKS: John Borrows is another great Anishinaabe scholar; he believes in the ongoing process of story. In *Drawing Out Law*, he shows how stories emerge from everyday experiences, and how stories can be used to guide the contemporary creation of Indigenous law. He continually shows that Anishinaabeg storytelling is a theoretical process that hasn't ended for Anishinaabeg; it's an ongoing process. It makes me think of a quote by Amanda Cobb that I really love: "Sovereignty is both the story or journey itself and what we journey towards." Borrows's work reminds us that what it means to be Anishinaabeg is still being defined; it is still a journey, an ongoing process. We're not only telling the stories that we've carried for generations, but we're also being gifted with and creating new stories all the time.

NJS: We certainly are scholars in the early part of our careers, and following a trail set forth by a very rich intellectual Anishinaabeg ancestry. At the same time, we come from three different Anishinaabeg communities with very different historical experiences and knowledge keepers. Many of our contributors also come from radically different spaces and places from our own too. I wonder if we could say briefly what, in terms of our personal experience and community contexts—how the idea of *Centering Anishinaabeg Studies* was guided by our understandings of story.

HKS: Good point. A lot of my academic work has really been provoked, sustained, or answered by stories. Oftentimes I hear a story and I end up applying that story to certain questions I am thinking about in other contexts. When I was first interested in issues of treaty rights and questioned what Ojibwa concepts of nationhood and land rights were in the nineteenth century, it was only after I returned to stories that I came to understand the complexity of some of these questions. When studying Anishinaabemowin in college, I was struck by the relationship between language and stories. It is in the etymology and rich meanings in specific words that stories are embedded, and this helped me appreciate the multiple ways in which stories function, as well as their power to provoke. It's in the transmission of stories, from one person to another, that the *aadizookaan* or "spirit" of the story is recognized and uncovered—even if sometimes only partially. Stories, I believe, give us so much insight into how Anishinaabe people understand the world; they teach us how to see and understand and listen and learn, and then, finally, express ourselves.

JD: When I was doing my graduate work, I was looking at Anishinaabe identity within the legal context and how tribal citizenship came to be created and regulated. I was interested in how Anishinaabe people defined and asserted identity in other ways than those imposed upon them. So, I started looking to stories locally, to people from my home at White Earth—like Gerald Vizenor, Ignatia Broker, and Kim Blaeser—and I was amazed by the rich heritage of written literature we have, and how it shapes and informs identity. Of course, identity and citizenship are complex and controversial issues with a wide range of very diverse opinions, but what I've found is that stories do some of the hard work in finding fundamental values that can guide us. For instance, Gerald Vizenor's concept of survivance has been very useful for my work because it both embraces change and envisions continuance. Stories encourage listeners and readers to look inward to find plausible solutions. That's what I hope for the collection: that stories are understood as something continually applicable, not something stuck in the past. Also, contemporary stories are just as applicable and useful as "traditional" ones.

NJS: I grew up on the former St. Peter's Indian Settlement, sometimes called "Little Peguis." It is a community that was illegally and unjustly removed by the Canadian government in 1907 to benefit settlers in southern Manitoba. Over three-quarters of our community was forced to move several hundred miles north, to what is now known as Peguis Indian Reserve. Some of us stayed and squatted on land once our own, including members of my family. Growing up, I lived in a community enveloped by legacies of erasure. St. Peter's is a community with no "official" name, representation, and certainly without recognition by anyone outside of ourselves. We even struggle with our northern relations to recognize that we are a part of them. I learned about the history of St. Peter's not through books, classrooms, or in schools I attended, but in the stories I heard at the friendship center, bingo hall, and at family picnics. These were transformative; they were tales filled with anger, irony, and beauty. And, despite such violence in our history, lots of laughter. These, to me, embodied the ongoing spirit of my community: a place that continues because people simply refuse to stop telling stories. I've used this to guide my work and research. Anishinaabeg stories, to me, are about generation and regeneration.

HKS: I also see Anishinaabeg stories as methods that teach us how to survive in an ever-changing environment. There is so much change and adaption going on in many of these stories. The power of them reside in these abilities; they are the greatest tools our people have to survive and live.

NJS: We see in our contributions in this book many suggestions that Anishinaabeg stories are vessels of intellectual life. They are *methods*, to use Heidi's word. What are some that assisted in our editing and selection process in *Centering Anishinaabeg Studies*?

JD: The intellectual possibilities in Anishinaabeg stories, the methods, are endless. I find LeAnne Howe's concept of tribalography useful in encapsulating what I understand these to be. Tribalography is the idea that Native stories take all different forms and often combine aspects of history, memoir, law, and other things. Tribalography unseats history as this unbiased authority and allows us more control over our stories. It relates back to the idea of us creating our own past and our own future, and this idea that it isn't necessarily predetermined. Our lives aren't tragic victimization narratives. Stories provide us with infinite possibilities because we acknowledge that they have a creative aspect; they aren't lists of "facts."

HKS: Like Howe, Jean O'Brien disrupts previous understandings of history in her recent book *Firsting and Lasting*. She beautifully shows how history is collection of stories, both *real* and *imagined*, demonstrating how local historians were recording narratives that essentially wrote Indian people out of existence. They convinced themselves that authentic Indians no longer existed. These were the stories they told, that they wrote, that became history. I think in the same way we see so many scholars trying to get us to think broadly about the power and function of stories, we see scholars like O'Brien talking about how history is story. We can't take history at face value, as a kind of empirical, objective form of knowledge. Just like our examination of stories, these histories also convey certain kinds of values and ideas.

JD: Yes, regardless of the type of narrative, regardless of how we want to categorize it, there are always these embedded values. Jace Weaver has argued: "I do not believe that there is any scholarship that is value-neutral. All scholarship, every academically attested to 'fact,' serves some political agenda."

NJS: I think that the creation, maintenance, and continuation of relationships are the centers of Anishinaabeg Studies. Stories actualize the infinite connections that make up Anishinaabeg culture and community, not only individually and amongst our varied communities, but with non-Anishinaabeg, with animals and plants and manitous and *zhaaganashag* and all of creation. Stories are strands that connect Anishinaabeg with everything around us, across space, time, and geography. They are gifts. The act of storytelling is also imaginative: it's what our ancestors did not only to create relationships with the world around them, but because they envisioned us here and now and wished to have a relationship with us. In a similar vein, we tell stories now for people who are coming, Anishinaabe youth like my daughter, and her children and grandchildren. That's why this work, for me, is so important, because it has an opportunity to have a life, a role to play in continuing the lives of future Anishinaabeg. Storytelling is an intellectual act that is both an inheritance and a responsibility.

HKS: There is some recent debate amongst Anishinaabeg scholars about the ways in which knowledge embedded within Anishinaabeg stories can be applied to contemporary and critical issues facing Anishinaabeg communities. We should speak about the ways in which Anishinaabeg stories not only are things but *do things*, like provoke action, embody sovereignty, or structure social and political institutions. We've spoken about the definitions of Anishinaabe, but what do we think about this? Can Anishinaabeg stories address challenges facing Anishinaabeg communities like poverty and unemployment?

NJS: I got an example, but I warn you, I'm starting with a discussion I had on Facebook.

HKS: I'm really glad Facebook made it into these discussions. In the future, there will be a story called "When Nenaboozhoo Discovers Facebook."

JD: Wow, just imagine what a great story that will be.

NJS: So, one day, I posted as my status: "How do we create strong and healthy Anishinaabeg communities?" I got several interesting responses, but the most striking was from my Anishinaabemowin teacher who said: "Start with the Creation Story." I thought about what she meant—about all of the versions I have read, heard, and known. All of the answers, I realized, are in that story. There is this amazing version of the Creation Story by the painter Daphne Odjig in a mural standing in the Manitoba Museum in Winnipeg, Manitoba, Canada. It's called *The Creation of the World.* In that mural are teachings that educate about the history of the geography of Manitoba, of that territory being at the bottom of this great melting iceberg that created the Great Lake Agassiz (which encompassed much of North America). There are also stories in that mural about our responsibilities as Anishinaabeg and non-Anishinaabeg signatories to Treaty One. There are also stories about Anishinaabeg aesthetics, European surrealism and cubism, and intercultural negotiation. There are stories about Odjig's historical witnessing of the removal of the Chemawiwin Cree from their homelands when their lands were flooded for a governmental damming project, and what they did to re-create their lives. There are stories about our relationships with Naanaboozhoo and Aki, with muskrats and turtles, with spirits and humanity. There are prophecies in that mural. Every single real-life struggle encountered by Anishinaabeg in Manitoba (and elsewhere) is talked about in that version of the Creation Story—from colonization to poverty, to environmental degradation, to language revitalization. It's a remarkable work. Now, whenever I think about issues facing Anishinaabeg Studies, I go back to thinking about our Creation Story. And it all started from Facebook. [*laughing*]

HKS: These stories are about what it means to be Anishinaabe. In my own work looking at Anishinaabe conceptions of sovereignty, I argue that the word for sovereignty in Anishinaabemowin is *Anishinaabe.* Our stories tell us who we are as a people, as nations. They outline the relationships that we have, to one another, to our place, to people, to our experiences and our ancestors' experiences too. Stories can guide us, serve as a lens for us to understand our social and political structures. When we look to stories, we begin to not only have a richer understanding of the contemporary kind of social and legal traditions in operation today in Anishinaabe country, but also those that we're able to enact. I think it's in these rich stories then that we can also come to understand how we can build mutually beneficial and healthy relationships today. We have high suicide rates among our youth, high rates of domestic violence, and other issues because there is a real divide between the kinds of values and ideals conveyed in our stories and the kinds of actions playing out in Anishinaabe country today. By looking to these stories, we can understand not only how to survive, but also how to thrive.

NJS: There are many studies that conclude that youth who are exposed to Anishinaabeg language and literature—and gain pride in their cultural inheritances—also gain values of resilience and self-worth. These possibilities are available through Anishinaabeg stories.

HKS: I think so. It is said that the goal or function of Anishinaabe life is to understand our purpose in this world: *ando-bawaajigeyan*, seek your dream or purpose. I think a way for us to get at that, a way for us to leave our own footprints for others to step in and then extend their own, is through stories. And that's what I think is so rich about many of the stories cited by our contributors in this collection: that they recognize the relationships we have to one another and our own self. It's not about creating a kind of singular identity, a singular Anishinaabe.

There's a reason why storytellers will often not tell you what these stories mean, because the idea is that we'll bring our own interpretations and ideas and language, and that can lend insight into addressing the contemporary challenges facing our communities.

JD: Thinking about how stories can be used to address contemporary issues draws me back to the idea of nationhood and relationships. What I want to talk a little bit about is the writing of the White Earth Constitution in 2009. At one of the Constitutional Conventions I gave a presentation on the story of Shingebiss and how we might apply the principles of perseverance and autonomy in that story to constitutional reform. I argued that we could use Shingebiss as a model for our actions. So that story of Shingebiss is embedded in our story of constitutional reform. The political document we developed is, in some ways, a creation story. We discussed how we could make the document reflect our values, our rights, and our responsibilities. We had to figure out how to articulate a vision of family, identity, and citizenship in the rigid structure of a constitution, which by nature is a relatively short document. Gerald Vizenor was a Constitutional Delegate and the Principal Writer of the Constitution. [He discusses this in an interview with James MacKay in this collection.] Many compromises were made along the way, but the Constitution is one example of a new story that we're telling now—one that envisions the future and asserts our sovereignty, and one that includes some of our older stories like Shingebiss. It's an act of survivance. It's an ongoing process.

NJS: And a story that will be told for years to come. So, as we conclude, what are some of the themes you see emerging from this collection? We now have a community formed from this book, thinking about story and its impacts and influences on Anishinaabeg Studies. What future relationships and trends do you see coming from our future readers, scholars, kin?

HKS: I think what comes out of this anthology is that stories are essential to understanding what it means to be Anishinaabe. Stories suggest the ideals we want to work towards. As we've all stated, this embodies and actualizes sovereignty and processes of self-determination. Vine Deloria Jr. has argued that "'Sovereignty' is a useful word to describe the process of growth and awareness that characterizes a group of people working toward and achieving maturity. Sovereignty, in the final instance, can be said to consist more of continued cultural integrity than of political powers and to the degree that a nation loses its sense of cultural identity, to that degree it suffers a loss of sovereignty." I think stories provide us a sense of cultural identity and direction toward achieving maturity.

NJS: I see new directions being provoked in the interests of continuing a great path our people have been following for generations. I see this book as participating in the continuation of our traditions, our ceremonies, our lives. I see it supporting the work of communities continuing to heal and, as Heidi has said, to survive and thrive. We're not perfect people by any means . . . and this is not a perfect book. But this collection of voices is part of a continuing conversation. All of our contributors may not agree, but they are all still invited to come and sit around the fire and have an opportunity to offer their words and ideas.

JD: I look forward to this collection contributing to the developing field of Anishinaabe Studies, but also engaging with American Indian Studies and Indigenous Studies. Tribal-centric views are not formed in isolation; in fact, I would argue that nothing exists in isolation. I don't agree with the idea that some things and ideas are "hybrid" and others are "pure." Purity is nonexistent, but that does not mean that distinct tribal perspectives are. I hope that we see the continued development of Anishinaabeg Studies, Choctaw Studies, Navajo Studies, and so on—in conversation with each other as well as with American Indian Studies and disciplines like history, English, and political science.

We hope *Centering Anishinaabeg Studies* offers new pathways for Anishinaabeg Studies. When editing the essays in *Centering Anishinaabeg Studies*, we encouraged conversation and a critical awareness of the contexts that resulted in divergent and interesting points of view. We wanted story-centered theories of Anishinaabeg Studies that imagined, constructed, and unified Anishinaabeg expressions, but weren't afraid of how stories also deconstructed, destroyed, and divided. Anishinaabeg stories, we believe, can create and transcend, affirm and deny—they have abilities to do all sorts of things, sometimes all at the same time. Thinking of all of these as part of the whole is the challenge set before us as inheritors of a great Anishinaabeg narrative tradition. We invited contributors to engage with the idea of story in multifaceted meanings. We didn't want to limit story just to the idea of traditional stories, or really even just to literature. We asked contributors to conceptualize story broadly and then think of the various ways in which they might use story within their work. We wanted them to then consider how story may serve as a center for Anishinaabeg Studies. In the end, we got a diverse body of essays that used "story" in the conventional and classical sense, as well as paintings, poetry, essay, song, and legal documents. If you think about all of the senses of narrative available in Anishinaabeg communities, all belong to a dynamic and complex sense of Anishinaabeg story.

What emerged are themes based in history, expression, earth, and values that span the beauty of Anishinaabeg life. We have grouped them into offerings that we believe encapsulate much of what we know as Anishinaabeg stories, which conveniently fell into what we affectionately referred to as "The 7 R's": Roots, Relationships, Revelations, Resiliency, Resistance, Reclamation, and Reflection. These R's do not, of course, include everything Anishinaabeg stories hold. In addition, the chapters and sections overlap and interact with each other, creating connections and dialogue.

It takes a village, and in that spirit, we say *chi-miigwech* to Gordon Henry Jr., the reviewers, and all of the contributors for seeing this process through, and for their ideas, perspectives, and engagement in this ongoing dialogue about the meaning, function, and application of stories. We also give tremendous thanks to our many elders, teachers, colleagues, relations, and friends who made *Centering Anishinaabeg Studies* possible. We continue to gain inspiration from all of you in this work and others. And, last but not least, we acknowledge our families—for without you none of this would be possible, or purposeful.

So, for now, we offer these words—and look forward to more. *Miigwech*.

Eko-bezhig Bagijigan

Stories as Roots

ANISHINAABEG STORIES ARE ROOTS; THEY ARE BOTH THE ORIGINS
and the imaginings of what it means to be a participant in an ever-changing
and vibrant culture in humanity. In the same vein, stories can serve as a
foundation and framework for the field of Anishinaabeg Studies, providing
both a methodological and theoretical approach to our scholarship. They
embody ideas and systems that form the basis for law, values, and community. Stories are rich and complex creations that allow for the growth and
vitality of diverse and disparate ways of understanding the world.

Basil Johnston outlines this in his essay "Is That All There Is? Tribal
Literature." Seen by many as one of the roots and foundations of the field
of Anishinaabeg Studies, it is fitting that we begin with one of our greatest
intellectual elders—for he is cited by contributors throughout this collection and countless others for the stories he tells. Johnston delineates how
stories hold deep knowledge about Anishinaabe perceptions, values, and
worldviews. His essay is a call in response to a curious young boy who, having grown bored of studying Indian cultures, asks him: "Is that all there is
to Indians?" Using examples in Anishinaabeg language and literature, Johnston argues that mainstream approaches ossify Anishinaabeg culture, and
asks that critical lenses focus on the intricacies of expression to understand
Anishinaabeg aesthetics, politics, and values. Like traditional creation stories and teachings, so too do Johnston's words not only teach us where we
come from but also illuminate where we can go as a field.

Heid Erdrich, in her essay "*Name*: Literary Ancestry as Presence," also
demonstrates that stories are foundational to the field of Anishinaabeg Studies. She claims the importance of understanding Anishinaabeg intellectual
and literary history, arguing that stories serve as signs or marks of our presence, functioning much like landmarks on a map. Her essay demonstrates
how stories can be seen both as persistence and continuance, "a presence that
is at once new and at the same time based in an Ojibwe epistemology as old

as petroglyphs." In doing so, Erdrich beautifully illustrates how contemporary storymaking is connected to the recovery of historic literary traditions. She unearths works that came before, extends the path with her footprints, and calls on others to take part in this literary motion as well. Erdrich's essay shows how story functions as an intellectual ancestry for the field, noting that "ancestry is everything to Ojibwe people."

Margret Noori's essay *"Beshaabiiag G'gikenmaaigowag*: Comets of Knowledge" recognizes that some roots of Anishinaabe story are contained within Anishinaabemowin, our ancestral language. She explains that action is the foundation of Anishinaabeg stories, and Anishinaabemowin, as a verb-based language, lends tremendous insight into the way these stories move and create. Much like Johnston, Noori outlines how literatures in Anishinaabemowin can serve as a window to Anishinaabe worldview, demonstrating how it contains subtle elements that reveal Anishinaabeg constructions of their relationship to all of creation. Noori's essay encourages us to consider how stories in Anishinaabemowin may be foundational to the field as they illuminate how we order our world.

Is That All There Is?
Tribal Literature

BASIL H. JOHNSTON

IN THE EARLY SIXTIES, KAHN-TINETA HORN, A YOUNG MOHAWK model, got the attention of the Canadian press (media), not only because of her beauty, but because of her articulation of Indian grievances and her demands for justice. Soon after, Red Power was organized, threatening to use force. Academics and scholars, anxious and curious to know what provoked the Indians, organized a series of conferences and teach-ins to explore the issues. Even children wanted to know. So for their enlightenment, experts wrote dozens of books. Universities and colleges began Native studies courses. Ministries of education, advised by a battery of consultants, adjusted their curriculum guidelines to allow units of study on the Native peoples of this continent. And school projects were conducted for the benefit of children between ten and thirteen years of age.

One such project at the Churchill Avenue Public School in North York, Ontario, lasted six weeks, and the staff and students who had taken part mounted a display as a grand finale to their studies. And a fine display it was, in the school's library.

In front of a canvas tent that looked like a teepee stood a grim chief, face painted in warlike colors and arms folded. On his head he wore a headdress made of construction paper. A label pinned to his vest bore the name Blackfoot. I made straight for the chief.

"How!" I greeted the chief, holding up my hand at the same time as a gesture of friendship.

Instead of returning the greeting, the chief looked at me quizzically.

"How come you look so unhappy?" I asked him.

"Sir! I'm bored," the chief replied.

"How so, Chief?"

"Sir, don't tell anybody, but I'm bored. I'm tired of Indians. That's all we've studied for six weeks. I thought they'd be interesting when we started, because I always thought that Indians were neat. At the start of the course, we had to choose to do a special project from food preparation, transportation, dwellings, social organization, clothing, and hunting and fishing. I chose dwellings"—and here the chief exhaled in exasperation—"and that's all me and my team studied for six weeks: teepees, wigwams, longhouses, igloos. We read books, encyclopedias, went to the library to do research, looked at pictures, drew pictures. Then we had to make one. Sir, I'm bored."

"Didn't you learn anything else about Indians, Chief?"

"No sir, there was nothing else . . . Sir? . . . Is that all there is to Indians?"

Little has changed since that evening in 1973. Books still present Native peoples in terms of their physical existence, as if Indians were incapable of meditating upon or grasping the abstract. Courses of study in the public school system, without other sources of information, had to adhere to the format, pattern, and content set down in books. Students studied *Kaw-lijas*, wooden Indians who were incapable of love or laughter; or Tontos, if you will, whose sole skills were to make fires and to perform other servile duties for the Lone Ranger—an inarticulate Tonto, his speech limited to "Ugh!" "Kimo Sabe," and "How."

Despite all the research and the fieldwork conducted by anthropologists, ethnologists, and linguists, Indians remain "The Unknown Peoples," as Professor George E. Tait of the University of Toronto so aptly titled his book written in 1973.

Not even Indian Affairs of Canada, with its more than two centuries of experience with Natives, with its array of experts and consultants, with its unlimited funds, seems to have learned anything about its constituents, if we are to assess them by their latest publication, titled *The Canadian Indian*. One would think that the Honourable William McKnight, then minister of Indian and Northern Affairs, under whose authority the book was published in 1986, should know by now that the Indians who often come to Ottawa do not arrive on horseback, do not slay one of the RCMP mounts and cook it on the steps of the Parliament Buildings. Moreover, most Indians he has seen and met were not dressed in loincloths, nor did they sleep in teepees. Yet he authorized the publication of a book bereft of any originality or imagination, a book that perpetuated the notion and the image that the Indians had not advanced one step since contact, but are still living as they had 150, even 300 years ago. There was not a word about Native thought, literature, institutions, contributions in music, art, theatre. But that's to be expected of Indian Affairs—to know next to nothing about their constituents.

Where did the author or authors of this latest publication by Indian Affairs get their information? The selected readings listed at the back of the book provide a clue: Frances Densmore, Harold Driver, Philip Drucker, Frederick W. Hodge, Diamond Jenness, Reginald and Gladys Laubin, Frank G. Speck, Bruce G. Trigger, George Woodcock, Harold A. Innis, Calvin Martin, E. Palmer Patterson—eminent scholars, none of whom spoke or attempted to learn the language of any of the Indian nations about which they were writing. Modern scholars, because they are not required by their universities to learn, are no more proficient in a Native language than were their predecessors.

Herein, I submit, is the nub and the rub. Without the benefit of knowing the language of the Indian nation that they are investigating, scholars can never get into their minds the heart and soul and spirit of a culture and understand the Native's perceptions and interpretations. The scholar must confine his research and studies to the material, physical culture, subsistence patterns, and family relationships.

Without knowing the spiritual and the intellectual, aesthetic sides of Indian culture, the scholar cannot furnish what that little grade-five youngster and others like him wanted to know about Indians.

Admitting his boredom was that grade-five youngster's way of expressing his disappointment with the substance of the course that he and his colleagues had been made to endure. In another sense, it was a plea for other knowledge that would quench his curiosity and challenge his intellect.

Students such as he, as well as adults, are interested in the character, intellect, soul, spirit, heart of people of other races and cultures. They want to know what other people believe in; what they understand; what they expect and hope for in this life and in the next; how they keep law and order and harmony within the family and community; how and why they celebrated ceremonies; what made them proud, ashamed; what made them happy, what sad. Whether the young understand what they want to know and learn does not matter much; they still want to know in order to enrich their own insights and broaden their outlooks.

But unless scholars and writers know the literature of the peoples that they are studying or writing about, they cannot provide what their students and readers are seeking and deserving of.

There is, fortunately, enough literature, both oral and written, available for scholarly study, but it has for the most part been neglected. Myths, legends, and songs have not been regenerated and set in modern terms to earn immortalization in poetry, dramatization in plays, or romanticization in novels.

What has prevented the acceptance of Indian literature as a serious and legitimate expression of Native thought and experience has been indifferent and inferior translation, a lack of understanding and interest in the culture, and a notion that it has little of importance to offer to the larger white culture.

In offering you a brief sketch—no more than a glimpse, as it were—of my tribe's culture, I am doing no more than what any one of you would do were you to be asked, "What is your culture? Would you explain it?" I would expect you to reply, "Read my literature, and you will get to know something of my thoughts, my convictions, my aspirations, my feelings, sentiments, expectations, whatever I cherish or abominate."

First, let me offer you an observation about my language, for the simple reason that language and literature are inseparable, though they are too often taught as separate entities. They belong together.

In my tribal language, all words have three levels of meaning: There is the surface meaning that everyone instantly understands. Beneath this meaning is a more fundamental meaning derived from the prefixes and their combinations with other terms. Underlying both is the philosophical meaning.

Take the word "Anishinaubae." That is what the members of the nation, now known as Chippewa in the United States or Ojibway in Canada, called themselves. It referred to a member of the tribe. It was the answer given to the question "What are you?" But it was more than just a term of identification. It meant, "I am a person of good intent, a person of worth," and it reflected what the people thought of themselves, and of human nature: that all humans are essentially, fundamentally good. Let's separate that one word into its two terms—the first, *Onishishih*, meaning good, fine, beautiful, excellent; and the second, *naubae*, meaning being, male, human species. Even together they do not yield the meaning "good intention." It is only by examining the stories of Nanabush, the tribe's central and principal mythical figure who represents all men and all women, that the term Anishinaubae begins to make sense. Nanabush was always full of good intentions, ergo the people of the tribe. The Anishinaubae perceived themselves as people who intended good and therefore were of merit and worth. From this perception they drew a strong sense of pride, as well as a firm sense of place in the community. This influenced their notion of independence.

Let's take another word, the word for truth. When we say "w'daeb-awae," we mean he or she is telling the truth, is correct, is right. But the expression is not merely an affirmation of a speaker's veracity. It is as well a philosophical proposition, in the saying of which a speaker casts his words and his voice as far as his perception and his vocabulary will enable him or her;

it is a denial that there is such a thing as absolute truth—that the best and most the speaker can achieve and a listener expect is the highest degree of accuracy. Somehow that one expression, *w'daeb-awae*, sets the limits to a single statement, as well as setting limits to truth and the scope and exercise of speech.

One other word: "to know." We say "w'kikaendaun" to convey the idea that he or she "knows." Without going into the etymological derivations, suffice it to say that when the speaker assures someone that he knows it, that person is saying that the notion, image, idea, fact that that person has in mind corresponds and is similar to what he or she has already seen, heard, touched, tasted, or smelled. That person's knowledge may not be exact, but similar to that which has been instilled and impressed in his or her mind and recalled from memory.

The stories that make up our tribal literature are no different from the words in our language. Both have many meanings and applications, as well as bearing tribal perceptions, values, and outlooks.

Let us begin at the beginning with the tribe's story of creation, which precedes all other stories in the natural order. Creation stories provide insights into what races and nations understand of human nature; ours is no different in this respect.

This is our creation story. Kitchi-manitou beheld a vision. From this vision, the Great Mystery—for that is the essential and fundamental meaning of Kitchi-manitou, and not spirit, as is often understood—created the sun and the stars, the land and the waters, and all the creatures and beings, seen and unseen, that inhabit the earth, the seas, and the skies. The Creation was devastated by a flood. Only the manitous, creatures, and beings who dwelt in the waters were spared. All others perished.

In the heavens dwelt a manitou, Geezhigo-quae (Sky-woman). During the cataclysm upon the earth, Geezhigo-quae became pregnant. The creatures adrift upon the seas prevailed upon the giant turtle to offer his back as a haven for Geezhigo-quae. They then invited her to come down.

Resting on the giant turtle's back, Geezhigo-quae asked for soil.

One after another, water creatures dove into the depths to retrieve a morsel of soil. Not one returned with a particle of soil. They all offered an excuse: too deep, too dark, too cold, there are evil manitous keeping watch. Last to descend was the muskrat. He returned with a small knot of earth.

With the particle of mud retrieved by the muskrat, Geezhigo-quae re-created an island and the world as we know it. On the island she created over the giant turtle's shell, Geezhigo-quae gave birth to twins who begot the tribe called the Anishinaubaeg.

Millennia later, the tribe dreamed Nanabush into being. Nanabush represented themselves and what they understood of human nature. One day his world too was flooded. Like Geezhigo-quae, Nanabush re-created his world from a morsel of soil retrieved from the depths of the sea.

As a factual account of the origin of the world and of being, the story has no more basis than the biblical story of creation and the flood. But the story represents a belief in God, the Creator, a Kitchi-manitou, the Great Mystery. It also represents a belief that Kitchi-manitou sought within himself, his own being, a vision. Or perhaps it came from within his being, and Kitchi-manitou created what was beheld and set it into motion. Even the lesser manitous, such as Geezhigo-quae and Nanabush, must seek a morsel of soil with which to create and re-create their world, their spheres. So men and women must seek within themselves the talent or the potential, and afterward create their own worlds and their own spheres, and a purpose to give meaning to their lives.

The people begotten by Geezhigo-quae on that mythological island called themselves Anishinaubaeg, the good beings who meant well and were human beings, therefore fundamentally good. But they also knew that men and women were often deflected from fulfilling their good intentions and prevented from living up to their dreams and visions, not out of any inherent evil, but rather from something outside of themselves. Nanabush also represented this aspect of human nature. Many times Nanabush or the Anishinaubaeg fail to carry out a noble purpose. Despite this, he is not rendered as evil or wicked, but remains fundamentally and essentially good.

Men and women intend what is good, but they forget. The story called "The Man, the Snake, and the Fox" exemplifies this aspect of human nature.

In its abbreviated form, the story is as follows: A hunter left his lodge and his family at daybreak to go in search of game to feed his wife and his children. As he proceeded through the forest, the hunter saw deer, but each time they were out of range of his weapon.

Late in the afternoon, discouraged and weary, he heard faint cries in the distance. Forgetting his low spirits and fatigue, he set out with renewed optimism and vigor in the direction of the cries. Yet the nearer he drew to the source of the cries, the more daunted was the hunter by the dreadful screams. Only the thought of his family's needs drove him forward, otherwise he might have turned away.

At last he came to a glade. The screams came from a thicket on the opposite side. The hunter, bow and arrow drawn and ready, made his way forward cautiously.

To his horror, the hunter saw an immense serpent tangled fast in a thicket as a fish is caught in the webbing of a net. The monster writhed and roared and twisted. He struggled to break free.

The man recoiled in horror. Before he could back away, the snake saw him.

"Friend!" the snake addressed the man.

The man fell in a heap on the ground the moment that the snake spoke. When he came to, much later, the snake pleaded with the man to set him free. For some time the man refused, but eventually he relented. He was persuaded by the monster's plea that he too, though a serpent, had no less right to life than did the man. And the serpent promised not to injure the man on his release. The hunter was convinced.

The snake sprang on his deliverer the moment the last vine was cut away.

It was like thunder as the man and the snake struggled. Nearby a little fox heard the uproar. Never having seen such a spectacle, the fox settled down to watch. Immediately he realized that the man was about to be killed.

Why were the snake and the man locked in mortal struggle? The little fox shouted for an explanation. The man and the snake stopped.

The hunter gasped out his story, then the snake gave his version. Pretending not to understand the snake's explanation, the fox beguiled the aggressor into returning to the thicket to act out his side of the story.

The snake entangled himself once more.

Realizing that he had been delivered from the edge of death by the fox, the man was greatly moved. He felt bound to show his gratitude in some tangible way. The fox assured him that no requital was required. Nevertheless the hunter persisted. How might he, the hunter, perform some favor on behalf of the fox?

Not only was there no need, the fox explained, there was nothing that the man could do for the fox; there was not a thing that the fox needed or desired of human beings. However, if it would make the man happier, the fox suggested that the man might feed him should he ever have need.

Nothing would please the man more than to perform some good for his deliverer; it was the least that he could do for a friend who had done so much.

Some years later, the hunter shot a little fox who had been helping himself to the family storage. As the man drew his knife to finish off the thief, the little fox gasped, "Don't you remember?"

That no snakes as monstrous as the one in the story are to be found on this continent makes no difference to youngsters' sense of outrage over the treachery of the snake and the forgetfulness of the man; nor does the exercise of speech that enables the snake and the fox to communicate with the hunter and each other prevent the young from being moved to compassion for the fox. Their sense of justice and fairness bears them over the anomalies in the story.

Before the last words, "Don't you remember?" have echoed away, the young begin to ask questions. "Why? Why did the man not recognize the fox? Why did he forget? How did the man feel afterwards? Why did the snake attack the man? Why did the snake break his promise? Why didn't the man leave the snake where he was? Do animals really have as much right to live as human beings do?"

Indians cared, loved as passionately as other people.

The story called "The Weeping Pine" raises the same questions about love and marriage, and the span of both, that have been asked by philosophers, poets, and lovers of every race and generation. It does not pretend to give answers to these age-old questions beyond suggesting that love may bloom even in circumstances where it is least expected to flower and endure. But owing to shoddy translation, the story has been presented as an explanation for the origin of pine trees.

According to the story, the elders of a village came to a certain young woman's home where she lived with her parents, brothers, and sisters. They had come to let her family know that they had chosen her to be the new wife to an old man. This particular man had been without a friend since the death of his first wife some years before. The old man was described as good-natured and kind. As one who had done much to benefit the tribe in his youth, the old man deserved something in return from his neighbors. In the opinion of the elders, the most fitting reward the old man could have was a wife. In their judgment, the young woman they had chosen would be a suitable companion for the old man.

They assured her that the tribe would see to it that they never had need.

Because this sort of marriage was a matter that the young woman had not considered, it was unexpected. The delegation understood this. They did not demand an immediate answer, but allowed the young woman a few days in which to make up her mind.

The young woman cried when the delegation left. She didn't want to marry that man—that old man whose days were all but over and who could never look after her. She had, like every young girl her age, hoped to marry someone young, full of promise—someone she would love and who would love her in return. Besides, it was too soon. How could she, not yet eighteen, be a companion to an old man of seventy or more. The disparity was too great.

At first her parents, too, were aggrieved. But soon after, they prevailed upon her to defer to the wishes of the elders, and her father delivered word of their daughter's consent to the elders.

But neither the disparity in age nor the preference of the young girl not to enter into a loveless marriage were too great; in the years that followed, she came to love this old man. And they had many children.

Thirty years later the old man died.

On the final day of the four-day watch, the mourners went home, but the widow made no move to rise. She continued to keen and rock back and forth in great sorrow.

"Come mother, let us go home," her children urged, offering to assist her to her feet and to support her on their way home.

"No! No! Leave me. Go," she said.

"Mother! Please. Come home with us," her children pleaded. Nothing they said could persuade their mother to leave.

"No. You go home. This is where I belong. Leave me."

Her children prayed she would relent—give in to the cold and hunger. They went home, but they did not leave their mother alone. During the next few days, a son or daughter was always at her side, watching with her and entreating her to come home. They tried to comfort her with their own love and care, assuring her that her wound would pass and heal. They even brought her food and drink to sustain her. She refused everything.

As their mother grew weaker with each passing day, the children besought the elders to intercede on their behalf. Perhaps the elders could prevail on their mother.

But the elders shook their heads and said, "If that is what she wants, there is nothing that you can do to change her mind. Leave her be. She wants to be with him. Leave her. It's better that way."

And so the family ceased to press their mother to come home, though they still kept watch with her. They watched until she, too, died by the graveside of her husband, their father.

Using the term "grandchild" that all elders used in referring to the young, the elder who presided over the woman's wake said, "Our granddaughter's love did not cease with death, but continues into the next life."

The next spring, a small plant grew out of the grave of the woman. Many years later, as the sons, daughters, and grandchildren gathered at the graveside of their parents, they felt a mist fall upon their faces and their arms. "It is Mother shedding tears of love for Dad," cried one daughter.

And it is so. On certain days, spruces and pines shed a mist of tears of love.

By remaining at her husband's graveside until she too died, the woman fulfilled the implied promise, "whither thou goest, there too will I go," contained in the term *weedjeewaugun*, companion in life, our word for spouse.

As she wept for her love, she must have wept for the love of her children. Their love threatened to break that bond that held her to her husband. No! She would not let even death part her from the man to whom she had given her heart, her soul, her spirit forever.

It is unlikely that the woman ever uttered more than "K'zaugin" (I love you) during her marriage. In this respect she was no different from most other women, or men for that matter, who are not endowed with the poetic gift, though they feel and love with equal passion and depth. *K'zaugin* said everything. I love you, today, tomorrow, forever. It expressed everything that the finest poets ever wrote, and everything that the unpoetic ever thought and felt but could not put into rhyme or rhythm.

Name'
Literary Ancestry as Presence

HEID E. ERDRICH

Mewenzha Anishnaabeg megwa babamiiaayaawaad
Long ago the Anishinaabeg while they were moving around

gii babaname'wag e-wii enji daapinamaagozig
they were leaving a presence while transporting things

gii babamiiayaawag niswaak ge kwa naanwaak ge minik miinwaa
they were travelling for up to [a] three to five year period of time and

*neyap ji ge gii azhegiiwewaad gaa ge pii aayaawaad ji
nagadanendamowaad da giimiiwaad.*
returned (that) was where they went home when
they were keeping in mind where they deserted.

—ROGER ROULETTE "*NOONGWA E-ANISHINAABEMJIG*:
PEOPLE WHO SPEAK ANSHINAABEMOWIN TODAY"

IN JOINING THIS CONVERSATION CENTERING ANISHINAABEG STUD-
ies, I want to position my comments to be understood as a *writerly*
response—the response of an Anishinaabe poet-critic. I assert that when
we read, we read from where we are and from *who* we are. If we are from
Anishinaabe people and places, we read from there. Our experiences as
Anishinaabe people are vastly varied, but still we read others like us with

a distinct understanding of our shared place, particularly our place in land and language. As a poet and playwright, I believe we are not alone in our reading, and so not alone in our writing. We write into and out of a great telling that brings us stories and songs, that teaches us to look and listen. This is not some mystic tradition; it is simply how it is to be aware of where you are, who you are, and who your people are when they create with words.

In awareness of who we are, and as we follow the path of early Ojibwe writers,[1] I choose to be guided by a metaphor that involves a play between the notion of landmark literary works and the pictographic marks/signs/presence that Anishinaabe people left/leave/find on rock and elsewhere. This metaphor arises from an Anishinaabe-centered epistemology that relates writing with landmark, and marking with ongoing presence in place. The Anishinaabe word name' is a verb transitive animate and means to "find/leave signs of somebody's presence."[2] While engaging in research in order to recover an Ojibwe tradition of writing in English, I find landmarks of literature, signs of presence, and draw them toward my understanding of the Anishinaabe word name'.[3] It seems apt: What helps us know a place? Landmarks. What helps us know a people? The marks/signs they leave, that we find. These marks and landmarks help us follow their path across a landscape of time. Further, as Roulette suggests above, the verb name' implies presence. When we find what another leaves, we are connected across time. Name' is the perfect metaphor for the Anishinaabe poet-critic to employ in a search for literary ancestry. We follow our literary ancestors—not with a destination in mind, not with intent to claim territory, but because we want to know who has gone before us, who now guides us. We take comfort in their signs of presence along our way. Name' speaks beyond the usual sense of landmark and the geographical and political notions of mapping—which is ideal, because not only are maps hard to fold up, we'd rather stop to ask directions. You get a lot of good stories that way.

OJIBWE LITERARY ANCESTORS

For Native American creative writers, writing into a specific cultural, tribal, or national tradition is an assertion of literary sovereignty. But in order to write in or out of our literary tradition in English, we have to first recover that tradition. Robert Warrior's *Tribal Secrets: Recovering American Indian Intellectual Traditions* marked the path both into the past and toward the future of Native American literature. Born in 1963, I became a reader of

Native American literature in the late 1970s. In the late 1980s I became a writer. In *Tribal Secrets*, Warrior notes the 1960s–1990s as an important time for the rise of Native American literature. However, in the 1970s, becoming a reader of Native American literature was no small act. What I now think of as my literary history—Native American in general and Ojibwe literary history in particular—was buried or was just being written. I can remember a time when I was aware of only a very few books written by American Indians, and one of those, a brief history of the Turtle Mountain Band, was written by my grandfather, Aunnishenauby/Patrick Gourneau.[4] As Warrior recalls: "Twenty-five years ago, building a library of America Indian writers from books in print would have taken up no more than a few feet of shelf space."[5] Without knowledge of the full heritage of writers like us who had come before us, a generation of new Native American writers began their careers and those shelves filled up: "With the emergence of literally hundreds of writers since and the reprinting of many authors from before 1968, the yield now is yards and yards."[6]

Those bookshelves filled up in part because Native American scholars such as Warrior retrieved work from the past and aligned works across tribes and cultures that created the appearance of one ethnic literature called Native American literature. However, the gathering together of books written by authors with similar backgrounds does not create the conversant literature that other literary movements in English have produced. My college training taught me to examine the ways literary works spoke from one author to another across generations—how authors expanded one another's ideas and created visions of humanity that also resounded decades later. This was the English literary tradition I fell in love with and yearned to become a part of in some small way. But there was no Ojibwe or even Native American literary genealogy for me to follow. Native American writers of my generation were introduced to a rich English literary tradition that had no parallel within Native American literature. Even if we were aware of the literary tradition in our own cultures and languages, our oral literatures, almost all Native American authors wrote solely in English, and connections between the oral and written traditions were still obscure. An absence persisted. A question nagged: What would we become part of as writers? What gathered our literary tribe?

In order to answer that absence and fill it with signs of presence, to enact *name*, we need to recognize landmark works of literature in the Ojibwe-English tradition. As an author whose work centers on Anishinaabe presence, the work of early Ojibwe writers enriches my own awareness of literature, and influences the ways my own creative work makes a path within the landscape that their writing has mapped for me. Cataloging and responding to our literary ancestors creates a path toward a recovered literary tradition in English. We also see where paths diverge, and where it gets difficult to mark that path. Earlier scholarship tells us what these Ojibwe literary ancestors wrote, but not how they wrote, their influences, motivations, aesthetic—these are all up to the current generation of Anishinaabe writers and scholars to recover, where they can. However, until relatively recently, recovering the connections between Native American writers that would create a literary tradition seemed unlikely. In 1995 Warrior stated that "the past century has featured two periods (1890–1925 and 1961–1973) in which Native writers associated closely with one another" and two other periods (1925–1961 and 1973 to the present) marked by "a lack of associative cohesion."[7] Yet when we focus on Ojibwe writers, we can mark association between authors as early as the 1830s.

Ojibwe authors have been connected across a large geographic territory for the past two centuries, continuing and maintaining a literary tradition within North American literature in English for a considerable time. We can determine connections between early Ojibwe writers as well as mark common subjects and modes of expression. Early Ojibwe writers of the mid-1800s are related literally[8] and *literarily*. Two of the earliest and best known Ojibwe writers, Keh-ke-wa-guo-na-ba/Peter Jones and Kah-ge-ga-gah-bowh/George Copway, both authored works for church use and served as translators in other capacities, including treaty negotiations. Scholar Bernd C. Peyer describes Kah-ge-ga-gah-bowh/Copway's career as "markedly influenced" by Jones.[9] However it is unclear whether that influence was on the missionary career or the evolution of the writer. The two are hard to untwine. Another writer of the era, Maungwudaus/George Henry, was the brother of Keh-ke-wa-guo-na-ba/Peter Jones, who included translations by Maungwudaus and a third brother, John Jones, in his own 1839 publication *Nugumouinun genumugumouat igiu anishinabeg anumiajig*.

In 1847 the best known of the nineteenth-century Ojibwe writers, Kah-ge-ga-gah-bowh/Copway, published *The Life, History and Travels of Kah-ge-ga-gah-bowh (George Copway), a Young Indian Chief of the Ojibwa Nation*. Copway spoke to enormous crowds, reprinted his book seven times, and enjoyed considerable, though brief, fame.[10] My own reading of Kah-ge-ga-gah-bowh is of a remarkable author who managed, without denying the humanity of Ojibwe people or the culpability of the Europeans who brought pain to his people, to write as both a Christian and an Ojibwe. He showed national/tribal pride, and his work also asserts the longtime literacy of the Ojibwe by explaining the "picture writing," which he declared as useful as English writing.[11] Kah-ge-ga-gah-bowh also authored the political document *Organization of a New Indian Territory, East of the Missouri River*, in 1850. Kah-ge-ga-gah-bowh's political writings contribute to a parallel tradition of Ojibwe writers turning to political purpose, which included Keh-ke-wa-guo-na-ba and Maungwudaus, and which continues today with the work of Winona LaDuke, who has run for vice president of the United States, and that of Gerald Vizenor, who has assisted his band, the White Earth Anishinaabe, in revising their constitution.

In recovering an Ojibwe-English literature, we have not scrabbled together obscure texts by writers who held no connection to, or influences on, English literature in general. Kah-ge-ga-gah-bowh met the poet Henry Wadsworth Longfellow and the scholar Henry Rowe Schoolcraft.[12] While Bame-wa-wa-ge-zhik-a-quay/Jane Johnston Schoolcraft is considered the earliest Ojibwe writer, her mother, Ozhaguscoddaywayquay/Susan Johnston, had an important literary role as well: She told her stories to her son-in-law, Henry Rowe Schoolcraft, for his own books, and it was from Schoolcraft that Longfellow took his notes for his poem *The Song of Hiawatha*.[13] Ozhaguscoddaywayquay and her daughter, Bame-wa-wa-ge-zhik-a-quay, should be recognized as significantly contributing to the larger English literary tradition and to the American literary tradition in one of its defining poetic works.

In 1987, Gerald Vizenor wrote that "the Ojibwe claim more published writers than any other tribe on this continent." He included nineteenth-century authors Copway and William Warren in his anthology *Touchwood: A Collection of Ojibway Prose*.[14] Scholar A. LaVonne Ruoff presented Keh-ke-wa-guo-na-ba/Jones in a brief mention in her 1990 bibliography.[15] Knowing a little of those three authors made me eager to read more "old" writers. I wanted to find Ojibwe who wrote in a personally expressive manner—my literary ancestors. My research in bibliographies, archives, libraries, and databases[16] led me to a dozen nineteenth-century Ojibwe writers[17] and another half-dozen Ojibwe who were published between 1900 and 1960. Listing them is like making a map for today's Anishinaabe writers; we can point to them as landmarks, encountering their works as marks/signs of their presence: Bame-wa-wa-ge-zhik-a-quay/Jane Johnston Schoolcraft, in *Muzzeniegun*, 1826–1827; Maungwudaus/George Henry, *An Account of the Chippewa who have been Traveling Among the Whites . . .* 1848; John Couchois Wright, *The Ottawan*, 1885; Andrew J. Blackbird, *History of the Ottawa and Chippewa Indians of Michigan*, 1887; Eliza Morrison, *A Little*

History of My Forest Life, 1894; Theodore H. Beaulieu, *The Progress*, 1884–1886, 1888, 1902–1904; John Couchois Wright, *Stories of the Crooked Tree*, 1915, *Northern Breezes*, 1917, *The Great Myth*, 1922; Annette Leevier, *Psychic Experience of an Indian Princess*, 1920; Noodin/Joseph Northrup, *Wawina*, 1937; Wa-be-no O-pee-chee/Jeanne L'strange Cappel, *Chippewa Tales* and *Chippewa Tales Vol. II.*, 1930 and 1931; John Couchois Wright, *Chicago Jig: Legend of the Indian Paradise*, 1935, *Scenic Michigan in Verse*, 1939; Way Quah Giizhig/John Rogers, *A Chippewa Speaks*, 1957; Ralph E. McCarry, *Reminiscences by Chief White Wolf of the Chippewa*, 1957.

Not all of these writers wrote well, or even in a way that makes Anishinaabe readers comfortable today. Nonetheless, I was happy to learn of them all and expect many more are out there yet to meet. Sometimes we encounter *name'* not as marks, not points for a map, but rather the moment when we find others beckoning. They give us courage and comfort along this path. They tell us of someone's presence here, someone who has come before us, so even in writing, we know we are in Anishinaabe Aking and we are headed the right way.

Given how relatively few writers there were, we find great diversity in our literary ancestry. Early Ojibwe authors can be seen as writing in and out of several modes, often overlapping: translators expressing Ojibwe history, culture, and tradition; authors of political documents and petitions; poets and translators of hymns; givers of accounts, narratives, even "tales" from traditional Ojibwe literature. Many wrote as bilingual writers and as such began the tradition of Ojibwe writing within English literature. Ojibwe authors enact a traditional literary motion that I see embodied in the Ojibwe word *name'*, (to find/leave signs of a being's presence) which is a stem word meaning "traces."[18] To be sure, my perspective is of one just learning Anishinaabe language, but ever since I first learned of the word *name'*, I've been reminded of Ojibwe poet-scholar Gerald Vizenor's concept of *survivance*.[19] The concept implied in *name'* and in *survivance* seem very alike. I want to draw them together in this Anishinaabe-centered reading/writing where the two concepts might resonate. Both suggest an ongoing presence of Anishinaabe making. Vizenor's survivance is drawn toward story as persistence and resistance, a postcolonial response as well as a tradition, and *name'* implies a being, a spirit, inherently present in the traces left, such as in the signs or writing.[20] Both concepts suggest an Ojibwe-centered notion of literature as persistence and continuance, a presence that is at once new and at the same time based in an Ojibwe epistemology as old as petroglyphs. In recovering and reviewing Ojibwe writing and placing myself within that tradition, I, and other Ojibwe writers, take part in such literary motion as well.

TWO LITERARY ANCESTORS: BAME-WA-WA-GE-ZHIK-A-QUAY/JANE JOHNSTON SCHOOLCRAFT AND MAUNGWUDAUS/GEORGE HENRY

Two nineteenth-century Ojibwe writers play a particularly important role in my research and in my creative writing: Bame-wa-wa-ge-zhik-a-quay/Jane Johnston Schoolcraft, and the former missionary Maungwudaus/George Henry. I came to my appreciation of these two authors, and to an evolution of my reading for an Ojibwe-English literary tradition, in the context of reading the nineteenth-century Anishinaabe authors I've listed. I was looking for personal expression, something close to what we now think of as literary. Bame-wa-wa-ge-zhik-a-quay's poetry and prose, along with travel writing by Maungwudaus, struck me as more like the personal, creative expression of today's writers than the work of other early Ojibwe authors or even those who followed such writers as William Warren. Bame-wa-wa-ge-zhik-a-quay and Maungwudaus seemed like mentors and guides for my own work. They became my literary ancestors. Both of these two figures inspired my own writing, and eventually, using research regarding their lives and work, I felt myself joining an Ojibwe poetic tradition started by Bame-wa-wa-ge-zhik-a-quay, and I found myself in collaboration with Maungwudaus as I wrote an entire play around the few pages of his writing that still exist from the 1840s.

Because Bame-wa-wa-ge-zhik-a-quay was female and a poet, I identify closely with her, but perhaps not in a conventional way. Researching her work and life inspired me to create just a single poem, and an elegy at that. Yet the path she marks for me is an important one: Bame-wa-wa-ge-zhik-a-quay was the first poet to write in both English and Ojibwe, and it is from her bilingual writing that I take inspiration. She is author of the earliest literary works by an Ojibwe writer.[21] Her poems and traditional tales, both in English and Ojibwe, were published by her husband, the noted ethnographer Henry Rowe Schoolcraft, in a magazine the couple edited and distributed by subscription. The magazine, *The Literary Voyager*, also known by its Ojibwe title *Muzzeniegun*, was published in fifteen volumes between 1826 and 1827. A definitive collection of the works of Bame-wa-wa-ge-zhik-a-quay is minutely researched and presented by critic Robert Dale Parker as *The Sound the Stars Make Rushing Through the Sky: The Poetry of Jane Johnston Schoolcraft*, from University of Pennsylvania Press, 2007. Importantly, Parker's book marks early Ojibwe literature as worthy of in-depth study and further consideration as part of American literature in general.

Parker's work on Bame-wa-wa-ge-zhik-a-quay brings her into a current conversation that satisfies my long interest in this important literary figure and Ojibwe woman. In the late 1990s I found copies of *Muzzeniegun* while visiting the library at Ober's Island on Rainy Lake in Minnesota. I later learned Bame-wa-wa-ge-zhik-a-quay had authored several of the poems and stories under pseudonyms that appeared in *Muzzeniegun* in 1826 and 1827. Her poetic style, well within the standard of American literature of her day, had a romantic ring and would be considered sentimental by current standards. Her subjects, however, resonate even today: the death of a child, the weight of depression, absent love, and sisterly affections. She also presents a version of her grandfather's war song and death song, no doubt received from her mother, Ozhaguscoddaywayquay, who was daughter of the famed Chief Waubojeeg. The fact that Bame-wa-wa-ge-zhik-a-quay recast Ojibwe songs as poems, wrote about her Ojibwe lineage, and took care to give attribution (in the Ojibwe manner of saying who "gave" the song or story) reveals a sensibility deeply within an Ojibwe literary tradition.

As a poet and as an Ojibwe writer, what fascinates me about Bame-wa-wa-ge-zhik-a-quay is that she wrote in Ojibwe as well as English and included Ojibwe words in her poems in English. Further, she wrote some works entirely in Ojibwe.[22] Her sensibility meets mine in that I recognize her experiences as deeply connected to an Ojibwe homeland. One of my favorite poems of hers is "To the Pine Tree," which is subtitled "on first seeing it / on returning from Europe." The poem excites my sense of what it means to be both of the North American continent, from Anishinaabe Aking, and from European ancestry. In reading the poem as Parker presents it, I am thrilled to see Ojibwe take precedence over English as Bame-wa-wa-ge-zhik-a-quay first expresses the poem in her Indigenous language:

To the Pine Tree
on first seeing it
on returning from Europe

Shing wauk! Shing wauk! nin ge ik id,
Waish kee wau bum ug, shing wauk
Tuh quish in aun nau aub, ain dak nuk i yaun.
Shing wauk, shing wauk no sa
Shi e gwuh ke do dis au naun
Kau gega way zhau wus co zid.

Mes ah nah, shi egwuh tah gwish en aung
Sin da mik ke aum baun
Kag ait suh, ne meen wain dum

Me nah wau, wau bun dah maun
Gi yut wi au, wau bun dah maun een
Shing wauk, shing wauk no sa
Shi e gwuh ke do dis an naun.

Ka ween ga go, kau wau bun duh e yun
Tib isht co, izz henau gooz ze no an
Shing wauk wah zhau wush co zid
Ween Ait ah kwanaudj e we we
Kau ge gay wa zhau soush ko zid

In presenting the English version, Parker titles it "translation," further suggesting that Bame-wa-wa-ge-zhik-a-quay's primary creative mode was, at least in this instance, in Ojibwe language, and that English was secondary—the translation, not the original expression.

In noting her choices within the translation to English, I hear the tight rhyme, the couplets that simply do not exist in the original Ojibwemowin. To today's ear, those couplets hurt. The sing-songy quality makes the poem sentimental, and the exclamation points jar. But the tight rhyme also reveals Bame-wa-wa-ge-zhik-a-quay's ability, her ease with the poetic craft of her time and her literary understanding of her genre. In short, the poem is a good example of verse of her day.

The pine! the pine! I eager cried,
The pine, my father! see it stand,
As first that cherished tree I spied,
Returning to my native land.
The pine! the pine! oh lovely scene!
The pine, that is forever green.

Ah beauteous tree! ah happy sight!
That greets me on my native strand
And hails me, with a friend's delight,
To my own dear bright mother land
Oh 'tis to me a heart-sweet scene,
The pine—the pine! that's ever green.

Not all the trees of England bright,
Not Erin's lawns of green and light
Are half so sweet to memory's eye,

As this dear type of northern sky
Oh 'tis to me a heart-sweet scene,
The pine—the pine! that ever green.

In contrast, the Ojibwe version of the poem uses subtle repetitions and a return to the phrase "Shing wauk, shing wauk" that strike me as mirroring the sound the pines would make. To my ear, as one recovering the language, Ojibwe employs onomatopoetic devices, especially in the names of living creatures. The tree hushes with the long *sheee* sound, and what might read as a harsh "wauk" is likely a low, soothing sound more like "wug." To anyone who has ever listened to pines in the wind, the very name *shing wauk* is a reminder of that comforting sound.

Much as the poem pains the ear of a contemporary poet used to free verse and more subtle forms, I am thrilled to see a poet of the 1820s using the phrase "native land" in clear pride, in direct contrast to "England bright" and "Erin's lawns," meaning Ireland, her father's homeland. A further and more telling contrast in the Anishinaabemowin original is her use of "no sa," a somewhat archaic term for father also used by Longfellow in his poem of the same era,[23] meaning father, but tied grammatically to the pine tree to give a sense of the land as patrimony or fatherland perhaps. Bame-wa-wa-ge-zhik-a-quay, expert in both languages, provides today's new generation of poets, those just relearning Anishinaabemowin, abundant inspiration that comes to us across more than a century of obscurity. Along the path toward an English-Ojibwe literature, Bame-wa-wa-ge-zhik-a-quay greatly comforts us with this *name'*, the sign of her presence in our literary landscape.

Bame-wa-wa-ge-zhik-a-quay died at age forty-two. She was not laid to rest in her homeland near the white pines she loved, near Lake Michigan. She died without her husband or children nearby. I learned these things before I began my formal research, and I recognized a tragedy in her life that I wanted to mark with a poem. Although I have not visited it except virtually, I found an image of her grave in a church cemetery in Ontario.[24] Her headstone contains a lengthy inscription, including a sonnet by her husband, which I quote. I use a partial version of the actual inscription as epigraph, and quote from Schoolcraft's sonnet within the body of the poem:

IN SEARCH OF JANE'S GRAVE

> *In memory of Jane, wife of Henry R. Schoolcraft, Esq., born at St. Mary's*
> *Falls, 1800; died at Dundas, May 22nd, 1842, in the arms of her sister,*
> *during a visit at the house of the rector of this church, while her husband*
> *was in England and her children at a distant school. She was the eldest*
> *daughter of John Johnston, Esq., and Susan, daughter of Waubojeeg,*
> *a celebrated war chief and civil ruler of the Odjibwa Tribe.*

—INSCRIPTION AT JANE JOHNSTON SCHOOLCRAFT'S GRAVE

Woman of the Sound the Stars Make Rushing Through the Sky,
Bamewawagezhikaquay, her headstone should have said.
But her name splits, eclipsed by his,
her co-author and husband.
Jane, wife of, it reads,
followed by a sonnet,
tightly rhymed to fit lines
together to say she died *bland*
and sure of immortality:
She smiled to quit a world of tears.

If only the words left us were hers.
Literary Grandmother,
first Ojibwe, mixed-blood,
Native, First Nations, Indian writer.
Mother poetess.

True, her verse hurts like 1830.
She kept current, do not doubt it,
wrote no worse than Longfellow,
who took her mother's family stories
(as offered by her husband, Schoolcraft)
and Hiawatha-ed the heck out of them.

In a small town cemetery, I thought
I'd found you, our literary Sky Woman.
Someone re-created your grave,
The sonnet at least, minus your name,
but nearer to your girlhood home

where you were known and loved as
Woman of the Sound the Heavens Make.

Dear Jane, hushing pines along the lake
should have sung you rest eternally—
peaceful on the point, Michigan
beating blue and flecked,
rushing like stars to the shore.

Bame-wa-wa-ge-zhik-a-quay's life and work give me a literary ancestor with
whom I can identify as a woman, as an Ojibwe with a Euro-American father,
and as a poet. However, the early Ojibwe writer who most intrigues me is
nothing like me in literary style or history.

In 1848, Maungwudaus published a brief narrative titled *An Account of
the Chippewa Indians, Who Have Been Travelling among the Whites, in the
United States, England, Ireland, Scotland, France, and Belgium; With Very
Interesting Incidents in Relation to the General Characteristics of the English,
Irish, Scotch, French, and Americans, with Regard to Their Hospitality, Peculiarities, etc.* In creating his curious and opinionated narrative of his travels,
Maungwudaus became our first Ojibwe literary ancestor to express himself
in prose in a deeply personal and original manner. In his work we hear a
strong and clear voice that unabashedly sees Europe from an Ojibwe center.
Maungwudaus's voice acts as a landmark on the path I travel toward discovery of Ojibwe literary history, and where I sense reciprocal *name'*/sign/mark/
presence. In the Newberry Library in Chicago, Maungwudaus spoke to me
across time. But why him? Why he to me?

I came to believe that he went to Europe out of curiosity and adventure,
as much as in hopes of making money along with his family and other tribal
members who accompanied him as a performing troupe. To me, curiosity is
a particularly *writerly* trait, and so, as an author, I relate to Maungwudaus as
fellow seeker and traveler.

The ways he differs from other Ojibwe writers of his times interests me
as well. Although Maungwudaus's 1848 publication makes him the first
Native American travel writer, remarkably he was not the only early Ojibwe
travel writer. Kah-ge-ga-gah-bowh/Copway wrote of his travels in Europe in
his 1851 *Running Sketches of Men and Places, in England, France, Germany,
Belgium, and Scotland.* Kah-ge-ga-gah-bowh records his impressions of London and other cities in Europe, but with less curiosity and detail than I read
in Maungwudaus's account. Perhaps this is because the very different purpose of the trips taken by these two Ojibwe men necessarily resulted in very

different accounts. Kah-ge-ga-gah-bowh and Maungwudaus's own brother, Keh-ke-wa-guo-na-ba, traveled to Europe as preachers between 1830 and 1840.[25] Given the times, it is not surprising that trips to raise money for missions would sometimes include Native American converts, and that they would write of their travels. But European travel by Native Americans for other than church business must have been exceedingly rare—I can think of no example other than Maungwudaus. His motives for European travel, according to his own 1848 narrative, seem personal, and perhaps even what we might think of as self-promotional today—exactly the stuff of contemporary memoir or travel writing.

I found Maungwudaus an intriguing subject. His singular journey, the tragedy of it, and Maungwudaus's connection to the painter George Catlin seemed extraordinary and improbable to me. I could not believe I had not heard more about this man. Yet, works directing attention to early Native American authors before Peyer's 2007 anthology, which contains Maungwudaus's narrative, made little or no reference to Maungwudaus. This is perhaps because his contribution is slight—a travel account no longer than a pamphlet, hymns, political documents, and some letters. But there may be other reasons literary criticism has failed to recognize the contribution of missionary writers and those who came from the missionary tradition. Critic Randall Moon, writing about American Indian writer and preacher William Apess, expresses a resistance to an Indigenous missionary writer: "I sense a political unease over Apess because he writes too much like a white person, with no trace of a Native 'voice,' and too Christianized to be recognized as an 'authentic' representative of Native America." But why should a voice rising out of Native American experience, especially one so clear and particular as Maungwudaus's, be ignored? Moon, in discussing Apess, suggests the problem is purely political, and I agree. In studying other narrative traditions arising out of particular cultural backgrounds, I find that all genres of early writing are embraced regardless of the political stance they seem to take. Moon compares the situation to the study of slave narratives now commonly read for their resistance to the hegemony from within, and he remarks that "it is interesting that critics would be blind to the same kind of strategies of resistance by Native American writers in the Nineteenth Century."[26]

Perhaps because I read Maungwudaus as one writer can read another, with sympathy for the task and admiration for the accomplishment, the "strategies of resistance" in Maungwudaus's work came clear to me immediately. His ways of resisting hegemony are apparent in the very title of his narrative: *An Account of the Chippewa Indians, Who Have Been Travelling among the Whites, in the United States, England, Ireland, Scotland, France,*

and Belgium; With Very Interesting Incidents in Relation to the General Char-
acteristics of the English, Irish, Scotch, French, and Americans, with Regard to
Their Hospitality, Peculiarities, etc. In pronouncing that he would characterize "the English, Irish, Scotch, French, and Americans" in regard to their
"Peculiarities," Maungwudaus enacts a resistance. He looks back on the
"other," who has, for so long, gazed upon Indigenous people with curiosity
and detachment. Although his status as a trained missionary might make
him less acceptable politically, he takes on the task of turning the tables
on two centuries of dominant discourse with particular intensity, a distinct
voice, and a humor that attracted me enormously.

   I could not immediately address how little critical attention was paid
to Maungwudaus, but I could allow him into my creative process. When
Maungwudaus quietly interjected his descriptions of the English men as
whiskered as black squirrels and English women as *too weak to carry their*
own babies, I was hooked. He allowed me a glimpse of an early Ojibwe-
centered view of Europeans that excited my imagination. In response to
my research and reading of this nineteenth-century Ojibwe author, and as
an act of intellectual recovery, I wrote *Curiosities: A Play in Two Centuries.*
Although I was inspired by historical research to write this play about the
life of Maungwudaus, I did so in a spirit of collaboration by including his
actual writing in the script. My play asserts that the heart of Maungwudaus's
story is his curiosity about Europeans, and theirs about the Ojibwe. That
sense of wonder, consternation, and incongruity forms the core of my play.
The lines of the character Maungwudaus are composed of his actual words
with only the very slightest exceptions—literally changing a word or two. I
state this fact in the preface to the script and the program handed out before
the play. I also acknowledge that the lines for the character George Catlin
are taken out of Catlin's actual journals.[27]

   Maungwudaus spoke to me across years, signing found presence/*name*',
sharing with me the most poignant memories of losing seven members of his
group to European diseases. His accounts of their deaths are restrained, but
for each he marked a place of burial—for his wife, children, and his medicine
man. A central part of my creative addition to Maungwudaus's words were
moments I created to allow the contemporary characters to enact Ojibwe
cultural practice of making offerings for the dead—indicated by the passing
of baskets of sweets and tobacco to the audience. In this way, I created an
ephemeral memorial to those who died and were left behind in Europe. At
times I sense that those acts were the reason I made the work. I sensed that
those lost Ojibwe needed to come home through their images. The play is
intended to use images of visual works based on this man and the family

he lost. In the notes to the play, I make clear the irony that Maungwudaus suffered poverty and ignominy in life, and yet he is the subject of a painting that sold at auction for millions of dollars and that was later retrieved at an unknown price by the Canadian government and then deemed a national treasure.[28] Part of the intention of my play was to create another image of this man so his memory becomes an Ojibwe national treasure as well.

As I said at the opening of this essay, we do not write alone. We write into and out of a great telling that brings us stories and songs, that teaches us to look and listen. The script for *Curiosities* is made in order to include collaboration from the players, including performance of dance, song, poetry, spoken word, and presentation of artwork as created during the play or via projection. In my 2010 script, Gordon Henry Jr. contributed the opening speech, which I selected from his dramatic work titled *Ghost Supper Karaoke*. Margaret Noori contributed much of the Anishinaabemowin translation of lines as well as lyrics to songs. Mike Zimmerman was also instrumental in translating Maungwudaus's speech. I consider this play an ongoing collaborative act, allowing players to improvise according to their varied talents and abilities with Ojibwe language. In this sense, and in the play's treatment of the passage of time, the form of this work is both contemporary and traditional. The movement in time is inspired, in part, by the British playwright Caryl Churchill's *Far Away*, and by Greek tradition as well. There's a chorus of sorts, and stage directions for movement left, right, and center suggest strophe and antistrophe. The risky element of the play is that performers become a 1840s-era Ojibwe performance troupe and return to the present day repeatedly—an aspect that is communicated in notes to the audience.

The script also moves through multiple media, suggesting that Ojibwe hymns can be played from available collections and/or sung aloud, and it is indeed possible to find and sing hymns actually written or translated by Maungwudaus. One such hymn is included in the text of the play. In the 2010 production of *Curiosities*, I created slides to run in the background to suggest setting changes via historical and contemporary images. Several images of Maungwudaus are available online, including daguerreotypes and a portrait by the noted Canadian artist Paul Kane. I used those toward the end of the play to reinforce the actuality of the character portrayed. George Catlin's paintings and journal sketches illustrated some scenes, particularly when images of the actual persons in Maungwudaus's narrative could also be projected. Sketches attributed to Say-say-gon (who traveled with Maungwudaus), included in Catlin's journals, were projected in scenes narrated by Say-say-gon's character, and I took his lines from stories Catlin attributed directly to Say-say-gon.

The following excerpt is from Act 1. The action takes place just as a group of Natives of varying appearances and ages mistake Maungwudaus for a street person:

[*Acting impatiently, one of the group pays bus fare for Maungwudaus. Group, close together as if holding bus rails. Maungwudaus staggers as he speaks.*]

Maungwudaus: Like mosquitoes in America in the summer season, so are the people in this city, in their numbers, and biting one another to get a living. Many very rich, and many very poor; about 900 births and about 1100 deaths every week in this city alone.

[*Maungwudaus sways unsupported while group holds rails.*]

Maungwudaus: Many ladies and gentlemen ride about in carriages. The carriages, servants, and horses are covered with gold and silver. Hundreds of them walk about in the parks, the servants leading little dogs behind them to air them.

[*He stoops to read a sign as a voice offstage says*]

Voice: This seat is reserved for handicapped, elderly people or others who may need assistance and for pregnant women.

[*Maungwudaus sways and leans toward the group.*]

Maungwudaus: The English women cannot walk alone; they must always be assisted by the men. They make their husbands carry their babies for them when walking.

[*After a time, group begins to depart bus.*]

2-Troupe/Say-say-gon: [*to group*] Hold up a minute. Here you go, old-timer—or ghost or whatever. [*Takes out a package of Prince Albert, offers to Maungwudaus.*]

1-Troupe: *Maajan!*

[*Maungwudaus makes hand movements to shoo him away, then seems sorry.*]

4-Troupe: Please? *Daga.*

3-Troupe: Don't make him leave . . .

[*Maungwudaus, happy with gift, shows off the tobacco.*]

Maungwudaus: Prince Albert is a handsome and well built man. They took us into the Queen's house. She is a small woman but handsome.

[*pointedly looks around at the ladies assembled*] There are many handsomer women than she is.

[*laughter*]

1-Troupe: Yeah, you met Prince Albert and Queen Victoria . . .

Maungwudaus: Her house is large, quiet country inside of it . . . [*becomes animated as he speaks.*] When she goes out she has a great many warriors before and behind, guarding her; most of them seven feet tall. Their coats and caps are of steel; long white horse-hair in waves on their heads. They wear long boots, long gloves, and white buckskin breeches . . . They do not shave the upper part of their mouths, but let the beards grow long, and this makes them look fierce and savage like our American dogs when carrying black squirrels in their mouths.

[*All laugh.*]

Because my portrait of Maungwudaus comes through his own words, my ability to create around established dialogue depended upon the implied setting of my play. Writing characters into the places this man once walked, and in sites he wondered at and where he mourned, I hope to suggest to my audience the amazed traveler. I wanted to convey what Maungwudaus risked and gained in his travels. I wished to pay my coauthor, Maungwudaus, due respect by paying respects to those he lost and had to leave so far from their native land.

In recovering an Ojibwe literary tradition, we Anishinaabe writers can note important works created from within our own culture group, from our close relatives, all the way back to very early in Native American literary history. Knowing we had others come before us makes room for today's authors. In responding to the work and lives of two literary figures, Bamewa-wa-ge-zhik-a-quay and Maungwudaus, I find myself on the path they marked for me. I find signs of their presence/*name'* to answer an absence:

this is survivance. Having ancestry is everything to Ojibwe people, and having literary ancestors makes a tradition of which we can be proud, and to which we feel a responsibility. Ojibwe writers today can honor the past, an important Ojibwe value, now that we can know our early writers. We can do so by reading and responding to these early voices. This is what I set out to do in my creative work. I write, and will continue to write, in conversation with other Ojibwe writers, scholars, artists—thinkers. The purpose for my providing critical context is, in no small part, to show how that context increasingly moves toward an Anishinaabe center.

NOTES

1. In my literary-critical work, I often use *Ojibwe* (rather than Anishinaabe) because the term *Ojibwe* makes clear that I mean the particular group rather than Odawa (Ottawa) or Potawatomi, who also consider themselves Anishinaabe. Also, *Ojibwe* allows me some objective space. This is a stylistic choice and does not suggest that others should follow suit or even accept my use of the term *Ojibwe*.

2. John D. Nichols and Earl Nyholm, *A Concise Dictionary of Minnesota Ojibwe* (Minneapolis: University of Minnesota Press, 1995), 91.

3. My understanding of this verb (*name*) is informed by conversations with Tobasonakwut Kinew/Peter Kelly (March 2003) and Margaret Noori, who recorded Roger Roulette's use of the verb (June 2011). The word seems to be associated, at least connotatively, with ways of marking presence, such as Ojibwe rock paintings. Perhaps there is some relation to the Anishinaabemowin word for sturgeon, *name/namewag*, a component of the pigment used to make rock paintings, according to Louise Erdrich's *Books and Islands in Ojibwe Country* (Washington, DC: National Geographic Society, 2003). Another of several similar Anishinaabe words that have *name'* at the root is *nameyaagonagishin*, meaning "leaves an imprint on the snow" according to the Kwayaciiwin.com dictionary, http://www.kwayaciiwin .com/dictionary (accessed October 11, 2011). Such words make me wonder if the idea of "imprint" as related to "sign" is not also contained in *name'*.

4. Aun nish e naubay (Patrick Gourneau), *History of the Turtle Mountain Band of Chippewa Indians* (Belcourt, ND: Gourneau 1970). This book was published in seven editions by my grandfather, and in an 8th and 9th edition (the final in 1993) by Charles Gourneau, my uncle.

5. Robert Warrior. *Tribal Secrets: Recovering American Indian Intellectual Traditions* (Minneapolis: University of Minnesota Press, 1995), xvi.

6. Warrior, *Tribal Secrets*, xvi.

7. Ibid., 3.

8. Penny Patrone, *First People, First Voices* (Toronto: University of Toronto Press, 1984). Patrone states that Jones and Henry had the same mother, and describes the relationship as half-brother. Maungwudaus/Henry, in his letter from Paris ca. 1844, hails Jones as "Brother."

9. Bernd C. Peyer, ed. *American Indian Nonfiction: An Anthology of Writings, 1760s–1930s* (Norman: University of Oklahoma Press, 2007), 14.

10. Donald B. Smith, in *Life, Letters, and Speeches—George Copway (Kahgegahbowh)*, ed. LaVonne Brown Ruoff (Lincoln: University of Nebraska Press, 1997), 23–48.

11. George Copway, *Touchwood: A Collection of Ojibway Prose* (Minneapolis: New Rivers Press, 1987), 84.

12. Smith, *Life, Letters, and Speeches*, 54.

13. Chase S. Osborn and Stellanova, *Schoolcraft, Longfellow, and Hiawatha* (Lancaster, PA: Jacques Cattell Press, 1942), 404.

14. Gerald Vizenor, ed., *Touchwood: A Collection of Ojibway Prose* (Minneapolis: New Rivers Press, 1987).

15. A. LaVonne Brown Ruoff, *American Indian Literatures: An Introduction, Bibliographic Review, and Selected Bibliography* (New York: Modern Language Association of America, 1990).

16. Newberry Library in Chicago, the Minnesota Historical Society archives in St. Paul, and the Native American Press Archives in Little Rock, Arkansas. Libraries accessed electronically include Victoria University Special Collections and the Clarke Historical Library at the Central Michigan University Library (Mount Pleasant).

17. Including authors who described themselves as both Ojibwe (or Chippewa) and Ottawa/Odawa. Excluding William Jones, who was Fox.

18. University of Minnesota, *The Ojibwe Peoples Dictionary*, available at http://ojibwe.lib.umn.edu/main-entry/name-vta.

19. Vizenor does not supply a quick definition of survivance in his own work, but by now I think my audience is familiar with his concept. Deborah L. Masden's *Understanding Gerald Vizenor* (Columbia: University of South Carolina Press, 2009) describes survivance as a "term for the resistant survival of tribal people," which might suffice, although I think Masden's definition lacks the sense of ongoing survival Vizenor intended.

20. Conversation with Anishinaabemowin teacher Tobasonakwut Kinew/Peter Kelly, March 2003.

21. Robert Dale Parker, *The Sound the Stars Make Rushing Through the Sky: The Poetry of Jane Johnston Schoolcraft* (Philadelphia: University of Pennsylvania Press, 2007). Robert Dale Parker has set 1820 as the earliest date of surviving poems by Bame-wa-wa-ge-zhik-a-quay.

22. Parker, *The Sound the Stars Make*, 2007.

23. Personal knowledge. The Native Languages of America website includes "no sa" (meaning father) in a comparative chart of Ojibwe phrases used by Longfellow, at http://www.native-languages.org/hiawatha.htm.

24. Janet Carnochan, *Graves and Inscriptions in the Niagara Pennisula*, http://www.sandycline.com/history/grave3.html (accessed April 2004).

25. Kah-ge-ga-gah-bowh and Maungwudaus's own brother, Keh-ke-wa-guo-na-ba, traveled to Europe as preachers between 1830 and 1840.

26. Randall Moon, "William Apess and Writing White," *Studies in American Indian Literature* (Winter 1993).

27. George Catlin, *Catlin's notes of eight years' travels and residence in Europe: with his North American Indian collection. With anecdotes and incidents of the travels and adventures of three different parties of American Indians whom he introduced to the courts of England, France, and Belgium*, 2 vols. (London: By the author, 1848).

28. "Will 'Maungwudaus' Leave Canada?" *Ambassadors Magazine* 7, no. 15 (2002): 22.

RESOURCES

Aun-nish-e-nauby/Gourneau, Patrick. *History of the Turtle Mountain Band of Chippewa Indians*. Belcourt, ND: Gourneau, 1970.

Bame-wa-wa-ge-zhik-a-quay/Schoolcraft, Jane Johnston. *The Literary Voyager or Muzzeniegun*. East Lansing: Michigan State University Press, 1962.

Beaulieu, Theodore H. "The Shaking Tent," and other stories. In *The Progress (White Earth, MN)*, 1886–1889, 1902–1904.

———. *The Land Allotment Question of the Chippewas*. G.D. Hamilton Printer, 1900.

Blackbird, Andrew J. *History of the Ottawa and Chippewa Indians of Michigan*. Ypsilanti, MI: Ypsilantian Job Printing House, 1887.

Catlin, George. *Catlin's notes of eight years' travels and residence in Europe: with his North American Indian collection. With anecdotes and incidents of the travels and adventures of three different parties of American Indians whom he introduced to the courts of England, France, and Belgium*. 2 vols. London: George Catlin, 1848.

Churchill, Caryl. *Far Away.* London: Nick Hern Books, 2003.

Erdrich, Louise. *Books and Islands in Ojibwe Country.* Washington, DC: National Geographic Society, 2003.

Kahgegagahbowh/Copway, George. *The Life, History and Travels of Kah-ge-ga-gah-bowh (George Copway), a Young Indian Chief of the Ojebwa Nation.* New York: Weed and Parsons, 1847.

———. *Organization of a New Indian Territory, East of the Missouri River.* New York: S. W. Benedict, 1850.

———. *Recollections of a Forest Life, or The Life and Travels of Kah-Ge-Ga-Gah-Bowh.* London: C. Gilpin, 1851.

———. *Running Sketches of Men and Places, in England, France, Germany, Belgium, and Scotland.* New York: J.C. Riker, 1851.

———. *The Traditional History and Characteristic Sketches of the Ojibway Nation.* Boston: Benjamin B. Mussey, 1850.

Keh-ke-wa-guo-na-ba/Jones, Peter. *Nugumouinun genumugumouat igiu anishinabeg anumiajig.* Boston: Crocker & Brewster, 1836.

———. "Removal of the River Credit Indians." *(Ontario) Christian Guardian,* 1848.

Leevier, Annette. *Psychic Experience of an Indian Princess.* Los Angeles: Austin, 1920.

Longfellow, Henry Wadsworth. *The Song of Hiawatha.* Boston: Ticknor and Fields, 1856.

Maungwudaus/Henry, George. *An Account of the Chippewa Indians, Who Have Been Travelling among the Whites, in the United States, England, Ireland, Scotland, France, and Belgium; With Very Interesting Incidents in Relation to the General Characteristics of the English, Irish, Scotch, French, and Americans, with Regard to Their Hospitality, Peculiarities, etc.* Boston: George Henry, 1848.

McCarry, Ralph E. *Reminiscences by Chief White Wolf of the Chippewa.* Sault Ste. Marie: Sault News Print Co., 1957.

Morrison, Eliza. *A Little History of My Forest Life: An Indian-White Autobiography.* Edited by Victoria Brehm. Tustin, MI: Ladyslipper Press, 2002.

Nichols, John D., and Earl Nyholm. *A Concise Dictionary of Minnesota Ojibwe.* Minneapolis: University of Minnesota Press, 1995.

Noodin/Northrup, Joseph (Chief Northwind). *Wawina: The Beautiful Story of an Indian Princess.* Carlton, MN: W.H. Hassing, 1937.

O-pee-chee, Wa-be-no/Cappel, Jeanne L'strange. *Chippewa Tales.* Los Angeles: Wetzel Publishing Co., 1930.

———. *Chippewa Tales Vol. 2.* Los Angeles: Wetzel Publishing Co., 1931.

Osborn, Chase S., and Stellanova. *Schoolcraft, Longfellow, and Hiawatha.* Lancaster, PA: Jacques Cattell Press, 1942.

Patrone, Penny. *First People, First Voices.* Toronto: University of Toronto Press, 1984.

Peyer, Bernd C., ed. *American Indian Nonfiction: An Anthology of Writings, 1760s–1930s.* Norman: University of Oklahoma Press, 2007.

Roulette, Roger. "Noongwa e-Anishinaabemjig: People Who Speak Anshinaabemowin Today." http://www.umich.edu/~ojibwe/stories/roulette.html (accessed June 2011).

Ruoff, LaVonne Brown. *American Indian Literatures: An Introduction, Bibliographic Review, and Selected Bibliography.* New York: Modern Language Association of America, 1990.

Vizenor, Gerald, ed. *Touchwood: A Collection of Ojibway Prose.* Minneapolis: New Rivers Press, 1987.

Warren, William Whipple. *History of the Ojibways, Based on Traditions and Oral Statements.* Collections of the Minnesota Historical Society 5. St. Paul, Minnesota, 1885.

Warrior, Robert. *Tribal Secrets: Recovering American Indian Intellectual Traditions.* Minneapolis: University of Minnesota Press, 1995.

Way Quah Giizhig/Rogers, John. *A Chippewa Speaks.* 1957; reprinted as *Red World and White: Memories of a Chippewa Boyhood.* Norman: University of Oklahoma Press, 1974.

Wright, John Couchois. *Chicago Jig: Legend of the Indian Paradise.* Alma, MI: Babcock & Babcock, 1935.

———. *The Great Myth.* Lansing, MI: Michigan Education Company, 1922.

———. *Northern Breezes.* Harbor Springs, MI: Self-published, 1917.

———. *The Ottawan, a short history of the villages and resorts surrounding Little Traverse Bay and the Indian legends connected therewith.* Harbor Springs, MI: The Author, 1895.

———. *Scenic Michigan in Verse.* Ithaca, MI: Gratiot County Herald, 1939.

———. *Stories of the Crooked Tree.* Harbor Springs, MI: Lakeside Press, 1915.

Beshaabiiag G'gikenmaaigowag
Comets of Knowledge

MARGARET NOORI

AT THE SANILAC PETROGLYPHS SITE, IN WHAT IS NOW MICHIGAN, A figure with a bow and arrow is carved into a stone. It is an image at least three centuries old. According to Anishinaabe teachers, the arrow is not aimed at prey, but is instead a metaphor representing the transfer of information. In its tip are stories, epiphanies, and glimpses of eternity, passed from one generation to the next. These intergenerational ways of understanding are complex, interconnected, and reflected in both Anishinaabe texts of long ago and text being written today. Knowledge recorded in the original language preserves subtle, hard-to-translate ideas. Through indigenous language, meaning can be transferred, like that shot of knowledge, from one generation to the next. For instance, consider the lack of a specific target. The hunter is not aiming at an object. And there is no noun for "knowledge" in the verb-based Anishinaabe language. In place of a single target word or definition, there are instead verbs bound with prefixes and suffixes indicating what is known and who is knowing. Follow, for example, the root word *giken* in several sentences about knowing:

Chizhaazhaagwa gikenjigewag. Long ago they were knowing.
   N'gii gikenimaaigoonanig jibwaa bi dagoshinoying. They knew us before we arrived.
   G'gii gikendamowaad ezhi aadiizookewaad. They knew the way to make stories.
   Gikendaagwad. It was simply known.

These verbs and the way they can be woven together are an integral part of the Anishinaabe network of knowledge, a system of connections between language and conscious or subconscious beliefs. Connections lost in the translation to English are regained when read, and then written, in Anishinaabemowin. It is important to define and discuss indigenous culture using primary, untranslated sources. It is equally as important to consider new untranslated sources as a continuing record of cultural perspectives.

One specific subject of ancient and contemporary Anishinaabe narratives is the relationship between the people and their natural surroundings. In the notably verb-based language of Anishinaabemowin, no single noun equates with the concept of "nature." There is no Lady of the Lake, no Green Goddess, and rarely is a personification of Mother Nature employed. Even those who attempt to translate the idea of "Mother Nature" offer such words as *shkaakaamikwe* or *maazikaamikwe*, neither of which contains the word "mother."[1] Readers find in older texts a concept of nature that encompasses the people's relationship with the land, the trees, the water, and the weather. Keeping in mind this theme of "nature," it is an interesting case study to travel from primary texts to contemporary poetry. Traces of older ideas and narratives can be differently identified through Anishinaabemowin. Contemporary poets who use the old language are compelled by structure and definition to also adhere to an older aesthetic, especially when choosing a traditional theme such as nature.

The sources in this limited discussion range in date from the early 1900s to the present and include the words of men and women from First Nations and reservations in Ontario, Michigan, Minnesota, and Saskatchewan. The range of voices across genders, generations, and locations is intentional. Throughout the process of colonization, identity and specificity were eroded. While pan-tribal Indian and Aboriginal politics could not have succeeded without intertribal cooperation, there is also a point at which nationalism results in self-destructive separatism. Both extremes lead to unrealistic readings and do not serve contemporary writers well. Not all myths and stories are shared by all nations; nor are all dialects and narrative structures unique isolates of the separate communities that exist today. However, in the words of Anishinaabe speakers we find a lingua franca, easily understood by fluent listeners and writers. Unfortunately, all too soon, a time will come when the keepers of the language have always been bilingual. The ability to carry Anishinaabe cultural identity forward depends on the networks of understanding and access built across time.

As we explore the way the Anishinaabe speak and write about nature, it is important to keep in mind the way the Anishinaabeg traditionally tell stories; it is to ask, *Aanii gaa ezhiwebag?* What happened? What did the people and animals do? What was the relationship of the Anishinaabeg to the space and sparks around them? How did the Anishinaabeg discuss the relationships between humans, animals, and forces not seen? These four ways of describing events correspond to the four dominant verb forms in the language, which all speakers navigate by instinct and all learners must understand to become proficient. Perhaps coincidentally, they echo earth's four seasons, four cardinal directions, and other scientific realities used as cultural mnemonic structures. Without question, the attention to action rather than description, and the focus on pronouns over nouns creates a backdrop for understanding that differs from anything English or other Indo-European languages can offer.

Gregor McGregor of Whitefish River First Nation was an adult when he told stories to Leonard Bloomfield in the 1950s. In his stories, readers find a tangible, practical connection to the environment and to the *manidoog*, or spirits. The connection between the land and the people in one of his stories is not anthropomorphic or romanticized, but matter-of-fact and based on an event that was recorded in rock. In fact, the spirit of this story is part of the rock. Nothing about the event is described as surprising or unusual; the rock is not personified. The spirit remains inhuman, without gender or voice.

> *Ningoding   giiwenh   Anishinaabeg   bimishkaawaad   omaa   ziibiing Adikamegoshii-ziihiing.*
>
> As the story goes, the Indians were once paddling their canoes here in the river, in Whitefish River. . . .
>
> *Mii imaa gii-waabamaawaad manidoon ashidaabikishininid.*
>
> That's where they saw a Manitou lying connected to a rock. . . .
>
> *Iniw manidoon niizh mii gaye go gii-mazinibiiwaawaad iniw manidoon.*
>
> They drew pictures of two of those manitous.
>
> *Onaman dash ezhinikaazod waabigan mii iniw gaa-aabaji'aawaajin igiw Anishinaabeg gii-ozhibi-iwaawaad iniw manidoon.*
>
> The clay, which the Indians used when they pictured the manitous, is called vermilion.
>
> *Geyabi noongom naanoomaya naagozibaniig igiw manidoog.*
>
> Even now or a little while ago those manitous were visible.[2]

No time is spent describing the images in detail; instead the focus is on the act of creating the images, leaving a record of the presence. In the Anishinaabemowin text, the obvious connections between the verb *waabamaawaad* (they see them) and the image producing *waabigan* (clay) can be heard. These words also relate to *waabishkaa* (white) and *waabanang* (in the east). The morpheme *waab* is recognizable and connects the idea of sight and symbol to color and space. In this text the science is a part of the story. The story explains that a *manidoo* was seen first with eyes only, and then, through visual literacy, it became connected to the landscape and made permanent. The land then becomes a map of understanding, and the task of the Anishinaabeg is to record what is seen through narrative and image.

Another narrator who discusses the way the spirit is connected to the earth is Angeline Williams, Biidaasigekwe, who was born in Manistique, Michigan, in 1869 and lived most of her life on Sugar Island, just east of Sault Ste. Marie. In 1941, when she was seventy-three, she was interviewed by Charles Voegelin and Leonard Bloomfield. The transcription of those conversations was published as a volume edited by John Nichols in 1991. Although the primary aim of the linguists was to examine her grammar and vocabulary, her stories reveal some of the ways the landscape was a part of life. Williams refers to the way trees were used as signs and often signifiers of important events and ideas. She describes the way trees were named, marked, or became part of the lives of mythic and real characters in her stories. In "Nenabush and the Ducks," Nenabush ends a series of exploits with a bleeding ass, which has turned into a second face. As he runs along the banks of the river, his graphic and physical interaction with the plants give several trees their names.

> *Mitigoonsan gii-ani-giziishin gaa-inaakizod. Gii-miskwiiwi. Gomaapiich miinawaa naageya'iing noopiming gii-ani-izhaa. Mii miinawaa gii-dibaabandizod. Mii gii-ni-noojimod. Bangii eta omigii . . . Miskwaabiimizhiins giga-izhinikaanigoom. Miinawaa gomaapiich aniw gichi-mitigoonsan gaa-inaad: "Gaye giinawaa gigi-izhinikaazom gichi-miskwaabiimizh. Gaye wii gedaganagekwak daa-izhinikaadewan anonda mitigoonsan. Nizhigosag aakoshkadewaad oga-mashkikiwaaboo kaadaanaawaan."*
>
> As he went along he scraped against bushes where he was burnt. He was all bloody. In time he went along to another place farther up from the water. He looked at himself once more. Now he was all well. He had only a small scar . . . Little Red Willow you will be called. After a time he said also to those larger bushes, "You for your part will be called Big Red Willow. And these bushes here will be called Spotted Bark. When My Aunts have a stomach ache they will make a medicinal drink of them."[3]

This traditional tale not only explains how it is that Nenabush was saved from remaining "two-faced" forever. The text in Anishinaabemowin also makes the connection between *miskwiiwi* (the bleeding) and *miskwaabiimizhiins* (the name of the willow). This could also be because both blood and the willow's bark are *miskwaa* (red), but the connection between all of the words, symptom, tree, and color, is one that is not echoed exactly in English. The last line of this story teaches a related lesson in the language by referencing the *mashkikiwaaboo* (medicine), which is a word related structurally to both *mashkawizi* (to be strong), *aki* (the earth) and *akina* (all). Stories of nature often center on healing, but as evidenced by this and other examples, the healing is earned and remembered, not miraculous and benevolent. The medicine is connected to the land and everything else.

We also find connections to the natural world in the stories of Andrew Medler, who was born in Saginaw, Michigan, but lived most of his adult life on Walpole Island, Ontario. As a child he spent three years at the infamous Carlisle Indian School, and later played in a band at the Chicago 1893 World's Fair.[4] His words demonstrate the level of detail used when speaking of nature, and explain how the water was a source of information for the Anishinaabeg. In Medler's story, a young boy learns from an older man how to see a connection between turbulent water and oncoming storms. The very short story also demonstrates the way everything is related and can be described. He includes the depth of snow, location of the well relative to the lake, and the arc of seasonal shifts.

Ngoding ngii-nokiinaaba giiwednong gbe-bboon. Pii dash menookmig, Ziis-baakdoke-giizis egoojing, gii-gsinaamgad. Gii-shpaagnagaa. Nsing ekoozdeng gii-piitaagnagaa. Ggizheb dash ngii-naadinbiish. Maa dash endhamaang dkibi aabtawdaaki yaamgad, besho yaag nbiish. Eni-dgoshnaan wiinaagmi iw nbiish endhamaang. Ge go dbi wnjijwang ge wii go bkwebiigmi. Maanoo dash go naa bangii aabtooshkin niimbaagning ngii-gwaabhaan. Ngii-maajiidoon endaay-aang. Ngii-wiindmawaag, "Gnabaj waya wesiinh yaadig maa ndahbaaning." Aw dash kiwenziinh gii-giigdo, "Aanii dash?" Mii dash gaa-nag, "Waabndamog ow nbiish ezhnaagwak." "Aa nii nga-waabndaan," kido dash aw kiwenziinh. Wgii-waabndaan dash. Mii dash ekdod, "Ji-bwaa-niizhgon'gak wii-bi-gchi-nimkiikaa." Ngii-maajaa dash ge-nokiiyaan. Miinwaa gaa-waabang eshkam gii-aabwaa. Mii dash enaagshig eshkam gii-gchiaabwaag. Ge go mii gii-waabndamaan waas-mowaad giw Nimkiig. Eni-dbikak mii gii-noondwangdwaa Nimkiig, ge go giigchi-nimkiikaag. Gegzhebaawgak goon kina gii-nkaabaawe. Mii eta nbiish gaa bmijwang gegzhebaawgak.

Once I was working in the North all winter. Then when the spring was at hand, in the month of March, there was cold weather. There was deep snow. The snow was three feet deep. In the morning I fetched water. The spring from which we got the water was halfway up a hill, near a lake. When I got there the water in our spring was dirty. Also, the place from which it flowed had muddied water. Nevertheless I dipped up a little, half a filling, in the pail. I took it to our house. I said to them, "It seems as if there may be some creature in the spring from which we get water." Then the old man spoke: "How is that?" I said to him, "Look at the way this water looks." "Well let me take a look at it," said the old man. Then he looked at it. This was what he said: "Before two days have passed there will be a big thunderstorm." Then I went off to work. The next day the weather was warmer. Then in the evening it began to get very warm, and then I saw lightning. When night came we heard the Thunders, and there was a great thunderstorm. By morning all the snow had melted away. Only then did the water flow, in the morning.[5]

The description in Anishinaabemowin of the shift in weather is subtle and precise. The atmosphere not only gets warmer, *gii aabwaa*, there is a warm wind that strengthens when the thunders arrive, leading to a combination that produces lightning. Most interestingly he says, *gii-waabndamaan waasmowaad giw Nimkiig* (I saw the lightning in Thunder), in a way that implies the lightning has a simple relationship with the viewer. This is made clear by his use of *waabndaa*, an inanimate transitive verb. However, the Nimkiig, the Thunders, are more complex. The verb he uses to describe hearing them is a transitive animate verb. More important than any implication of "animacy," which many speakers say is an inaccurate term, the switch in verb types shows that there is a difference between lightning and thunder. This is a cultural perspective not clear in English, and one that relates to other words and stories. The Nimkiig, Thunders, are recognized and are "beings" that have an impact on Anishinaabeg life. Their very name, *nimkiig*, sounds like the words *animikawe* (to leave tracks) and *animiko* (to turn something). These concepts of etymology and aesthetics can only be found when simple stories of science and the environment are told in the original language.

A storyteller who lived a bit later and farther west corroborates the connections between narratives of nature and practical science. Naawakamigookwe, Maud Kegg, was born in 1904 and was raised by her maternal grandparents, Margaret and John Pine, on the shores of Portage Lake in Minnesota. She married Martin Kegg in 1920 and lived much of her life on the Mille Lacs Reservation. Like others, Maud Kegg tells the stories she was told, and they in turn teach much about the way the landscape was perceived. In "Gegoo Gi-madwesing Zaaga'iganiing/What Goes Clink in the Lake" she describes one man's ability to interact with a creature of nature, not quite human and yet more than plant or animal.

Bezhig giiwenh a'aw akiwenzii ezhi-maajaad, naadid mashkiki. Miish giiwenh iwidi jiigibiig ezhi-namadabid giiwenh, ezhi-nagamod manidoo-nagamonan, ingoji-sh igo niiwin, niiwin nagamonan, iniw manidoo-nagamonan. Mii giiwenh ezhi-maajijiwang i'iw zaaga'igaans. Miish giiwenh ingoding, ingoding igo, mii imaa awiiya ezhi-mookiid. Onikaa miinawaa oshtigwaani, akina sa go ezhi-naagozid igo Anishinaabe, mii ezhi-naagozid. Miish giiwenh ezhi-maajtaad manashkikiwed onikaaning, maagizhaa gaye oshtigwaanining, akina go gegoo miinawaa go imaa okaakiganaaning, miinawaa go okaadining. Akina go, mii ezh-balwe'ang giiwenh, mii I'iw wegodogwen dinowa.

One old man went to get medicine. He sat right on the lake shore and sang spiritual songs there, about four of them. That lake started to whirl. Then somebody came up from the water. He had arms and a head and was just like what a human being looks like. Then the old man started making medicine from the other one's arms, maybe his head, all over, even from his chest and legs. He started taking chunks from here and there of I don't know what.[6]

Reading the story in Anishinaabemowin, the physical connection between land, life, and medicine is emphasized. The medicine was made from *onikaaning* (his arms), *okaakiganaaning* (his chest), and *okaadinin* (his legs). The morpheme these words share is *kaan*, which is also the word for bone and a close cognate to the term *niikaan*, a term used to describe a male friend in a ritual setting, also now used as a communal refrain at some ceremonial gatherings. Reading this story in Anishinaabemowin, connections can be made between bones, bodies, and ceremonial medicine. Certainly, these same connections could be made in English, but they are irrefutable in Anishinaabemowin.

Naawakamigookwe speaks of medicine again in the story "Webinige-giizis (Throw Away Moon)" when she says:

Miish giiwenh awiiya aakozid—dibi go ji-aakozid, okaading, onikaang, opikwanaang—mii mitigoons we'o-izhi-bookobidoowaad. Miish iwidi asemaan ezhi-agwapinaawaad iwidi ishkweyayi'ii. Mii ezhi-biibaagiwaad, mii iwidi gwayak a'aw giizis agoojing. Mii iwidi epagidoowaad. "Niwebinaan indaakozi-win," mii giiwenh ikidowaad.

It is said that if someone is sick—I don't know where he'd be sick in his leg or arm or his back then they go and break off a stick. There at the end they tie tobacco. Then they call out straight up in the sky at the moon. That's where they throw it. I throw away my illness, that's what they say.[7]

This short description of ritual healing relies on parts of nature combined, the *mitigoons* (branch) and *asemaan* (tobacco), and a gesture of sending thoughts across the sky, to the *giizis* (sun). Interestingly, the term for moon, *dibikigiizis*—literally, the night sun—is not used. The text clearly says only "giizis," which means only "sun," but as part of the title and the name of a month means "moon." Again, the connection between the sun and moon can be stated as part of Anishinaabe literature, but it is also embedded in the language, implying an understanding of the moon and sun as related opposites marking cycles in time and space. In these networks of understanding, we see the Anishinaabe view of nature.

As explained by these storytellers, nature is sustenance, and due to its significance it must be understood as precisely as possible. The relationship between the land and the people is not one of mystery and superstition, but one of habit and description. Across Anishinaabe Akiig, which would be the traditional territory of the people prior to the existence of the United States and Canada, the same metaphors are used to convey a belief in sustainable stewardship. The gifts of the land are often described as a garden or field that must be tended, and for which the people must give thanks. A member of the Garden River First Nation in Ontario, Dan Pine Sr. lived from 1900 until 1992 and was considered a great storyteller and healer. His views of the Anishinaabeg connection to the land reaffirm the belief that the earth is a *kitigan* (field) of resources. Recently, the Ojibwe Cultural Foundation published transcriptions of his story "Anishinaabe Amiikan," in which Pine explains the *Anishinaabe odi ezhi-aayaawin*, or traditional way of life. According to Pine, long ago:

> *Gii kendan kina gegoo Mnidoon ga miingojin, ga tamaagjin ma akiing.*
> He knew what the Creator gave him, what was on the earth for him.
> *Gii miigwechwige pane . . .*
> He always gave thanks . . .
> *Gii wii jiindaan kina gegoo.*
> He was connected to everything.
> *Mii go bi-gshkozid bi-zaaghiwed giizis, mii go gewii kizheb paamse ma giizhaa nkweshkwaad mishoomsan, waawiijiwgojin gbe giizhig.*
>
> He would rise as soon as the sun came up, and go for a walk to meet with his Grandfather who was going to walk with him all day.
> *Aan, ni-naakshig ni-bnghishmod giizis, mii go miinwaa oodi.*
> By evening as the sun is about to set, it is the same thing.
> *Mii kina gegoo mkwendang ga-zhichgesig gaazhi wnijged.*
> There he remembers the things that he did not carry out, his faults.
> *Kina go gegoo mii ma temgadnig.*
> Everything is there, this is where it is.
> *Gii aahaabwewendizo ma, jibwaa bngishmod giizis . . .*
> That is where he forgave himself, before the sun went down . . .

Gezhi wii ji bmaadsiindang kina gego mishoomsan, gookmisan aki ngooki.
He knew how to live with everything, his grandfather, and his grandmother, the earth.[8]

Later he says:

Mshkiki wdi-zhnikaadaanaawaa, wa dnawo bemaadis kina miijim aawan enji-wiisniimgag.
They call it medicine, that kind of person, it is all food that nourishes itself.
Aki aawan wi, enji-mno-yaamgag mii nikeyaa gaa-zhi-zhichgaademgag, gaa-zhigoowiing ji-zhayaaying, ji-zhi-bmaadsiiying.
It is the soil, that is why it is good, it was made this way, we were made to live that way, this way of life.
Kina gego gii-zhichgaademad.
Everything was made.
Dbishkoo gchi-gtigaan, gnimaa ge gdaa-kid.
Just like the big field, you might say.
Mii ezhnaagog aki.
That is how the earth looks.
Giinwinh dash maa gadaa biitaanaa g-wiisnimin maa.
That is us that live in it and are nourished by it.
Ka mno-yaamin, ka-zaaghidmin.
We will live in harmony and we will love each other.[9]

Pine emphasizes the connection between humans and nature and the need to give thanks for the gifts of the *kitiganan* (fields).

The same ideas about gifts from the earth and need for thanks and humility can be found in communities hundreds of miles away. Roger Roulette is a linguist and teacher in Winnipeg who carries many of the old words and old ways of thinking. His story of the origins of Anishinaabe ceremony begins with someone who is hungry and finds a moose. In the story, the moose is killed and prepared before the hunter continues on to find other gifts in a great *kitigan.*

Megwaa babimosed, ogii-waabandaanan iinzan gitigaanensan.
While he was walking along, he noticed some gardens/vegetables.
Niibowa iinzan gitigaanensan ogii-waabandaanan.
He saw many vegetables.
Mii gaa-izhi-gidakiid ini gitigaanensan.
He then harvested the vegetables.

Wiinge iinzan gii-jiikendam.
He apparently was delighted.
Misakamig gegoon iinzan ogii-ayaanan.
He had plenty of things.
Awenen miigwech ge-inag, wegodogwen miigwech ge-idamaan iinzan inendam.
Who should be thanked, he didn't know what to thank, he was thinking.
Mii-sa miziwe ayinaabi.
He looked all over.
Gaan awiyan owaabamaasiin.
He saw no one.
Mii-sa inendam onjida ji-miigwechiwi'idamaan gegoo.
He then thought, I must give thanks to something.
Miisa ezhi-odaapinang aanind moonzowi-wiiyaas.
Then he took some moose meat.
Miinawaa ezhi-odaapinaad aanind ozigwaakominan.
Again, he proceeded to take some saskatoons.
mii-sa ishkwaach ezhi-odaapinang aanind gitigaanensan.
He then took the last of the vegetables.
Gii-ishkwaa odaapinang gakina wiisiniwin, gaa-izhi-atood jiigaatigong.
After he took all the food, he leaned against the tree.
Miigwech ikido iinzan bekish ayinaabi.
He apparently said thank you while he was looking around.
Mii-sa eni-izhi-maajaad.
He then proceeded to leave.
Mii i'imaa iinzan gaa-onjisemagak nanaakongewin.
This, is where giving honour/religion, came from.[10]

Roger's story echoes the idea that nature is abundant, but must be carefully harvested in a sustainable and respectful manner.

Roger is also one of the storytellers who speaks of what happens when the natural order of things is disturbed. He doesn't reference a "Mother Earth" figure, but rather a living source who aids the survival of the Anishinaabe. Gezhizhwazh is "a hero in Ojibwe legends" known for her "cleverness and her own sacrifice to battle these wiindigog." The *wiindigog* are creatures of the far north that represent all that opposes health and survival. During a CBC radio show, Maureen Matthews interviewed Roger and Caroline Anderson, from the Ojibwe Reserve at Fairford, in Northern Manitoba, who told a story about Gezhizhwazh. As Maureen explained, "The name means 'to try to cut,' and it refers to her willingness to be snacked upon by cannibals while she is waiting to murder them."

Ngoji iidog gii-bi-onji-bagamigoziwag ongo wiindigoog. Mii omaa gii-ayaawag. Gii-ayaagaansiinowag iidog aaniish nishtam ishkoniganensan ono gii-ayaagaansiinowag Anishinaabeg. Mii gaa-izhi-bagamigoziitaagowaad ini aya'aa wiindigoo. Bezhig ikwezensan gii-nawapowag. E-bimi-gojigaamoonaawaad ogii-gaagiishkizhwaawaan. Mii Gojizhwaazh ogii-izhinikaanaawaan.

Mii 'awe Gojizhwaazh, mii aazha ozhigewag imaa ini Anishinaabe' odoodisaawaa' ongo Wiindigoog. Mii ezhi-anoonaawaad mii 'awe Gojizhwaazh. Gegoo odanoonaawaan ji-naajibatwaadaminind ji-awi-gagwedwenid. Ah, ikido iinzan mii d'aw Gojizhwaazh, Wiindigoog ongo gaa-odisinekwaa. Ozhiitaag! Giwii-amwagoowag noo'om gaa-dibikag ikido iinzan. Aazha iinzan ezhi-ozhiitaawaad. Gichi-bagwaanegamig iidog ogii-ayaanaawaa. Iidog ezhi-ozhitoowaad wedi zhoonzhaakowaabaawajigewag. Bi-biindigaawaad ini Wiindigoog ji-biindigeyaaboononid. Zhigwa omaa ogii-nepiiminaanaawaan waagaakwadoon ji-onji-niiwana'waawaad.

Mii aazha geget. Mii goda wiin a'a Gojizhwaazh, Gojizhwaazh bi-giiwen. Gegoo miinawaa giga-inaajim odinaawaan iinzan. Mii aazha Gojizhwaazh gii-ishkwaa-dibaajimod o'o. Miisa eni-izhi-giiwebatood. Na, mii zhigo gaa-izhi-ozhiitaakanda'waawaad, mii gaa-izhi-maaji-biindigeyaaboonowaad iidog. Apane iidog akawe bakite'aawaad waagaakwadoon ono Wiindigoo'.

Mii 'iwe gaawin aapiji nimaaminonendanzii aaniin gaa-ani-inaadizookaagoowaang. Mii dash wiin igo iwe eko-maamikawiyaan.

Roger's abridged version of Caroline's story explains:

The story goes . . . she sacrificed herself to be taken by the Wiindigoo because they were going toward where the Ojibwe people were living. And there was a band of them. So she thought, if she sacrificed herself to be taken by the Wiindigoo, in that way, she'd have an eye on them, of what they were going to do, what their plans were, even though during the time she was with them, they would cut pieces of her and eat parts of her. But in order to save her own people, the Anishinaabe, she would be taken as lunch. And then she knew their plan. So, when she had the chance to go to the Anishinaabe village, she told them what the Wiindigoo's plans were. She wanted to be the first one to strike, and she also showed the Anishinaabe how to kill the Wiindigoo. And she's seen as a hero because she was the main killer of Wiindigoo. And that's the story.[11]

Stories of balance and disturbance, harmony and discord, calm springs and terrifying thunders are all part of the Anishinaabe tradition. As with any language, single words contain vast ideas. The concepts that surface when speaking of nature are the ones shot forward in time like an ancient arrow:

waabigan could be defined as a light mark in the dark earth; *miskwaasiniin* is a swampy place where the earth bleeds; *giizis* is an arc of time between dawn and sunset guided by a grandfather sun and later an alter night sun, the moon; and *maashkiki* is that which comes from the earth and provides strength as medicine. These are the ideas contemporary writers include when writing in Anishinaabemowin, and doing so in the language is arguably the most efficient route to the truth.

One example of a second-language writer using the language of her teachers is Kateri Akiwenzie-Damm. She says, "I write to tell something of who we are, to know myself, to remember, to celebrate life, to transform the injustice and hatred and lovelessness around me into something creative and positive. I am inspired by the land, by my ancestors, by the friends and lovers and enemies who have been my teachers."[12] Hers is clearly a postcolonial voice grappling with the difficulty of two languages. Her poems, as translated by her teacher Basil Johnston, are works of collaboration across subjects and generations. In perfect balance, they write of love and nature, both as raw and real as life itself. The poem "Benae Anami-auzoowin/ Partridge Hymn" is one that expresses literal and figurative hunger and does it with a different clarity in Anishinaabemowin compared to English. The drumming, *medawaewae*, is a serious and ceremonial sound, not the standard *dewegan*. The possessive noun that in English reads, "my love" is actually the statement "I am loving you" in Anishinaabemowin.

> *Baeshoowitiwishin*
> Come to me
> *K'zaugi-in*
> My love
> *K'd'minido-waewaemin*
> I am calling
>
> *Babaum-itoowishin*
> Hear my song
> *Ae-izhi-anami-auziyaun*
> Sweet one
> *Medawaewae-aungissaeyaun*
> I am drumming
>
> *Maewishkoohnssing*
> In the reeds

Kbaubee-in
dear one
K'zaugi-in
I am waiting

Baeshoowitiwishin
Come to me
K'd'minido-waewaemin
My love
K'zaugi-in
I am calling[13]

In another poem written by Akiwenzie-Damm and translated by Johnston, the same interplay between languages is evident. The translation is correct in spirit, but the world of one poem is not the world of another. In "Nindo-waewaemauh Ishkotae-benaessih/Calling Thunderbird," the term selected for Thunderbird, which connects back to earlier stories, is not the usual *Niimkiig*, but rather *Ishkotae-benaessih*, a bird of fire. The desire to connect is as intense as described by Pine and Roulette. Yet, as this contemporary woman describes her desires through metaphors of nature, the ancient lesson of life is quite clear. The sense of relationships based on survival is evident, and there are layers in this poem of two worlds, two languages, that would be lost if only the English were available.

N'cheebitauk-doonaewutch; tibishko
My lips are dry
Anaukunushkook zhaushaub-waukishinoowaut gooning
Reeds piercing late winter snow
Yaushkawaewae-ishkauwut; mee ae-izhi
Rattling your name
Gauskawaewaeminaun
In the cold wind blasting
Kissin-aunimuk
From my lungs

Tipaubauwizhishin
Rain into me, love
Tipaubauwizhishin
Rain into me

N'cheeby-tauk-anikae
My arms are dry
Nkunimun zagazoowaeitaenoon
Bones bereft of marrow
Nweeyoowim inautaeshimooh
This flesh is a shadow
Keen nakae
Stretching toward your body
Bunu-inaeniminaun
Brittle so brittle your memory

Tipaubauwizhishin
Rain into me, love
Tipaubauwizhishin
Rain into me

Naunauwi-zeepeengawae
My eyes are dry
Iskutae-tigawaeyauh
Riverbeds cracked by the sun
Bunaussin mitauwun
Dust settling in stillness
Nindo-naewautoot oshki-zeepeekaun
Thirsting for fresh streams
Tchi aundji-igiyaun
To revive me

Tipaubauwizhishin
Rain into me, love
Tipaubauwizhishin
Rain into me
N'zaugaidjinaewiss
My womb is dry
Pushkawau-dauwingauh
Earth unseeded
Weesigau-kummikau
My soil bitter tasting
Bawaussin
fallen
Baussi-kummikauh
fallow

Tipaubauwizhishin
Rain into me, love
Tipaubauwizhishin
Rain into me[14]

Although there has been a resurgence of teaching, the language still hovers on the brink of extinction. Few teachers have time to write intentional verse, but there are some. James Shawana is one. Originally from Wikwemikong, and currently a teacher in Ontario, Shawana writes songs and verse to reinforce his lessons and express his love of the land and language. His poem "Mino Gizhebaawin/It's a Good Morning" is an example of simple, yet powerful observation. Like the songs collected and verse written by Vizenor, Shawana's words connect nature and the human experience as well as any imagist verse.

Nongo, kizheb, aabiji mino kizhebaawin.
Today, this morning, it is a very good day.
Jiigbiig daa'aa.
I have the beach.
Noondwaa Pichi.
I hear the robin.
Noondaan biish.
I hear the water.
Noogkaamgaa.
All is soft.
Mishomis, Giizis, waase'waachge.
Grandfather Sun shines.
Mino kizhebaawin
It is a good day.[15]

At the same time in another place, Jim Northrup, columnist, storyteller, playwright, and poet, decided to try writing in Ojibwe in 2002. His poem "Dash" asks and answers the questions that ripple across generations.

Dash Iskigamiziganing
Then at the Sugar Bush
Nimbiindaakoojige
I make an offering of tobacco
Ninga-naadoobii iwidi noopiming wayiiba
I'll gather sap in the woods soon
Aaniin apii waa-ozhiga'igeyan iwidi Gwaaba'iganing dash
When will you tap trees over there in Sawyer? Then . . .

Mii bijiinag i'iw apii baadaajimowaad aandegwag dash
At the exact time the crows arrive telling news . . . then
Mii zhigwa oshki-ziigwang
When it is a new Spring
Aaniin dash apane wenji-izhichigeyan i'iw dash
Why do you always do this . . . then?
Apane nimishoomisiban apane gii-izhichige dash
Always my grandfather who is gone always did this . . . then
Awenen ge-wiidookawik iskigamizigeyan dash
Who will help you at your Sugar Bush . . . then?
Indinawemaaganig miinawaa dash niwiijiiwaagan dash
My relatives and my partner . . . then
Awenen waa-mawadisik iskigamizigeyan dash
Who will visit you at your sugar bush . . . then?
Awegwen iidog dash
I don't know who . . . then
Aaniin dash apane wenji-izhichigeyan dash
Why do you always do this . . . then?
Niniijaanisag miinawaa dash noozhishenyag miinawaa dash
For my children and my grandchildren . . . then
akina Anishinaabeg niigaan igo ani-nitaa-iskigamizigewag dash
for all the Anishinaabeg to show them how to make syrup . . . then
Awegonen waa-aabajitooyan iwidi iskigamiziganing dash
What will you use over there at the sugar bush . . . then?
Ninga-aabajitoon asema dash ininaatigoog dash bagone'igan dash
I will use tobacco then maple trees then a drill then
negwaakwaanan dash ziinzibaakwadwaaboo dash iskigamiziganaak dash
taps then maple sap then a frame for the kettle then
okaadakik dash misan dash iskigamigani-ishkode dash zhingobaandag dash
the kettle then firewood then a fire for boiling sap then balsam branches then
dibaajimowinan dash
stories then
Mii iw
That is it
Mii sa iw
That is really it[16]

As I became more fluent in the language, although I will always be a student, I answered his example and began a dialogue of my own. In one of his columns, he told how someone asked: *"Aaniidash aanind ininatigo-ziigwaagamide makadeagame miinwaa aanind nangagame?* Why is some maple syrup dark and some light?" His reply, "*Baam enji dibikad aanind ndo'zaawaa.* Because some we boil at night" became the basis for the poem "Dibiki-Ziigwaagaame/ Night Syrup."

> *Ziigwaagame n'daagwaagominaan*
> I stir syrup into
> *makademashkikiabo miinwaa*
> coffee and
> *kwejimdizo, "Wenesh e-naagamig*
> I ask myself "What
> *dibikiziigwaagame?"*
> does night syrup taste like?"
> *Gete-misaabe-zekwekik ina?*
> The ancient iron kettle?
> *Giiwedinong giizhik ina?*
> Northern cedar?
> *Zagaswans ina?*
> A bit of smoke?
> *maage*
> or
> *Enangwiiganing aandeg ina?*
> The wing of a crow?
> *Moozo akiianzo shkiijigan ina?*
> The brown eye of a moose?
> *Oshki miikans-maamad tigwaking ina?*
> A new path in the woods?
> *Ode noondan abita-dibikong ina?*
> Hearing a heart beat at midnight?
> *Miidash nsostooyaanh*
> And then I understand
> *wiishkobii-kade-aagamide*
> sweet dark syrup
> *bimaadiziwin e-naagamig.*
> tastes like life.

A few years later, I was able to write "Bizindaanmaad/Wind Sound" to explain what the wind, the pines, and continual presence mean to the Anishinaabe. In this poem, not only was it important to convey the correct meaning, but also the sound. A *zhingwag* (pine) should sound like a pine, and the wind does not just come and go, it takes the old variety of forms that hearken back to stories of Medler and others. Ultimately, wisdom is held in the bones, and in the balance of life, in the solid earth that gives structure to our body, which is mostly water. We house our spark of identity within us until we walk on. And the wind can either feed our flame or extinguish it.

Noodin nd'noondaan nanagoodinong
I hear the wind sometimes
Pii "ziiziigwaa" nagamowaad zhingwag
When the pines sing "ziiziigwaa"
Pii shkwandamag mawiiwaad
When the doors cry
Pii baapagishkaawaad waasechiganag
When the windows shake
Miidash gwekaanimad, boonaanimad nengatch piitaanimad
Then the wind shifts, lets up and slows to a new speed
Noongwa jiisakinini da shkitoon weweni jiisakaanke
Now the tent shaker can carefully build his tent
Miidash maajigaaskanozwaad noodinong
And the wordless whispers begin in the wind
Gekaajigba wiindamaaiyangidwa bimaadiziig ezhi-wiindeying
The old ones tell us to live as we are named
Miikojiinangidwa debwemigad nikananannig
And we feel their wisdom in our bones

At other times, I try to justify the classics of two worlds, writing answers unheard to such poets as Wendell Berry, whose poem "The Peace of Wild Things" has a view of nature that contrasts sharply with the one that can be written in Anishinaabemowin. "Gidiskinaadaa Mitigwaaking/Woodland Liberty" offers a new view of the woods and nature, not as benign and less complex than "civilization," but richly diverse, a system with which a person can interact and come to understand the universe more deeply and completely. With respect for the many wise teachings that emphasize scientific reality over precious romantic descriptions, the poem ends with an Anishinaabe view of the constellations Orion and the Pleiades, and a brave walk into a place that evokes the name of a great Anishinaabe leader.[17]

Pii dibikong gaashkendamyaanh miinwaa goshkoziyaanh
When in the night I am weary and awake wondering
endigwenh waa ezhichigewag bgoji Anishinaabensag odenang,
what the wild young Anishinaabeg of the cities will do,

mitigwaaking izhaayaanh miinwaa anweshinyaanh.
into the woods I go and rest.
Nd'mawadishaag zhingwaakwag miinwaa okikaandagoog
I visit with the white pines and the jack pines.
Nd'bizindaawaag zhashagiwag miinwaa ajiijaakwag.
I listen to the herons and the cranes.
Nd'maatookinaag zaagaa'igan ogaawag miinwaa apakweshkwayag.
I share the lake waters with the walleye and the cattails.
Nd'waabaandaanan wesiinhyag miikanag miinwaa nakwejinaanig
I marvel at the complexity of wild paths and webs woven.
Miidash pii bidaaban niswi giosewag miinwaa
Then when the dawn hides the three hunters
niizhwaaswi nimisenhyag dibiki-giizhigong gaazhad
and seven sisters of the night sky
baabimoseyaanh nikeye naawakwe zoonide'eyaanh.
I walk bravely toward the noonday.

Lastly, the connection to nature is also attached to politics and current events. The way the urban welfare state connects with the reservation economy, a vast oil spill in the Gulf of Mexico, and the diversity of homeless people are all subjects of "Bemidjigoding/In the Center of the City." Anishinaabe connections can be found in the term for Americans, the matter-of-fact description of water pollution, and allusions to mothers raising more children than their own. Real mothers are communal; the earth can be a mother in English, but is a struggling ecosystem in Anishinaabemowin, a place where the mer-people cannot survive.

Bemidjigoding
pii nkomisinaanig gashwaanaanig aayaawaad
Chimookiman-chiis teg
miinwaa amoo bagosendaawaad.

In the center of the city
where grandmamas are mamas
there is government cheese
and families of bees speaking dance in the hives.

Ishkonigoning
nandawendamigonanig

sugaswaawaad, sostamowaad
pii dash Anishinaabemowaad gaye.

In the center of the rez
where everyone is a cousin
there is still smoke in the lungs
but some hope for the words rushing out.

Kchigamigong zhawanong
Baashkidemagad
Chizebwized mishepisshu
Nibaanikewag gaawiin geyabi aayaasiiwag.

In the center of the ocean
the miscarriage continues
visible from space draining
the umbilical base of the Mississippi.

Nd'enendaming
nimkiikaa
anongkeyaanh dibang
giikaamagwa chigimag.

In the center of my mind
circuits are shorted
constellations of thought assemble
against all that screams around me.

Giishpin boonigidetawagwa
nitam ensa gizheb
debwewaamdizo, debwewaabmaainan
dibishko inini nameying azhigan ina?

Can noticing be the first act
empty of others' intentions
focused on everyone and no one
like the man who lives under the bridge?

N'ga miijin Chimookiman-chiis
zhabwitooyaan gete-ikidowinan

anamataw biish
miinwaa kidoyaanh "aanii" inini nameying azhigan.

I will eat more government cheese
snatch the ancestors' words from the smoke
pray for the waves to separate from the methane
and say hello to the man under the bridge.

Like the one carved in stone, the students and teachers of one generation who aim at the future send forth knowledge. All of us are children, really, gathering our quiver of thoughts, stringing them carefully on a bent bow, and aiming them into the future, hoping a connection will be made. In "Shoot the Wintermaker," Maud Kegg says:

> *Mii giiwenh mewinzha Anishinaabeg giikajiwaad onzaam ginwenzh bibooninig.*
> *Mii giiwenh mitigwaabikawaawaad iniw abinoojiinyan. Miish ezhi-inaawaad:*
> *"Ishpiming iwidi o-ina'en. Bimo gaabiboonoke." Miish giiwenh ingiw gwiiwiz-*
> *ensag zaagiziba'idiwaad, mii iwidi ishpiming ina'ewaad. Mii iidog bimwaawaad*
> *iniw gaabiboonoken. Miish giiwneh geget ezhi-aabawaag.*
>
> It's long ago and the Indians are cold because the winter is too long. They make bows for the children. They tell them: "Go and shoot up in the sky. Shoot the Wintermaker." The children go outside and aim skywards. They shoot the Wintermaker. And sure enough it warms up.[18]

By reading and writing in Anishinaabemowin, we are able to use sounds, morphemes, and transitive animate constructions that do not even exist in English. It is in this way that we can free ourselves from the expectations and limitations of American literature, Native literature, even nature writing, and create Anishinaabe narratives—each voice unique, yet connected to all the ones before and reaching toward those to follow. As we continue to record and explore the connection between the Anishinaabeg and nature, may we remain good listeners, to the past and in the present, and to the whispers of generations to come.

NOTES

1. Basil Johnston and other Ontario storytellers, including Isaac Pitawankwat, use these terms, but in conversations they have led me to understand these

words as implications of the idea of one who creates, makes new, or provides for life.

2. John D. Nichols, *An Ojibwe Text Anthology* (London, ON: Centre for Research and Teaching of Canadian Native Languages, 1988), 200.

3. Angeline Williams, Leonard Bloomfield, and John Nichols, *The Dog's Children* (Winnipeg: University of Manitoba Press, 1991), 22–23.

4. Medler, in Rand Valentine, *Weshki-Bmaadzijig Ji-Noondmowaad/That the Young Might Hear: The Stories of Andrew Medler as Recorded by Leonard Bloomfield* (Manitoba: University of Manitoba, Department of Native Studies), *Algonquian and Iroquoian Linguistics*, vols. 23–26 (1998): 17.

5. Ibid., 113–15.

6. Maud Kegg and John D. Nichols, *Memories of an Ojibwe Childhood* (Minneapolis: University of Minnesota Press, 1993), 156–57.

7. Maud Kegg, "Nookomis gaa-inaajimotawid/What My Grandmother Told Me," *Oshkaabewis Native Journal* 1, no. 2 (Spring 1990): 94–95.

8. Dan Pine, "Anishinaabe Miikan," *Ojibwe Cultural Foundation Newsletter* 5, no. 3 (May 2010).

9. Dan Pine, "Anishinaabe Miikan," *Ojibwe Cultural Foundation Newsletter* 5, no. 5 (July 2010).

10. Personal communication, April 2, 2011.

11. Maureen Matthews et al., "Mother Earth," transcript, IDEAS, CBC Radio One, June 2003.

12. Akiwenzie-damm, in Blaeser, *Stories Migrating Home: A Collection of Anishinaabe Prose* (Bemidji, MN: Loonfeather Press, 1999), 229.

13. Kimberly Blaeser, ed., *Traces in Blood, Bone, and Stone: Contemporary Ojibwe Poetry* (Bemidji, MN: Loonfeather Press, 2006), 8.

14. Ibid., 10.

15. Personal communication, April 2012.

16. Allison Adelle Hedge Coke, *Sing: Poetry from the Indigenous* Americas (Tucson: University of Arizona Press, 2011), 186.

17. Naawagiizhig (Noonday) was a well-known Michigan chief in the early 1800s, and the surname Naokwegijig is still common throughout Ontario.

18. Kegg, "Nookomis gaa-inaajimotawid/What My Grandmother Told Me," 106–7.

RESOURCES

Blaeser, Kimberly M. *Stories Migrating Home: A Collection of Anishinaabe Prose.* Bemidji, MN: Loonfeather Press, 1999.

Blaeser, Kimberly M. *Traces in Blood, Bone and Stone: Contemporary Ojibwe Poetry.* Bemidji, MN: Loonfeather Press, 2006.

Hedge Coke, Allison Adelle. *Sing: Poetry from the Indigenous Americas.* Tucson: University of Arizona Press, 2011.

Eagle, Melvin. "Gekendaasojig/The Wise Ones." (Bemidji, MN: Bemidji State University, American Indian Studies). *Oshkaabewis Native Journal* 5, no. 1 (Spring 1998).

Kegg, Maud. "Nookomis gaa-inaajimotawid/What My Grandmother Told Me." (Bemidji, MN: Bemidji State University, American Indian Studies). *Oshkaabewis Native Journal* 1, no. 2 (Spring 1990).

Kegg, Maud, and John D. Nichols. *Memories of an Ojibwe Childhood.* Minneapolis: University of Minnesota Press, 1993.

Matthews, Maureen, with Stan Cuthand and Roger Roulette. "Mother Earth." IDEAS, CBC Radio One, June 2003.

Nichols, John D. *An Ojibwe Text Anthology.* London, ON: Centre for Research and Teaching of Canadian Native Languages, University of Western Ontario, 1988.

Pine, Dan. "Anishinaabe Miikan M'Chigeeng," *Ojibwe Cultural Foundation Newsletter* 5, nos. 3 and 5 (2010).

Thornton, Russell, ed. *Studying Native America: Problems and Prospects.* Madison: University of Wisconsin Press, 1998.

Valentine, Rand, ed. and annotated. *Weshki-Bmaadzijig Ji-Noondmowaad/That the Young Might Hear: The Stories of Andrew Medler as Recorded by Leonard Bloomfield.* Manitoba: University of Manitoba, Department of Native Studies. *Algonquian and Iroquoian Linguistics*, vols. 23–26 (1998).

Williams, Angeline, Leonard Bloomfield, and John Nichols. *The Dog's Children.* Winnipeg: University of Manitoba Press, 1991.

Eko-niizh Bagijigan
Stories as Relationships

ANISHINAABEG STORIES ARE EMBEDDED IN RELATIONSHIPS AND relationship-making practices—they institute them, explain them, and/or define them. Many see stories as the living strands (indeed, even living beings themselves) that constitute the relationships Anishinaabeg hold between themselves and with all of Creation. Much like the connections they embody, these are complicated, specific, and intricate acts that describe an ever-changing and fluid exchange that requires constant care and consideration. Stories can also challenge and destabilize relationships, with sometimes positive or negative consequences. With a focus on values like respect and responsibility, however, many Anishinaabeg stories embody interest in forging healthy communities to benefit Anishinaabeg and the world around them.

Accounting for the spirit within stories, Eva Garroutte and Kathleen Westcott advocate that we remain ever aware of the living relationship between stories and the field of Anishinaabeg Studies. In their essay "'The Story Is a Living Being': Companionship with Stories in Anishinaabeg Studies," they caution us to use care in our application of stories as a center, to ensure that we do not repeat the errors of past scholarship that has misconstrued, appropriated, and objectified stories. They ask the important question "Do frameworks for working with sacred stories assist or challenge those who wish to be their good companions?" Concluding with a beautiful example of story, they gesture to a meaningful method of intercultural and mutual exchange that models the responsibilities we have to stories.

Niigaanwewidam James Sinclair, in his essay "*K'zaugin*: Storying Ourselves into Life," asks us to consider how the field of Anishinaabeg Studies might look if we conceived the field through *zaagi'*, love. Performing a close reading of Basil Johnston's essay "Is That All There Is? Tribal Literature," Sinclair suggests that Anishinaabeg language and literature gesture towards a methodology that provides a "pathway out of many ossifying approaches that continue to plague our field, and towards considerations of the intricate narrative processes of Anishinaabeg culture- and community-making that constitute us as a people." Citing Johnston's context and practice as a model, Sinclair demonstrates how love inspires Anishinaabeg to maintain connections and communication with one another, even in the face of violence, disagreement, and continual migration. These are crucial for us to come together and recognize our responsibilities and ties to one another—much like the healthy relationships gestured to by one of our creative and critical ancestors.

Thomas Peacock furthers this discussion in "Teaching as Story," explaining how stories can be employed as pedagogy. Extending the question of how stories may serve as a methodological and theoretical framework for the field of Anishinaabeg Studies, Peacock illustrates the ways stories teach, and proposes that *to teach is to story*. Stories, as living entities, are capable of inspiring action. By letting stories "work on" non-Indian students preparing to be teachers, they are able to "experience"—briefly and empathically—what it means to be Anishinaabeg. In doing so, stories challenge a conventional educational curriculum that has often fixed Native peoples in the past and/or erased them from historical and political narratives altogether. Prospective teachers, armed with this knowledge, can then confront the reality that the Anishinaabeg are real, dynamic, and contemporary peoples.

The Story Is a Living Being

Companionship with Stories in Anishinaabeg Studies

EVA MARIE GARROUTTE AND
KATHLEEN DELORES WESTCOTT

> *Mythic thought is the way traditional people think today and the way*
> *others thought in the past. It is a reasonable way of ordering the world*
> *that presupposes that any activity can happen again. Thus, the telling of a*
> *cosmogonic myth continues creation. . . . The retelling of the myth animates*
> *the story and makes it all happen again—on another sphere of existence,*
> *but not so far away that such power could not break through into our own*
> *plane of being. . . . Myths are true in that sense. They pulse in the telling of*
> *them. The language is vibrant in a sacred way.*
>
> —MAUREEN KORP, *THE SACRED GEOGRAPHY*
> *OF THE AMERICAN MOUND BUILDERS*

THE CURRENT VOLUME INVITES READERS TO CONSIDER WHETHER THE
emerging field of Anishinaabeg Studies can center itself on stories, and what
kinds of questions a field so positioned might undertake. An invigorating
invitation, it raises complex issues. Scholars have contributed a considerable
body of research on Native American stories. Yet such research has often
yielded results that those stories' caretakers find unsatisfying. The excellent
collection edited by Phyllis Morrow and William Schneider, *When Our
Words Return: Writing, Hearing, and Remembering Oral Traditions of Alaska
and the Yukon* (1995), offers a compendium of common critiques. Some
contributors offer concern about scholarly approaches that overanalyze and

"tear apart" stories, become preoccupied with hidden meanings, and exclude Native voices—or include them in ways that strip their authority. Others express frustration with researchers who demand disclosure, misconstrue themes, appropriate and objectify, or impose ill-fitting analytic categories. This is a partial list.

Such criticisms suggest that past encounters between scholarship and Native American stories have gone badly wrong. Can scholars of Anishinaabeg Studies hope for different outcomes as they attempt to place stories at the center of this emerging field? That depends, we suggest, on the intellectual tools they use to engage stories.

For many decades, researchers have applied the perspective of "narratology" to interpret and theorize stories. Directing particular attention to issues of story structure, narratology has influenced scholarship not only within literary criticism, but in anthropology, psychology, and sociology. Still, the approach has critics. Some, like leading narratologist Arthur Frank, observe in his discipline the same analytic heavy-handedness that troubles storytellers. Frank's response directs the analytic gaze away from excessive attention to structural elements and toward the *capacities* of stories: "The study of stories that I propose," he writes, "is less about finding themes and more about asking what stories do, which is inform human life."[1]

Even more importantly, Frank argues for "dialogical" approaches. In place of analysis that "asserts rather than engages," Frank urges practices that avoid "finalizing" stories, tidying them away via imposed intellectual frameworks that appear to speak the last interpretive word. "Dialogue," Frank writes, "implies an ethical demand for openness to the difference of the other, both recognizing what is different and also respecting the need to sustain the difference, not assimilate or finalize it." By inviting many voices, dialogical approaches honor "humans' necessary, inescapable, sometimes beneficial but too often imperfect companionship with stories." Such approaches, Frank proposes, may even "improve the terms of that companionship."[2]

Dialogical narratology promises new possibilities for the intersection between scholarship and stories that scholars in Anishinaabeg Studies invite. Yet they will wish to proceed advisedly. Issues surrounding stories understood as myths—the sacred stories described in some Anishinaabe traditions as living entities—invite particular consideration. This chapter ponders the *consequences* of looking to narratological approaches for the tools Anishinaabeg Studies will use to construe stories. How might these perspectives, even the dialogical varieties, *affect* stories? How do the possible outcomes differ from the consequences accruing within the perspectives that storytellers themselves bring? How, in short, do frameworks for working with sacred stories assist or challenge those who wish to be their good companions?

We proceed via an analytic approach that places an Anishinaabe myth at the center. We begin by presenting a sacred story retold by Anishinaabe/ Cree elder Kathleen Westcott. We then examine two exemplary *narratives*, by which we mean sets of resources from which speakers build up and grapple with individual stories. Our selected narratives represent two important perspectives that define ideas about stories and what they do; one is carried by narratologist Arthur Frank, and one by the storyteller herself. After describing our narratives, we consider how each serves as a starting point for engaging Anishinaabe myths. But first: the sacred story that will focus our remarks throughout this chapter.

AN ANISHINAABE STORY RETOLD BY KATHLEEN WESTCOTT

This section presents a sacred story, introduced and retold by Anishinaabe/ Cree storyteller Kathleen Westcott. The myth is an excerpt from a longer telling that we have previously published. We have elsewhere described the distinctive methodology for collection and presentation by which we generated this material; in the barest terms, our approach included a series of audiotaped interviews, followed by joint inspection of resulting transcripts, along with extensive consultation during writing.[3] Because Anishinaabeg conventionally distinguish personal remarks or reports of more ordinary human experience (*tabatcámaowin*) from sacred stories (*atíso'kanak*),[4] the following passage does the same. Regular font indicates when the storyteller references her ideas, while italics signal the transition to myth.

> This story was given by an elder whose name is Ignatia Broker.[5] I just now went out and offered tobacco with the understanding that the story is a living being. It's alive. So it's important to follow the principle of reciprocity: by giving a gift and asking the story to impart itself to us in a way that will help us gain insight and knowledge, and perhaps even wisdom. Ignatia gave this story for that purpose. . . . So I've made an offering to the story. I consider the offering a form of food. This is a way that I express gratitude to Ignatia and to the story. So, let's just begin.
>
> *This story takes place among the Anishnaabe people of the Great Lakes region, many hundreds of years ago. It begins at a time of year when the snow is melted and the rivers are running. It's a story about a young woman in her early 30's, her*

husband, her children, and her village. This young woman and her husband were looked upon by their people as very admirable because the bond of marriage between them was pure. It was joyous and effortless—their friendship, their intimacy as a couple, their pleasure in being parents, their regard for the older generation, their responsibility toward the elders and toward their community.

In this particular season, which was early to mid-spring, the husband prepared to go on a fishing trip with other men from their village. They set off early in the morning. His wife continued with the day, gathering firewood, tending their children, preparing meals. It was maple-sugaring time, so those activities were also taking place. The day went on with bright sun. There was a warming wind and high hopes for a new year. There was a lot of gratitude among the people for having made it through the winter, for the food stores having lasted long enough.

At the end of the day, the men returned in their canoes to the river's edge where the village was newly established. But there was a heaviness in their bodies as they got out of the canoes. The women came to the edge of the river to help unload the day's catch. It then became apparent that there was somebody missing. The young woman who is the subject of this story realized very quickly that her husband hadn't returned. She heard the story about how he had been pulled under the current and drowned. It was an unusual event. No one could save him.

Her grief began as everyone expected it to, and followed its normal course through all of the ritual and ceremonial procedures: through the burial, through the giveaway, through the cutting of her hair, through one year of carrying her husband's personal bundle. In all these traditional ways, she observed his absence for an entire year. But in this story, the year passed, and the woman was as deeply in grief as at the first moment of learning about the loss of her husband. She had taken care of her children for that entire year and met all her ceremonial responsibilities. But the whole time she felt that she'd walked about quite numb. So after the year-end feast that would usually have ended her year of mourning, she left the village. She walked away, walking into the woods, where she found a particular tree that she felt drawn to. She sat down with her back to the tree, isolating herself. She stayed there season upon season: through spring, through summer, through fall, and through winter. The people of the village took care of her children. They kept her wood stores up, gathered her food. They brought small offerings out to her. When the weather got cold, she would return to her lodge to sleep and later return to the tree, speaking to no one.

Of course, after a time, the elders of the community were deeply concerned. So they came together and they inquired among each other, "What are we witnessing here?" What they learned was that this woman was acting in her own purity and goodness, her own ability. The elders acknowledged among each other, "She's thinking. She's thinking on our behalf. She is working on this carefully within her *heart. This wouldn't be happening if there weren't something coming our way that we need to be prepared for. She's been called to go out and to learn about it."* The elders continued, *"We have to support her as though she's in a prolonged search for guidance, for communion. We may not even be alive when whatever it is she's seeking to prepare us for occurs."* But they were excited to simply back this woman and support her. They reminded the people in the village to keep up what they were already doing. They realized that there was great purpose in her behavior and that they must uphold her well.

A second year passed. It came to be about mid-June. The woman was still sitting there against this tree. And one day, early in the morning, she heard somebody speaking to her, which was very unusual. This hadn't occurred for this entire time. She hears a voice, she looks around, but she really can't see anybody. She eases her body back against the same tree—then she hears the voice again. Only this time she not only hears the sound of the voice but she feels the vibration of the voice, pulsating through her spine. She realizes the tree is talking to her.

Now, anyone listening to the story will understand the tree isn't audibly talking. Instead, their minds have become one, the mind of the woman and the mind of the tree. There's a communion occurring here. The woman and the tree are sharing the energy of thought. And the tree is saying, *"My Granddaughter, I've held you all these months. I've come to know you well. I've come to know your devotion to your people and the strong bond that you carry with your husband. I know that you've lost your will to live and that your desire to drop your body and cross over to join your husband is strong. At the same time, your desire to be of some use to your people is also strong, and it has always been there. You've always connected this desire with your marriage. But I've come to know you well, Granddaughter, and to love you well. I want you to stand. I want you to stand tall, turn around and face me."* Which the woman does.

The tree continues, *"I'm going to show you something about myself. I'm going to share my own self with you by giving you some of my own skin. First, I am going to teach you how to strike my skin."* She does that. The woman strikes the skin—the bark of the tree—and she strikes it in a particular way causing the skin to just flip right off! Then this blessed tree says, *"I am giving you the skin of my very being and I'm going to teach you to cut it in a certain way. . . . I'm going to teach you to go to some of the other ones in the Plant Nation in these woods. You will gather basswood for sewing and willow for framing. . . . You will continue to gather my skin for the body of these baskets that I'm going to teach you to make. They'll be fine and strong, and they'll have great beauty."*

So for several days, the woman and the tree worked together closely. The first birch-bark baskets emerge out of their work. They are glistening in the sun—golden, radiant, functional, beautiful. Then the woman sits. She looks at what they've done.

She sighs at the beauty of it, feeling the joy alive in her heart again. The tree speaks to her again through her mind, saying, "My granddaughter, do you notice that your will to live has returned to you out of your own dignity, your own integrity, out of your desire to help your people, and your willingness to stay alive? You've learned a new skill and you're learning to come into relationship with me, in a manner not unlike your relationship with your husband. Now, I want you to go back to your people. When you have returned to your people, I want you to give these baskets to them as a gift, so that their life will be more beautiful, and a little easier. As you continue to make them, they will continue to provide for you the way your husband once did, and you will continue to live in good relationship with all life.[6] You will be able to care for your children."

So the woman picked up three baskets. She walked back to the village. She was quite radiant but also very humble and grateful. It was the elders that saw her coming first. They stood together to greet her and to welcome her back. And the moment they saw the baskets, without really even knowing the use that they would have and the ease that they would bring, they saw the beauty of them, and their hearts filled with understanding. The woman told the story about the gift she'd been given, and how she'd been restored with the will to live: how she'd been brought back into relationship through knowledge and skill to a purposeful life. She continued to make the baskets. She taught her children how to make them. The tree had given her the way to make offerings and the songs to sing—everything that was necessary to do this work in a sacred way. She passed all this on, and it continues to be passed on to this day. Mii'iw.[7]

ENGAGING ANISHINAABE STORIES: TWO NARRATIVES

The current volume envisions Anishinaabeg Studies as an academic subfield oriented around stories. This goal promises to draw stories, including myths such as the one related above, even more fully into academic discourse. This process implies an encounter between stories and specific *narratives*, which are distinct from stories. While stories feature devices such as protagonist and plot, narratives resemble rules of grammar; they influence the *kinds* of stories that can be told.[8] Any analysis of stories likewise requires a guiding narrative, and we have set ourselves to compare two exemplars. One of these exemplary narratives resides within a body of narratological writing; the other resides in the orally transmitted perspectives of a traditional storyteller. After first supplying an overview of each narrative, we then ask how the assumptions characterizing each might bear consequences for the Anishinaabe story retold above.

Arthur Frank: A Narratological Perspective

The first narrative is represented by the published corpus of influential narratologist Arthur Frank, an impressive body of work that spans decades and culminates in the recent volume titled *Letting Stories Breathe* (2010).[9] Stories, in the narrative that Frank labels "socio-narratology," behave in many ways like living things; they operate as powerful forces influencing how humans inhabit the world. Stories can "emplot" individual lives and "instigate" social change, always "affecting what people are able to see as real, as possible, and as worth doing or best avoided." Stories "may not actually breathe," Frank concedes, "but they can animate."[10]

An especially important function of stories is to enable humans to envision "possible lives." This observation prompts Frank to stipulate for socio-narratology an unabashedly moral goal: to enrich and improve human life by introducing people to more stories, more perspectives, more ways of thinking and being. It is this "dialogic" predisposition that most distinguishes Frank's socio-narratology from older perspectives in narratology, making it a suitable exemplary narrative by which to examine the promise of newer narratological frameworks for Anishinaabeg Studies.[11]

Kathleen Westcott: An Anishinaabe Storytelling Perspective

Our second exemplary narrative is constituted in the remarks of storyteller Kathleen Westcott. This narrative appears in unpublished transcripts of interviews conducted between chapter coauthors in March and April 2005 and is supplemented by subsequent consultations. Like Frank's socio-narratology, Westcott's narrative highlights the tremendous power of stories. A central function of stories, in her narrative, is to "position" hearers; they "shape consciousness and shape choices." They engender "ways of being in the world" that attend to specific possibilities. These include the experiences attributed to the woman in the Anishinaabe myth: "Stories keep the door open for the perception and occurrence of those kinds of experiences."

Also, like Frank's socio-narratology, Westcott's narrative endows stories with capacities shared by living things. She illustrates with an analogy:

> Here's a way to think about [sacred] stories. Suppose you have a garden planted. It exists regardless of who knows about it. At every moment, things are changing all around the garden. The light and the weather are in flux. There may be different animals coming and going. But that garden will hold its shape and size, its directional orientation. It will also influence the conditions of the day, the region, the people. It's like that with a story. Even when no one is visiting the story, it is living. . . . It's a living part of its living context.

Such a story, Westcott concludes, "participates in that river of life that flows into and through every being, in every moment of our lives. That river endows all forms of life with the Great Mystery." This phrase, "the Great Mystery" (or sometimes "The Mystery"), translates the Anishinaabe phrase *Kitchi Manitou*, the generative, abundant force that creates, animates, and lovingly expresses itself through everything in the cosmos.

The vital qualities of stories enable them to work "co-creatively" with hearers, Westcott continues, helping to mold the shape of the world. And they imply that stories do not reduce to their constituent parts. "I was taught . . . that the story is a living being. It's not an entity in the way that, say, a bear is—because it's carried on the word. The story is able to procreate through the telling, but it is not identical with the words that people use to tell it." The living nature of stories even enables modes of interaction beyond narration: "Even at times when my purpose is not to tell the story, I may enter the story; I watch it and listen to it."

Emanating from a storyteller who has dedicated her life to the understanding of her tribe's cultural traditions, Westcott's remarks constitute a suitable exemplary narrative that promises to illuminate ideas and values typically missing from scholarship on Native American stories. While we make no claim that her narrative somehow represents *the* Anishinaabe perspective, it is *one* such perspective that shares features of worldviews described by students of Anishinaabe philosophies.[12]

ANALYSIS: THREE DOMAINS OF NARRATIVE ASSUMPTIONS

The analytic practice that we apply in relating the two narratives described above to the Anishinaabe myth follows a strategy that Arthur Frank has, himself, recommended. This approach, widely endorsed in the sociology of knowledge, urges attention to the fundamental, often unarticulated, *assumptions* that are embedded in narratives. The value of this approach,

Frank suggests, is that it opens to discussion the particular construction of the world and its possibilities—the "preferred reality" that assumptions evoke and reinforce.[13]

We identify three areas of assumption that reflect interest in the capacities of stories and that receive treatment in both our exemplary narratives. These domains suggest ideas about what stories *do*, with particular regard to *social relationships, human perceptions,* and *material reality.* Examining each domain in turn, we consider implications of divergent assumptions for the Anishinaabe myth. What type of engagements do these assumptions enable and disenable? What do they permit the myth to do—or prevent it from doing?

Stories and Social Relationships

Among the powers of stories upon which Frank dwells throughout his published work is their ability to "make life social."[14] Stories create bonds by bridging subjectivities, allowing people to "make inferences from other minds."[15] The "illness narratives" that commanded Frank's attention in his influential study *The Wounded Storyteller* represent a type of storytelling that enables especially significant social interactions. While illness often sets the sufferer apart in dramatic ways, stories empower him to become a "communicative" or "dyadic body," a deeply relational self. Storytelling, Frank argues, "is one medium through which the dyadic body both offers its own pain and receives the reassurance that others recognize what afflicts it."[16]

Such remarks depend upon fundamental assumptions in the philosophy of mind: illness stories become important because they allow people to confront the fundamental separateness, and thus unknowability, of other subjectivities. They are vehicles by which isolated subjects invite others to *imagine themselves* into their experience. Stories, in this view, address a troubling human problem: "The dyadic relation is the recognition that even though the other body is outside of mine, 'over against me,' this other *has to do with me, as I with it.*"[17] Even though human minds remain irremediably separate from each other, the ill may achieve a deep understanding that human subjectivities *are* finally united, after a fashion, in the experience of suffering and mortality. By narrating their hard-won knowledge, the ill contrive an empathic bridge: "a vision of the inter-human."[18]

Westcott's narrative also attends to the relevance of storytelling for making life social, while nevertheless making distinctive assumptions about the relationship of human subjectivities to each other. "The minute humans take on a form [at birth]," this storyteller observes, "they start experiencing being separate. The perception of isolation resides very deeply within humans who have been born." Yet this perception does not exhaust the truth about human subjectivity: "Some worldviews accept that human minds really *are* separate," Westcott continues. "But they're not." This latter assumption enables Westcott to construe her Anishinaabe myth in ways that some audiences fail to consider:

> Many times a non-Native audience will hear this story from what I think of as a Euro-American perspective. To me, it seems they imagine that the woman was going out *alone*—into isolation or into herself. But that's not what happened. That woman was engaging in an act of co-creation *through her kinship ties*. . . . She was undertaking a co-creative process that engaged her in her deep, *interrelated* self.

Notably, the deep interrelationships for which Westcott's assumptions provide include, but extend beyond, the joining of strictly human subjectivities. "That story shows us someone who is engaging not just her kinship ties with humans, but with *other beings*—specifically, with the trees."

The extension of social relationships beyond human communities carries further implications for one's ability to construe what comes next in the myth. This, in Westcott's conclusion, is literal transformation: "That woman was *remade*." As she elaborates:

> In her social and cultural relations, and even in her *body*, that woman became as much a part of the forest as she was human. She gained access to parts of reality that aren't usually available to humans—knowledge that comes from another level of beings. . . . She came to know herself as part of that continuous river of life that flows through everything—humans, animals, trees, even life that hasn't yet taken on a physical body. At the same time, that process was actually deepening her humanity. It awakened her . . . more deeply, more compassionately, to service in the human community where she lived.

Insofar as Frank's assumptions require stories to help people proceed *as if* they could participate in other subjectivities, they solve a problem that does not exist in Westcott's narrative. By the assumptions that our storyteller brings to her myth, it becomes possible to hear it as "bearing testimony to the phenomenon of infinite communion, and to the outcome of all minds merging and becoming of one mind—becoming *not* separate." It becomes possible to conceive a potentiality in stories for social relationships that far exceeds Frank's "vision of the inter-human."

Stories and Human Perception

Other assumptions suggested in Frank's socio-narratology characterize human subjectivities as not only isolated from each other, but as separated, likewise, from the world of objects. Direct perceptions of objective reality are impossible, such that the external world becomes available only via intermediating "representations." This state of affairs implies a dilemma: "If the human condition is to experience the real through its representations, those representations are not necessarily distorting. But neither are they the real itself."[19] Representations are unreliable guides, raising always the possibility that they obscure as well as reveal.

By such assumptions, stories function as a special type of representation. Just as stories fill the gulf between human minds, they stand in the gap between observing minds and the world beyond, shaping what is taken in. In this view, the repertoire of stories that people carry about does not merely *guide* perception, but creates what Frank (extending Bourdieu) calls "narrative habitus"—dispositions to perceive in particular ways. "[A] crucial aspect of habitus [is] its deceptive transparency. Looking out through that filter or grid, there seems to be only the world as it is, appearing as if unfiltered." More accurately, the habitus is a "screen." It is "the set of representations that comes between the listener and any new story," determining what will be heard, unheard, or adapted.[20]

By filtering perception, stories do not, Frank adds, behave as "characters"—a category that he reserves for beings distinguished by intention and motive. As collections of signs, stories behave only as "actors"—forces that influence human outcomes, although not through sentience or will. Still, the relation of stories to human perception is decisive. While stories operate only through the humans who tell them, humans rely on stories to realize their humanity. The relationship of stories to humans, Frank concludes, is "symbiotic."[21]

The narrative supplied by our Anishinaabe storyteller reflected different assumptions about that role of stories in human perception. Notably, these do not rule out the possibility of unmediated interactions with reality beyond the human mind. Westcott describes such interactions as "original perception"—and her narrative assumes that a principal function of stories is to *conduct people to* that experience. "Story," Westcott explained, "has the ability to hold you in a state where you can engage in *original perception*—by which I mean the perception of life before it moves into form." The process of the storyteller, she continues, is

> the same one used by someone who has the ability, among Anishnaabeg, to be a namer. Suppose there's a baby born, and the parents take the child to a namer. The namer doesn't look at the child as she is after birth; he travels to the pathway by which that child came *into* form. He goes *before* conception and witnesses the attributes the child brought *to* conception; the child's name presents there. So the namer exercises penetrating insight into the character and destiny of the child. [In that same way] the storyteller, through the vehicle of story, allows himself to be in an aspect of creation *before* form. Our Anishnaabe stories allow people to know the essential attributes of things.

By such assumptions, stories do not *filter* human perception, but *focus* it. Stories, Westcott concludes, "allow people to enter into The Mystery." Stories perform this function because, in contrast with Frank's "actors"—effectual but impersonal forces—the story conceived in Westcott's assumptions "*embodies* motivation and intention." As a manifestation of The Mystery, story even

> has a life purpose. It doesn't fully realize itself without human involvement. The same thing is said in Indian Country about traditional medicines: plants can have healing attributes—but unless they're used in relationship with someone who is ill, they never get realized. It's the same with sacred stories. Stories work together with humans to realize their life purpose.

If Frank's assumptions favor the conclusion that the relationship of humans to stories is "symbiotic" in a metaphorical sense, Westcott labels it "reciprocal" in a literal sense.

Stories and Material Reality

A last divergence of assumption between socio-narratologist and storyteller suggests itself in Frank's discussion of relationships between stories and material reality. Such relationships, Frank emphasizes, are profound. "Contemporary sociologists argue that stories mobilize social movements, and stories send nations off to war." Stories even "perform themselves into the material world"—not only "in the form of social relations, but also in the form of machines, architectural arrangements, bodies, and all the rest."

Ultimately, however, stories in Frank's narrative are "semiotic in their being," and this assumption imposes strict limits: material reality exercises powers that stories cannot dispel.[22]

The trajectory of a serious illness frequently serves Frank as a proto-typical example of the limitations of stories. The teller of an illness story, as Frank writes in *At the Will of the Body*, speaks from a longing "to touch others and perhaps to make a difference in the unfolding of their stories." Such hopes notwithstanding, stories confront a material world characterized often by implacable forces. Thus, "the responsibility of the ill . . . is not to get well, but to express their illness well. And the two have nothing to do with each other."[23] As Frank summarizes in later work: "Bodies get well or die, often regardless of the stories being told about them."[24]

The assumptions of our Anishinaabe storyteller admit other possibilities. In her remarks, the story does not exist apart from, but in intense interaction with other aspects of reality. Choosing, like Frank, the example of illness to illustrate her point, Westcott observes that stories *heal*, and that this is evident in her myth. That story, she explains, shows a woman, guided by traditional stories, who moves into wholeness through an experience that might be diagnosed today as the mental illness of clinical depression. Westcott's assumptions then carry her farther. In the same way, she says, "story can also alter *physical* forms." She continues:

> Ceremonialists from different tribes treat illness differently, but I see similarities [in how they proceed]. Indigenous approaches, including among the Anishnaabeg, often recognize the necessity to dissolve the structure that defines the illness and dissolve the structure that defines the treatment. Those outcomes are often sought in ceremony, through songs that tell the tribe's creation story. Those stories take the person rhythmically, energetically, back to the first moments of creation when no illnesses were *there*. The quality of song and the quality of drumming can allow the person treated to become completely resonant to that which the song ensures. And then the illness falls away! It doesn't have anything to adhere to any more.

When healing is accomplished, "the person may collapse right during the ceremony because the illness has just slipped away. The pattern of it has been broken down through the telling of the creation story, which caused the person to travel back to The Beginning—[to the time of first creation] when illness didn't exist."

Here, the story affects not only the world that people *experience*—Frank's "semiotic" domain in which stories, like other "representations," reside. Story affects the fundamental reality in which creation *happens*—is *always* happening because the mythical moment of origin is not subject to the rules of temporality. Unlike Frank's stories, which ultimately bow to forces beyond themselves, Westcott's myths can prevail even over stubborn, "material" reality. They prevail by continuously reinvigorating the perfection of the earliest beginning, calling it forth in ways that literally create and re-create the world.

THE CONSEQUENCES OF NARRATIVES

Of course, the assumptions we have discussed as embedded in Arthur Frank's socio-narratology correspond to a larger intellectual context. This context—a "preferred reality" in Frank's language—unifies even very divergent schools of narratology, and many other intellectual fields besides.[25] This context may be labeled by names such as "epistemological dualism" and "indirect realism"; we prefer "representationalism." While there are many versions of representationalism, we intend contexts oriented to the fundamental idea in the philosophy of mind "that the mental and the physical—or mind and body or mind and brain—are, in some sense, radically different kinds of thing."[26] A product of Western philosophical heritage, representationalism is traceable to Descartes but has even earlier roots in the thought of Plato and Aristotle.[27]

The assumptions that Westcott articulates also invoke a larger context of assumption—a preferred reality the epigraph to this chapter labels "mythic thinking." As with Frank's representationalism, elements of mythic reality among the Anishinaabeg have been described. Anthropologist Irving Hallowell, for example, characterized an Anishinaabe worldview wherein social relations include a large category of both human and other-than-human "persons," and wherein myth functions as a conscious, vital entity possessing the power to create the world.[28]

Accordingly, the value of our discussions is not that they add something new to the characterization of social scientific or mythic thought. Instead, having highlighted assumptions that underwrite the two narratives we have examined, we invite readers to return to the question with which we began. If scholars in the emerging field of Anishinaabeg Studies choose to work with sacred stories using conventional intellectual tools—tools we represent here with the exemplar of Arthur Frank's socio-narratology—what outcomes might they anticipate? Do such narratives promise to make them, in Frank's phrase, good companions to stories?

On the one hand, narratological approaches such as Frank's invite readers to take stories seriously; they ask us to listen long and carefully. And they provide a host of useful concepts to assist in those efforts; an example is the typology that Frank develops in *The Wounded Storyteller*, which helps readers appreciate the extent to which Westcott's Anishinaabe myth twines together elements of "quest," "restitution," and "chaos" stories, and how such threads link it to stories from other cultures and times. Even more, the analytic practices recommended throughout Frank's narrative strive honestly to mitigate unequal power relations between those who speak with academic expertise and those who do not. It warns analysts that "theoretical frameworks are not the truth of the stories. . . . The frameworks . . . are only a means of heightening attention to stories that are their own truth."[29]

At the same time, we may properly remember that socio-narratology directs analysts to concern ourselves with the *capacities* of stories; it encourages us to ask always what stories *do*. If we take this instruction a step further, we find ourselves asking what stories are *able* to do when contextualized within particular narratives. The answers deserve sober attention.

Our analysis suggests that the capacities of stories, including the Anishinaabe myth at the heart of this chapter, differ depending on the narrative within which they move. Retold within narratives characterized by representational assumptions, including Frank's socio-narratology, Westcott's story has the power to reveal an extraordinary woman: a perseverant soul whose sensibility values and feels profoundly connected to the natural world. It supplies a strong metaphor for that connection by showing forth an individual who, by mining her culture's traditions, engages with the natural world in ways that resemble interactions with beings that manifest motivation and intention. It leads audiences to appreciate how such personal qualities might make adversity into an ethical opportunity with intergenerational consequences. It suggests deep wisdom about the therapeutic potential of introspection, quietude, and creative process. These are not trivial accomplishments.

Yet to the extent that it moves only within the confines of representational assumptions, the Anishinaabe myth *loses* the capacity to evoke a mythic reality. It loses the ability to testify to possibilities for being in the world as a relative within an infinitely extended web of human and other-than-human relationships. It does not lead its hearers to conclude that they can move beyond empathic awareness to become of *one mind with* other beings. It fails to teach an audience that they can be fully transformed by such relationships. It no longer bears witness to "original perceptions" or to the possibility of a world remade in story. In short, narratives grounded in representational assumptions rob this myth of powers for which Westcott's narrative allows. In so doing, these conventional narratives for guiding scholarly engagement with stories disenable "possible lives."[30] They foreclose specifically upon lives lived in the expectation and experience of oneness, of communion, of co-creation with The Mystery. When scholars of Anishinaabeg Studies choose the analytic tools that they will bring to their work with stories, they would do well to consider whether these are sacrifices they are willing to make.

CONCLUSION

Previous research on Native American stories has been carried out within a range of narrative frameworks. While narratology, in all its variants, constitutes one important framework, the representational assumptions that we have discussed prevail in others as well; they inform many, if not most, of the intellectual frameworks that contemporary scholars bring to their work. The Anishinaabeg Studies envisioned in this volume promises to open stories to even more intense engagement with such narratives. As researchers in the new field select different analytic tools, our remarks suggest that they should not make choices without realizing that these will affect what their stories can *do*: those stories' ability to evoke realities and to illuminate possible lives.

Such decisions can rightly recall Arthur Frank's remarks on the companionship of humans with stories, especially his reminder that "good companions take care of each other."[31] We encourage scholars in Anishinaabeg Studies (and other fields defined by the perspectives of indigenous peoples) to persevere in interrogating the assumptions characterizing the narratives that they will use in working with stories, especially sacred myths. Perhaps they will even continue, at the right time, to develop analytic practices that proceed from careful reflection on assumptions found in narratives carried by Anishinaabe storytellers and other culture bearers. This, we suggest, represents a promising route to fruitful, protective companionship with tribal stories.

NOTES

1. Arthur Frank, *Letting Stories Breathe: A Socio-Narratology* (Chicago: University of Chicago Press, 2010), 2.

2. Ibid., 2, 193, 198.

3. Eva Marie Garroutte and Kathleen Delores Westcott, "'The Stories Are Very Powerful': A Native American Perspective on Health, Illness, and Narrative," in *Religion and Healing in Native America*, ed. Suzanne Crawford (Westport, CT: Praeger, 2008), 163–84.

4. Irving Hallowell, "Ojibwa Ontology, Behavior, and World View," in *Contributions to Ojibwe Studies: Essays, 1934-1972*, eds. Jennifer S. H. Brown and Susan Elaine Gray (Lincoln, NE: University of Nebraska, 2010), 542.

5. A late and respected elder and teacher of the White Earth reservation, Broker is also known for her novel *Night Flying Woman.*

6. The word *bimaadizinwin* translates as "to live in good relationship with all life." This "central goal" of life among Anishinaabeg has been interpreted to imply outcomes including "longevity, health and freedom from misfortune"— all of which depend upon personal effort and the "cooperation of *both* human and other-than-human persons"; Hallowell, "Ojibwa Ontology, Behavior, and World View," 559.

7. *Mii'iw* is an Anishinaabe word for concluding remarks. It may be translated, "This is what I have to say."

8. Anne Harrington, *The Cure Within: A History of Mind-Body Medicine* (New York: Norton, 2008).

9. Frank has fully explicated and named his distinctive analytic framework only in a recent volume. Earlier publications nevertheless prefigure later ideas to an extent that encourages us to consider *three* of this researcher's book-length publications as constituting a single narrative, which we refer to as socio-narratology. In addition to the recent *Letting Stories Breathe* (2010), our discussions draw on *The Wounded Storyteller* (1997), Frank's systematic exploration of "illness narratives," and *At the Will of the Body* (1991), his sociological reflection on his own experience with cancer.

10. Frank, *Letting Stories Breathe*, 3.

11. Ibid., 18, 202.

12. For example, Hallowell, "Ojibwa Ontology, Behavior, and World View."

13. Arthur Frank, "Why Study People's Stories? The Dialogical Ethics of Narrative Analysis," *International Journal of Qualitative Methods* 1, no. 1 (2002): 109–17, available at http://ejournals.library.ualberta.ca/index.php/IJQM/article/view/4616, p. 14.

14. Ibid., 20.

15. Ibid., 86, quoting Brian Boyd.

16. Arthur Frank, *The Wounded Storyteller: Body, Illness, and Ethics* (Chicago: University of Chicago Press, 1997), 36.

17. Ibid., 35, quoting Martin Buber.

18. Ibid., 178.
19. Frank, *Letting Stories Breathe*, 89.
20. Ibid., 56, 57.
21. Ibid., 31, 37.
22. Ibid., 3, 42–44.
23. Arthur Frank, *At the Will of the Body: Reflections on Illness* (Boston: Houghton Mifflin, 1991), 127.
24. Frank, *Letting Stories Breathe*, 123.
25. Frank, "Why Study People's Stories?"
26. Howard Robinson, "Dualism."
27. W.J.T. Mitchell, "Representation."
28. Hallowell, "Ojibwa Ontology, Behavior, and World View."
29. Frank, *The Wounded Storyteller*, 24.
30. Frank, *Letting Stories Breathe*, 18.
31. Ibid., 43.

RESOURCES

Frank, Arthur W. *At the Will of the Body: Reflections on Illness.* Boston: Houghton Mifflin, 1991.

———. *Letting Stories Breathe: A Socio-Narratology.* Chicago: University of Chicago Press, 2010.

———. "Why Study People's Stories? The Dialogical Ethics of Narrative Analysis." *International Journal of Qualitative Methods* 1, no. 1 (2002): 109–17. Available at http://ejournals.library.ualberta.ca/index.php/IJQM/article/view/4616.

———. *The Wounded Storyteller: Body, Illness, and Ethics.* Chicago: University of Chicago Press, 1997.

Garroutte, Eva Marie, and Kathleen Delores Westcott. "'The Stories Are Very Powerful': A Native American Perspective on Health, Illness, and Narrative." In *Religion and Healing in Native America*, ed. Suzanne Crawford, 163–84. Westport, CT: Praeger, 2008.

Hallowell, Irving. "Ojibwa Ontology, Behavior, and World View." In *Contributions to Ojibwe Studies: Essays, 1934-1972*, eds. Jennifer S. H. Brown and Susan Elaine Gray, 535–68. Lincoln, NE: University of Nebraska, 2010.

Harrington, Anne. *The Cure Within: A History of Mind-Body Medicine.* New York: Norton, 2008.

Korp, Maureen. *The Sacred Geography of the American Mound Builders.* Lewiston, NY: Edwin Mellen, 1990.

Mitchell, W.J.T. "Representation." In *Critical Terms for Literary Study*, ed. F. Lentricchia and T. McLaughlin, 11–22. Chicago: University of Chicago Press, 1990.

Morrow, Phyllis, and William Schneider, eds. *When Our Words Return: Writing, Hearing, and Remembering Oral Traditions of Alaska and the Yukon*. Logan: Utah State University Press, 1995.

Robinson, Howard. "Dualism." In *The Stanford Encyclopedia of Philosophy*, ed. Edward N. Zalta. Fall 2009. http://plato.stanford.edu/archives/fall2009/entries/dualism/.

K'zaugin
Storying Ourselves into Life

NIIGAANWEWIDAM JAMES SINCLAIR

*The following does not apply to just one
Anishinaubae, but to all, every single one.*

—BASIL H. JOHNSTON, *TALES OF THE ANISHINAUBAEK*

IN JUNE 2010, THE FIRST OF SEVEN NATIONAL EVENTS FOR THE
Truth and Reconciliation Commission (TRC)[1] was held in Winnipeg,
Manitoba, Canada.[2] Held to honor the experiences of Indian Residential
School (IRS)[3] survivors and disseminate information to the public about
the legacies of these schools, the four-day event was attended by over 40,000
people. The event was as diverse as it was dynamic, with IRS attendees, their
families, and Canadians sharing their stories and reflecting during public and
private presentations, facilitated discussions, an academic conference, and a
host of other critical and creative forums. Hundreds of political and spiritual leaders, politicians, and advocates—including the national chief of the
Assembly of First Nations, Shawn Atleo, and Governor General Michaëlle
Jean—showed up. Some came to protest the event. Others arrived to listen,
watch, and learn.

On June 17, a gala evening was held, featuring five Indigenous authors
from all over Canada: Joseph Boyden, Rosanna Deerchild, Richard Van
Camp, Beatrice Mosionier (formerly Culleton), and Basil Johnston. The
event, entitled "Writing Truth, Imagining Reconciliation," showcased these
writers reading from their books, sharing new work, and detailing stories
about ancestors, relatives, and others affected by the schools. Tears, laughter,
and truth filled the theater. It was an inspiring night.

While all brought important perspectives, Johnston's presentation was the most poignant. It wasn't just what he said that left the biggest impression, though; it was *the way* Johnston delivered his presentation. Unlike his fellow writers, the storyteller and elder from Neyaashiinigmiing (Cape Croker) carried no papers or books to the podium—just an eagle feather. Then, narrating from memory, he told a single story over forty-five minutes. A story, he described it, about love.

It was a self-portrait, spanning eighty years. He spoke of his birth, his parents, being taken to Spanish Residential School when he was ten years old. He bravely recounted being punished for speaking Anishinaabemowin,[4] enduring an oppressive and demeaning curriculum, and experiencing brutal sexual and physical abuse at the hands of classmates and clergy. He described how these events introduced burdens and beliefs—namely that he was flawed, unimportant, and unworthy. These manifested themselves throughout his life, leaving long-term effects that only increased when he finished school and moved to Toronto. Insecurities and self-loathing soon became loneliness, self-defeat, and reclusiveness. He could, at times, keep these feelings at bay—particularly when he wrote or met old school friends from Spanish. The latter were gifts of relief and respite, experiences he encapsulated in his collection *Indian School Days*. The dark memories and emotions, however, would eventually and inevitably return.

It was when Lucie entered his life that a long journey towards clarity, recovery, and strength began. Meeting her at a church dance, he gathered enough courage to ask her to join him on the floor. They danced, dated, and grew enamored with one another—their affection culminating when Lucie said, "I love you" for the first time. These words, Johnston described, changed everything. They challenged him to encounter his past, take his place in the present, and face his future. They gave him a family, a home, and the strength to eventually disclose to Lucie, in the thirty-ninth year of their marriage, what had happened to him at Spanish. It was also through these words that he found strength and support to continue after she passed away a few years later. It was through "I love you" that he discovered that he was worthy and capable of beauty, possibility, and power. In the end, this is Johnston's story—and I hope I've done it a bit of justice here—but if readers want to understand more, he's written about it elsewhere.[5]

When he finished, the audience gave Johnston a five-minute standing ovation.

His fellow authors embraced him backstage. He returned for an encore (when does *that* happen at a literary reading?). The moment was powerful beyond what words can express. I've heard some tell how Johnston's story reminded them of the power of resilience, the healing powers of community, or the value of family. Others talk about how it demonstrates wisdom, beauty, and bravery. No doubt there are many more interpretations. As for me, I continue to reflect on it—now years later—and learn.[6]

In spring 1991, just months after one of the most resistant and activist periods involving Indigenous peoples in Canadian history, Basil Johnston published "Is That All There Is? Tribal Literature" in *Canadian Literature: A Quarterly of Criticism and Review*, one of the most widely respected academic journals in Canada.[7] We are honored that he has given permission to republish it in *Centering Anishinaabeg Studies*. I propose that this essay, from one of our greatest ancestral intellectuals and elders, provides a framework in which "story" can be understood in Anishinaabeg Studies through an Anishinaabeg-specific methodology of *zaagi'*, love. As Johnston uncovers, love is embedded throughout Anishinaabeg language and literature, illustrating how we are a people *making* life as much as *living* life. Conceiving our field through *zaagi'*, I argue, provides a pathway out of many ossifying approaches that continue to plague our field, and towards considerations of the intricate narrative processes of Anishinaabeg culture- and community-making that constitute us as a people. In "Is That All There Is? Tribal Literature," Johnston encourages us to think of ourselves, our nation, and our stories as verbs as much as nouns—vessels of life. The act of story- and relationship-making among ourselves and with others is therefore an act of love; it is what maintains us, (re-)creates us, and ultimately, what defines us as Anishinaabeg.

In "Is That All There Is?" Johnston shares an experience he had during the "Red Power" era, with a young boy dressed as a chief at a public display of his class's projects about Native peoples in Canada. As Johnston narrates, the young student is dissatisfied and "bored" by his research and reading about Indians (and particularly their "dwellings"). Asking the student if he learned anything else, the boy replies: "No sir, there was nothing else . . . Sir? . . . Is that all there is to Indians?" Using this experience as a broader example of Canada's historical treatment of Native cultures, Johnston summarizes that for Canadian schoolchildren,

> little has changed since that evening in 1973. Books still present Native people in terms of their physical existence as if Indians were incapable of meditating upon or grasping the abstract. Courses of study in the public school system, without other sources of information, had to adhere to the format, pattern, and

content set in books. Students studied *Kaw-lijas*, wooden Indians, who were incapable of love or laughter; or Tontos, if you will, whose sole skill were to make fires and to perform other servile duties for the Lone Ranger; an inarticulate Tonto, his speech limited to "Ugh!" "Kimo Sabe," and "How."

Johnston goes on to turn his sights on government and academia—the bodies responsible for these curricula. Condemning "Indian Affairs of Canada, with its more than two centuries of experience with natives," as an institution that continues to rely on myopic stereotypes and "know[s] next to nothing about their constituents," Johnston claims that the lion's share of the blame belongs to "eminent scholars." It is irresponsible academics, he accuses, who sanitize, objectify, and misrepresent Native cultures and ultimately justify an ongoing colonial process.

To rectify this, Johnston stridently advocates that scholars become fluent in two Indigenous knowledge systems: language and literature. Anishinaabe "language and literature are inseparable," Johnston writes, "though they are too often taught as separate entities. They belong together." Of language, Johnston argues that linguistic fluency is *the* primary method through which one must understand Native cultures, positing that "Without the benefit of knowing the language of the Indian nation that they are investigating, scholars can never get into their minds, the heart and soul and the spirit of a culture and understand the Native's perceptions and interpretations. The scholar must confine his research and studies to the material, physical culture, subsistence patterns, and family relationships." On the topic of literature, Johnston is somewhat less prescriptive and more descriptive, arguing that

> There is, fortunately, enough literature, both oral and written, available for scholarly study, but it has for the most part been neglected. Myths, legends, and songs have not been regenerated and set in modern terms to earn immortalization in poetry, dramatization in plays, or romanticization in novels.
>
> What has prevented the acceptance of Indian literature as a serious and legitimate expression of Native thought and experience has been indifferent and inferior translation, a lack of understanding and interest in the culture, and a notion that it has little of importance to offer to the larger white culture.

Then Johnston's article takes a dramatic turn, translating several words from Anishinaabemowin to English and telling three interdependent and interesting stories—narrated with virtually no explanation. It is a powerful, and perhaps perplexing, journey for readers, ending with Johnston explaining the meaning of *K'zaugin* (I love you) in the context of a story called "The Weeping Pine."

I say that it may be perplexing, but I'm really only guessing. Scholars—in virtually all treatments of his work—have generally not given Johnston's writings ample critical consideration. For example, turn to most books, articles, or essays where he is cited: almost unilaterally, scholars quote Johnston as if his words are timeless and the letter of the law in all things Anishinaabeg. Or, just consider the amount of times *Ojibway Heritage* (1976), *Ojibway Ceremonies* (1982), or *The Manitous: The Supernatural World of the Ojibway* (1995) are cited to make arguments about something called "the Anishinaabeg worldview"—irrespective of subjectivity, history, or geography (or worse, as if they were saying the same thing). Or, see how many times Johnston's Nanabush or Nana'b'oozoo stories (notice the spelling differences) are anthologized, referenced, and used to make singular claims on Native "tricksters," humor, or politics. It's as if any time scholars need to make a claim regarding Anishinaabeg identity or culture, they simply pull out a Johnston reference. Admittedly, I've been a bit guilty of this myself, too.

It's not that there isn't evidence of a wide-ranging Anishinaabeg sense of culture and story at work in Johnston's writings (which I discuss in a moment). It's that this is done when his very words direct readers to a far more nuanced reading. While perhaps well-intentioned, Johnston's criticisms of "eminent scholars" who perform "indifferent and inferior translation," demonstrate "a lack of understanding and interest in the culture," and embody "a notion that it has little of importance to offer to the larger white culture" could also be applied to many who cite his work. They, too, ossify some of his ideas, separate them from their contexts, and deny them the important historical, political, and geographical locations they reside within. This is unfortunate—and rather unfair—placing Johnston's contributions in a sort of easily referenced, simplistic, and essentialized stasis. It's time this changed.

To understand Johnston's essay, though, it's perhaps good to view other Anishinaabeg who are doing similar work. In his 2010 book *X-Marks: Native Signatures of Assent*, Leech Lake Anishinaabe and Dakota critic Scott Richard Lyons calls for an end to the "perennial question, what is an Indian?" Instead of asking a question fraught with essentialist motives and interested in pinpointing elements and factors that make up Indianness, he suggests, "that we turn our attention instead to the social processes that create intersubjective Indian identities. This would mean a move away from conceptions of Indians as 'things' and toward a deeper analysis of Indians as human beings who *do* things—things like asserting identity, defining identity, contesting identity, and so forth—under given historical conditions."[8]

As Lyons argues, this movement away from "being" to "doing" reflects more accurately the cultural practices and processes that make up Indian—I will use "Indigenous"—existence. Indigenous identity, he argues, is always changing, in flux, and being remade, reinvented, reconstructed. This doesn't mean that tradition, ceremonies, and certain sets of principles and values don't carry weight, but that certain parts are negotiable and move over time. This is not a new idea or call—scholars such as Emma LaRocque, Simon Ortiz, Robert Warrior, Lee Maracle, and Craig Womack have made similar claims—but Lyons takes it a step further, arguing that the creation of "intersubjective Indian identities" is itself Anishinaabeg.

A basis for Lyons is found in the lexicon and structure of Anishinaabemowin, which he uses throughout *X-Marks* to introduce cultural arguments. He argues that Anishinaabemowin is "constituted by verbs on the move" and words that embody "the desire to produce more life."[9] This is best articulated in the term "anishinaabe bimaadizi, or 'living as an Indian' . . . used to describe the general state of someone being alive, and it possesses connotations of movement that can be understood in a physical sense."[10] An Anishinaabe existence, according to this understanding of the language, is much more about *making* life than *having* life. It is more about respectfully participating with forces in the universe rather than assuming domination over, and autonomy from, entities within it. The former adopts a relational framework with humans as one part of a life-making system; the latter presumes an anthropocentric perspective where existence is an inherited right. As life is constantly moving, fluid, and interconnected, the most meaningful relationship with it is to embody these same principles in a reciprocal and ecological exchange. Lyons concludes that "Perhaps it would not be going too far to suggest that Ojibwe speakers do not have a culture at all. Rather, it may be more accurate to say that they spend their time *culturing . . .* producing more life, living in a sustainable manner as part of the flow of nature—and never separate from it."[11] Lyons then uses this cultural principle (and others) to suggest pathways of Indigenous nationhood, sovereignty, and citizenship.

What's interesting is that the very question Lyons calls for an end to in *X-Marks* is virtually the same one Johnston addresses in "Is That All There Is? Tribal Literature." In the article, Johnston responds to the question "What is your culture? Would you explain it?" by offering a "brief sketch, no more than a glimpse." He argues that this is demonstrated in the "inseparable" nature of Anishinaabeg language and literature and then gives a quick language lesson through three words: "Anishinaubae," "'w'daeb-awae," and "'w'kikaendaun." Terms in Anishinaabemowin, Johnston points out, "have three levels of meaning" that consist of "the surface meaning that everyone instantly understands. Beneath this meaning is a more fundamental meaning derived from the prefixes and their combinations with other terms. Underlying both is the philosophical meaning." Unlike Lyons, who calls for an end to the "perennial question, what is an Indian?" Johnston is interested in trying to find some kind of answer to it. This is an interesting difference.

In fact, Johnston is so committed throughout "Is That All There Is?" to answer the question first asked by the little boy, he provides several entryways to describe "my tribe's culture." In terms of the "surface" and "fundamental" meanings for his Anishinaabemowin word list, they are:

- "Anishinaubae" means "I am a person of good intent, a person of worth," and is made up of "Onishishih" (meaning "good, fine, beautiful, excellent") and "naubae" (meaning "being, male, human species");
- "w'daeb-awae" means "truth . . . he or she is telling the truth, is correct, is right";
- and "w'kikaendaun" means "to know . . . that he or she knows."

Of course, the "fundamental" levels of these words are also deeply contextual—relying on how, where, and when the words are used in sentences, by which speaker, and for what purpose. Their translation into English inevitably influences this as well.[12]

Johnston's third level—the "philosophical meaning"—is where things get really interesting. As Johnston explains, the "surface" and "fundamental" meanings of words in Anishinaabemowin are not enough to convey their fullest expressions. It is in *how they are used, what they do, and how they convey experience* that they find their deepest meaning. In other words, it is in how words are expressed, how they participate in the universe, and what principles can be gained through their use. For example, in "Anishinaubae," one understands the meaning of "I am a person of good intent, a person of worth" in the context of the "stories of Nanabush, the tribe's central and principle mythical figure who represents all men and all women." Since "Nanabush was always full of good intentions," these narratives therefore show evidence of how "the Anishinaubae perceived themselves as people who intended good and therefore were of merit and worth."

Most striking is that Johnston describes "Anishinaubae" as a noun *and* a verb. The word refers not only to a group of people, but a set of actions and beliefs that constitute the term itself. These actions and beliefs form the basis of who the "Anishinaubae" are, and their relationships, both among themselves and with beings throughout the universe, as "from this perception they drew a strong sense of pride as well as a firm sense of place in the community. This influenced their notion of independence." The "philosophical meaning" of Anishinaubae therefore is deeply embedded in narrative acts of intention, perspective, and community-making. To Johnston, Anishinaubae is not only a name of an identifiable group, but a way of life—a way of stories.

This is furthered in the "philosophical meaning[s]" of "w'daeb-awae" and "w'kikaendaun," two words that first appear to be verbs. Here, Johnston reverses the process he followed with "Anishinaubae." "W'daeb-awae" is truth as *it is perceived to be by the speaker of that truth*. It is "a denial that there is such a thing as absolute truth; that the best and most the speaker can achieve and a listener expect is the highest degree of accuracy." This definition is active as well. It positions truth as subjective, relative, and mobile—leaving room for other truths. "W'kikaendaun" is knowing as *it is experienced by the speaker of that knowledge*. It is distinctly tied to sense perception and prior influence, and "may not be exact, but similar to that which has been instilled and impressed in his or her mind and recalled from memory." This idea of "knowing" is active, experiential, limited by past knowledge, and expandable. While clearly verbs, Johnston importantly frames "w'daeb-awae" and "w'kikaendaun" as claims, things that carry weight in the world. Anyone who has been in a courtroom, classroom, or living room knows that statements of "truth" and "knowing" impact the lives and realities of people. "W'daeb-awae" and "w'kikaendaun" are verbs *and* nouns. Like "Anishinaubae," they are concepts in an ongoing and storied process of life-making.

The question, one might ask, is why doesn't Johnston simply do what Lyons does, and explain to the reader why the question is inherently faulty? The answer, I suggest, lies in the journey Johnston is trying to inspire. By ideologically and rhetorically connecting three central ideas through his definitions of "Anishinaubae," "w'daeb-awae" and "w'kikaendaun," Johnston takes the reader on a brief walk through Anishinaabemowin. Like a tour guide, he shows how his ancestral language is filled with subjective noun/verb terms and based in multiply-derived intentions, perspectives, and experiences. These words, at their very core, undergird an autonomous position (Johnston calls it "independence") and end with the suggestion that there is such a thing as Anishinaabeg identity—rather *identities*—and these are related to the existences of other identities. Without telling the reader that the question is baseless and providing evidence why, Johnston gestures to how readers can uncover tools for discovering this on their own.

At the same time, Johnston provides a fairly radical way to conceive of Anishinaabeg identity, culture, and community. According to him,

Anishinaabeg are a body of diverse people embodying countless subjectivities, experiences, and perspectives that together enact an autonomous language and literature which forms relationships among themselves and with others. What makes Anishinaabeg who they are, according to Johnston, are their negotiable, multiple, and fallible truths—constantly emerging and based in principles of complexity—and their inherent and ongoing ties to one another in a trajectory of continued, collective existence. Like Lyons in *X-Marks*, Johnston frames Anishinaabeg as engaged in a constantly changing and complicated cultural process, embedded in creating life in a diverse and mysterious universe. What is slightly different is that Johnston works with the very question Lyons abhors, attempting to empower others to discover this mobile sense of Anishinaabeg peoplehood from where they stand. Rather then dictating where the questioner should begin, Johnston works with where they are, employing a rhetorically interesting and contextual strategy of relationship-making.[13]

This returns us to Johnston's eagle feather. Feathers, as anyone knows, enable eagles to fly—but explaining exactly how this is is almost impossible. In his 2011 collection *One Story, One Song*, Wabaseemoong Anishinaabeg writer Richard Wagamese points out: "There are no flying lessons. One day the young eaglets stand at the rim of their nest with their whole world in front of them. They can hear the call of their parents high above. To fulfill their destiny and become who they were created to be, each of them must make that first frightening jump, test their ability to fly."[14] Watching them one afternoon with his elder Jack Kakakaway, Wagamese recounts that he learns that an eagle spends an entire lifetime learning to fly—a mastery that looks effortless but "doesn't come easily" as

> Each eagle feather is made up of thousands of tiny filaments, Jack said, and the eagle has to control them all, whether the wind is blowing or the air is still. Only that skill will keep the eagle aloft. Just as importantly, the eagle must learn how to see the world, reading the treetops and the grasses for information."[15]

Like the eagle feather he held that night at the TRC event, I believe that Johnston was employing a tactic similar to the one he used in "Is That All There Is?" reminding all of us who were listening that night—Anishinaabeg and non-Anishinaabeg—that we are made up of thousands of tiny (and virtually unexplainable) filaments that constitute unique parts of a system that together make up a crucial, interconnected process of making our universe fly.[16] One strand of a feather cannot control another; they must simply do their job and rely on others to do their work. At the same time, and like our many separate yet interconnected communities, it is important for each filament to understand something about what the other does, so we can all understand where we are going. While each are separate parts, we need to respect the other strands, support them, and together we will all carry our collective weight.

Johnston doesn't stop here, though. He then narrates three stories: the Anishinaube story of creation; "The Man, the Snake, and the Fox"; and "The Weeping Pine." The first is "our creation story," a narrative that explains how the world was created after "Kitchi-manitou beheld a vision"; how a pregnant Geezhigo-quae and the muskrat re-created the world "with a small knot of earth"; how she gave birth to "twins who begot the tribe called the Anishinaubaeg"; why the Anishinaubaeg "dreamed Nanabush into being"; and how Nanabush "recreated his world from a morsel of soil retrieved from the depths of the sea." "The Man, the Snake, and the Fox" is a story about a hunter who is tricked and almost killed by an "immense serpent," until he is saved by a fox. In return, the fox wants nothing until the man insists and agrees to "feed him should he ever have need." Unfortunately, some years later, the hunter shoots "a little fox who had been helping himself to the family storage. As the man drew his knife to finish off the thief, the little fox gasped, 'Don't you remember?'" The last story, of "The Weeping Pine," is a narrative about a young woman's arranged marriage to an old man who she at first resists but grows to love—so much so that she refuses to leave (and in fact perishes at) his grave. Soon after, a "small plant grew out of the grave of that woman," producing mist that reminds her children of the love she held for her husband, which lives on today in "spruces and pines [that] shed a mist of tears of love." These are complex and multilayered stories (and I encourage readers to read them for themselves), but I'd like to follow Johnston's directive by employing his critical strategy and suggesting some three levels of meaning in them.

Examining the "surface meaning" of the Anishinaubae story of creation is fairly straightforward—as Johnston tells it to us. Just as he does earlier, he introduces a process-based method of analysis, walking readers through the text before encouraging independent exploration. Speaking of the creation story, it is a "factual account of the origin of the world and of being" and doesn't discount or have "[any] more basis than the biblical story of creation and the flood." The story "represents a belief in God, the creator, a Kitchi-manitou, the Great Mystery. It also represents a belief that Kitchi-Manitou sought within himself, his own being, a vision. Or perhaps it came from within his being, and Kitchi-manitou created what was beheld and set it into motion."

The "fundamental meaning" of the narrative ("derived from the prefixes and the combinations with other terms") is also described by Johnston. As he writes, the "story of creation . . . precedes all other stories in the natural order." It is, in linguistic terms, a prefix; every story, idea, or experience that emerges afterwards for the Anishinaubae is shaped by this one. This is rather simple (it is, after all, a creation story), but Johnston, I believe, is pointing to more. A prefix, according to most dictionaries, helps create a noun, and is an "element placed at the beginning of a word or stem to adjust or modify its meaning"; and it is also a verb—meaning literally to "pre-fix," to "fix, appoint, or determine beforehand."[17] If we are to look at what immediately precedes this story in "Is That All There Is? Tribal Literature," it's the word-list defini-tions Johnston offers—which I've argued suggest that notions of nouns and verbs are intertwined in Anishinaabemowin, and Anishinaabeg are equipped with a constantly changing culture embedded in creating life. Johnston is rearticulating his main thesis, that "language and literature are inseparable." The story of creation therefore is innately tied to the lessons he just wrote about in "Is That All There Is?" Like "Anishinaubae," "w'daeb-awae," and "w'kikaendaun," the story is relative to other truths, always changing, and known according to memory and ongoing experience. It is an ongoing story told in moments of subjectivity and context. It is a verb, an action.

And an action based in a place and a time—a noun. At the time of the publishing of "Is That All There Is?" in spring 1991, Indigenous peoples in Canada had just emerged from the "Oka Crisis," a 270-year conflict over land between the Kanien'kehaka (Haudenosaunee) people of Kanehsatà:ke and Canadian settlers. It was an event that culminated in a 78-day stand-off between Onkwehonwe and the Canadian military, which unfortunately ended in violence.[18] It's not that the event was a surprise, as Nishnaabeg scholar Leanne Simpson writes, for it "confirmed everything" Indigenous peoples knew: "that given the opportunity, Canada would not hesitate to use its military power to crush Indigenous nations and our aspirations to be peaceful, responsible, self-determining neighbours."[19] Still, and up against tremendous force and odds, Indigenous resistance and agency at Oka was effective, impactful, and inspiring. It was, as Simpson describes, similar to

> throwing a stone into a body of water. The stone and the act of throwing, represents both intent and action. The impact upon the water is the result of that action. When the stone hits the water, there is an immediate and dramatic impact. There is sound and displacement.
>
> But long after the stone sinks to the bottom, the concentric waves of displaced water radiate outward, carrying the impact of the action through

time and space. The impact of the initial disruption is carried across different realms by these concentric rings, interacting with the other elements of Creation in synergy.[20]

These concentric circles inspired more movements in the interests of Indigenous resurgence and revitalization, much of which reverberates today. "When the Onkwehonwe collectively threw their stone into the lake in the summer of 1990," Simpson concludes, "there was no telling the tremendous gift and opportunity they gave to Indigenous Peoples. . . . The summer the Kanien'kehaka took on the Canadian army and won continues to inspire. It continues to bring us hope."[21]

But the Oka Crisis was not without its own stones thrown in the water, its own prefixes. The trauma of many centuries of colonial invasion in the Americas, and the memories and experiences it brings, is an ongoing story well known by Indigenous peoples. So are our many resistances. As Beausoleil Anishinaabe writer Wanda Nanibush reminds us:

> The stand that the Kanien'kehaka took in the Pines was also a traumatic event for the community and for all of us who acted in solidarity. It connects to a list of colonial traumas like "Starlight tours of Saskatoon," "Ipperwash," "Burnt Church," "500 missing and murdered Aboriginal women," "Trail of Tears," "Residential Schools," and many, many more. These specific events become part of a larger collective history of colonialism and our resistance to it. Each new colonial event brings up a prior trauma, something almost forgotten, repressed or something that has been attempted to be erased.[22]

Johnston begins "Is That All There Is?" by citing Red Power, the revitalization movement that forced schools, governments, and academics to recognize Indigenous peoples as worthy of consideration. Unfortunately, as he also points out, these examinations have failed to represent Indigenous peoples and cultures—and particularly the Anishinaabeg—accurately. This is manifested in everything the little boy from Churchill Avenue Public School is bored with, provoking him to ask "Is that all there is?" Instead of turning away from the little "chief" or chastising him, Johnston however does something truly revolutionary: He listens. He learns. He forms a relationship with him—accepting what the boy has to say, and turning his words into a "stone in the water" that creates concentric and reverberating circles throughout his life. This is evidenced by the many times Johnston repeats this story throughout his literary career.[23] In his preface to *The Manitous*, for example, he even claims the boy's words as inspiration for *Ojibway Heritage* and *Ojibway Ceremonies*, along with other books and articles.[24]

This brings us to the "philosophical meaning" of Johnston's story of creation. Again, Johnston explains this to the reader—that all beings, Kitchi-manitou, animals, "lesser manitous," and others, "seek a morsel of soil with which to create and recreate their world, their spheres. So men and women must seek within themselves the talent of the potential and afterward create their own worlds and their own spheres and a purpose to give meaning to their lives." For Johnston, it is in story that relationships are possible and morsels of soil are made available so Anishinaabeg culture and identity can be created. It is in story that the possibilities within "Anishinaubae," "w'daeb-awae," and "w'kikaendaun" empower a process of life-making that is as much about doing as being. It is in stories like the little chief asking, "Is that all there is?"—in Red Power, in the Oka Crisis, and so on—that stones are thrown into the water, and resistance is enacted and inspired. It is in story that Anishinaabeg exist. And where does this all begin? The story of creation. Among many things, Johnston shows how this narrative—embodied through his version—can be considered not only as full of timeless values and concepts, but also as a specified history, land claim, law, artistic expression, call to action, and example of subjectivity from Johnston's own life and experience. This story is not only a prefix for Anishinaabeg, but for Johnston himself (more on this below).

The next two stories are somewhat more subjective, and Johnston leaves most of this hard work to the reader (although he does mention "justice and fairness" as an important theme). In this I assert that he is gesturing that others must find their own "morsels of soil," but in this vein I'd like to suggest a few I believe are available. "The Man, the Snake, and the Fox" ends with a series of questions that suggest it is about trust and relationships between the three beings in the story. In many ways, it is about the power of stories: following them, being tricked by them (and almost paying for it with your life), witnessing the power of them (to even trick a trickster), and forgetting them (which seems to result in the worst punishments of all—death, anger, regret). Johnston's emphasis here, I believe, is about responsibilities embedded in storied relationships. The hunter, for example, neglects his responsibility to the fox by forgetting their story, so their relationship is severed, just as his relationship with the serpent is broken when he is told a false story. He repeats the story of the snake and has isolated himself (and will likely die if faced with a similar situation). While trying to support his family, he violates a sacred trust by forgetting about his interdependence on others.

It's hard—especially considering the prefix of all that has come before this story—to not see "The Man, the Snake, and the Fox" in the context of Indigenous-settler relations in Canada, the United States, and elsewhere. Many of these conflicts emerge from a competition between stories—competing stories, sharing stories, rejecting stories, and everything in between. As Johnston points out, claims—for the Anishinaabeg anyway—do not exist in a vacuum. They are nouns that are verbs, verbs that are nouns. They have relations with the universe around them. By prefixing the story of "The Man, the Snake, and the Fox" through listing a long process of Indigenous resistance to colonialism, it's only a stone's throw (pun intended) to see a reference here. There are certainly a lot of conniving, bloodthirsty serpents Indigenous peoples have faced and should be resisted.

There are also many foxes who shouldn't be forgotten. This is part of why I believe Johnston is both dedicated to articulating processes embedded in Anishinaabeg culture and gesturing to ways they can be engaged on their own—even if this is complicated and difficult. As my colleague Damien Lee puts it succinctly in his essay "Echoes of Impermanence: Kahnehsatà:ke, Bimaadiziwin and the Idea of Canada":

> As Anishinabek, we are seeking to transform our current relationship with Canada. Like our Onkwehonwe sisters and brothers, we are not seeking to defeat Canada, but instead we seek to revitalize and live in the spirit of co-existence embodied in our treaties and worldview. Currently, Canada does not uphold its treaty responsibilities, opting instead to negate Onkwehonwe self-determination and to oppress Indigenous Nations with the Indian Act. Transformation for us means co-existing with dignity, not winning or losing. It also means re-establishing balance through healthy relationships with Canadians.[25]

It is my hope that we as Anishinaabeg remember our commitments to the fox, because you never know when you are going to be tricked by a serpent. If we don't respect who foxes are and where they come from, they might not always be there to hear us, help us, or ask, "Is that all there is to Indians?" In other words, we should be patient, understanding, and remember our commitments and responsibilities. These memories and experiences are what I believe Johnston means when he describes Anishinaabeg as people with "good intention"—that we must live with integrity, respect, and honor both ourselves and those around us. Johnston's message is that focusing on responsibilities can revitalize and strengthen Indigenous communities and transform Indigenous-settler relationships so that colonial violence can be engaged in a meaningful fashion. It's not about "winning or losing," but the journey together.

Crucial to this storied relationship is language. Most interesting is that Johnston writes "Is That All There Is?"—and makes a demand that scholars learn Anishinaabemowin—in English. He also chooses to explain Anishinaabeg concepts in it while refusing to lament the failures of English to convey them. While Anishinaabemowin clearly has critical and embedded concepts and ideas that are valuable and worth fully understanding, Johnston stubbornly refuses to throw up his hands and claim incommensurability when speaking in English. This doesn't mean that he doesn't make a profound argument for the importance and value of Anishinaabemowin—in fact he demands that scholars become fluent in it—but that he is interested in dialogue, exchange, a *relationship*. The path to a "balanced" and "healthy" relationship is possible if we can speak to one another using our own languages. In fact, a relationship with English is critical for most Anishinaabeg too, as the majority of us continue to relearn Anishinaabemowin. As Johnston puts it, one must know the languages and literatures of the people one is investigating in order to understand them. This isn't a ringing endorsement of English; rather, it is an honest treatment of it, as well as a reminder to those of us still learning languages that each have intellectual, useful, and important concepts that help us understand the universe and ourselves in unique ways.

The last story is by far the most perplexing—but perhaps now that I've arrived at it, is also the most evident. It's a story about love: its immense power, beauty, and possibility. Again, it's very hard not to see this story as referencing Johnston's own life, his own discoveries about love, and hearing the transformative words of "K'zaugin" (I love you) from the lips of Lucie—but I don't want to speak for him. No story is ever truly autobiographical, but in the context of his story at the TRC national event, it's a beautiful possibility.

In "The Weeping Pine," Johnston provides us with no easy answers, just the story. As he encourages us to do throughout "Is That All There Is?" we must find our own answers, our own "morsels of soil," and consider the impacts and responsibilities that these leave us with. As for me, I read "The Weeping Pine" as being about how love takes hard work. It is not found in the instantaneous endings of fairy tales, but is something that demands time, space, and constant and consistent communication. The young woman does not at first love the old man, but after years of commitment grows to. She loves him so much, in fact, that she builds a family, community, and life with him. She even forsakes her children and dies to be with him. Her love is what ensures her permanent presence on earth, in the "small plant" that grows from it. Love is not solely the physical, unconditional, lusty romp we see in Hollywood movies (although perhaps a fun part of it!), but a relationship filled with respect for, patience with, and responsibilities to another person. It's about listening and learning, even if the person you are communicating with is not doing the same. The question, undoubtedly, is how you can love another being when they are so drastically different. There are no easy answers on how to love someone else. Sometimes love, for example, involves protecting yourself and others you love, too. Love is something that involves a never-ending struggle with yourself, someone else, and entities throughout the universe in a process of life-making.

It's easy to see how love can bring Anishinaabeg together: in ceremonies, classrooms, and countless instances of community. A true commitment to *k'zaugin* is in seeing how it can inspire Anishinaabeg to maintain connections with one another even as we disagree, grow apart, and travel in different directions. Maintaining the teachings of *k'zaugin* might just be the greatest challenge Anishinaabeg face in the coming years. *K'zaugin* can inspire us to continue to tell each other our perspectives, share food with family members and relations, and join together in times of struggle and resistance. *K'zaugin* can assist us in learning how to speak to one another in our many languages, and to listen, always listen. *K'zaugin* is what can maintain and define our many responsibilities to one another, and ensure that we speak to each other with honesty, commitment, and truth—even if this results in disagreement. *K'zaugin* can also assist our continuation into the multiple, diverse, and complex community we are, always have been, and will continue to be as Anishinaabeg. *K'zaugin* is what will enable us to throw pebbles in the water and create waves of story that will inspire us to continue Anishinaabe existence forever.

In my studies of Anishinaabemowin, what strikes me about *zaagi'* is how it also means "to treasure" and is part of so many words that talk about growth and expansion, such as *zaagigi* (sprout, grow out), *zaagijiwan* (flow out) and *zaagidenaniweni* (stick out one's tongue).[26] *Zaagi'* is also a transitive animate verb, which uses the second-person singular *gii-* instead of the first person *nii-*, which is kind of like saying, "(You) do *x* to me."[27] *K'zaugin* might also mean: *You grow in me.* What is fascinating—and a little risqué—is that this also represents *lovemaking*, an action and a thing in its own right. Sex, especially when love is involved, is definitely a noun and a verb too. Anishinaabeg lovemaking is also life-making—the idea of each of us being a part of one another in all of our complexities, and creating a beautiful and dynamic Anishinaabeg world together. This is precisely the kind of responsible, ethical, and dynamic Anishinaabeg community I want to be a part of.

This is articulated beautifully in "K'zaugi-in, I Love You, My Soul Is Open for You," a poem Johnston wrote to accompany a 2000 art exhibit featuring Norval Morrisseau's paintings. After describing two people who enter one another's "heart and soul," he concludes by stating:

Hand locked in hand, hearts entwined
We set upon the Path of Life
Our dreams now one
Our steps true and measured
You love mine; mine yours
To help me know myself, the world.
You and Kitchi-Manitou
And to walk on into the world of dream
and beyond.[28]

Our Anishinaabe language and literature, filled with love, is what inspires us to walk and grow together along a diverse and complex Path of Life, from this existence to the next.

K'zaugin is what can guide Anishinaabeg Studies. Love is what inspires Johnston to keep Anishinaabemowin and Anishinaabeg stories alive, and encourage (even demand) others to learn from them. Love is what lives in Johnston's work and his investments in speaking to, and advocating for, himself, his family, his people. Love is what inspires him to take up the call for resistance to colonialism and "independence." Love is what will ensure that his life continues well beyond his own, in the work of all of us—like here, in *Centering Anishinaabeg Studies*. His love, a model for our love for one another, is what can feed, support, and ensure our responsibility to one another, ensuring that we as Anishinaabeg will continue to speak our languages and tell our stories for many years. Love is also how we can assure a future for our children, alongside and with others—who depend on working with us to keep this world going. It is how we can live *anishinaabe bimaadizi*, create and re-create Anishinaabeg culture and community, and make more life. As Johnston concludes in "Is That All There Is?," "K'zaugin said everything. I love you, today, tomorrow, forever."

Love is where we will find our morsel of soil to remember, live, and thrive as Anishinaabeg.

Ho! Ho! Miigwech Basil for culturing, storying, and encouraging the rest of us to produce more life. *Gi ga waabamin miniwaa, ndinawemaagan.*

NOTES

1. According to the website of the Truth and Reconciliation Commission of Canada, its "mandate [is] to learn the truth about what happened in the

residential schools and to inform all Canadians about what happened in the schools. The Commission will document the truth of what happened by relying on records held by those who operated and funded the schools, testimony from officials of the institutions that operated the schools, and experiences reported by survivors, their families, communities and anyone personally affected by the residential school experience and its subsequent impacts.

"The Commission hopes to guide and inspire First Nations, Inuit, and Métis peoples and Canadians in a process of truth and healing leading toward reconciliation and renewed relationships based on mutual understanding and respect.

"The Commission views reconciliation as an ongoing individual and collective process that will require participation from all those affected by the residential school experience. This includes First Nations, Inuit, and Métis former students, their families, communities, religious groups, former Indian Residential School employees, government, and the people of Canada."

For more, see http://www.trc.ca.

2. According to the TRC website, the national events "are a mechanism through which the truth and reconciliation process will engage the Canadian public and provide education about the IRS system, the experience of former students and their families, and the ongoing legacies of the institutions." The other six events were held across Canada. For more, see http://www.trcnational events.ca.

3. From the 1870s to 1996, over 130 residential schools—predominantly church-run and legislated by the federal government—operated across Canada. They were designed to assimilate Indigenous children into the Canadian sociocultural and religious mainstream by "removing" the Indian in the child. More than 150,000 First Nations, Métis, and Inuit children attended these schools (most times forcibly so), often far away from their home communities. They were indoctrinated with a foreign and ideologically based curriculum, endured often unsanitary and inappropriate labor, were forced to speak English and attend church, were punished if they spoke their tribal languages or practiced their culture, and were refused access to their relatives, elders, and parents. Many also endured horrific acts of sexual and physical abuse. An estimated 80,000 former students are alive today. As a direct result of these institutions, the ongoing legacies of residential schools continue throughout these survivors and their communities, contributing to many social issues within them. For more on this, see J. R. Miller's *Shingwauk's Vision: A History of Native Residential Schools* (Toronto: University of Toronto Press, 1996), or John Milloy's *A National Crime: The Canadian Government and the Residential School System, 1879 to 1986* (Winnipeg: University of Manitoba Press, 1999).

Throughout the 1990s, former residential school students (with the support of allies, their families, political agencies, and lawyers) took the federal government and the churches to court seeking compensation for the harm caused by residential schools. Their cases led to the Indian Residential Schools Settlement Agreement, the largest class-action settlement in Canadian history. As well as providing financial compensation to former students, the agreement established the Truth and Reconciliation Commission of Canada, with a budget of $60 million and a mandate of five years. In addition, on June 11, 2008, Prime Minister Stephen Harper, on behalf of the Government of Canada, delivered a formal apology in the national House of Commons to former students, their families, and their communities for Canada's role in the operation of the residential schools.

4. While Johnston uses the phonetic system when writing in Anishinaabemowin (and I leave his system intact when quoting him), I will utilize the Fiero writing system. I am aware of Johnston's distaste for the Fiero writing system, which he describes in *Anishinaubae Thesaurus* (East Lansing: Michigan State University Press, 2006). I use it not to be disrespectful, but as the system I am most familiar with, have been taught, and utilize in the interests of communication with a broad Anishinaabeg audience.

5. Basil H. Johnston, "Foreword," in Sam McKegney's *Magic Weapons: Aboriginal Writers Remaking Community after Residential School* (Winnipeg: University of Manitoba Press, 2007), vii–xv.

6. A *gichi-miigwech* to Basil Johnston for agreeing to read my overview of his presentation. Any errors are my own.

7. Basil H. Johnston, "Is That All There Is? Tribal Literature," *Canadian Literature: A Quarterly of Criticism and Review* 128 (Spring 1991): 54–62. There is admittedly a bit of uncertainty, even from my discussions with Johnston, regarding the dates during which "Is That All There Is? Tribal Literature" was written. Johnston identifies it as copyrighted in 1989 in *Think Indian: Languages Are Beyond Price* (Wiarton, ON: Kegedonce Press, 2011), for instance. Johnston did, however, explain to me informally that he edited it over the following two years, culminating in the 1991 publication in *Canadian Literature*. In fact, Johnston has edited it subsequently in other publications. All references to the article are to the 1991 version, which we have republished in *Centering Anishinaabeg Studies*.

8. Scott Richard Lyons, *X-Marks: Native Signatures of Assent* (Minneapolis: University of Minnesota Press, 2010), 59.

9. Ibid., 4, 87.

10. Ibid., 87.

11. Ibid., 88.

12. As Johnston points out, translations of Anishinaabemowin into English are usually indirect, often requiring more than one descriptor. While notable, this feature is hardly specific to Anishinaabeg contexts, and—while utilized by many in Indigenous Studies to lament the absolute failures of English to carry any meanings of Indigenous languages—is a "straw man" argument. Similar statements, for example, could be made of exchanges between many languages (even European ones) and English. No language is directly transferable, and multiple words are almost always needed when translating languages. This is an example, I argue, of Johnston gesturing towards a relational, dynamic, and culturally based method of communication in Anishinaabeg expression that is not erased during translation.

13. In Lyons's defense, *X-Marks* reflects a different context and purpose too, proposing "modern" ways of conceiving of Indigenous nationhood, sovereignty, and citizenship. His is more of a treatise (and, in the context of 2010 in the United States, a quite necessary one), while Johnston's "Is That All There Is? Tribal Literature" is more of an act of diplomacy (which, in the context of 1991 in Canada, is equally necessary). These two rhetorical differences in doing similar work, however, are notable in the ways in which both books are interested in particular relationships with readers and the intellectual community. Both scholars are undoubtedly brave and bold in what they are proposing and envisioning for Anishinaabeg studies.

14. Richard Wagamese, *One Story, One Song* (Vancouver: Douglas & Mcintyre, 2011), 22–23.

15. Ibid., 22.

16. Johnston also identifies that eagle "feathers are emblems of courage and foresight and wisdom" in *Honour Earth Mother: Mino-audjaudauh Mizzu-kummik-Quae* (Wiarton, ON: Kegedonce Press, 2003), 88. While in this book he gestures to an Anishinaabeg-specific understanding of eagles in this context, it is relatable and a part of the universal usage I argue he employs here.

17. *Oxford English Dictionary Online*, "prefix," at http://www.oed.com (accessed December 7, 2010). "Prefix" can also be an adjective: "fixed beforehand."

18. The Oka Crisis was an over two-centuries land dispute between the Kanien'kehaka (Mohawk, or Haudenosaunee) people of Kanehsatà:ke and settler Canadians (specifically from the town of Oka, Quebec) that culminated in an armed standoff that began on July 11, 1990, and lasted until September 26, 1990. Similar standoffs and actions were taken across Canada, and specifically by Haudenosaunee relations at Kahnawà:ke and Akwesasne. It drew international attention to Indigenous land grievances in Canada, and galvanized an entire Indigenous political and activist movement in Canada

still being felt today. It was a peaceful protest that quickly escalated, as Lac Du Flambeau scholar Gail Guthrie Valaskakis documents in *Indian Country: Essays on Contemporary Native Culture* (Waterloo, ON: Wilfrid Laurier University Press, 2005): "The seeds of conflict were sown when land claims were ignored in a move to extend a golf course into the grounds of an ancient Indian cemetery in Kanehsatake, a patchwork of Mohawk reserve land intertwined with the town of Oka, forty eight kilometers from Montreal. Women who were cousins or clan mothers sat in "the Pines" where the cemetery is located, through the media silence of a restless winter. Their vigil was vocal but peaceful, a statement of heritage and heresy voiced without the guns that attract media attention. Winter dissolved into spring and then summer. In June, when the weary voices of the women in the Pines became shrill, the mayor of Oka obtained an injunction against the protestors and summoned police to remove them. The women called upon Mohawk warriors to defend their vigil, to resist their removal from consecrated land; and the festering wounds of Kanehsatake transformed from a campfire into a barricade" (37).

Many are uncomfortable with the term "Oka Crisis" and prefer the descriptor "resistance at Kanehsatà:ke." For more on the conflict, see Alanis Obomsawin's excellent documentary entitled *Kanehsatake: 270 Years of Resistance* (National Film Board of Canada, 1993).

19. Leanne Simpson, "Niimkiig," in *This Is an Honour Song: Twenty Years since the Blockades*, ed. Leanne Simpson and Kiera L. Ladner (Winnipeg: Arbeiter Ring, 2010), 16.

20. Ibid., 17.

21. Ibid., 17–18.

22. Wanda Nanibush, "Love and Other Resistances: Responding to Kanehsatà:ke through Artistic Practice," in *This Is an Honour Song: Twenty Years since the Blockades*, ed. Leanne Simpson and Kiera L. Ladner (Winnipeg: Arbeiter Ring, 2010), 171.

23. This is evidenced in the countless times Johnston has told the story of the young "chief." While I've heard him tell it many times (including the night of the TRC gala event), he retells it in the foreword to McKegney's *Magic Weapons* (Winnipeg: University of Manitoba Press, 2007), in his "Contributor's Note" in *Our Story: Aboriginal Voices on Canada's Past* (Toronto: Doubleday, 2004), and in *The Manitous: The Spiritual World of the Ojibway* (St. Paul: Minnesota Historical Press, 1995).

24. Basil Johnston, *The Manitous: The Spiritual World of the Ojibway* (St. Paul, MN: Minnesota Historical Press, 1995), xii.

25. Damien Lee, "Echoes of Impermanence: Kanehsatà:ke, Bimaadiziwin and the Idea of Canada," in *This Is an Honour Song: Twenty Years since the Blockades*,

ed. Leanne Simpson and Kiera L. Ladner (Winnipeg: Arbeiter Ring, 2010), 241.

26. John D. Nichols and Earl Nyholm, *A Concise Dictionary of Minnesota Ojibwe* (Minneapolis: University of Minnesota Press, 1995), 123.

27. Ibid., xvii.

28. Basil H. Johnston, "K'Zaugi-in: I Love You, My Soul Is Open for You," in *The Art of Norval Morrisseau, The Writings of Basil Johnston* (Calgary, BC: Glenbow Museum, 1999), 12.

Teaching as Story

THOMAS PEACOCK

Young and old asked:
Who gave me
The breath of life
My frame of flesh?
. . .
Who gave to us
The gifts we do not own
But borrow and pass on?
Who made us one?
Who set the Path of Souls?
Who carved the Land of Peace?
Who?

As the young asked, the old men and old women thought about these
matters. They gave their answers and explanations in the form of stories,
songs, prayers, rituals, and ceremonies.

BASIL JOHNSTON, *OJIBWAY HERITAGE*

ORAL STORIES ARE AMONG HUMANKIND'S OLDEST WAY OF TEACHING, helping traditional societies make sense of things, giving meaning to their experience, and explaining both the known and unknown. Today, stories are often used as both primary and supplemental instructional materials. Stories can give the experiential knowledge necessary for solving complex problems, and provide context for students who lack direct experience.[1]

In teacher education programs, stories can help prospective teachers problem-solve and vicariously experience issues of learning and teaching, and understand the complex societal, institutional, community, family, and personal issues their future pupils must deal with. Stories may be particularly useful in preparing non-Native teacher candidates to be better teachers of Native students, because many non-Natives lack the direct real-life experiences to relate to the issues facing many Native students.[2] The stories may also be helpful to Native teacher candidates, because they may be better able to relate to the issues and situations portrayed in the stories. Moreover, accompanying stories with a hands-on kinesthetic activity models a traditional way of teaching used in many Native cultures.[3] This paper describes the use of stories and a hands-on activity to prepare teachers of Native students.

BACKGROUND

Stories have been the means by which many traditional cultures asked questions, explored issues, engaged in debates, and taught values and attitudes. In many traditional cultures, stories as well the characters in them were (and still are) sometimes viewed as possessing spirit, so accuracy and respect were of utmost importance for the storyteller.[4] Moreover, as stories were sometimes the primary means of conveying history and other important teachings, it was incumbent on the storyteller to protect them from change.[5]

Traditional Ojibwe people told stories, legends, and history for their amusement as well as for teaching. Storytelling was most often done in the lodges during the evenings, accompanied by the preparation of clothing and household items, the mending of fishnets and hunting equipment, and making playthings for the young. The topics of these stories touched all aspects of Ojibwe life:

> There is not a lake or mountain that has not been connected with some story of delight or wonder, and nearly every beast and bird is the subject of the story-teller, being said to have transformed itself at some prior time into some mysterious formation—of men going to live in the stars, and of imaginary beings in the air, whose rushing passage roars in the distant whirlwinds. These legends have an important bearing on the character of the children of our nation. The fire-blaze is endeared to them in after years by a thousand happy recollections.[6]

Ethnographer Inez Hilger chronicled Ojibwe life in *Chippewa Child Life and Its Cultural Background*, capturing some of the reasons and ways of stories. As she records from informants:

> My mother used to tell us stories that taught us to do right; my father, when he was old, told stories only occasionally to his grandchildren. . . . Years ago when we were young, we often sat around in a circle while an old person in the group talked, telling us what was ahead of us; what we should do to live good lives. . . . Boys as young as seven were made to go where the old men were talking to listen to them; parents made the children go. Old men usually talked to boys, and old women to girls. . . . A grandfather often took a grandson when his voice began to change and preached to him. This was done especially in the evening but at any time of the year.[7]

How to conduct oneself, what constituted acceptable character, the attributes of acceptable behavior and quality were all contained in story meanings.[8] Elders were most often the tellers of the stories because their knowledge of the Path of Life gave them the experience and qualities for teaching younger adults and children wisdom, knowledge, patience, and generosity:

> And if the stories that have come down to us are to be examined, they will be found to be simple yet complex. They are simple in the sense that they appeal to the very young; complex in terms of the scope and depth and number of themes in each. . . . A story well told should have at least four levels of meaning: enjoyment, moral teaching, philosophic, and metaphysical.[9]

The lessons in the stories were conveyed indirectly. Listeners would draw their own conclusions with no attempts to directly impose meaning. Seemingly simple teachings, such as stories about why birch trees have black marks, or when the rabbit ate all the roses, contained deeper meanings as well—about ridiculing, and the responsibility of humankind to protect our elder brothers, the plant beings. Young and old alike learned according to their cognitive ability and developmental level. Each story contained a gift for each listener in the form of individual interpretation. With maturation, the stories, oft-repeated in the lodges, assumed deeper meanings:

> Hunger, courage, generosity, fidelity, the quality of existence, transformation, history and all matters related to life and being, matters that engaged the fascination of manhood. From the story-teller, the young gained insights into life. It was through story that the people grew in understanding.[10]

USING STORIES IN TEACHING

Stories can enrich teaching lessons. Jonassen and Hernandez-Serrano provide some rationale for using stories in teaching:[11]

> Stories are the most natural and powerful formalism for storing and describing experiential knowledge that is essential to problem solving. The rationale and means for analyzing, organizing, and presenting stories to support problem solving are defined by case-based reasoning. Problems are solved by retrieving similar past experiences in the form of stories, and applying the lessons learned from those stories to the new problem.[12]

Jonassen and Hernandez-Serrano go on to note that the skills and techniques of traditional expertise, particularly as they are being taught in schools, do not match the complexity found in many fields, including education. Students are trained to work on problems that are decontextualized and well structured, while problems in real-life situations are typically complex and ill-structured.[13] As a result, a mismatch often occurs between the kinds of problem solving learned in formal settings, and the methods used to solve real-life problems. While using stories cannot replace real-life experience, they can help fill the gap by offering context, complexity, and "messiness."

For students with little direct experience in the field, stories can offer a window into real-life experience, allowing them to gain insight vicariously,[14] and making them better decision makers in determining course of action.[15] Stories also allow for the authentic exploration of experience from a particular perspective,[16] helping students to see other views of the forest of reality, other fractions of the truth.

Stories also serve as important reminders of our own experiences, facilitating our ability to relate to and empathize with the characters and situations provided in the story, and more importantly, with real people in similar situations. J. Clifford has stated that "Any story has the propensity to generate another story in the mind of the reader (or hearer), to repeat and displace some prior story."[17] Stories can be almost metaphoric, whereby students see patterns or associations in their own experience, which they will combine to generate their own unique meanings.[18] So, as stories can serve to facilitate one's understanding of their own life experiences, they also facilitate the planning of one's future actions.[19] Moreover, by being able to relate to another's story, individuals will be better able to articulate their own identity to others through a series of interconnected stories.[20]

Stories also foster our ability to negotiate and renegotiate meanings, and assist in assessing the pros and cons of things.[21] Stories can help us find our place in a culture.[22] Stories help us interpret meaning,[23] develop explanations for things, and expand our knowledge of human diversity, human action, intentionality, and temporality.[24] Stories help us to remember the unusual.[25]

USING STORIES AND A KINESTHETIC ACTIVITY TO TRAIN TEACHERS OF NATIVE CHILDREN

Many Native people still learn their way in life though stories, so I have chosen to use fictional, contemporary stories about Ojibwe people in my teaching to introduce concepts, model a traditional way of teaching, and give context to issues in Native education. The use of stories reflects both Ojibwe standpoint epistemology (a way of viewing the world) and female narrative discourse.[26]

The stories allow the reader (or listener) to view the issues Native students face in school and life from an Ojibwe perspective—a perspective that is rich in metaphor, and runs counter to a more Euro-Western linear reporting of data, facts, and findings. Along the way, I tell my own personal story, as well as allow students to share their own. During the course of storytelling, the class is also engaged in a hands-on kinesthetic activity—be it a beading project, making bark containers, carving the cedar knockers used to harvest wild rice, or making dream catchers. Having students actively engaged in making something models a way of teaching used in the Ojibwe lodges of generations past, when stories were told in the evenings while our ancestors were engaged in repairs and crafts. Non-Native students, most with little knowledge of Ojibwe reality, come away from the lessons having vicariously experienced some of the real issues facing many Native students in today's schools, homes, and communities. Native teacher candidates partake in a way of teaching and learning many are familiar with. The craft item they produce is a concrete, tangible product and serves as a reminder of their experience. I call this approach to instruction "teaching as story."

An Example of Teaching as Story

An illustration of this approach to teaching is a story found in the opening pages of my text *Gekinoo'imaagejig, The Ones Who Teach*. I will paraphrase it in the following pages. This narrative is also often accompanied by a sock-beading activity. The main character in the story, Deacon Kingfisher, is a fluent Ojibwe speaker who has Down's syndrome. The story begins with Deacon's grandparents being killed in an automobile accident, leaving him without adult care, and with a community mourning the loss of their two remaining fluent Ojibwe speakers and teachers. David, the Native home-school coordinator, must become the Ojibwe language teacher, even though he is not a fluent speaker. Along the way in the story, he discovers that Deacon Kingfisher is a fluent speaker, and tries to get him hired as his teacher's aide. Intended for use in training special-education teachers who work in Ojibwe communities, the story introduces students to real issues that impact contemporary Ojibwe communities and their young people, particularly language loss and how Ojibwe communities deal with individuals with cognitive disabilities.

All the while that students are reading the story aloud to each other, they are guided by the instructor to bead a pair of socks. The beading, reading, and discussion of the issues in the case takes one-and-a-half to two hours.

The lessons in the story begin straightaway by introducing readers to the real issues of language loss confronting many Ojibwe communities, in the context of a school and community confronted with the death of its only remaining language speakers and teachers. It starts like this:

We've been at a loss here at Pine Bend School ever since the elder Kingfishers were killed at Roy's Point in an accident with a drunk driver. That idiot drove straight through the stop sign like a bat out of hell and plowed into them sideways. It was a white guy who was shacking up with some Sisseton woman that moved onto our rez a year or so ago and got one of the low rent units. That asshole lived, of course, but we lost those two precious elders. As least they went quick, the EMTs said.

You see, Joe and Shanud Kingfisher were our Ojibwe culture and language elder teachers. They came in twice a week and taught the language to our elementary and high school kids. And now, without them, we don't have anybody to properly teach it, and just the thought of it makes me so afraid for our people. Because without the language passing down to the young generation, who is going to say those prayers to our Creator at our gatherings and ceremonies? The prayers can only be done in the language. Who is going to do the pipe ceremonies? That can only be done in the language as well. And who is going to do namings, and teach the young people about the healing plants, or the prayers and songs that go along with the practicing of skills like parching wild rice and making bark baskets and trapping? Joe did namings. He was the only one on our rez who had that gift. Shanud made the most beautiful black ash baskets. Very few people practice that craft anymore. I suppose skills like ricing and making maple syrup and stuff like that will survive in spite of the language, but wouldn't it be so much richer to know these things within the context of our Ojibwe language? To know the songs and prayers that should be said for the rice, or for the harvest of maple syrup? Without those two elder teachers, our community, our whole future as Native people, is in jeopardy. They were the last two people in our community, as far as I know, who were fluent Ojibwe speakers. At least as far as I am concerned, without our language we are just brown white people.

The story and its lessons continue when David, the Native home-school coordinator, finds himself having to teach the language, and feeling woefully inadequate because he lacks fluency:

After the accident I took the elder Kingfishers' place in the classroom as the children's teacher. I feel so inadequate there, because I know just a small fraction of what those two elders knew. And the young ones know, they do, how important that language is, because they remind me all the time. The other day one of the little ones came up to me after class, and he asked me something.

"David," he said (they call me David), "could you give me my Ojibwe name?"

"I would be honored to do that if I could," I said, "but I don't have that gift. Maybe when I get older I will. But right now, I can't do that."

The little boy walked away from me so disappointed, and the look on his face just said it all as far as I am concerned.

Now it's like a race, you know, to learn the language.

Little does David know that Deacon Kingfisher, who was being cared for by his grandparents before their death in the accident, is a fluent speaker, having been raised in the language:

I been learning Niibish [a dog, his friend] to speak and now he knows too.

"*Umbe, Niibish!*" (Come, Niibish).

"*Neebish, namadabi.*" (Niibish, sit.)

My Grampa Nimishoo and Gramma Nokoo always talked it to me. When I see them in my head they talk it to me.

And even more, Deacon, who has been visiting his grandmother's friend Olivia, is also relearning the language as a result of her visits with Deacon.

The following scene reinforces the Ojibwe belief that the language is always inside us, and that we need to bring it out:

> I gode over to 'Livia's lots, me and Niibish, so we can watch her TV. I told her I been learning Niibish the language. And she says a long time ago she used to know it but it's been too long. So I started talking and pretty soon now she's talking with me that way. She says it's coming back inside her.

One evening while going to the store, David stops alongside the road to say hello to Deacon, who is speaking (in Ojibwe) to Niibish (his dog friend) and doesn't notice David. Stunned, David drives off, but later goes to visit Deacon:

> Later that evening I went over to elderly housing to visit him. I brought that sacred *asema* (tobacco) with me. He was in a pair of Tigger pajamas when he answered his door.
>
> "*Aniin ezhi a ya yan?*" I said. How are you doing?
> "*Nimino aya, geendush?*" he replied. I'm fine, and you?
> "*Nimino aya,*" I said back to him. I'm fine as well.
> "*Nimiwendum wabaminan,*" he replied. I'm happy to see you.
> "*Gidojibwem, ina?*" he asked. Do you speak Ojibwe?
> "*Eya, baangi nindojibwem.*" Yes, a little Ojibwe I speak.
>
> I asked him that night if he would be my teacher. And when he said he would, I gave him that sacred *asema*, tobacco, and he accepted it.
>
> I've known Deacon nearly my entire life, and for most of it I just thought he was a gentle and happy-go-lucky person who happened to have special needs. I never thought that he would possess the knowledge and ability that I have spent much of my adult life trying to get. Until now, I'd always measured him by his limitations.

The story's lessons continue when David attempts to hire Deacon as a teacher's aide to accompany him in the classroom, only to find the parent committee tabling his request because they have concerns with having someone with Down's syndrome teaching the children. This issue highlights the ignorance many adults have about persons with cognitive disabilities. Undeterred, David lobbies the parent committee behind the back of its chairperson, and approaches them again with the request to hire Deacon. This time, however, he has an ally, Olivia, a respected elder in the community. Olivia enters the meeting and, when allowed, speaks to them as only a respected elder can:

"The last item on our agenda tonight is to reconsider the hiring of Deacon Kingfisher as Ojibwe language teacher aide."

'Livia stood then.

"I'd like to address the committee," she said.

Then she spoke to us in the language.

And her voice was at once so strong and forceful and gentle and sincere, and her message carried in it all the dreams of our ancestors who had walked on through the ages. She talked for a long time and then she sat down.

Then I told them what she said.

As a result of Olivia's intervention, Deacon Kingfisher, a fluent Ojibwe speaker who happens to have Down's syndrome, is allowed to become a teacher:

Me and 'Livia and Davey's teachers, Niibish. We teach that tongue to the little ones.

DISCUSSION

Using contemporary Ojibwe stories to train teacher candidates about the issues facing Native students has proven to be an effective instructional method. Stories like those found in *Gekinoo'imaagejig, The Ones Who Teach* introduce important concepts of Ojibwe culture (using stories to teach important life lessons, the ways traditional Ojibwe communities dealt with persons with disabilities, issues of language loss). Stories, combined with a hands-on kinesthetic activity model a traditional Ojibwe way of teaching,[27] reflecting both Ojibwe standpoint epistemology and female narrative discourse.[28]

The stories provide context, a view into a window of reality, a world inherently complex, ill-structured,[29] and different from that of many non-Native people. This fits Jonassen and Hernandez-Serrano's assertion[30] that using stories helps with real-life problem solving because it poses issues in their complexity. Teacher candidates gain insight about Ojibwe life vicariously.[31] The stories allow readers (or listeners) to view reality from a (Ojibwe) perspective other than one's own.[32] Perhaps more importantly, using stories reminds teacher candidates of their own life experiences, something Clifford noted was important in developing empathy toward others.[33] Ojibwe-based stories help teacher candidates to relate to and empathize with Ojibwe young people and the issues (racism in all its forms, cultural conflict, multigenerational grief, multiple trauma, identity, resilience, poverty, achievement and attendance, learning styles, etc.) they are confronted with.

SUMMARY

As an Ojibwe and a teacher, I always tell part of my life story along with the fictional cases the students read about and discuss. I am a part of the story, having struggled through many of the same issues as the fictional characters in my stories. My very existence is living proof that overcoming the difficulties of being a Native in mainstream America is possible. And I ask my students to share their own stories as well, so they become a part of the story.

The classroom discussions resulting from using stories are heartfelt and often emotional. I want it that way because I feel good teaching must engage students on an emotional level. There is much at stake. Our children and grandchildren, nephews and nieces continue to struggle in their homes, communities, schools, and society.

I do this for them. *Mi-iw* (that is all).

NOTES

1. D. Jonassen and J. Herandez-Serrano, "Case-based Reasoning and Instructional Design: Using Stories to Support Problem Solving," *Educational Technology Research and Development* 50, no. 2 (2002): 65–77.

2. L. Miller Cleary and T. Peacock, *Collected Wisdom: American Indian Education* (Needham Heights, MA: Allyn and Bacon, 1998).

3. E. Albert and T. Peacock, "Teaching as Story," *Proceedings of the 1999 International Indigenous Conference on Education* (Hilo: University of Hawaii, 2000).

4. Sunwolf, "The Pedagogical and Persuasive Effects of Native American Lesson Stories, Sufi Wisdom Tales, and African Dilemma Tales," *Howard Journal of Communication* 10, no. 1 (1999): 47–71.

5. Sunwolf, "Pedagogical and Persuasive Effects."

6. G. Copway, "The Traditional History and Characteristic Sketches of the Ojibway Nation," in *Touchwood*, ed. Gerald Vizenor (St. Paul, MN: Touchwood Press, 1987), 72–73.

7. Inez Hilger, *Chippewa Child Life and Its Cultural Background* (St. Paul: Minnesota Historical Society Press, 1992), 57.

8. Johnston, *Ojibway Heritage.*

9. Ibid., 69–70.

10. Ibid., 122–23.

11. Jonassen and Herandez-Serrano, "Case-based Reasoning."

12. Ibid., 65.

13. Ibid.

14. Ibid.; J. Bruner, *Actual Minds, Possible Worlds* (Cambridge, MA: Harvard University Press, 1986).

15. D. Polkinghorne, *Narrative Knowing and the Human Sciences* (Albany: State University of New York Press, 1988).

16. H. McEwan and K. Egan, *Narrative in Teaching, Learning, and Research* (New York: Teachers College Press, 1995).

17. J. Clifford, "On Ethnographic Allegory," in *Writing Culture: The Poetics and Politics of Ethnography*, ed. J. Clifford and G. E. Marcus (Berkeley: University of California Press, 1986), 100.

18. Cleary and Peacock, *Collected Wisdom.*

19. Polkinghorne, *Narrative Knowing.*

20. Polkinghorne, *Narrative Knowing*; R. Schafer, "Narration in the Psychoanalytic Dialogue," in *On Narrative*, ed. W.J.T. Mitchell (Chicago: University of Chicago Press, 1981); Cleary and Peacock, *Collected Wisdom.*

21. J. Bruner, *Actual Minds, Possible Worlds* (Cambridge, MA: Harvard University Press, 1986).

22. Ibid.; H. White, "The Value of Narrativity in the Presentation of Reality," in *On Narrative*, ed. W.J.T. Mitchell (Chicago: University of Chicago Press, 1981).

23. S. Gudmundsdottir, "The Narrative Nature of Pedagogical Content Knowledge," in *Narrative in Teaching, Learning, and Research*, ed. H. McEwan and K. Egan (New York: Teachers College Press, 1995).

24. Bruner, *Actual Minds, Possible Worlds*; M. Huberman, "Working with Life-History Narratives," in *Narrative in Teaching, Learning, and Research*, ed. H. McEwan and K. Egan (New York: Teachers College Press, 1995).

25. Bruner, *Actual Minds, Possible Worlds*; R. Schank, *Dynamic Memory Revisited* (Cambridge: Cambridge University Press, 1999).

26. Cleary and Peacock, *Collected Wisdom.*

27. As noted by Johnston, *Ojibway Heritage.*

28. Cleary and Peacock, *Collected Wisdom.*

29. As noted by Jonassen and Hernandez-Serrano, "Case-based Reasoning."

30. Ibid.

31. As noted by Jonassen and Hernandez-Serrano, "Case-based Reasoning"; Bruner, *Actual Minds, Possible Worlds.*

32. McEwan and Egan, *Narrative in Teaching, Learning, and Research.*
33. Clifford, "On Ethnographic Allegory."

RESOURCES

Albert, E., and T. Peacock. "Teaching as Story." *Proceedings of the 1999 International Indigenous Conference on Education.* Hilo: University of Hawaii, 2000.

Bergstrom, A., L. Miller Cleary, and T. Peacock. *The Seventh Generation: Native Youth Speak about Finding the Good Path.* Charleston, WV: ERIC Clearinghouse on Rural and Small Schools, 2003.

Bruner, J. *Actual Minds, Possible Worlds.* Cambridge, MA: Harvard University Press, 1986.

Cleary, L. Miller, and T. Peacock. *Collected Wisdom: American Indian Education.* Needham Heights, MA: Allyn and Bacon, 1998.

———"Disseminating American Indian Educational Research through Stories: A Case against Academic Discourse." *Journal of American Indian Education* 37, no. 1 (1997): 7–15.

Clifford, J. "On Ethnographic Allegory." In *Writing Culture: The Poetics and Politics of Ethnography*, ed. J. Clifford and G. E. Marcus, 98–121. Berkeley: University of California Press, 1986.

Copway, G. "The Traditional History and Characteristic Sketches of the Ojibway Nation." In *Touchwood*, ed. Gerald Vizenor, 59–89. St. Paul, MN: Touchwood Press, 1987.

Gudmundsdottir, S. "The Narrative Nature of Pedagogical Content Knowledge." In *Narrative in Teaching, Learning, and Research*, ed. H. McEwan and K. Egan. New York: Teachers College Press, 1995.

Hilger, I. *Chippewa Child Life and Its Cultural Background.* St. Paul: Minnesota Historical Society Press, 1992.

Huberman, M. "Working with Life-History Narratives." In *Narrative in Teaching, Learning, and Research*, ed. H. McEwan and K. Egan. New York: Teachers College Press, 1995.

Jonassen, D., and J. Hernandez-Serrano. "Case-based Reasoning and Instructional Design: Using Stories to Support Problem Solving." *Educational Technology Research and Development* 50, no. 2 (2002): 65–77.

Johnston, B. *Ojibway Heritage.* Lincoln: University of Nebraska Press, 1976.

McEwan, H., and K. Egan. *Narrative in Teaching, Learning, and Research.* New York: Teachers College Press, 1995.

Peacock, T., and M. Wisuri. *The Good Path.* Afton, MN: Afton Historical Society Press, 2002.

Peacock, T. *Gekinoo'imaagejig, The Ones Who Teach.* Pembroke, NC: Pembroke Magazine, 2006.

Polkinghorne, D. *Narrative Knowing and the Human Sciences.* Albany: State University of New York Press, 1988.

Schafer, R. "Narration in the Psychoanalytic Dialogue." In *On Narrative*, ed. W.J.T. Mitchell. Chicago: University of Chicago Press, 1981.

Schank, R. *Dynamic Memory Revisited.* Cambridge: Cambridge University Press, 1999.

Sunwolf. "The Pedagogical and Persuasive Effects of Native American Lesson Stories, Sufi Wisdom Tales, and African Dilemma Tales." *Howard Journal of Communications* 10, no. 1 (1999): 47–71.

White, H. "The Value of Narrativity in the Presentation of Reality." In *On Narrative*, ed. W.J.T. Mitchell. Chicago: University of Chicago Press, 1981.

Eko-niswi Bagijigan

Stories as Revelations

ANISHINAABEG STORIES REVEAL, ILLUMINATE, AND MAKE KNOWN THE complexities of Anishinaabeg being—a crucial contribution to humanity. By placing stories at the center of the field, a dynamic and thought-provoking set of questions emerge and, along with these, potential new insights. Stories suggest new pathways to Anishinaabeg Studies, forming the basis for the complex, rich, and nuanced answers to some of the most critical questions posed within Anishinaabeg communities. They open doorways, clear paths, and gesture to ways in which Anishinaabeg Studies can be centered as a whole.

Cary Miller demonstrates how centering the field with stories reveals a complex kinship network at work within Anishinaabeg societies. Her essay "Every Dream Is a Prophecy: Rethinking Revitalization—Dreams, Prophets, and Routinized Cultural Evolution" uncovers how many scholarly works on historic religious movements, visions, and revitalization prophets have failed to fully consider the relationship between dreams, Anishinaabeg, *manidoog*, and the natural world. Consequently, much scholarship has overemphasized particular prophets and movements as new and transformative, instead of recognizing how they fit into a larger Anishinaabe understanding of the world—in which dreams formed a large part of everyday practice. Through examples, Miller encourages us to consider dreams as stories that work(ed) each night to inform, instruct, and illuminate all kinds of possibilities for Anishinaabeg.

"Constitutional Narratives: A Conversation with Gerald Vizenor" centers around a May 2010 interview by European University Cyprus professor James Mackay with writer and scholar Gerald Vizenor. Vizenor tells the story of constitutional reform at White Earth and the nation's new constitution—of which Vizenor was Principal Writer. Within the larger trajectory of Vizenor's work, the two discuss how a constitution is both a document and a story, revealing how Anishinaabeg imagine our world through a sense of belonging and identity. The document narrates these aspirations and goals. As Vizenor reminds us: "Constitutions are created as narratives and ratified as political documents of governance." This collective essay demonstrates the formidable possibilities that stories generate for the field of Anishinaabeg Studies and for Anishinaabeg nationhood(s) more broadly.

Julie Pelletier, in her essay "And the Easter Bunny Dies: Old Traditions from New Stories," shows how stories, when utilized as a methodology, uncover the relationship of storymaking to concepts of tradition and cultural perseverance and innovation. Placing stories and storymaking at the center, Pelletier reveals how tribal expectations are perceived and received by elders. Furthermore, she displays how storymaking allows elders to resist these conceptions by inverting narratives to reveal a different set of expectations that institute new ways of thinking that challenge historical accounts of colonialism faced by Anishinaabeg and other communities. Pelletier suggests that these narratives support assertions of authenticity, sovereignty, and self-determination critical to Anishinaabeg nationhood, while recognizing the diversity, adaptability, and resiliency of an all-too-often ignored people.

Every Dream Is a Prophecy

Rethinking Revitalization—Dreams,
Prophets, and Routinized Cultural
Evolution

CARY MILLER

THE ANISHINAABE WORLDVIEW, THROUGH STORIES, CEREMONY, AND tradition, emphasizes the importance of reciprocal social relationships that extend the notion of kin far beyond biological relatives, the need for gifts or blessings from *manidoog* (spirit-like beings outside of oneself), the permeable line between animals and *manidoog,* and the close relationship between the Anishinaabe people and the natural world around them. Understanding the full extent of these relationships requires a reevaluation of the nature of revitalization prophets, visions, and religious movements among Ojibwe communities in the early nineteenth century. Visions requiring new personal practices as a part of building personal relationships with the *manidoog* were continuous, as were visions that incorporated the actions of others, such as the visions that inspired war parties. The creation of the world itself was an action Kitche Manido pursued in response to a vision, according to author Basil Johnston—an action that the Ojibwe emulated through seeking dreams at puberty that would direct them as they looked to the future.[1] Bishop Frederick Baraga commented that dreams were so important that the Ojibwe debated "passionately among themselves about the meaning of dreams, and often their entire life and actions are ruled by dreams."[2] Prophetic dreams formed such an important part of life, that at some point nearly everyone could be said to have received this form of spiritual guidance in their lives. In other words, prophets were a common, everyday occurrence. The almost routine appearance of lesser-known religious movements within Anishinaabeg tradition shows the regular transmission of new ceremonies and moral correctives from the spirit realm to human communities to be a normal corrective, only rarely emerging beyond the boundaries of the band or village in which it originated. The importance of this is that they paved the way for acceptance when larger movements did arise, and they represent the dynamic responsiveness to change inherent in Anishinaabeg religion. An examination of the context of Anishinaabeg interaction with the spirit world, as well as specific "new" ceremonies given to them at various points in time, will demonstrate the relative regularity of what Western scholars have referred to as "prophets."

Anthropologist Anthony F. C. Wallace's paradigm suggests that revitalization movements can be defined as "deliberate, organized conscious effort by members of a society to construct a more satisfying culture."[3] As such, the members of the cultural system itself must feel that their society, or some major aspect of it, is unsatisfactory and requires innovations that will result in a new cultural system with new relationships and new traits. In presenting this theory, he sought to present an alternative scenario to passive culture change through evolution, drift, diffusion, or acculturation by suggesting that revitalization movements were proactive internal attempts to ease feelings of cultural disruption through consciously directed change.[4] However, in his theory Wallace seems to overlook the degree to which such vision seeking is culturally ingrained, routinized activity in Eastern woodland societies generally, and in Anishinaabe communities in particular, despite the fact that he has commented on such traditions as commonplace elsewhere.[5] For Anishinaabe communities, prophetic prediction formed a part of everyday life, from hunting to marriage to war, to such an extent that anthropologist A. Irving Hallowell has stated that dream experiences lead "directly to the heart of [their] cognitive orientation toward the world."[6] As a result, while widely influential prophets, like widely influential chiefs, were unusual, and to some extent driven by the context of contemporary events, prophecy and innovation themselves are deeply rooted cultural traditions within the Anishinaabe cosmos. This expectation of prophecy in their midst in an ongoing and unfolding way means that the true basis for wide acceptance of any given visionary was a result of established social processes and ingrained cultural norms.

Anishinaabeg peoples valued social relationships established through gift exchange with human and *manidoog* that promised to aid them in basic subsistence, and to achieve the Ojibwe moral ideal, *mino-bimaadiziwin*, or life lived well, comprised of longevity, good health, and freedom from misfortune.[7] *Mino-bimaadiziwin* "involves not only prescribed behaviors, but commitment to relations with the other persons of the cosmos, for only under their tutelage can one find the strength one needs to live well."[8] However, the Anishinaabeg lived in a very harsh environment. Starvation in the late winter months always threatened *mino-bimaadiziwin*. The only way to ensure *mino-bimaadiziwin* in all seasons was through establishing relationships of interdependency as widely as possible—including extended family in neighboring communities, and spiritual entities. In obtaining human assistance through the expansion of social networks to new families and communities, one also allied with those other-than-human persons who aided them. However, these alliances needed close supervision, because community members could jeopardize relations with *manidoog* beings if they ceased to maintain accepted standards of personal and social conduct. The standards applied to mutual obligations between human beings also applied to the reciprocal obligations between humans and all other inhabitants of the cosmos.

These *manidoog*, often understood as "grandfathers" of animal species or personification of natural phenomena, are more adept at survival due to the gifts the Creator gave them, and thus are stronger and more powerful than the Ojibwe people. Since they are, however, participants in the same moral order, they share their gifts, abilities, knowledge, and power with their human "grandchildren" in return for demonstrations of gratitude expressed through taboo or ceremonial observances the individual agrees to perform.[9] Returning to Johnston's rendition of the Anishinaabe creation myth, when Gichi-Manidoo, the Creator, made the universe, that one[10] had a vivid vision of the universe, which that one brought into being. In the process, Gichi-Manidoo imbued the *manidoog* beings and forces with immortality, virtue, and wisdom, and implanted them, to various degrees, into beings and objects. The act of creation is the ultimate selfless gift, a use of the Creator's power purely to benefit others, and a gift so awesome that it can never be fully reciprocated. In honor of this first gift, all beings in creation emulate the selfless sharing of Gichi-Manidoo. The *manidoog* give gifts to needy humans, and humans give gifts to others and show respect to those who have aided them. The Creator did not bring into existence a predetermined creation, but rather entrusted all beings with not only purpose but also free will. Those who shared their gifts or blessings did so out of free will, and on the same basis could also withhold them.[11] The clearest demonstration of power was lack of dependence—hence, the animal and plant beings had more power than humans, as they could exist independently of humans with little difficulty, while humans were exceedingly dependent upon them.

Following this act of creation, oral tradition frequently describes spiritual gifts as flowing from one entity to another, with the more powerful bestowing a part of his/her own power as a gift or blessing to one who is in need. These stories portray the basic state of human life as one that evoked the pity of other humans and other more powerful spirit beings who shared these gifts and blessings with them. To some extent, this was a regular part of everyday experience, because human beings were dependent on such gifts to the point of being "in constant need of help from birth to death."[12] Such help was perceived as so essential that no performance of any kind of task, whether in the service of subsistence, war, peace, or even love, was interpreted as due to an individual's own abilities or efforts.[13] Humans were expected to seek dreams and visions that would ensure their future happiness and success in life.

Oral tradition provides a road map to a culture's worldview, but religious performances and testimonies of religious experience or phenomena constituted additional "empirical" sources of knowledge and authority that further reinforced a particular perception of the cosmos.[14] Peter Berger and Thomas Luckmann suggest that the process of socialization within a culture, usually during one's formative years, "convinces the individual that the way he or she has been taught to view the world is the way the world really is."[15] At birth, the family gave gifts to an elder who had the ability to learn a child's name through dreams. These initial gifts disbursed by the family on the child's behalf started the individual on their lifelong journey of forming relationships with the other beings that occupied the Anishinaabeg world. This elder would hereafter be considered family to the named, with all the obligations that entailed, and the spirit who aided the elder would help protect the child as well. Once children were old enough, their parents encouraged them to begin fasting and seeking dreams to establish their own connections with the spirit world.[16] Anishinaabeg individuals approached both human and *manidoog* beings with requests for pity or to receive a blessing: "to be pitiable . . . seems to be the correct state for a person who wishes to receive a gift of power—a promise of help in getting through life. . . . Such gifts consisted of specific powers, abilities to perform life's jobs both great and small; in short, they consisted of the requisite 'necessaries' in order. . . . to survive."[17]

When dreams brought blessings, there were conditions for using them.[18] Those who received them had to exercise them appropriately without wasting the gift, and had to maintain a proper attitude of respect and gratitude for their benefactor's benevolence.[19] Others who mimicked songs or actions that connected one to power, without the proper permission or instruction, received no power and often made fools of themselves. Even worse, those who used the gifts flowing through them improperly could expect their actions to backfire and injure either the user or others close to them. This attitude of respect included not being greedy. One could be greedy for power just as one could be greedy for material objects, and both these foibles constituted inappropriate moral and social behavior. Overfasting to obtain connections with more powerful *manidoog* is portrayed in Ojibwe oral tradition as another form of greed, which generally resulted in negative outcomes. Such actions, for example, could bring a person so closely in touch with the spirit realm that their humanity became altogether lost.[20] As a result of this constant contact with the sacred, the defining element of tradition ceases to be a continuity of doctrine over time and instead becomes a continuity of contact with the sacred. Authority rests in the realm perceived by the senses of the soul, populated by ageless *manidoog* that act both in the oral tradition and in everyday life, and with those Anishinaabeg who have most successfully interacted with these beings over time.

At puberty, families isolated girls in a small wigwam some distance from the main lodge during their first menses, and isolated boys for as long as ten days with blackened faces in the forest to fast and meditate to prepare themselves to dream.[21] While this seclusion was important for girls, who also could receive very powerful dreams or visions at this time, their generative abilities demonstrated through childbirth rendered the need for a powerful vision less necessary. For boys, however, the dreams or visions they received at this time could determine their future roles in society. To secure their aid, it was necessary to become "pitiful," like those who received help in myth to overcome hunger or other dire circumstances. As a result, these young people would go without food and blacken their faces, sometimes for as long as a week to ten days, so as to demonstrate their need and pitiful condition. It was assumed that the *manidoog*, recognizing the immaturity and weakened state of their human grandchildren, were willing to share their strength, power, and knowledge with them so that they might achieve *mino-bimaadiziwin*. They took "pity" on them, visited them through dream or vision, and became their "guardian spirits."[22] As scholar Susan Grey has identified, "The puberty fast undergone by young boys, institutionalized the importance of dreaming; this was the time when the [*manidoog*] who would bless and aid the boys throughout their lives were attained. As far as Ojibwa people were concerned, men were rendered practically powerless without these 'grandfathers,' especially if they aspired to lead religious ceremonies or be especially good hunters."[23]

While these dreams were not shared publicly unless the vision carried a public obligation, the community would recognize that an individual had received power through behavioral changes and/or alterations in their ritual obligations as required by the reciprocal agreement made with those *mani-doog* who offered their help in an individual's dream or vision.[24] This means that a degree of individual variation in religious practice was not only tolerated, but expected as a demonstration of one's personal access to other than human power. Further, the Anishinaabe did not distinguish people by their occupation, but rather by the kind of power they had received through their dreams.[25] Individuals seeking to serve in certain professions were expected to dream to receive an initial calling to their new role as a healer, warrior, *medewid*, or *jossakid*, and to continue dreaming to demonstrate their continued abilities in these areas. Before healers began doctoring, the dream experience had to be related, and war parties each day discussed the dreams of the war leader and the warriors who followed him to ensure that they were still guaranteed the support of the *manidoog* for a positive outcome.[26] Headmen of family groups received knowledge of threats to their family members through dream, whether indications of enemy hostility in the physical or the spiritual realm.[27] Scholar Michael Angel goes so far as to state that collectively, the community viewed these individuals as powerful for the abilities they had received from the *manidoog* through dreams that kept the various forces of the universe in equilibrium.[28] In short, prophetic dreaming was a necessary part of human activity and expected on a fairly regular basis.

Oral tradition provides many examples of individuals acting upon obligations given to them in dream. In addition to the story related above concerning the act of creation, the migration story of the Anishinaabe peoples tells that seven prophets came among the people indicating that the people should move from their homes on the Atlantic down the St. Lawrence Seaway and into the western Great Lakes until they reached the place where the food grew on the water—the wild rice. This we know the Anishinaabeg did over a long period that included seven stops along the route, which are still geographically identifiable today from the clues given in these stories. The stories of how the *Midewiwin* and the water drum came to Anishinaabeg people similarly involve individuals who are transported to the spirit realm to receive teachings and ceremonies that will improve the lives of the Anishinaabeg.[29] A story of how the Anishinaabeg first came into contact with Europeans, written down in the early nineteenth century by Henry Rowe Schoolcraft, also demonstrates this process:

A principal man of the Medawewin named Masewapega, dreamed a dream, in which he beheld spirits in the shape of men, but having white skins, and their heads were covered. They approached him with a smile on the face, and the hands extended. This dream he told to the principal men of his tribe in a council, and over a feast to his dream-spirit. He informed them that the spirits he had seen in his dream resided in the east, and that he would go and find them. For one year Masewapega prepared for his journey. He made a strong canoe, and dried meat for his wappo, and with only his wife as a companion he left Lapointe to go and find the spirits he had seen in his dream. He went down the Great Lake and entered into a river that flowed towards the rising of the sun. He passed through tribes . . . that spoke different languages. At last when the river had become wide, and like a lake, he found on the banks one night as he encamped, a hut built of logs, and the stumps of large trees that had been cut by other and sharper instruments than their . . . axes. The signs thus discovered were apparently two winters old. Much encouraged, Masewapega continued his course downstream, and the next day again came to another deserted log hut. The third day he saw another log hut, from the chimney of which arose a smoke. It was occupied by the white spirits of his dream, who came out and cordially welcomed him with a shake of the hand. When he returned to his people, he brought the presents he had received of an axe, a knife, beads, and some scarlet cloth, which he had carefully secured in his medicine-bag, and brought safely to Moningwanakauning. Collecting his people to council, he showed them the sacred presents of the white spirits. The next season, numbers followed Masewapega on his second visit to the whites. They carried with them many beaver skins, and returned with the fire-arms that from this time made them the terror of their enemies. From this time the dispersion of the tribe from Lapointe can be dated. The Indians say 8 generations or "string of lives" ago, which, estimating an Indian generation by 35 years, would make 280 years ago.[30]

Here we see Masewapega not only receive a dream directing him to take an action, which he pursued on behalf of the people, we also get a glimpse of the sociopolitical process by which the community vetted such visions and the actions they inspired. He told his dream to the principal men of his tribe in a council at which they also partook of a feast to Masewapega's dream spirit. He then prepared for a year before setting out on his journey—providing ample time for the village to intercede should they find his actions based on his dream inappropriate. Upon his return, he again called the council together and showed them the results of his trip, encouraging more to make the journey with him the following year.

This process of taking dreams that addressed public concerns to the village council for review appears not only in myth but also in John Tanner's narrative of Anishinaabe life in the late eighteenth and early nineteenth centuries. The child of Kentucky settlers, Tanner was abducted by a war party around the age of seven, was adopted by an Ottawa family, and lived and married among the Anishinaabe—returning east only at middle age after spending at least thirty years in Anishinaabe communities. Tanner's narrative presents many examples of dreams used to predict the location of game, to direct parties of war, and to warn the wary of imminent danger. He also presents several examples of prophets—most of whom never gain influence beyond a band, or even a war party or hunting group. But their frequency does demonstrate how common such individuals were in Ojibwe society, and how easily people accepted them.

Leaving aside occasional dreamers like his mother Netnokwe, who frequently predicted the location of game when hunters struggled to find it, and the influence of the Shawnee Prophet in Ojibwe country, Tanner refers to at least three other prophets just among the few bands where he spent most of his adult life. He related two separate occasions in his village when the village council was summoned to listen to an individual's vision that had ramifications for the entire community.[31] While Tanner's account contains few dates, his narrative, written in middle age, was first published in 1830, so these events, which he witnessed as an adult with a family, likely took place in the first or second decade of the 1800s.

The first local prophet he discussed is Aguskogaut, a leader of the Muskego whom Tanner and his brother accompanied on a war party. Little is said of the vision ceremonies or moral code of this particular prophet, but given the religious expectations for a war leader, the fact that a prophet would lead a war party is not unusual. Dreams and visions usually played an important role in spurring an individual to organize a war party, to decide who should go, and to determine when or where the battle would take place. Good dreams were of paramount importance for the success of the war party, and indeed, a war leader often began contemplating a war party because of a dream. Once the leader made the decision to begin war preparations, he withdrew from his family into a separate lodge. He then began singing songs to bring additional dreams and strengthen his connections with the *manidoog* that promised him aid in battle. In his dreams, his slain relatives visited him to harden his resolve, and his *manidoog* provided him with useful information, such as where to procure food along the way to enemy territories, how to find the enemy camp, and how to ensure a surprise attack when he did. Dreams might also reveal how many of the enemy a man would kill.[32] A clear dream assured the war leader that he and the war party would go and return safely. A vague dream warned that he would lose some men.[33] Others noticing his preparations would begin to stop by and listen to his intentions and the dreams that supported them. If others agreed with his course of action and found inspiration in their own dreams, they joined the war leader in his seclusion and song. The war leaders also developed a plan of operations and sent out tobacco and/or a war pipe stem to men of various villages inviting them to take part in the campaign.[34] If enough men accepted the tobacco to join the war party, and the war leaders agreed on all parts of the plan, they set a date for departure.[35] While this process demonstrates the very egalitarian opportunity to become a war leader based on visionary experience, it also shows the long process of community ratification and acceptance before such a venture could be successful. If others did not believe in his dreams, there would be no war party.

Such advance warning was necessary so that the participating warriors could also begin preparing themselves spiritually by fasting, dreaming, and refraining from sexual intercourse. They occasionally dropped in on the war leader to have him evaluate their dreams. One of ethnographer Ruth Landes's informants explained, "The leader could not take [just] anyone at all. He had to know their power."[36] If the war leader rejected the vision a warrior brought to him, the leader sent him back to try again.[37] On one occasion, an older man felt confident in joining a war party because he had dreamed of a large bull buffalo. The war leader, and even the other warriors, attempted to dissuade him from the expedition, "because the buffalo is not like a small bird. . . . It is big and can be seen easily." The old man went anyway, was shot full of arrows, and died.[38] Dreams were not just common, but required for success in warfare, and likely Tanner was hopeful, when he joined a war party led by a prophet, that success would be assured.

However, those following a visionary war leader could also doubt the power of his visions. While on their way to seek out the enemy, Aguskogaut's war party fell apart and returned home. An old man called Ahtekoons (Little Caribou) made a *Kozaubunzichegun*, or divination, and announced afterwards that a large band of Dakotah warriors were coming directly towards them, so that the war party needed to change course to avoid meeting them and attack their villages as planned. Ahtekoons further asserted that if the group instead set out to meet these approaching Dakotah warriors, "we should be cut off, to a man." Another influential man in the war party, Tabushshah, believed Ahtekoons and wished to change the direction in which they traveled, but the Muskego chief, and the Muskegoes generally, would not listen to him. The result was widespread discontent and gradual abandonment of Aguskogaut, whose visions they now doubted.[39]

The second local prophet Tanner encountered was a man called Aiskaw-ba-wis, whom Tanner described as a poor hunter, and whose children began to suffer from hunger following the death of his wife. Ais-kaw-ba-wis also called the *kijianishinaabeg* together, by which time Tanner was apparently counted among them as one of the most successful hunters in the village and head of his own extended family household. Tanner related that Ais-kaw-ba-wis announced to the *kijianishinaabeg* that he had been favored by a new revelation from the Great Spirit. He showed them a round ball of earth, about four or five inches in diameter, rolled smooth and smeared with red paint. This ball, he said, had been given to him by the Great Spirit, who took pity on him while he cried and sang and prayed in his lodge. The Great Spirit told him, "I give you this ball, and as you see it is clean and new, I give it to you for your business to make the whole earth like it, even as it was when Nanabush first made it. All old things must be destroyed and done away; everything must be made anew and to your hands, Ais-kaw-ba-wis, I commit this great work." In the usual private conversations following the meeting, Tanner expressed that he did not believe these visions, although it seems apparent that many of the other *kijianishinaabeg* accepted the vision and followed the influence of Ais-kaw-ba-wis for some time. Tanner stated that he "hesitated not to ridicule his pretentions wherever I went," and subsequently suggested that Ais-kaw-ba-wis used his position to call frequent community feasts to compensate for his poor abilities as a hunter. Nevertheless, Ais-kaw-ba-wis "gained a powerful ascendancy over the minds of the Indians," so that Tanner found that all his "efforts in opposition to him were in vain." In fact, Ais-kaw-ba-wis was eventually able to turn even Tanner's in-laws against him by accusing him of sorcery, and forced Tanner to leave the community for a time.[40]

In Tanner's third story concerning a local prophet, he recounts how a man named Manito-o-geezhik disappeared for a year, and when he returned, claimed to have visited the abode of the Great Spirit, who gave him instructions to share with the community. In the spring of the year when the men of several villages had assembled at the Pembinah trading house, those present were called together to hear this new message. Manito-o-geezhik must have previously obtained the backing of the chief, or *ogimaa*, and headmen, or *kijianishinaabeg*, for his visions, as the leading men "built a great lodge and called all the men together to receive some information concerning the newly revealed will of the Great Spirit." Further, the *ogimaa* Little Clam led the meeting, explaining why he had called it, singing, praying, and explaining the vision Manito-o-geezhik had received. In this example, the *ogimaa* and *kijianishinaabeg* play a very clear role in sanctioning new religious ideas brought to the community and persuading others to follow the vision. Little Clam himself, rather than the prophet, is the one who explains the vision.

Later, when another leader, Eshkibagikoonzh of Leech Lake, arrived at Pembinah with the hunters of his band, he also had a lodge built and invited all the men still at the post to hear him lend his support to the recent visions of Manito-o-geezhik.[41] We know little about what this vision entailed for the community, as Tanner only stated that the injunctions communicated to them were "of a kind to be permanently and valuably useful to them," including refraining from theft, fraud, and alcohol. Likely these are social concerns the *ogimaa* and *kijianishinaabeg* wished to see observed in any case, which quickly caused them to support Manito-o-geezhik. Tanner related that this vision resulted in "more orderly conduct" and "somewhat amended condition" of his village over the next two or three years.[42] Tanner provides no explanation for why Manito-o-geezhik's ceremonies and moral observances were eventually abandoned.

The arrival of an envoy of the Shawnee Prophet, Tenskwatawa, to the village where Tanner lived followed the same procedures as the local prophets mentioned above in seeking village acceptance of his message. The envoy, much like the war leader's assistants discussed earlier, first sought to smoke with Tanner and the other *kijianishinaabeg* of his community to win their support.[43] Then, as with the local prophets Tanner encountered, a long lodge was built, and the rest of the people were called to hear the message of this prophet and embrace it.[44] While Tanner describes the influence of the Shawnee Prophet as extensive among the Anishinaabe, and we know that many important leaders such as Eshkibagikoonzh accepted his teachings, Tanner asserts that "it was not the common impression among them that his doctrines had any tendency to unite them in the accomplishment of any human purpose."[45] Rather, the impact of the prophet was expressed in changed moral behavior throughout the villages he visited over the next few years—until these behaviors were gradually abandoned.[46]

These examples from oral tradition, and Tanner's narrative of mythical, local, and intertribal prophets demonstrate that prophecy was common, prophets were readily accepted, and specific processes existed to ratify and adopt these religious innovations within Anishinaabe communities. The proof of their ability as prophets derived not from their claim of prophetic authority or the newness or oldness of what they proposed to the community, but from whether it satisfied the community-sanctioned goals that dreamers and prophets had always satisfied. Did the taboos and ceremonies of these prophets bring success in hunting and war, prevent hunger and witchcraft, keep the people healthy and the universe in equilibrium? The Anishinaabe employed this litmus test to all dreams of all dreamers, from the young girl who dreamed of her husband or her first child's name, to the war leader whose dreams predicted the direction and number of their enemies, to the prophet who proposed actions the whole community must observe. While these traditions led to localized moral changes in daily practice, for the most part they did not espouse or generate collective political or military action, even in the case of the widespread acceptance of the vision of the Shawnee Prophet. Everyone dreamed, and dreams were necessary to ensure success in all aspects of life. Leaders encouraged their people to accept and adopt the prophetic visions they found to contain beneficial practices for the community. These dreams and the prophetic traditions they produced were not a shock, were not an abrupt transition, did not create a new "gestalt," but rather were a common, routine, and expected part of Anishinaabe life.

NOTES

1. Basil Johnston, *The Manitous: The Spiritual World of the Ojibway* (Toronto: Key Porter Books Limited, 1995), 2.
2. Frederick Baraga, *Short History of the North American Indians*, trans. and ed. Graham MacDonald (Calgary: University of Calgary Press, 2004), 143–44.
3. Anthony F. C. Wallace, "Revitalization Movements," in *Revitalizations and Mazeways: Essays on Culture Change* (Lincoln: University of Nebraska Press, 2003), 1:10.
4. Wallace, "Revitalization Movements," 10.
5. Anthony F .C. Wallace, *The Death and Rebirth of the Seneca* (1969; New York: Vintage Books, 1972).
6. A. Irving Hallowell, *The Ojibwa of Berens River Manitoba: Ethnography into History* (New York: Harcourt Brace Jovanovich, 1992), 97–98.
7. Thomas W. Overholt and J. Baird Callicott, *Clothed in Fur and Other Tales: An Introduction to an Ojibwa World View* (Lanham, MD: University Press of America, 1982), 151.
8. Theresa S. Smith, *Island of the Anishinaabeg: Thunderers and Water Monsters in the Traditional Ojibwe Life-World* (Boise: University of Idaho Press, 1995), 183.
9. Hallowell, *The Ojibwa of Berens River Manitoba*, 91.
10. Johnston, *Manitous*, 2. In the Ojibwe language, the third-person pronoun is the same for both genders. The male/female gender of Kitchi-Manitou is not identified in the language and is discussed as a truly balanced being. Basil Johnston also refers to Gitchi-Manidoo as neither male nor female.
11. Johnston, *Manitous*, xxi, 2–4.

12. A. Irving Hallowell, "Myth, Culture, and Personality," *American Anthropologist* 49 (1947): 551; Overholt and Callicott, *Clothed in Fur and Other Tales*, 141.

13. Hallowell, "Myth, Culture, and Personality," 551.

14. A. Irving Hallowell, "Some Empirical Aspects of Northern Saulteux Religion," *American Anthropologist* 36 (1934): 392–93.

15. Peter Berger and Thomas Luckmann, *The Social Construction of Reality* (Garden City, NY: Doubleday, 1967), 135.

16. Timothy G. Roufs, *The Anishinabe of the Minnesota Chippewa Tribe* (Phoenix: Indian Tribal Series, 1975), 9.

17. Mary Black-Rogers, "Starving and Survival in the Subarctic Fur Trade: A Case for Contextual Semantics," in *Le Castor Fait Tout: Selected Papers of the Fifth North American Fur Trade Conference, 1985*, ed. Toby Morantz, Bruce Trigger, and Louise Dechêne (Montreal: Lake St. Louis Historical Society, 1987), 367.

18. Overholt and Callicott, *Clothed in Fur and Other Tales*, 161.

19. Ibid., 144, 146–47.

20. A. Irving Hallowell, "Ojibwa Ontology, Behavior, and World View," in *Teachings from the American Earth: Indian Religion and Philosophy*, ed. Dennis Tedlock and Barbara Tedlock (New York: Liverwright, 1975), 172–73.

21. Roufs, *The Anishinabe of the Minnesota Chippewa Tribe*, 9.

22. Hallowell, *The Ojibwa of Berens River Manitoba*, 87–88.

23. Susan Gray, *"I Will Fear No Evil": Ojibwa-Missionary Encounters along the Berens River, 1875–1940* (Calgary: University of Alberta Press, 2006), 33.

24. Michael Angel, *Preserving the Sacred: Historical Perspectives on the Ojibwa Midewiwin* (Winnipeg: University of Manitoba Press, 2002), 28.

25. Ibid., 30.

26. Ruth Landes, *Ojibwa Sociology* (New York: Columbia University Press, 1937), 115–16.

27. Edward S. Rogers, *The Round Lake Ojibwa* (Ottawa: Ontario Department of Lands and Forests for Royal Ontario Museum, 1962), D5.

28. Angel, *Preserving the Sacred*, 30.

29. Edward Benton-Banai, *The Mishomis Book: The Voice of the Ojibway* (St. Paul, MN: Red School House, 1988).

30. Henry Rowe Schoolcraft, *History, Condition and Prospects of the Indian Tribes of the United States* (Philadelphia: Lippincott, Grambo & Co., 1852), 144.

31. John Tanner, *The Falcon* (New York: Penguin Books, 1994), 111, 169–70, 185–86.

32. Johann Georg Kohl, *Kitchi-Gami: Life among the Lake Superior Ojibway*, trans. Lascelles Wraxall, 1860; reprint with introduction by Robert Bieder

and additional translations by Ralf Neufang and Urlike Bocker (St. Paul: Minnesota Historical Society Press, 1985), 341–43; Landes, *Ojibwa Sociology*, 118–19.

33. Landes, *Ojibwa Sociology*, 118–19.
34. Kohl, *Kitchi-Gami*, 342–43; Sherman Hall and William T. Boutwell, "Communication from Messers Hall and Boutwell Dated at La Pointe, Feb 7, 1833," *Missionary Herald* 29 (September 1833): 316.
35. Kohl, *Kitchi-Gami*, 342–43.
36. Landes, *Ojibwa Sociology*, 118–19.
37. Ibid., 118–19.
38. Ibid., 119.
39. Tanner, *The Falcon*, 112.
40. Ibid., 186–93.
41. Ibid., 177.
42. Ibid., 169–70.
43. Ibid., 144.
44. Ibid., 145–46.
45. Ibid., 147.
46. Ibid., 147.

Constitutional Narratives
A Conversation with Gerald Vizenor

GERALD VIZENOR AND JAMES MACKAY

CONSTITUTIONAL VISIONS

Gerald Vizenor once stated that "there isn't any center to the world but a story."[1] His work denies origins and endings, celebrating unconventional flights of survivance and transmotion over the butterfly-case fixing of terminal identities. Strongly rooted in observation of White Earth and urban Indian experiences, Vizenor's acute critique has always been directed at dissolving those structures that prevent American Indians from creating stories of hope and futurity. His style, lambent and precise, was forged in the unusual meeting of seventeenth-century Japanese poetry, journalism's need to open the text to competing narratives, and the deep study of Anishinaabeg tradition and history first recorded in the volume *Summer in the Spring*.[2] Later infused with the tricky twists of postmodern theory, his language overturns expectations on the page, confronts settled truths, disrupts concepts that should surely be foundational to any sense of identity, and can leave even the subtlest readers gasping for mercy. Coinages and repurposings of words are put to use in dismantling ethnic certainties and liberal pieties as easily as they are aimed at racist stereotypes, false casino economies, and perpetrators of genocide.

All in all, Gerald Vizenor would seem an unlikely candidate to write as sober a document as a constitution.

Yet this curious turn in Vizenor's career, as Principal Writer of the proposed new Constitution of the White Earth Nation, should be seen as a return not just physically to White Earth, but also to the themes and attitudes of his earliest works. For example, the articles and stories collected in *The Everlasting Sky* and *Tribal Scenes and Ceremonies* evince a profound constitutionalism, in the common-language sense of reverence for the American Constitution, especially its negotiations between practical necessities and the necessity of justice.[3] In *The Everlasting Sky*, for example, Vizenor produces one of his many anecdotes about a tribal member standing up to and outwitting the U.S. judicial system. Finding conflicts between federal and state laws, and making them analogous to the blocking of a right to trial by jury, Loretta Beaulieu convinces a judge to set her free without a hearing. Vizenor unironically depicts Beaulieu as "a visionary defending the United States Constitution,"[4] and, as befits someone who at the time was an active member of the ACLU, he looks to the same Constitution as a potential source of true justice. Equally, his series of editorials on the American Indian Movement criticizes the "confrontation heroes" for indulging in symbolic battles at the expense of detailed and long-term engagement,[5] arguing that "Symbolic confrontations bring national attention to problems, but institutional changes require more than an audience with government authorities."[6] His inspiration for the form such institutional changes could take comes from sources such as Anishinaabe deputy sheriff Ira Isham's practice of "*restitutive* rather than *restorative* justice on the reservation,"[7] from William Lawrence and Lee Cook's campaigns against overdependence on federal largesse,[8] or from watching Russell Means's ill-fated attempts to replace corrupt democratic government at Pine Ridge with a hereditary oligarchy.[9]

That a constitution is a curious document is something I know only too well, coming originally from Britain (a country that never got around to codifying its arcane complexities in anything so vulgar as a single document), and living as I do in Cyprus (a country forced to suspend its constitution for thirty-five of the fifty years it has existed as an independent nation).[10] As can be seen from those examples—though one could equally consider the various Navajo constitutional crises[11]—a single constitution is strictly speaking *inessential* to the business of governance. Indeed, moving closer to the example at hand, one could even argue that a constitution, improperly framed, can be more damaging than none at all. Certainly community voices have been raised for years against the 1964 Revised Constitution and Bylaws of the Minnesota Chippewa Tribe, which binds six reservation communities together in a fundamentally undemocratic structure, enshrines nontraditional blood-quantum requirements that carry the potential to eliminate the tribe through exogamy, and centralizes all governing powers in a committee primarily designed for business concerns. But this is why constitutions are not, ultimately, only a matter for legal scholars. A good constitution may lay out a structure that creates the conditions for universal justice (whatever the community understands by that term), but what is at its heart is, must be, an idea of the community as a whole. The

Revised Constitution and Bylaws of the Minnesota Chippewa Tribe envisions Anishinaabe communities as little more than a profit-making entity with a racialized membership: it is this shrunken vision that makes it unfit for the purposes of democratic governance.

Consider, instead, the very name of the proposed replacement document: the Constitution of the White Earth Nation. A certain expression of inherent, immovable sovereignty—not separatist, not defiant (for the document purposefully reduces mention of the state and United States to almost zero), but a simple assertion of fact, followed in turn by the Preamble:

THE CONSTITUTION OF THE WHITE EARTH NATION PREAMBLE

The Anishinaabeg of the White Earth Nation are the successors of a great tradition of continental liberty, a native constitution of families, totemic associations. The Anishinaabeg create stories of natural reason, of courage, loyalty, humor, spiritual inspiration, survivance, reciprocal altruism, and native cultural sovereignty.

We the Anishinaabeg of the White Earth Nation in order to secure an inherent and essential sovereignty, to promote traditions of liberty, justice, peace, and reserve common resources, and to ensure the inalienable right of native governance for our posterity, do constitute, ordain and establish this Constitution of the White Earth Nation.

This is, evidently, an expansive vision upon which to build a nation. The approximately 19,000 White Earth citizens have a constitutional document that, for inspiring rhetoric, can hold its head up alongside that of any country in the world.[12] And, more than rhetoric, the Constitution puts forward practical steps to achieve its ideals: for instance mandating, in chapters 7–9, *mino-bimaadiziwin* ("to live a good life") as a fundamental purpose of nationhood, and creating community councils of elders and the young to attend to this aim. It separates powers into a three-branch structure (executive, legislative, judicial) and provides checks and balances to ensure, firstly, that all significant strands of community opinion are represented, and that secondly, no one party can dominate to the extent of creating one-party rule. It envisions a nation that is fundamentally open-ended, discursive, allowing of difference, allowing tradition to have a role without becoming the ultimate arbiter of all decision-making, even making space for groups to create their own definitions of voting communities with the permission of the majority.

The Constitution, though containing many recognizable Vizenorisms ("artistic irony," "survivance," "altruistic relations"), remains deeply entwined with White Earth history and culture. For example, in the first sentence, the Preamble overcomes fascistic biological definitions of membership in favor of relationships ("families") and traditional practice ("totemic"), while still through the use of an imprecise word ("associations") leaving open the possibility of new ways of belonging. Indirectly honoring imaginative forebears such as John Ka Ka Geesick and Charles Aubid, people secure in their understanding and inventive in their way of making the new world accommodate it, the Preamble creates a moral vision—surely that same moral vision espoused by the editors of *The Progress* a century before—and yet avoids moralism by simultaneously enshrining humor, spirituality, and natural reason as cultural lodes.[13]

This is an ongoing story, one that at the time of writing still has an uncertain outcome. The citizen referendum is being prepared for, with Constitutional Proposal Team member Jill Doerfler writing a series of articles in *Anishinaabeg Today*, explicating the finer points of the Constitution, and individual sections' effects and intentions. Meanwhile, an indignant resistance movement with a different view of Anishinaabeg identity—one that seems to me as an outsider to be dispiritingly based on resentment and victimhood rather than pride—protests against, among other things, the possibility of removing racial barriers to tribal membership.[14] Using the Internet and street protest, this group campaigns for a "No" vote, and only time will tell which side will prevail. However, the idealism of the Constitution, ratified by tribal delegates in a 16–8 vote, nevertheless will remain, whatever the outcome, an inspiring national vision.

CONSTITUTIONAL INTERVIEW

It seemed to me that with the events of the various convocations so fresh in mind—for every clause was discussed, fought over, and some eliminated, in a communal conversation to which all citizens and residents were at one point or another invited to contribute—the best way to work towards understanding this new and potentially central form of White Earth storying was to interview Vizenor himself about the process of writing it. The interview was conducted in his Santa Fe home on a Sunday in May 2010.

Gerald Vizenor is a magnificent subject—garrulous, wide-ranging, and with that best of all interviewee attributes, the ability to speak in complete, rounded sentences and paragraphs. His answer to my first, somewhat insipid question ran for thirty minutes without interruption, holding attention throughout. What follows is not a verbatim transcription of the interview, but rather an agreed-on text that has been through a complete rewrite.

James Mackay (JM): Gerald, would you please start by describing how you came to be involved in drafting the proposed Constitution of the White Earth Nation?

Gerald Vizenor (GV): The White Earth Reservation community has talked about a new constitution or changes in the government for more than ten years. The most critical discussions focused on how to change the constitution that had been established by the federal government. The federal constitution was imposed as an executive, corporate structure that governed six reservations in Minnesota. The Minnesota Chippewa Tribal Executive Committee of elected officials from each reservation serves as the government for six reservations, and that structure has become a problem over the years. White Earth, for instance, is one of the largest reservations, and must share decisions with the smaller reservations.

The federal government foisted the first constitution, and threatened some reservations with termination if they did not accept the corporate constitution. At the time, in the 1950s, the federal government actually terminated several reservations, so the threat could not be taken lightly. That is, the federal government withdrew services and support of some reservations that had been established by treaties. So, in a sense, the resistance to the federal constitution and the idea of a new constitution, or at least a serious change of the constitution, has been around for more than sixty years.

Erma Vizenor was elected tribal leader, or chief, about six years ago. She was the first woman elected as tribal chair of the White Earth Reservation, and she was the first leader of the reservation to initiate the idea of a new constitution. Erma, who was elected to a second term of office in 2008, was determined to reform the reservation government to better serve the citizens. She was, in this sense, a visionary leader, and truly dedicated to the fundamental improvement of the process of governance and the protection of the rights of reservation citizens.

Erma was very determined to change the government—not by radical means alone, but more by negotiation, by reasonable discussions with the executive council, and by a convincing argument and philosophy of reservation independence. She was determined to separate from the federal constitution of six reservations and create an independent government with a new constitution of the White Earth Nation. Naturally, this caused some people to worry about the established and familiar order of the tribal government. Erma has always presented her ideas openly, and has encouraged others to express their different and critical views of the proposed constitution. Even during the formal Constitutional Conventions, she invited many, many citizens who were worried about change, and concerned about the future of the reservation government, to participate in the public discussions.

She did not want anyone to feel they had been left out of the discussions, or their views ignored. Those critical discussions were necessary, and yet they were difficult, frustrating, and time-consuming.

Chief Erma Vizenor inspired me to become more active in reservation education and politics. I donated to the White Earth Tribal Community College, for instance, most of my library of books about native American Indians. Erma made it possible for native citizens to take pride in governance of the White Earth Reservation. More than that, she wanted citizens one day to be proud of the new Constitution of the White Earth Nation.

JM: Erma Vizenor, Gerald Vizenor: surely some relation?

GV: We are related by marriage. Erma's late husband was my father's cousin. Erma earned a doctorate from Harvard University and returned to work in educational administration on the reservation. She had previously been a teacher. We surely met more than forty years ago. I was working on the streets at the time, an advocate on the urban "reservation" in Minneapolis, but we did not get to know each other until about fifteen years ago when Erma invited me to meet with a group of native students in a special summer program.

JM: When did Erma contact you about working on the constitution?

GV: About four years ago. Erma decided to pursue the idea of a new constitution through formal Constitutional Conventions. So, she invited nominations of potential delegates from native communities on the White Earth Reservation, and enrolled members of the reservation from other communities in northern Minnesota.

JM: How many delegates were selected?

GV: There were forty duly sworn delegates, and the delegates solemnly promised to consider the themes, purposes, subjects, constituents, and other matters in the discussion of a new constitution. The delegates agreed to pursue the idea of a constitution, but not the specific form or character of such a document. That would be worked out in the discussions of the delegates at the Constitutional Conventions.

JM: You were a delegate at large?

GV: Yes, one of two or three delegates at large. I was teaching at the University of New Mexico at the time of the first convention, and then moved back to Minnesota. I was obligated to listen closely at the first convention, obviously, to be sure that my ideas about the constitution were not too abstract in the discussions with delegates and others who attended the conferences.

JM: And were they?

GV: No, not in the slightest. The ideas and sentiments of a new constitution were based on real experiences, and that reality was easy for me to articulate and share. You might say that my emotive comments were abstract in the sense that my most idealistic thoughts concentrated on human rights, survivance, and continental liberty.

JM: Survivance can be a slippery concept, with entire conferences and volumes devoted to its explication. How did the delegates respond?

GV: My idea of survivance, a sense of active presence over historical absence and victimry, and other idealist sentiments were understood and shared by most of the delegates. My thoughts about the constitution, and expressed at formal sessions with other delegates, were derived from my personal experiences working as an advocate for natives on the reservation, in nearby communities, and in Minneapolis.

I had directed a desegregation program, for instance, in the consolidated high school at Park Rapids, Minnesota. Native students from the reservation school at Pine Point were bused, starting in the seventh grade, to the consolidated school. That short distance was a critical separation from native community and family, and more than 90 percent of the native students did not graduate. The high dropout rate became a federal issue of segregation, and so a program of desegregation was funded in the school district. My experiences in that school, and in many other service programs, provided a significant cultural and emotive background to pursue the issues of a new constitution of independence. Experience, of course, is not enough to change institutions, but the conventions were open discussions by sworn delegates. The conventions, in other words, were not seminars. I did not mention any books, and only quoted selections from the United States Constitution and the Bill of Rights.

JM: How many conventions did you have?

GV: There were four Constitutional Conventions, and, to provide an ironic scene, the delegates gathered in a conference room at the Shooting Star Casino Hotel on the White Earth Reservation. The casino is actually located in Mahnomen, Minnesota. The first formal convention was held on October 19–20, 2007. I traveled from Albuquerque, New Mexico. The forty delegates were divided into eight groups, or discussion tables, five delegates in each group.

Erma introduced the broad objectives of sovereign governance and then invited the delegates to discuss the value of an independent constitution for the White Earth Reservation. That initial invitation to the delegates was obviously very complicated, but at the end of the first session there was a general consensus and outright enthusiasm for the idea that the delegates might construct the Constitution of the White Earth Nation. I cannot remember any delegate, for instance, who did not agree with the idea of independence and the declarative notion of a nation. Later, of course, there were serious concerns about the actual substantive meaning of a new constitution.

I was inspired and deeply moved by the experiences of the first convention. I drove home that night at the end of the convention with a sense of hope and excitement that the delegates might actually agree to create a new constitution. The ideals, adventure, encounters, and excitement of that first convention are truly memorable. There were many moments in the last two conventions, however, when my enthusiasm almost vanished over the nasty comments, obstructions, and hateful politics. I was most discouraged by the one or two delegates, and some visitors, who expressed hateful, racialist, and separatist attitudes.

Please remember that at the time of the first Constitutional Convention, the delegates were discussing the experiences, values, and concepts of an independent nation and a new constitution. I was a delegate, nothing more, and had no idea or conception of how or who would actually write the proposed document that we were discussing in our groups. I never thought about the actual creation of a constitution, except, of course, the history of the United States Constitution, and my early research on the military conditions at the end of the war and the construction under occupation of the Constitution of Japan.

In fact, I refused when, at the second convention, Erma Vizenor first asked me to be the Principal Writer. I agreed only to participate on an advisory committee. As it turned out, no one else would consider the responsibility to prepare even the first draft of the proposed constitution. Several delegates agreed only to serve on a committee. In other words, the actual composition of the constitution was considered a serious burden, too much to bear in ordinary time, and apparently no one was eager to confront the enemy politics of a new constitution. Erma, in the end, persuaded me to become the Principal Writer, probably because of my dedication to the process and my experience as a writer.

JM: Could you describe some of the issues that emerged in the early discussions? What were the most serious points discussed by the delegates?

GV: Yes, there were many concerns, as you can imagine, but the most significant question during the discussions at the first convention was about the definition of a citizen. That is, the critical and political issue of blood quantum, carried out by the federal government, compared to family descent. I thought at first that the blood-quantum issue would totally distract the delegates, but most of the delegates favored the straightforward definition of family descent as the means to determine official enrollment or citizenship in the White Earth Nation. Some of the delegates who opposed family descent were concerned that without the federal recognition of blood quantum, they might lose their rights to education, health care, and other services. These were very serious concerns, and could not be taken lightly.

There was much discussion about the definition of who would be recognized as a citizen of the reservation, and at the end of the second convention, the delegates were divided on the issue; slightly more than half of the delegates present voted for family descent based on the original families of the treaty reservation. Less than half of the delegates present voted to stay with the definition of blood quantum to determine citizenship. The delegates were unanimous in their rejection of the notion of "membership," and without objection adopted "citizen" as the reference to the constituents of the White Earth Nation.

I supported the definition of citizens based on family descent, and forcefully articulated my position in discussions with the other delegates, but I did not persist, however, because my health care and services were not provided on the reservation. My heath care was more secure, and that limited the relevance of my position. I pointed out that nothing would be lost and more respect earned by rejecting the racialist blood-quantum measures of native identity.

After several hours of intense discussions, those who supported the racial arithmetic of blood quantum became more determined, and a few delegates revealed critical racial views of intermarriage. Clearly we had reached the point when the discussions on the definition of citizenship were no longer productive.

Much later, as the Principal Writer of the Constitution, I was obliged to accommodate both views, that is, to articulate the support for family descent and also the protection of federal services based on blood quantum on the reservation. Some delegates were worried that recognition of family descent would increase the number of citizens and therefore reduce the available federal health care and other services on the reservation. These were significant concerns, and the sentiments continue to be controversial.

Chapter 2 of the Constitution, "Citizens of the White Earth Nation," contains two articles about the definition of citizens. The first article provides that *Citizens of the White Earth Nation shall be descendants of Anishinaabeg families and related by linear descent to enrolled members of the White Earth Reservation and Nation, according to genealogical documents, treaties and other agreements with the government of the United States.* The second article provides protection for those citizens who support the federal blood-quantum arithmetic. *Services and entitlements provided by government agencies to citizens, otherwise designated members of the White Earth Nation, shall be defined according to treaties, trusts, and diplomatic agreements, state and federal laws, rules and regulations, and in policies and procedures established by the government of the White Earth Nation.* These two articles of the new constitution were ratified, and serve the interests of those who define a citizen by family descent and those who rely on blood-quantum certificates. I wrote the articles without using the racialist words "blood quantum."

JM: When did you agree to be the Principal Writer, and how did you go about writing a new constitution? How did you first approach the complicated, and surely controversial, first draft of the constitution?

GV: Complicated, indeed, and the chapters, declarations, articles, and every sentence of the first draft became an anticipation of controversy. I was mistaken, because the discussions of the proposed constitution were actually very productive at the last Constitutional Convention. The delegates discussed each and every chapter, and only minor changes were suggested at the convention in preparation for a ratification vote.

The second Constitutional Convention was held on January 4–5, 2008, and nine months later the third Constitutional Convention met, on October 24–25, 2008. The Constitution of the White Earth Nation was ratified by the delegates at the fourth and final Constitutional Convention held on April 3–4, 2009.

Erma named me the Principal Writer of the proposed constitution, and she also established a committee of three advisors: Jill Doerfler, an assistant professor at the University of Minnesota, Duluth; JoAnne Stately; and Anita Fineday, chief tribal judge of the White Earth Nation. Jill Doerfler was a brilliant advisor, and by her knowledge and experience provided significant suggestions about the community councils and other matters. The final ratified version of the Constitution of the White Earth Nation was published in the reservation newspaper, *Anishinaabeg Today.*

JM: Please would you tell the story of the article allowing urban representation?

GV: Yes, the surprise article that had not been reviewed by anyone, not even Erma Vizenor. I was making the final minor corrections to the constitutional narrative, and decided to insert, as a teaser, an article about representation outside the reservation. Erma Vizenor and the advisory committee had no knowledge of the insertion until the moment it was read and discussed by the delegates. Erma searched through her copy of the draft constitution and obviously could not locate the article. I had written that the Legislative Council had the authority to appoint one ex officio representative from outside the reservation. My idea was to create the circumstances that would provide wider representation, and in time might result in an amendment to the constitution that would include elected members of the Legislative Council from outside the reservation.

I read the surprise article and waited for a critical response, but the delegates were silent. The surprise article was a calculated strategy to increase the number of representatives. I was worried the article would be rejected or become a distraction. I boldly reread the article and asked if there was a motion to approve the article. Yes, there was a motion, and then another delegate demanded that the motion be amended. I was certain the article was about to be revised and amended to death, but instead the delegate wanted to amend the article to state that the proposed representative be elected to the Legislative Council. That amendment was truly a great moment for me. What started as a surprise article to appoint an ex officio representative had become an elected member from outside the reservation. I asked for a second to approve the amended motion, only to be interrupted by another amendment. The second request for an amendment seemed more like an intrusion, but that was not the case. The second amendment changed the number of elected representatives from outside the reservation to two. I could not have been more pleased about any article in the constitution. My surprise article became an even greater surprise at the last Constitutional Convention.

Chapter 6, "Governance," provides in Article 7 that *Two citizens of the White Earth Nation shall be elected at large to serve constituencies outside the White Earth Reservation in the State of Minnesota.* On April 4, 2009, the delegates present voted to ratify the Constitution of the White Earth Nation.

JM: What sources did you consult in the final preparation and actual writing of the Constitution?

GV: The primary sources were the systematic summaries of delegate discussions. There were five delegates at each of eight tables, and each group presented a summary of the discussions at each convention. These general summaries about native rights and cultural values provided the premise and starting point of the constitution. I already mentioned the discussion of citizenship. Other significant cultural values discussed by the delegates focused on community councils, elections and representation, cultural sovereignty, judicial practices of reciprocity, and the significance of native concepts of nature, traditions, and totemic associations. The delegates also strongly supported the modern divisions of an elected government, the executive, legislative, and judicial. These divisions were considered critical to protect the rights of natives on the reservation. The divisions, of course, are the foundations of many modern constitutions and the Constitution of the United States.

The federal executive constitution was redundant, unclear, and almost unreadable by ordinary citizens. The federal constitution of the six reservations was constructed and imposed as an expediency by career bureaucrats who had no knowledge of the native people or place of governance. I made use of only a few relevant sections from the federal executive-style constitution, specifically those sections that were derived from early treaties. The White Earth Reservation is located in three counties in northern Minnesota. The legal boundary of the reservation was established in a federal treaty on March 19, 1867. The boundary has not changed, but the actual ownership of reservation land is only a fraction of the original treaty.

The Constitution of the United States became a general guide of prudent and practical public representations and governance, but the only specific references were secured, of course, from the Bill of Rights. The most difficult problem at first was to find a form, a direct language and structure to document the narratives of rights and duties of governance. I turned to the Constitution of Japan, one of the most recent democratic constitutions in the world, for the clarity of content, form, and structure.

JM: What did the Japanese document contribute?

GV: The Constitution of Japan provided uncomplicated chapters that described the modern practices of governance. I adapted the chapter style with thematic divisions, such as executive, legislative, judiciary, advisory councils, elections, citizenship, native rights, and the duties of elected representatives. My adaptation of this forthright and uncomplicated structure made it much easier for me to consider and organize specific chapters of independent governance. I then devised an organization strategy, an essential strategy to consider a wide range of practical and legal statements, provisions, and protections from many sources, including the summary of delegate discussions, treaty rights, the federal executive constitution, federal and international laws, and many other sources of modern native governance, preservation, and security.

The account of my structural strategy must be reduced to a general description, because the actual practice was much more complicated, a strategy that partly was created in the process. In other words, the narrative of the strategy is a native story. I cut out relevant statements and documents from many sources and then created categories of governance. I transcribed the sources once the hundreds of statements and documents were stacked in more than a dozen categories, such as councils, native rights, totemic association, free speech, artistic expression, possession of firearms, and the prohibition of banishment. That was a fundamental organization, and from the transcription the chapters of the constitution began to take shape. The duplications were combined or eliminated, and each chapter was rewritten for brevity and clarity.

The Preamble is two distinct paragraphs. The first paragraph declares that the *Anishinaabeg of the White Earth Nation are the successors of a great tradition of continental liberty, a native constitution of families, totemic associations. The Anishinaabeg create stories of natural reason, of courage, loyalty, humor, spiritual inspiration, survivance, reciprocal altruism, and native cultural sovereignty.* The second paragraph describes the ideals and provisions of native sovereignty. *We the Anishinaabeg of the White Earth Nation in order to secure an inherent and essential sovereignty, to promote traditions of liberty, justice, and peace, and reserve common resources, and to ensure the inalienable rights of native governance for our posterity, do constitute, ordain and establish this Constitution of the White Earth Nation.*

Erma Vizenor, Jill Doerfler, and the advisory committee met a few weeks before the fourth and final Constitutional Convention to review each and every chapter of my proposed Constitution. The document was basically complete, and after a hearty discussion, only minor changes were necessary. Anita Fineday, for instance, raised a rather tedious question about my reference to "continental liberty" in the Preamble. I explained that the native sentiment of my proposed narrative of a democratic constitution was not legalistic and must make use of expansive metaphors, and especially in the idealism of the Preamble.

I am convinced now that no one else could have written the Constitution that was ratified by the delegates. Only an active delegate could have created a narrative of native governance, and only someone with extensive experience as a creative and scholarly writer. I was seventy-four years old when the Constitution was ratified. A younger person might not have had the capacity to gather the intellectual energy, experience, political, practical, and literary, and the train of original philosophical values that were articulated in the Constitution of the White Earth Nation.

JM: Would you explain further your understanding of a constitution as a narrative?

GV: Constitutions are created as narratives and ratified as political documents of governance. The narratives of constitutions reveal the ethos, the specific cultural metaphors and linguistic references of a time, and the language of every constitution has a unique narrative style. Consider, for instance, the executive and bureaucratic metaphors of the federal corporate constitutions. The Constitution of the United States was created by a revolution, and pronounces the integrity of that revolution. The Constitution of Japan was created by a military order. General of the Army Douglas MacArthur, supreme commander of the Allied Powers in the occupation of Japan, directed his senior staff officers to create a draft of a constitution that renounced war, abolished feudalism, and provided suffrage for women and political parties. The document that was drafted in two weeks time became the Constitution of Japan.

The Constitution of the White Earth Nation is not a document of revolution, and it is not a document prepared by supreme military officers or federal bureaucrats. The Constitution was created in the spirit of resistance and independent governance, by the sentiments of native survivance, and by the inspiration and vision of the delegates and Erma Vizenor. There is no other constitution in the world that contains the profound sentiments of survivance, and native continental liberty.

NOTES

1. Laura Coltelli, *Winged Words: American Indian Writers Speak* (Lincoln: University of Nebraska Press, 1990), 156.
2. Gerald Vizenor, *Summer in the Spring: Lyric Poems of the Ojibway* (Minneapolis: Nodin Press, 1965).
3. Gerald Vizenor, *The Everlasting Sky: New Voices from the People Named the Chippewa* (New York: Crowell-Collier, 1972); Gerald Vizenor, *Tribal Scenes and Ceremonies* (Minneapolis: Nodin Press, 1976).
4. Vizenor, *The Everlasting Sky*, 111.
5. Vizenor, *Tribal Scenes and Ceremonies*, 49–80.
6. Ibid., 73.
7. Vizenor, *The Everlasting Sky*, 97.
8. Ibid., 83–92.
9. Vizenor, *Tribal Scenes and Ceremonies*, 74–77.
10. "What Britain does not have is a short single-volume constitution . . . the opinion of many commentators is that, without a formal codified structure, such 'unwritten constitutions' are untrustworthy, because they are confused, unclear and uncertain"; Colin Pilkington, *Politics Today Companion to the British Constitution* (Manchester: Manchester University Press, 1999), 2. For an overview of the effects of the ongoing occupation of Cyprus on its constitution, see Nikos Trimikliniotis, "Nationality and Citizenship in Cyprus since 1945: Communal Citizenship, Gendered Nationality and the Adventures of a Post-Colonial Subject in a Divided Country," in *Citizenship Policies in the New Europe*, ed. Rainer Baubock, Bernhard Perchinig, and Wiebke Sievers (Amsterdam: Amsterdam University Press, 2009), 390–94.
11. There have been three attempts to create a Navajo constitution—in 1934, 1953, and 1968. All three failed or were rejected. For brief summaries of this history, see Raymond Darrel Austin, *Navajo Courts and Navajo Common Law: A Tradition of Tribal Self-Governance* (Minneapolis: University of

Minnesota Press, 2009), 13–16; and David E. Wilkins, *The Navajo Political Experience* (Lanham, MD: Rowman & Littlefield, 2003), 106–7.

12. Population estimate from the "2010 State of the Tribe" address by Erma Vizenor, State of the Nation, Shooting Star Convention and Event Center, Mahnomen, MN, March 10, 2010, http://www.whiteearth.com/data/upfiles/files/April72010.pdf (accessed September 13, 2011), p. 2.

13. These figures are discussed in essays in various of Vizenor's works. For Aubid, see Gerald Vizenor, *Fugitive Poses: Native American Indian Scenes of Absence and Presence* (Lincoln: University of Nebraska Press, 1998), 167–69. For John Ka Ka Geesick, see Vizenor, *The Everlasting Sky*, 128–36. For the moral vision of *The Pioneer* editors, see Gerald Vizenor, "Aesthetics of Survivance: Literary Theory and Practice," in *Survivance: Narratives of Native Presence*, ed. Gerald Vizenor (Lincoln: University of Nebraska Press, 2008), 5–10 (a much expanded version of the essay "Tribal Newspapers," 1974, 159–66).

14. For more details of protests against Erma Vizenor and the constitution, see the online news stories from Riham Feshir, "Petition Aims to Oust Erma Vizenor," *DL-Online*, April 24, 2010, https://secure.forumcomm.com/?publisher_ID=5 (accessed September 13, 2011); and Tom Robertson, "Protesters Removed from White Earth Indian Reservation," Minnesota Public Radio News, July 14, 2010, http://minnesota.publicradio.org/display/web/2010/07/14/protesters-removed-from-white-earth-indian-reservation/ (accessed September 13, 2011).

RESOURCES

Austin, Raymond Darrel. *Navajo Courts and Navajo Common Law: A Tradition of Tribal Self-Governance.* Minneapolis: University of Minnesota Press, 2009.

Coltelli, Laura. *Winged Words: American Indian Writers Speak.* Lincoln: University of Nebraska Press, 1990.

"Constitution of the White Earth Nation." April 4, 2009. http://www.d.umn.edu/~amind/images/WECONSTITUTION.pdf (accessed September 13, 2011).

Doerfler, Jill. "Governance of the White Earth Nation." *Anishinaabeg Today* (White Earth, MN), October 6, 2010.

Feshir, Riham. "Petition Aims to Oust Erma Vizenor." *DL-Online*, April 24, 2010. https://secure.forumcomm.com/?publisher_ID=5 (accessed September 13, 2011).

Pilkington, Colin. *Politics Today Companion to the British Constitution.* Manchester: Manchester University Press, 1999.

"Revised Constitution and Bylaws of the Minnesota Chippewa Tribe." 2000. http://www.mnchippewatribe.org/constitution_revised.pdf (accessed September 13, 2011).

Robertson, Tom. "Protesters Removed from White Earth Indian Reservation." *Minnesota Public Radio News*, July 14, 2010. http://minnesota.publicradio.org/display/web/2010/07/14/protesters-removed-from-white-earth-indian-reservation/ (accessed September 13, 2011).

Trimikliniotis, Nikos. "Nationality and Citizenship in Cyprus since 1945: Communal Citizenship, Gendered Nationality and the Adventures of a Post-Colonial Subject in a Divided Country." In *Citizenship Policies in the New Europe*, ed. Rainer Baubock, Bernhard Perchinig, and Wiebke Sievers, 389–417. Amsterdam: Amsterdam University Press, 2009.

Vizenor, Erma J. "2010 State of the Tribe Address." 2010 State of the Nation, Shooting Star Convention and Event Center, Mahnomen, MN, March 10, 2010. http://www.whiteearth.com/data/upfiles/files/April72010.pdf (accessed September 13, 2011).

Vizenor, Gerald. "Aesthetics of Survivance: Literary Theory and Practice." In *Survivance: Narratives of Native Presence*, ed. Gerald Vizenor, 1–23. Lincoln: University of Nebraska Press, 2008.

———. *Fugitive Poses: Native American Indian Scenes of Absence and Presence*. Lincoln: University of Nebraska Press, 1998.

———. *Summer in the Spring: Lyric Poems of the Ojibway*. Minneapolis: Nodin Press, 1965.

———. *The Everlasting Sky: New Voices from the People Named the Chippewa*. New York: Crowell-Collier, 1972.

———. *Tribal Scenes and Ceremonies*. Minneapolis: Nodin Press, 1976.

Wilkins, David E. *The Navajo Political Experience*. Lanham, MD: Rowman & Littlefield, 2003.

And the Easter Bunny Dies
Old Traditions from New Stories

JULIE PELLETIER

THE FOURTH HILL

IN BASIL JOHNSTON'S *OJIBWA HERITAGE*, WEEGWAUSS (BIRCH) HAS A dream so troubling that he seeks guidance from Chejauk (Crane) on its meaning.[1] Chejauk listens and assures Weegwauss that he has had a good dream—a dream that tells the story of human life from beginning to end, through the four stages or hills: "For men and women to live out life in all its stages is to receive and possess nature's greatest gift."[2] Chejauk describes the characteristics of each stage as he understands them, concluding with the fourth stage:

> Old age is a gift of the Kitche Manitou. As such it is to be cherished; not disparaged. Even in old age, life's work is not finished. There is still much good that can be done for brothers in life. By living through all the stages and living out the visions, men and women know something of human nature and living and life. What they have come to know and abide by is wisdom. This is what they must pass on to those still to traverse the path of life and scale the mighty hills. Only when they finally vanish into the mists is the work over.[3]

In this chapter I will examine the role of elders, those tribal members who have reached the fourth hill, in one Anishinaabeg community at one moment in time. I look at what was expected of this age group and how these expectations shape tribal community interactions with elders. I examine how tribal expectations were perceived and received by elders. To illustrate both the usefulness of story as methodology in Anishinaabeg Studies and how story and storymaking relate to cultural perseverance, sovereignty issues, cultural innovation, and concepts of tradition, I turn to the stories of the storymakers themselves. Ironically, we begin with a story and an analysis of the role of storytelling and storymaking from a child, not an elder.

THE STORY OF SUSIE, A LITTLE INDIAN

> He just does Indian stuff, like fishing, and hunting, and growing a garden. He also plays tricks on us, like an Indian! And he tells stories, lots of stories!
>
> [Susie, age 8, July 20, 1994][4]

Susie was aware that I was interviewing people, and insisted on being included in my research.[5] When asked about her own identity, Susie stated that her grandfather, Joe, is an Indian, so that makes her an Indian. I then asked how she knew he is an Indian; could she tell me what makes him an Indian? Her reply, given without hesitation, is quoted above. She and other tribal children with whom I interacted had learned that identity as something that is inherited in an essential or biological way—Susie's grandfather is an Indian, so she is one as well, tracing her ancestry from her grandfather through her mother to herself.

When I asked Susie, "Are you an Indian?" the interview went like this:

Susie: "A little bit. If your mother is full Indian, you're ¼ Indian."
Julie: "Do you like being a little Indian?"
Susie: "Sorta."

At this point, Susie ended the interview because her mother (who was in the adjoining room) and I could no longer contain our laughter![6]

Susie and the other kids also saw tribal identity as practiced—"fishing and hunting, growing a garden . . . playing tricks . . . telling stories." When I asked Susie if her grandmother, Joe's wife, is an Indian, she responded thoughtfully, "I don't think so. She doesn't do tricks." The practices that Susie and others associated with Indian/Anishinaabeg identity could be part of the inherited identity, but in this instance, the practices were learned and passed on, through observation/instruction as well as through stories. Stories are carriers of content, and storytelling and storymaking are actions of practiced identity. And practiced or lived identity may be passed on deliberately, or, as one tribal member observed, "elders pass on knowledge without knowing it, such as trapping, snaring, etc."[7]

THE STORY OF JOE'S TRICKS

Susie was blessed with a grandfather, "Joe," who had a well-honed sense of humor. He was known for his practical jokes, with immediate family members often being the butt of elaborately planned and executed stories and tricks. Joe's tricks, jokes, and stories often targeted the stories and beliefs of the dominant culture. For example, before Easter one year, Joe killed a wild rabbit and froze it after painstakingly arranging it sitting on its haunches with a colored Easter egg between its front paws. The finishing touch was a ribbon tied in a bow around its neck. He then told Susie and his other grandchildren that they should not expect anything from the Easter Bunny since he had shot the fabled creature, "and the Easter Bunny died." They were accustomed to his tall tales and jokes, but ran screaming when he pulled the elaborately staged and very dead "Easter Bunny" out of his freezer.

Another time, Joe drove from house to house one Christmas Eve with a partially stuffed Santa suit protruding from his car trunk. He explained to his horrified grandchildren that he had heard an intruder on the roof and shot him, only to find that he had killed Santa Claus. These pranks might seem harsh to some, but the old man's family thought they were hilarious. So did his grandchildren, once they recovered from their shock—a process that was encouraged by teasing from their parents and other relatives. Having a sense of humor was a signifier of Indianness—being able to gracefully accept being the butt of a joke, a sign of character and self-control.

THE STORY OF BILL WHO FINDS WHAT HE HAD LOST

Bill and his wife, who is white, prided themselves on being modern and progressive. For them, being modern and progressive specifically meant that Bill did not behave in any way that would mark him as Indian—I would identify him as a "disconnected elder."[8] His wife, Jane, was a teacher in the local public school. Bill was of mixed Anishinaabeg and white ancestry, like many Soo Tribe members. Unlike his sister, however, Bill had denied his Indian ancestry until the 1990s.[9] I intended to interview Bill alone, but Jane insisted on remaining in the room and actively participated in the interview as well. Her comments were unsolicited but enlightening.

Bill was a retired state employee, married for more than thirty years, and the father of two children. He explained that it would have been "a bad idea" to let his employer know that he was an Indian, although he was often questioned about his dark skin, hair, and eyes. Like many Soo Tribe members, he explained his appearance as being owed to Italian ancestry.[10] Jane agreed that it was not good to be known as an Indian, but expanded the reasons for the subterfuge to include negative stereotypes about Indians. Jane did not identify these as stereotypes, however, but as truths, and she specifically applied them to Anishinaabeg students who were in her classroom, as well as to their parents. Bill's eyes remained fixed on the kitchen table during this monologue and he remained silent. Jane then stated that he was an exception who had done well in life with her guidance and assistance.

When Jane left the room to get us some refreshments, Bill regained his animation and spoke fondly of his mother and his memories of life with her and his sister. He expressed sorrow at having forgotten how to speak "Indian." Bill recounted his decision to apply for tribal membership, a decision supported by Jane. Having returned to the room, Jane explained that once she learned about the benefits their children would qualify for, such as the Michigan Indian Tuition Waiver, she convinced Bill to apply. Bill stated that the day he received his membership card was one of the happiest days of his life. He said it felt like he was closer to his deceased Anishinaabeg mother in some way. Jane looked sour at this point, and we quickly brought the interview to a close.

THE STORY OF JOE'S BRAIDS

Joe, who grew up on Sugar Island, surprised us both one day while telling me stories—I was a good audience because I was usually available, hadn't heard his stories a hundred times, and exhibited a level of gullibility irresistible to a practical joker and good storyteller.[11] We sat at the kitchen table in his dilapidated house, which was uncharacteristically quiet, with his wife off cleaning houses, the many children and grandchildren at work or school.

Instead of a funny story, Joe told me about the day his long braids were cut off. Town authorities were pressuring his parents to send him to the public school in the Soo. A regular passenger ferry across the St. Mary's River made his attendance at school possible.[12] Joe remembered being curious about school, and excited by his parents' descriptions of the toys and games they assured him were at the school. What he did not realize was that his hair must be cut. Every day, for as long as he could remember, his mother had combed out his long, thick black hair and carefully braided it, binding the ends with bits of thread, yarn, or sinew. Now his father offered him a rare treat, candy, and took him to the barbershop in the Soo.

Close to sixty years later, this man could remember and describe the unfamiliar smells of the barbershop, and the fear he felt when his father lifted him onto the big leather chair. With tears in his eyes, he recalled the feeling of his heavy braids sliding down past his shoulders to the floor. He vaguely remembered his father gathering the braids and wrapping them in a cloth to take home. He described feeling betrayed by his parents and hating his new school. At this point, the story seemed to be at an end. After a period of shared silence, I asked him if he became the class clown at his new school, and he said, yes, it was a way to get by. I then asked him if he had ever shared this story with his large family and he said, no. He did not like to talk about "the bad times" and was surprised that he had told me the story. A few minutes later, I knew he had regained his composure when he jokingly accused me of putting some kind of Micmac-patty-wack medicine in his tea, to make him reveal all of his secrets.[13]

ANALYZING STORIES AND STORYMAKING

Stories can promote a sense of identity and of belonging to a particular group or community. They can entertain, mystify, exoticize, and have been studied by generations of folklorists, historians, ethnohistorians, and anthropologists. But how might one utilize story as a methodology? An interest in looking at the strategic use of ritual, termed "ritualization," influences my approach.[14] Rather than focusing on describing rituals and ceremonies, I have analyzed how and why individuals and groups use ritual strategically. Examining the praxis of ritual reveals social conditions that the actor/individual/group is/are living in, and perhaps manipulating or solidifying. Anishinaabeg story as point of analysis and as methodology can be explored in a similar way. To do so requires positioning story as verb, as storymaking—which reveals the dynamic characteristics of conveying and creating and re-creating identity.

Storymaking and ritualization are particularly relevant in American Indigenous communities because of their relationship to the dominant culture. In a nation-state where legal Indigenous identity is legislated and defined by national policy, and in a tribe that has only had legal tribal recognition for a few short decades, the pressure to perform Anishinaabeg identity, often through ritual and ceremony, and to tell the story of the authentic Anishinaabeg identity of the Soo Tribe is tremendous. Pressure to participate in and support these efforts is put on elders in subtle and overt ways, as elders are perceived as the keepers of knowledge and tradition and, therefore, of Anishinaabeg identity. Stories and storymaking, like rituals and ritualization, can be a lens into the tribe's goals and strategies for expressing and teaching Anishinaabeg identity.

The tricks Joe played on his children and grandchildren were a sort of storymaking; he was participating in an old tradition—teaching lessons, poking fun at authority, matching wits—and doing so with new stories, that of the Easter Bunny and Santa Claus. There are many stories told by the Anishinaabeg about the *waboos* (Anishinaabeg for "rabbit")—he can be a trickster who gets into scrapes, is shamed, and is physically transformed (by having his ears lengthened, for example). But he is a survivor and has helped the Anishinaabeg survive by offering up every part of himself to be useful. When the *waboos* is Christianized, however, by becoming the Easter Bunny, he becomes vulnerable and is made a fool of in a way that he cannot survive—shot and popped into a freezer with an Easter egg between his paws and a bow around his neck. To my knowledge, Joe's Easter Bunny was not consumed, so was not useful in a "traditional" way. Yet Joe's storymaking in which he kills the Easter Bunny (and Santa) springs from an old tradition that is reinforced and handed down; it also expresses the Anishinaabeg identity, which in Joe's lifetime and before was almost extinguished in the Soo Tribe community.

Comparing the stories of Bill and Joe, men of similar ages, racial/tribal background, education, and work (Joe was a civil servant until he retired), is illuminating. First, questioning Joe about any serious matter was difficult because he was highly skilled at distracting and deflecting the conversation to safer, more humorous, and less personal topics. However, many of his jokes, pranks, and stories served a purpose and demonstrated his keen awareness of social, historical, and other forces that affected his life, and the lives of his family, friends, and community. I learned from other tribal members, including his family members, that Joe, like Bill, had suffered from prejudice and discrimination in his professional and personal life. Rosemary Gaskin told me that he was an active participant in the first powwow held in Sault Ste. Marie in the 1970s, a gathering that aroused anxiety and fear among local and national law enforcement.[15] There is, of course, a story to tell about this powwow, but it is Rosemary's story and will be told in due course.

Bill, like Joe, was an intelligent man, but I sensed that he had built a false story of himself and held onto it for so long that receiving concrete proof of his tribal identity in the form of his membership card broke down his strategic storymaking and left him groping for the remnants of Anishinaabeg memory, story, and language, even of self. Unlike Joe, he was doing so not only without the support of his spouse, but against her formidable resistance. In the privacy of my thoughts and field notes, I abandoned the pretense of scientific objectivity and silently urged Bill to revive his story with the help of his son and his sister, both at ease in their identity as Anishinaabeg. Joe may have been trapped in a different story, one that entangles Indianness with poverty—that is another story that I will tell as the outsider anthropologist.

Bill's experience is in many ways representative of the experiences of elders in the Soo Tribe. Many have passed for white, in the past, in order to accommodate themselves to the dominant culture, thereby gaining access to economic, political, and educational opportunities. They were encouraged by their parents to assimilate, to stop speaking Ojibwa, to be Christian, in order to survive and, perhaps, succeed in an often-hostile world. Several elders expressed sorrow at what they had lost by rejecting or hiding their Indian identity. These elders usually expressed guilt as well, a feeling that was exacerbated by the expectations of younger tribal members.

The elderly members were expected to possess traditional knowledge about Anishinaabeg life, from technical skills such as curing animals, to spiritual knowledge and skills. Some never learned these skills, and others had forgotten what they learned in their childhood. They expressed embarrassment and sadness when they could not pass on Anishinaabeg skills and knowledge to their children and grandchildren. Those elders who did retain traditional skills, such as basket making, beading, and sugaring, were valued and encouraged to share their skills with younger members of the tribe.

Other elders did not express sorrow or guilt about their lack of tribal knowledge or skills, and were quite pragmatic about the difficulties of the past. Many of the disconnected elders took a pragmatic approach to tribal membership, with the tribe serving as an additional socioeconomic support system. The experiences of tribal elders were diverse, so it is not surprising that their stories and storymaking, as well as their participation in ritual, at times did not resonate with or support the tribe's authenticity nation-building project, leaving elders simultaneously positioned at the center and at the periphery of tribal life.

A BRIEF STORY OF THE SOO TRIBE

The southern Anishinaabeg gathered regularly at the place of the rapids, Bawating, to take advantage of the natural bounty found there, and to avoid their Iroquois enemies to the south.[16] The French arrived in September 1641, renamed the area Sault (falling water or rapids) de Ste. Marie, and described a village of two thousand inhabitants.[17] Between 1893 and 1895, Charles Kawbawgam, descendant of chiefs from Sault Ste. Marie, told the story of a great peace council held at that location "in the time of [his] grandfather's father."[18] Hickerson argues that the Saulteur (as the local Anishinaabeg came to be known) "apparently comprised an amalgam of members of many clans; they existed, perhaps in some sense, as a symbol of the unity based on common language, culture, and traditions of all of them. In socioeconomic terms, the Saulteur proper formed the nuclear settlement for annual ceremonies, trade, renewal of alliances, and, to some extent, fishing."[19]

Danziger, on the other hand, describes the Anishinaabeg of Bawating as "probably an advance band of the westward-expanding Chippewa hunternomads."[20] The differences of these two scholars are both methodological and theoretical and fall mostly outside the confines of this work. However, Hickerson's analysis turns up in a bastardized form among critics of the Soo Tribe. Repeatedly during my fieldwork, individuals, Indian and non-Indian, referred to the Soo Tribe as "made-up," arguing that the tribe didn't really exist in the past, but is made up of a bunch of leftover people, many of whom are not "real" Indians.

Questions of authenticity for the Soo Tribe, as for the Mashantucket Pequots and many California tribes, are fueled in part by concerns about nation-building efforts related to economic development and political influence. A close reading of Hickerson's text reveals that he situates the Anishinaabeg of Sault Ste. Marie, as a symbol of unity, at the nuclear settlement for important events.[21] The people of the Soo, due to the long practice of gathering at Bawating, came to represent a mixed population, a situation that may have complicated their journey toward federal recognition as a tribe in contemporary times. An additional complication could have been lack of a land base—after three hundred years of colonization, the Anishinaabeg of Bawating had been pushed out of the way of "progress":

On December 24, 1953, the residents became the "Sugar Island Group of Chippewa Indians and Their Descendants." At that time, Sault Ste. Marie and Sugar Island contained no lands for their people, and the federal government considered them members of the Bay Mills Indian Community. The Descendants did not feel part of the Bay Mills Community, located 30 miles west of Sugar Island. Bay Mills had not extended services to the Sugar Island residents and had not represented their needs at Tribal council meetings. As a result, the Sugar Island Group pushed for recognition as a separate Tribe. Their actions were motivated by the impoverished community in which they lived. Many of their friends and family members lacked jobs and lived in inadequate homes, along unlit and unpaved streets.[22]

The tribal history expresses succinctly and poignantly the trauma and despair of their experience. The Soo Tribe achieved federal tribal recognition in 1972, and their economic well-being has been greatly enhanced by their recent success with casino gaming. Once a people without land and legal standing, the Soo Tribe came to dominate the economy of the Upper Peninsula of Michigan and to be increasingly in the public eye. By the 1990s, the story the tribe told of itself was of a progressive tribe rooted in tradition. Consequently, the tribe acted out this conceptualized Anishinaabeg identity through rituals for strategic purposes, including positioning themselves as authentically Indigenous.[23] They believed it was necessary to do so because their authenticity was challenged by representatives of the dominant culture, by other Michigan tribes, and, at times, by their own members.[24]

The tribe's decision to determine membership based on lineal descent was one source of criticism, as it meant that the size of the tribe increased rapidly in a relatively short period, as well as challenging ideas and policies about Indian identity tied to blood quantum. Having experienced a sudden increase in membership as well as in its economic success and political influence, the tribe sought ways to enhance a shared sense of tribal identity. As part of their efforts, the tribe encouraged the revitalization of ceremonies, rituals, and symbols, as well as the development of new ceremonies or new applications for rituals and ceremonies. Their response to criticisms and attacks on their authenticity included efforts to communicate their image, to tell the story of themselves as a progressive tribe rooted in tradition. This story and image was conveyed through the tribe's logo, which included images of clan totems or *dodems*, such as the bear and the deer, for example. Buildings and enterprises were given Anishinaabeg names, and events such as the opening of new enterprises were marked with feasts and prayers.

THE ROLE OF ELDERS IN THE SOO TRIBE'S STORY

The role of older members of the Soo Tribe was to link the tribe to an authentic past while celebrating the achievements of the present. The term "elder" is multivalent in American Indigenous communities. It may be used to refer to an age category, much as the term "senior citizen" has come to describe older people in the United States. Another meaning of the term "elder" is a person whose knowledge base and cosmology is tribally situated. He or she knows the history, traditions, and practices of the tribe and can serve as a teacher. Some are spiritual leaders as well, providing instruction and leadership in ceremonial settings, advising tribal leadership, or serving as the tribal leadership. In the Soo Tribe, the term "elder" was left somewhat ambiguous. The Soo Tribe recognized specific elders as possessing tribal historical and cultural knowledge and experience; these elders were revered and honored. Simultaneously, any tribal member who achieved a certain age was referred to as an elder, qualified for special privileges and programs, and in that way and others, they were shown respect and honor.[25]

Anthropologists doing research in communities often find older members to be excellent sources of information.[26] An older "informant," to use anthro jargon, can describe interrelationships of kinship and friendship, will have observed community change or stability over time, and may be able to guide the researcher and access networks. The classic approach, associated with Boas, was to gather stories that could be analyzed for content, or as text, or to categorize a culture. The stories could serve, intentionally or not, to exoticize the culture, and some writers and editors purposely packaged the stories—and, by association, the cultures—safely for general consumption; the same can be said of many anthropological studies of ritual and ceremony.[27] By looking at story and ritual as actions and practice, we seek to discern the intentions of the storyteller or storymaker, rather than collecting stories and rituals (and the people who perform them) as interesting cultural/historical artifacts.[28]

My interviews with some of the elders of the Soo Tribe provided valuable ethnographic material, much of it conveyed as story. The storytelling sessions often took on a ritual aspect, especially if I was talking to an elder. Traditionally, Anishinaabeg do not tell stories except in the winter. I was told that the manitous, or spirits, are asleep under the frozen ground then and will not hear their names being spoken. Drawing the attention of the manitous can be a risky business, so it is better not to take chances. Many tribal elders were willing to tell stories from their life in other seasons, as long as the stories did not involve any manitous. The tribe was engaged in a long-term project to record their elders' life stories, and elders volunteered as storytellers and cultural teachers at the tribal school.

The tribe's story of tribal solidarity and authenticity included the concept of the wise tribal elder. The wise tribal elder should possess cultural and ritual knowledge, as well as memories, that further enhance the tribe's identity. Elders found themselves cast in the role of spiritual leader or ritual specialist, whether they actually possessed this knowledge or not. Some acquiesced, including those who lacked the knowledge, background, or understanding. As shortcomings in knowledge or spiritual groundedness of certain "elders" became evident, they were less likely to be called upon to act in ceremonial ways, or to be asked for spiritual guidance or counsel. There were a few tribal elders who fulfilled the role of wise advisor with great knowledge and spiritual presence, and their words and actions represented cultural retention and survival of Anishinaabeg values and norms. However, most of the spiritual leaders (this was the title most commonly used for ritual specialists) in the Soo in the 1990s were thirty-five to forty-five years old. One confided that he was uncomfortable with his role at times, and with the requests for ceremonies made to him by people much older than himself.[29]

The elected leaders and younger traditionalists, like the spiritual leaders described above, actively encouraged involvement and public identification with the tribe by offering elders special privileges and programs—this also reflected Anishinaabeg respect for those who have reached the fourth hill.[30] For some elders, there was a shyness or timidity about expressing a tribal identity that had been thoroughly and sometimes brutally suppressed. Reflecting Anishinaabeg values of personal autonomy, elders might be coaxed to be involved, but they were not forced to participate or ostracized for remaining disconnected. This approach also reflected an awareness of, and sensitivity to, the assimilating and colonizing experiences that the older members of the community had undergone. Elderly members rarely shared painful memories of the past unless they were asked directly to focus on some negative experience. This reserve may have created tension between the younger traditionalists and the elderly, as the traditionalists were usually eager to discuss the injustices and inequities of the past. Several elderly members did tell me privately about some of their painful experiences, such as being sent away to boarding school, or being teased and abused by whites in town. But they were otherwise reluctant to add what they defined as their personal stories of suffering to the larger narrative of the tribe.

The younger traditionalists saw themselves as the spiritual and cultural conscience and memory of the tribe. This did not contradict their reverence for elders, who were one source of their knowledge concerning tribal traditions. They spent many hours visiting and informally interviewing the older people in the community, and often expressed a sense of urgency as tribal elders died, taking important knowledge and stories with them. But more than the loss of knowledge was also what I perceived as a loss of identity—that the sense of identity was tied up both in the knowledge and stories, and in those who held the knowledge and were the storytellers and storymakers.

The traditionalists initiated a number of projects to capture and preserve the memories and stories of the elders, including the life-history project.

They tried to ensure that older members were able to attend tribal events and ceremonies by arranging for transportation if necessary. They visited older members who were ill or dying and wanted traditional medicine and care. When Rosie Gaskin, an elder, became too ill to remain in her own home, she was admitted to a local nursing home. One or more traditionalists visited her every day, praying and singing and burning tobacco as an offering. She died soon after entering the nursing home, but the attentions of the traditionalists gave her great comfort in her final weeks. I expected the nursing-home staff to resist the burning of tobacco and other sacred plants, but they were supportive and respectful, as well as very interested in the ritual itself. This was an example of the tribe's story being told through a ritual that demonstrated the care and commitment Anishinaabeg had for a dying elder.

THE STORY OF ROSIE AND THE FBI

That Rosie Gaskin would die being comforted by the revitalized rituals of her tribe is fitting, since she played an important role in the tribe's early efforts to improve the lives of its members. A high-school dropout, she was convinced that education and self-respect were critically important and became a community organizer. When I met Rosie, she was sixty-four years old but looked much older. She was blind and on dialysis as a result of diabetes; she was virtually housebound, but remained passionately interested in the tribe's development. Our conversations were not only informative, but enjoyable, as she had a keen sense of humor and was a gifted storyteller and storymaker.

One day she told me her story of the first powwow in Sault Ste. Marie. It was 1972 during the Wounded Knee "episode"—this was Rosie's word for it, and she added with heavy sarcasm: "Nice word for what they were doing to us."[31] She helped raise gas money to send three local youth—Cathy LeBlanc, Butch Elliot, and Bucko Teeple—to South Dakota to see what they could do to help. A protection ceremony was done for the three, and the powwow was held upon their return. Rosie said that almost 4,000 people showed up. The Michigan State Police arrived; Rosie said that they feared insurrection, so she served them buffalo, wild rice, corn, and fish. Helicopters flew overhead taking photos during the parade, and men in dark suits walked through the parking areas noting license plate numbers; Rosie and others believed that the information gathered was added to FBI files on activist Indians. The American Indian Movement sent a seventeen-car caravan from Minnesota.

Eddie Benton-Banai, one of the founders of the American Indian Movement (AIM) was in one of the vehicles. When he was late arriving, Rosie and the other organizers became worried. Rosie walked up to the FBI and asked them point-blank where Eddie Benton-Banai was. The agent was so surprised by her question that he blurted out that Eddie's car had broken down in Marquette, Michigan. She said he even told her Eddie's hotel and room number. So she organized a "rescue operation" and sent a car to pick him up. Whether all of the details of Rosie's story are true or not is irrelevant, just as it is irrelevant whether or not Joe killed the Easter Bunny or Santa Claus. What is relevant is the storymaking, and Rosie's stories described the terrible conditions in which the Anishinaabeg in the Soo lived, as well as the beginnings of revitalization and identity- and nation-building. The story of Rosie taking on the dreaded FBI and tricking them so an AIM member could be rescued and welcomed into the Soo Tribe's community is a story of resistance laced with humor.

THE STORY OF MARY AND OTHER CHRISTIAN ELDERS

One commonly shared characteristic of tribal elders is their membership in Christian churches. They are more likely to practice a mainstream religion whether or not they participate in Anishinaabeg ceremonies and rituals. When asked if they saw this as a contradiction, they said they did not. They were aware of the disapproval of the younger traditionalists, but explained that for them, there was comfort in the rituals of the Catholic Church, for example, as there was in the Anishinaabeg rituals. A common statement was that there is only one Creator who is neither Christian nor Anishinaabeg, but rather is a being beyond those human distinctions.

This duality of belief systems created tension during public tribal rituals and revealed inconsistencies in the storymaking of the tribe. For example, in 1995 Mary Murray was one of the oldest people in the tribe and was responsible for the tribe's land base when they were seeking legal status as a tribe:

> In the late 1960's and early 1970's the Shunk Road and Marquette Avenue area in Sault Ste. Marie had no paved roads, it had no public housing, it provided

virtually no public or tribal services. The roads were so bad at times school buses wouldn't drive down it to pick up children for school. The city of Sault Ste. Marie did not provide water and sewer services to the Shunk Road area. Ditches were cesspools especially in the Spring and Fall. The Tribe had no land until Mary Murray (tribal member) donated 40 acres of land on Sugar Island. Most of the Marquette Avenue and Shunk Road area was either wetlands or swamp.[32]

Physically frail, she did not attend all tribal gatherings, so if she was present at a ceremony, Mary was usually asked to say a prayer. She invariably prayed in English and used Christian prayers, to the annoyance of the traditionalists and elected leaders who organized the public ceremony. They did not openly criticize her or any other elder who acted similarly, but resorted to making sarcastic comments meant to be heard by the sympathetic or discreet.

By using Christian prayers during Anishinaabeg rituals, Mary and other elderly members disrupted the story of cultural continuity and unity, a story told by the younger traditionalists and the elected leaders, particularly during ceremonies attended by non-Indians. Openly embracing Christianity challenged the hegemonic ritualization of the tribe. The elders who are involved in the spiritual life of the tribe expressed gratitude for being able to practice Anishinaabeg rituals openly. They described having to hide their sacred plants, drums, and other paraphernalia from both religious and secular authorities in the past. Even gathering in large groups could draw unwanted and sometimes dangerous attention. One elderly man described being chased through the swamp in the Indian neighborhood by white men who heard him and his cousins drumming and singing. He was unsure of the exact date, other than it was a couple of years after World War II.

MY STORY ABOUT JOE AND CHANGE

Some tribal elders struggled with the rapid pace of economic and social change in the tribe. Some did not want to leave their old homes, even those that are shacks. Their children and grandchildren begged them to move to better housing, even offering to build a new home on the same lot so they would feel at home. Joe's frustrated daughter commented to me that her parents seemed to believe that being poor was an integral part of being Indian. They were afraid that they would lose something of themselves, of their culture, by improving their economic situation. Joe's daughter was college-educated and familiar with the culture-of-poverty concept. Arguing this point did not convince either of her parents.

Joe expressed his own frustration one day after receiving a visit from a tribal housing representative who wanted permission to demolish his home and replace it with something better. In Joe's opinion, the tribe was more worried about its image and reputation than it was concerned about his welfare. He was aware that the elected leaders and some of the younger traditionalists were embarrassed by the poor condition of some private homes owned by tribal members and located near the reservation. They saw this as detracting from the overall success of the tribe.

In this particular instance, Joe's adult children purchased a prefabricated house for their parents and set it up on the large lot their parents own, after destroying several shacks and lean-tos to make room. They also removed truckloads of wood, metal and wire pieces, and old tires from the property, items that Joe had salvaged over the years. Joe and his wife were pleased that their children cared enough and were successful enough to purchase the new home. Joe was dismayed to see his "valuable stuff" being cleared away and hurriedly squirreled away some prized salvage material. He and Mrs. Joe refused to let their old house be torn down, however, and the children could not change their minds. The last time I visited the elderly couple in 1995, I found them continuing to live in their old, dangerously dilapidated house during the day while their children were at work. In the evenings, they entertained family and other visitors in the new house, carrying on a pretense that they had actually moved into the new house.

THE STORY PLAYS OUT

For involved elders, the tribe's financial success and accompanying support of Ojibwa cultural events was a great boon. They participated in sweats, talking circles, cultural and language workshops, naming ceremonies, funerals and weddings, as well as powwows. They were honored guests at feasts and all tribal gatherings and received a great deal of positive attention by joining in the ritualization efforts of the tribe. At the same time, their practices and beliefs could be out of sync with the tribe's authenticity work, as the tribe strove to emphasize, through story and ritual, its Anishinaabeg identity.[33] The articulation of Anishinaabeg values demonstrated through the high status of tribal elders was complicated by the long-term effects of colonization, as well as by the diverse experiences, personalities, and stories of the tribal elders themselves.

There was a sense of excitement and pride among involved elders. They had lived in poor housing and had struggled to find work. They and their loved ones struggled with substance abuse. They had seen so many of their people die of disease and the effects of lifelong poverty. Many of them dropped out of school—either from economic need, or to escape the discrimination of the educational system. What they witnessed happening in the tribe in the 1990s seemed, in their own words, "almost like a miracle." Tribal members were employed, the children could attend their own school, and the tribal community was joining together to hold ceremonies without fear of repercussions. Medical and substance-abuse treatment were available for all, and much of the substandard housing had been destroyed. All of these changes were incorporated into the Soo Tribe's storymaking, used to support assertions of authenticity, sovereignty, and self-determination. As positively as the tribe's socioeconomic success was perceived, it could also challenge assumptions held by non-Indians and Indians alike—the stories individuals had constructed to explain their lives and their place in the world.[34]

In Basil Johnston's *Ojibway Ceremonies*, an old woman describes the values of her people: courage, generosity, fortitude, patience, endurance, resourcefulness, and perseverance.[35] If "it is one's practice that determines one's identity,"[36] some could and have argued that many of the elders in the Soo Tribe are living an identity that is Indigenous in name only. I would argue that their practice, expressed through their stories, reveals values rooted in Anishinaabeg cosmology—endurance, perseverance, resourcefulness, and a commitment to family.[37]

NOTES

Acknowledgments: Niigaanwewidam James Sinclair, Becca Gercken, and Zachary Firestone provided invaluable comments and suggestions. I thank the editors for their vision in conceiving this project, and their trust in allowing a non-Anishinaabe to tell a story—*woliwon* (thank you). Any errors of fact or interpretation are mine. This chapter is drawn from my dissertation, and I am grateful to the Sault Ste. Marie Tribe of Chippewa Indians for funding my doctoral fieldwork. I also received support from the King-Chavez-Parks Future Faculty Fellowship.

1. Basil Johnston, *Ojibway Heritage* (New York: Columbia University Press, 1976), 109.
2. Ibid., 112.
3. Ibid., 118.
4. All informants' names except Rosemary (Rosie) Gaskin's are pseudonyms. Rosemary gave permission to use her name.
5. I had not intended to interview children; for one thing, I wasn't sure what they'd have to say about "tribal/Indian/Anishinaabeg identity." It turned out I was wrong. When I asked Anishinaabeg children about Indian identity, they were more likely to connect this aspect of their lives with their family than with any tribal structure. They told stories about their grandparents, their aunties and uncles, their parents and cousins, and described how their behavior, actions, and beliefs were what made these people and themselves Indian.
6. I made it up to Susie later that day by taking her out for ice cream and telling her that her contribution to my research was important and greatly appreciated. And it is!
7. Interview, July 7, 1994.
8. I am using Taiaiake Alfred's term. His discussion of First Nations identity resonates on the U.S. side of the border as well: "Another thing that must be acknowledged is that fact that many of our people are disconnected from the land and unfamiliar with their own Indigenous cultures and, because of this, they hold ideas about identity and their nationhood which reflect colonial attitudes and which have been shaped by the pressures of racism and assimilation"; Taiaiake Alfred, *First Nation Perspectives on Political Identity* (Ottawa: First Nations Assembly, 2009), 2.
9. Bill's older sister Emma was also interviewed; her story is not included here, but she did publicly self-identify as being of Indian descent throughout her lifetime.
10. I was not able to discover why Italian instead of French, which was more likely to be the source of the non-Indigenous ancestry.
11. Sugar Island is a small island in the St. Mary's River; its northern shoreline delineates the border between Canada and the United States. While the Bay Mills Indian Community has also claimed connections to the island, the Sault Ste. Marie Tribe of Chippewa Indians considers it under the tribe's control and representation.
12. Regular ferry service began in 1925. Prior to that time, rough rafts provided irregular movement to and from Sault Ste. Marie, Michigan; http://genealogy trails.com/mich/chippewa/citypayment.html.
13. As a person of Maliseet Mi'kmaq descent (Wesget Sipu of Maine), I was often teased and identified by the nickname "Micmac patty wack," an allusion to

the children's folk song or rhyme "nick nack patty (or paddy) wack, give a dog a bone" popularized by Burl Ives. This never failed to get a chuckle. I purposely added to the teasing by revealing that my son, when he was very young, innocently referred to us as the "Big Mac Tribe."

14. C. Bell, *Ritual Theory, Ritual Practice* (New York: Oxford University Press, 1992); C. Bell, *Ritual: Perspectives and Dimensions* (New York: Oxford University Press, 2009).

15. Interview, August 23, 1995.

16. E. J. Danziger Jr., *The Chippewas of Lake Superior* (Norman: University of Oklahoma Press, 1979); H. Hickerson, *The Chippewa and Their Neighbors: A Study in Ethnohistory* (1970; Prospect Heights, IL: Waveland Press, 1988); C. E. Cleland, *Rites of Conquest: The History and Culture of Michigan's Native Americans* (Ann Arbor: University of Michigan Press, 1992).

17. Danziger, *The Chippewas of Lake Superior.*

18. A. P. Bourgeois, ed., *Ojibwa Narratives of Charles and Charlotte Kawbawgam and Jacques LePique, 1893–1895* (Detroit: Wayne State University Press, 1994).

19. Hickerson, *The Chippewa and Their Neighbors*, 45.

20. Danziger, *The Chippewas of Lake Superior*, 26.

21. Hickerson's *The Chippewa and Their Neighbors: A Study in Ethnohistory*, originally published in 1970, was revised and expanded in 1988 with a "Review Essay and Bibliographical Supplement by Jennifer S. H. Brown and Laura L. Peers." See Brown and Peers's review essay for more on Hickerson's approach, strengths, and limitations of his original work. Cleland's description falls more in the Hickerson camp than in Danziger's and is found in an endnote: "The rapids of the Saint Marys [*sic*] River and the Straits of Mackinac seem to be places where people of otherwise independent bands joined forces to cooperate in the fall fish harvest"; C. E. Cleland, *Rites of Conquest*, 73.

22. "Tribal History 2010," available at www.saulttribe.org.

23. The strategic use of ritual, or ritualization, is at the core of my dissertation based on my fieldwork with the Sault Ste. Marie Chippewa Indians.

24. Verna Lawrence is one such tribal member. She denies the authenticity of the tribe, while being an enrolled member who once served on the tribe's elected board. Verna has been active in protesting against treaty rights, such as fishing, and earns a mention in L. Nesper's *The Walleye War: The Struggle for Ojibwe Spearfishing and Treaty Rights* (Lincoln: University of Nebraska Press, 2002).

25. I listened to many conversations among tribe members about "what is an elder?" Overwhelmingly, it was concluded that a "true" elder is someone who possesses traditional Anishinaabe knowledge, preferably has some grasp of

the Anishinaabemowin language—at least enough to be able to function in ceremonial settings—and whose character and actions make him or her identifiably Anishinaabe. Occasionally, as part of these conversations, someone would bring up questions or ideas about how to distinguish one from another—by using different terms, for example—but this idea was always discarded. One reason was that everyone concerned would have had to agree on who was a "true" elder and who was not, an approach that would have impinged upon individual autonomy, a highly held value. Perhaps more off-putting was the thought of offending older tribal members: not only would this go against another highly held value, it also brought up concerns and beliefs about witchcraft. One tribal member reported to me about being cautious around all of the older tribal members because they were more likely to know how to cause harm through magical or supernatural means. For the sake of simplicity, and in accordance with Soo Tribe customary usage, I am using the term "elder" ambiguously as well.

26. I could include folklorists, ethnohistorians, historians, and others in this category.

27. See Jay Miller's discussion of Mourning Dove's unsuccessful resistance to a editor's pressure to collect the (exotic) folktales of her tribe, the Okanagon from the Colville Reservation, when what she wanted to write was quite different. Christine Quintasket, as she was also known, did succeed in publishing a novel, *Cowega, the Half-Blood*, in 1927 (1990).

28. Criticisms of the Boasian approach must be tempered by the wealth of cultural data recorded by him and his students—cultural data that has at times enabled tribes to revitalize and, in some instances, relearn and reclaim ceremonies, rituals, even language. As a cultural relativist, Boas became unpopular in the United States for his vocal opposition to racism and other forms of oppression; within his profession, he became unpopular for his criticism of colleagues conducting research to support American military goals.

29. July 7, 1994.

30. Anishinaabeg, like many North American Indigenous peoples, understand the life course as a circle or as a series of steps or hills. The number four is also of great significance, referring to the four cardinal directions, the four sacred plants, the four colors, and so on. So to reach the fourth hill is to have achieved the life stage when one has gained wisdom from life's experiences, wisdom that can be shared for the benefit of the people.

31. Interview, August 23, 1995.

32. "Tribal History 2002," available at www.saulttribe.org.

33. Examples of public ceremonies adapted or innovated by the Soo Tribe included blessing their various ventures, sites, and events, including powwow

grounds, culture centers, schools, newly elected board members, and so on. One tribal member quipped that there wasn't an event that the tribe's spiritual leaders couldn't find a blessing for. See Barbara Myerhoff, *Number Our Days* (New York: E.P. Dutton, 1979), and Sally Moore, "Uncertainties in Situations, Indeterminacies in Culture," in *Symbol and Politics in Communal Ideology: Cases and Questions*, ed. S. F. Moore and B. G. Myerhoff (Ithaca, NY: Cornell University Press, 1975) for their work on ritual innovation.

34. Sociologists working in the Durkheim tradition would label this social phenomenon as *anomie*—a sense of normlessness, of having lost your place in the world, or of not recognizing the world in which you now live, which has changed dramatically and quickly.

35. B. Johnston, *Ojibway Ceremonies* (Lincoln: University of Nebraska Press), 35.

36. Alfred, *First Nation Perspectives on Political Identity*, 33.

37. In the mid '90s, I conducted fieldwork in the Upper Peninsula (UP) of Michigan with the Soo Tribe. While I have returned to the UP repeatedly since my original fieldwork, this account is based primarily on research done in the Soo Tribe's community in the 1990s. Culture is not static, and therefore the story is not static, so it is important for me to clearly identify the limitations and parameters of my account. My understanding is also shaped by my own standpoint (gender, age, social class, race/ethnicity, education, etc.), and others may interpret and describe the same relationships, events, and dynamics quite differently. I was remarkably fortunate to have the opportunity to interact with Soo Tribe members and to have my 1990s research funded primarily by the Soo Tribe. In return, I did an applied anthropological project for the tribe—a drop in the bucket compared to how I have benefited by completing my Ph.D. and building an academic career. I continue to "pay it forward" by contributing in the area of indigenous education and empowerment. Some tribal members were concerned about my research—suspicion of anthropologists is understandable considering the checkered history of anthropological involvement in Indigenous communities.

RESOURCES

Alfred, Taiaiake. *First Nation Perspectives on Political Identity.* First Nation Citizenship Research & Policy Series: Building towards Change. Ottawa: First Nations Assembly, 2009.

Bell, C. *Ritual: Perspectives and Dimensions.* New York: Oxford University Press, 2009.

———. *Ritual Theory, Ritual Practice.* New York and Oxford: Oxford University Press, 1992.

Benton-Banai, E. *The Mishomis Book: The Voice of the Ojibway.* St. Paul, MN: Red School House, 1988.

Bourgeois, A. P., ed. *Ojibwa Narratives of Charles and Charlotte Kawbawgam and Jacques LePique, 1893–1895.* Recorded with notes by Homer H. Kidder. Detroit: Wayne State University Press, 1994.

Brown, J.S.H., and L. L. Peers. "The Chippewa and Their Neighbors: A Critical Review." In *The Chippewa and Their Neighbors: A Study in Ethnohistory,* by Harold Hickerson, 135–46. Prospect Heights, IL: Waveland Press Inc., 1988.

Cleland, C. E. *Rites of Conquest: The History and Culture of Michigan's Native Americans.* Ann Arbor: University of Michigan Press, 1992.

Cornell, G. L. "Ojibway." In *People of the Three Fires: The Ottawa, Potawatomi, and Ojibway of Michigan.* Grand Rapids, MI: Grand Rapids Intertribal Council, 1986.

Danziger, E. J., Jr. *The Chippewas of Lake Superior.* Norman: University of Oklahoma Press, 1979.

Day, G., and B. G. Trigger. "Algonquin." In *The Northeast,* ed. B. G. Trigger. Vol. 5 of *Handbook of North American Indians,* general ed. W. Sturtevant, 792–97. Washington, DC: Smithsonian Institution, 1978.

Dewdney, S. *The Sacred Scrolls of the Southern Ojibway.* Toronto and Buffalo: University of Toronto Press, 1975.

Hallowell, A. I. *The Ojibwa of Berens River, Manitoba: Ethnography into History.* Fort Worth, TX: Harcourt Brace Jovanovich, 1992.

Hickerson, H. *The Chippewa and Their Neighbors: A Study in Ethnohistory.* 1970; Prospect Heights, IL: Waveland Press, 1988.

Johnston, B. *Ojibway Ceremonies.* Lincoln: University of Nebraska Press, 1990.

———. *Ojibway Heritage.* New York: Columbia University Press, 1976.

Miller, J. *Mourning Dove: A Salishan Autobiography.* Lincoln: University of Nebraska Press, 1990.

Moore, S. F. "Uncertainties in Situations, Indeterminacies in Culture." In *Symbol and Politics in Communal Ideology: Cases and Questions,* ed. S. F. Moore and B. G. Myerhoff, 210–39. Ithaca, NY: Cornell University Press, 1975.

Moore, S. F., and B. Myerhoff. "Secular Ritual: Forms and Meaning." Introduction to *Secular Ritual,* ed. S. F. Moore and B. G. Myerhoff, 3–24. Assen/Amsterdam: Van Gorcum, 1977.

Myerhoff, B. *Number Our Days.* New York: E.P. Dutton, 1979.

———. "We Don't Wrap Herring in a Printed Page: Fusion, Fictions and Continuity in Secular Ritual. In *Secular Ritual,* ed. S. F. Moore and B. G. Myerhoff, 199–226. Assen/Amsterdam: Van Gorcum, 1977.

Nesper, L. *The Walleye War: The Struggle for Ojibwe Spearfishing and Treaty Rights.* Lincoln: University of Nebraska Press, 2002.

Pelletier, J. "The Role of Ritual in a Contemporary Ojibwa Tribe." Ph.D. diss., Michigan State University, 2002.

Schechner, R. "Victor Turner's Last Adventure." Preface to *The Anthropology of Performance*, by Victor Turner, 7–20. New York: PAJ Publications, 1992.

Sault Ste. Marie Tribe of Chippewa Indians. "Tribal History." http://www.saulttribe .org (accessed November 20, 2002).

Sault Ste. Marie Tribe of Chippewa Indians website. http://www.saulttribe.com/ index.php?option=com_content&task=view&id=29&Itemid=205 (accessed August 11, 2010).

Thwaites, R. G., ed. *The Jesuit Relations and Allied Documents: Travels and Explorations of the Jesuit Missionaries in New France, 1610–1791.* Cleveland: Burrows Brothers, 1896–1901.

Warren, W. W. *History of the Ojibwa People.* 1885; St. Paul: Minnesota Historical Society Press, 1984.

Eko-niiwin Bagijigan
Stories as Resiliency

ANISHINAABEG STORIES ARE EXPRESSIONS OF RESILIENCY. IN REMEM-
bering, retelling, and remaking stories, Anishinaabeg storytellers enact
paths to cultural and political agency and resistance. Centering Anishinaabeg Studies with stories uncovers a longstanding and active history
of narrative continuance embodying Anishinaabeg practices and ways of
being—sometimes even in the most challenging of circumstances. In
traditional frameworks, this is often described as practices embodying *mino-
bimaadiziwin*, or "the good life." Resiliency is a hallmark of Anishinaabeg
life, embodied in the stories told by Anishinaabeg for generations and continuing into today.

Jill Doerfler, in her essay "'A Philosophy for Living': Ignatia Broker and
Constitutional Reform among the White Earth Anishinaabeg," proposes
that stories can reveal a framework for survivance, a theory proposed by
critic Gerald Vizenor. She notes that "Stories are both accounts and acts of
survivance. It is by knowing and telling our stories that the people of White
Earth can both imagine and construct the past, present, and future." Doerfler argues that stories contain the answers to fundamental questions like
"who are Anishinaabeg?" and "what does it mean to be Anishinaabeg?" Using
the work of noted storyteller Ignatia Broker, Doerfler argues that the act of
identity-making and storymaking are intricately connected, as evidenced in
the constitutional process undertaken by her community since 2007.

Matthew Fletcher, like Doerfler, advocates that change and adaptation
are critical for survivance. Fletcher, in his essay "'A Perfect Copy': Indian Culture and Tribal Law," applies David Treuer's assertion that "Native American
literature does not exist" to American Indian culture and tribal law, in order
to question whether tribal law is merely a good copy of Indigenous legal traditions. Fletcher argues that flexibility and fluidity is key to the integrity of
Anishinaabeg cultural traditions, noting that stories must change, grow, and
evolve to ensure our survival as a people and as nations. In the same way,

centering the field with stories also strengthens our resiliency by putting forward new and ever-changing narratives. These narratives not only reflect longstanding visions of what it means to be Anishinaabeg, but also makes space for and encourages new stories.

Melissa Nelson continues in this tradition in "The Hydromythology of the Anishinaabeg: Will Mishipizhu Survive Climate Change, or Is He Creating It?" She asserts that our stories will survive us, and thus can also teach us how to survive. Asking the critical question "Will Mishipizhu survive climate change, or is he creating it?" Nelson invites us to both reflect and reconsider the position and power of stories. She reminds us that human beings must reconsider our relationship to the environment, noting that our stories teach us how to relate to the earth respectfully and responsibly. Nelson gestures to the "rich cognitive and imaginative realities of Anishinaabeg hydromythology and how the continuation of these stories not only maintains Ojibwe identity and worldview but also may provide critical epistemological clues for how to creatively respond to the climate crisis affecting lands, waters, and peoples globally."

A Philosophy for Living
Ignatia Broker and Constitutional Reform among the White Earth Anishinaabeg

JILL DOERFLER

There was a knock, and Oona turned and saw a small girl in the doorway.
The child stood with eyes cast down just as Oona had stood before her
grandmother. Oona said, "Come in, my child, and speak if you wish to do so."
The child said, "My name is Mary in the English way, but in the language
of our people, I am called A-wa-sa-sa."
"And what is it you wish, my child?" asked Oona.
"I should like," said the child, "to hear the stories of our people."
Oona felt a joy in her spirit and a light on her face. She knew that the
Ojibway would forever be known in future years.

—IGNATIA BROKER, *NIGHT FLYING WOMAN*

RECENTLY, MANY NATIVE NATIONS HAVE BEGUN THE HISTORIC AND challenging process of constitutional reform. As Anishinaabe scholar Duane Champaign writes: "If tribal communities want to assert greater control over their economic, political, and cultural lives, they will need more effective forms of government. For many communities there is a growing sense of crisis and a movement to remake tribal constitutions."[1] On March 1, 2007, Dr. Erma Vizenor, chairwoman of the White Earth Tribal Council, gave the annual State of the Nation address at the Shooting Star Casino in Mahnomen, Minnesota. She formally announced her goal to begin the process of constitutional reform and to hold a Constitutional Convention in the fall. Vizenor noted that a clear separation of powers of the tribal government should be considered as well as the requirements for citizenship, stating, "As tribal membership continues to decline under the present one-fourth blood quantum requirement, we must decide eligibility for enrollment."[2] Between 2007 and 2009, four Constitutional Conventions were held; delegates voted to ratify the proposed constitution on April 4, 2009.[3]

The White Earth Nation is part of the Minnesota Chippewa Tribe (MCT), which was created under the Indian Reorganization Act (IRA). The MCT is an umbrella government with six member nations; each nation has a degree of autonomy, but is governed under the MCT constitution. Citizenship is regulated within the MCT constitution. Many Native nations have found IRA-style constitutions to be ineffective. Indeed, White Earth has found the MCT constitution to be restrictive. The requirement of one-quarter MCT blood for citizenship has literally divided families, with some qualifying for citizenship and others excluded. Additionally, the MCT constitution lists nine powers, some of which are "subject to the review of the Secretary of the Interior," the Tribal Executive Committee, and six powers of Reservation Business Committees.[4] White Earth, like many tribes with IRA constitutions, has found that the constitution does not reflect traditional values or practices, and consequently have wanted to write a constitution that reflects Anishinaabeg values and traditions.

One of the primary issues addressed in the 2007–present reform movement was tribal citizenship. The regulation and requirements for tribal citizenship vary from tribe to tribe and, in many cases, have been heavily influenced by the federal government. In fact, the elected leaders of the MCT spent many years during the 1940s and 1950s discussing how tribal citizenship should be regulated in the constitution. They passed several resolutions that required lineal descent; however, the secretary of the Interior rejected these resolutions and strongly suggested that blood quantum be used instead.[5] The elected leaders of the MCT, including those representing White Earth, did not want to use blood quantum as a requirement for tribal citizenship, because they were concerned that their children and grandchildren would potentially be excluded from citizenship under this rule, which would, in turn, erase their identity as Anishinaabe and American Indian for all legal purposes. Faced with strong Anishinaabeg opposition, the Bureau of Indian Affairs took drastic action. They threatened to stop providing services to the MCT if they did not use one-quarter blood quantum for tribal citizenship. Under this pressure, the elected leaders of MCT adopted a one-quarter blood quantum requirement in 1961. The U.S. secretary of the

Interior approved the change in 1963, and the constitution was amended to require one-quarter Minnesota Chippewa blood for tribal citizenship, but this has remained controversial.[6] After several ardent discussions on tribal citizenship during the 2007–2009 Constitutional Conventions, White Earth Constitutional Delegates agreed that family should form the base of the nation. The ratified Constitution of the White Earth Nation requires lineal descent for tribal citizenship.[7]

Not only does political history support lineal descent, but so too does the literary record; in fact, literature is one place where tribes who are engaged in the reform process can find fundamental values that can be employed as a means to guide the process of reform. For example, I will apply the values and beliefs delineated in White Earth Anishinaabe Ignatia Broker's 1983 narrative *Night Flying Woman: Sacred Stories of the Ojibwe* to provide guiding principles that are useful in creating citizenship requirements that are reflective of Anishinaabe values.[8]

Citizens form the foundation of nations; a nation cannot exist without citizens. Yet the regulation of citizenship is often controversial. Recently, in the United States, the 14th Amendment, which grants citizenship to all babies born within U.S. borders and was passed as a means to block states from preventing former slaves from becoming citizens, has come under attack. Some Americans argue that the babies of illegal immigrants should not be granted citizenship, but others maintain that changing the amendment could re-create a hereditary underclass.[9] Tribal nations have also had fierce debates on the issue of citizenship. Legal scholar Carol Goldberg has observed: "Indian nations' constitutional reform efforts encounter some of their most paralyzing conflicts over criteria for membership."[10] Tribal nations regulate citizenship in a variety of ways, and requirements have changed—in some cases dramatically—over time.[11] The influence of the United States has been significant.[12] With regard to citizenship requirements, Anishinaabe scholar Scott Lyons has argued, "It is absolutely essential that Indian nations devise their own criteria."[13] I wholeheartedly agree, but creating and agreeing upon the criteria for citizenship is no easy task. This is where turning to the literary record can be useful.

Stories have long served several important functions in Anishinaabe communities, including illustrating appropriate behavior and actions as well as views on life, death, and religion.[14] Written narratives have long been utilized by Anishinaabeg to argue political agendas or subvert the colonial histories created by the dominant society, and they are acts of survivance.[15] White Earth Anishinaabe scholar Gerald Vizenor brought the term "survivance" into wide use. The term is used in the Constitution of the White Earth

Nation, of which Vizenor was the Principal Writer. Vizenor has defined survivance in the context of the constitution.

> Survivance means more than the ordinary act of survival. Survivance is an active sense of native presence over absence, or sense of presence in native stories over absence of natives in histories. Survivance is a renunciation, or rejection, of political and cultural dominance, and the unbearable sentiments of tragedy and victimry. Survivance is native courage, spirit, and native traditions.[16]

Stories are both accounts and acts of survivance.

It is by knowing and telling our stories that the people of White Earth can both imagine and construct the past, present, and future. Indeed, in her poetry, White Earth Anishinaabe critic and creative writer Kimberly Blaeser has explored the connections between story and survivance. The last stanza of her poem "Surviving Winter or Old Stories We Tell Ourselves When Winter Is Coming" reads:

> I used to think we told these stories
> to learn to survive winter
> but now I know that winter comes
> so that we tell stories
> and learn to survive life.[17]

Attesting to the power of narrative, Blaeser's poem asserts that stories themselves aid in survival; stories do not only give instructions for physical survival, they tell us how to "survive life" and, perhaps, engage in acts of survivance.[18]

Correspondingly, Vizenor argues that one of the primary functions of Native American literature is to actively engage survivance. Vizenor sees literature as one of the primary venues through which American Indians can not only fight the terminal creeds produced by dominant society but also create new discourses that support the survivance of American Indians. Addressing the power of American Indian literatures, Vizenor writes: "The shadows and language of tribal poets and novelists could be the new ghost dance literature, the shadow of literature of liberation that enlivens tribal survivance."[19] Writing, reading, and listening to stories are acts of survivance, and through these actions not only do Anishinaabeg resist and refuse to accept the terminal histories of the dominant society, we also create our own stories, enacting the process of survivance. We engage in liberation from the terminal identities created by the U.S. government, and perpetuated by the dominant society, by telling our stories. The stories envision a new means to exist in the changing world. Broker's *Night Flying Woman* is a "liberation, and a visionary sovereignty" and "an act of survivance" that defies the colonial imposition of blood and race as a marker of identity.[20]

Blood quantum is a terminal creed designed to erase and eliminate American Indians. Defining American Indian identity on a racial basis has been a primary way the United States has used conceptions of identity to dispossess American Indians of their resources and erase their political obligations. Since the late nineteenth century, the United States has used blood quantum as the primary way of defining who is and who is not Indian.[21] In her interdisciplinary study of American Indian identity, *Real Indians*, sociologist Eva Garroutte notes:

> The original, stated intention of blood quantum distinctions was to determine the point at which the various responsibilities of the dominant society to Indian people ended. The ultimate and explicit federal intention was to use the blood quantum standard as a means to liquidate tribal lands and to eliminate government trust responsibility to tribes, along with entitlement programs, treaty rights, and reservations.[22]

Clearly, the federal government's use of blood quantum has not been an application of unbiased scientific fact, but rather a calculated political attempt to legally abolish American Indians and gain control of American Indian resources. Additionally, the federal government's attempt to define American Indians on a racial rather than political basis undercuts the sovereign right of American Indian nations to define their own citizenry. This is a serious and conspicuous attack on the sovereignty of Native nations and is nothing more than mathematical termination.

In *Night Flying Woman*, Broker challenges blood quantum, a foe that has been highly controversial and divisive. She utilizes story as a tool to critique the concept of blood quantum, and to assert Anishinaabe ways of determining and understanding identity that are not based on biological race. The story is an act of survivance because it resists pseudoscientific measures of blood, promotes Anishinaabe conceptions of identity, and emphasizes the continuance of families. In the narrative, Broker repeatedly asserts that "Ojibway tales teach a philosophy for living," and that "remembering our past and acting accordingly will ensure, that we, the Ojibway, will always people the earth."[23] I will apply these directives to citizenship requirements. Since 1963, White Earth, as a member nation of the Minnesota Chippewa Tribe, has used a minimum of one-quarter Minnesota Chippewa blood as the sole requirement for tribal citizenship. This requirement racializes Anishinaabe identity and does not correlate with Anishinaabe values.

Broker was born in 1919 on the White Earth Reservation and attended federal Indian boarding school at the Wahpeton Indian School in North Dakota, as well as Haskell Institute in Kansas. She lived most of her adult life in the Twin Cities of Minneapolis and St. Paul, Minnesota, and was very active in the urban Indian community. In the preface, Broker notes that she was motivated to write the book, in part, because her children and others were beginning to ask her many questions about the past so they could pass it on to their own children.[24] She further states that the children she sees have a "dubious but seeking to learn look, and I truly believe they are reaching back to learn those things of which they can be proud."[25] Broker writes: "I, myself, shall tell you what I have heard my grandmother tell and I shall try to speak in the way she did and use words that were hers."[26] She then addresses the readers as "my grandchildren" and writes: "I am glad that you, the young Ojibway of today, are seeking to learn the beliefs, the customs, and the practices of our people."[27] This technique draws readers close to Broker by constructing them as part of her family. Anishinaabeg who read the book and are excluded from tribal citizenship are pulled in and included through a familial relationship. Broker creates a world in which all Anishinaabeg are related, one family and one nation. In addition, Broker's position as the reader's grandmother puts her in a position of authority and respect. Broker welcomes the young Anishinaabeg to learn from her the traditions that were once passed on to her, and in doing so, she continues the oral tradition in written form. This is an act of survivance. Broker engages in continuance and resists the terminal creed of blood quantum.

Broker goes on to explain that she is describing the stories her great-great-grandmother shared with her about the ways in which their family adapted to changes during the tumultuous period surrounding the turn of the twentieth century. The narrative is focused on the life of her great-great-grandmother, Ni-bo-wi-se-gwe (Night Flying Woman) or Oona, as she was nicknamed, whose generation lived the experience of migrating to White Earth to claim allotments.[28] In reality, the relationship between Broker and Oona is more complex, and so we know that she is positioning herself strategically to convey her message in what she believes is the most effective manner. Broker is also more interested in demonstrating ideals for people to model, rather than accuracy.[29]

Broker's figurative and strategic position as the reader's grandmother allows her to effectively relay an important message, which she repeats throughout the narrative: "Ojibway tales teach a philosophy for living," and "It is important that you learn the past and act accordingly, for that will assure that we will always people the earth."[30] Here her directive to the reader to "learn the past and act accordingly" is a call to action. It is this action that will assure that Anishinaabe people will always endure. Likewise, Anishinaabe storyteller and writer Basil Johnston has argued, "It is not enough to listen to or to read or to understand the truths contained in stories; according to the elders the truths must be lived out and become part of the being of a person."[31] Broker is living out the truths in her story and encourages others to do the same. Additionally, Broker's use of the word "we" in the passage above further supports her efforts to draw in the reader and make them part of the story. This enlivens the story so that it is not just in the past but is ongoing—something the reader is participating in. In Broker's story, the future is dependent on both the way in which the past is remembered and contemporary actions. Readers are given a responsibility to learn a "philosophy for living" from her story. Broker believes that learning and applying this philosophy will enable Anishinaabeg to endure for all time. I have taken Broker's directive and read her story for the lessons it contains, with specific attention to identity and tribal citizenship. This essay is part of my own effort to live out Broker's philosophy, and an attempt to ensure that by learning about our past through story and taking action, we will always people the earth. A critical part of the way Anishinaabeg endure is through our distinct status as nations. While Anishinaabeg identity is multifaceted, tribal citizenship and political status is of decisive importance.

Early in the story, Broker repeats another important message from the introduction that connects to identity. Oona's namer, A-wa-sa-si, tells her, "Remembering our past and acting accordingly will ensure, that we, the Ojibway, will always people the earth."[32] Oona is honored to have been given such important words and responds, "I shall repeat them many times."[33] Of course, by including this exchange in the book, Broker is enacting Oona's promise to repeat the words. Anishinaabeg who read Broker's narrative are engaging in remembering the past, and they are also learning the philosophy for living contained within the narrative. Consequently, the reader is able to "act accordingly." I believe that the narrative contains important lessons regarding identity, and that Broker's assertion about acting accordingly is itself a message that speaks to how identity and tribal citizenship should be determined among the Anishinaabeg.

When A-wa-sa-si was very ill, she wanted to share important knowledge with Oona and requested that Oona continue the cycle by sharing the knowledge with others. A-wa-sa-si instructed Oona about proper Anishinaabe behavior, including respect for the earth, plant life, and animals as well as deference to elders. She emphasized the importance of sharing the harvest and offering thanks to Gitchi Manito. A-wa-sa-si ended her instructions by noting:

> These are the beliefs of our Ojibway people. We sustain the beliefs, and the beliefs sustain us. That is a circle. From seed to harvest, the life of the Ojibway is full and sufficient. This is what must not be lost, and this is what you must tell my grandchildren.[34]

Oona plans to pass on A-wa-sa-si's wise words. Broker passes on the instructions through the text. The beliefs and practices are emphasized as critical to remaining Anishinaabe. Balanced and reciprocal relationships are what sustain the Anishinaabe and make a circle. A-wa-sa-si is not concerned with race or biology and does not instruct Oona to pass on a message of racial purity. Unlike cultural practices and beliefs, blood quantum does not make a circle. Blood quantum creates a linear scale of authenticity and cannot sustain Anishinaabeg families or nations.

As the narrative continues, Broker captures the fear and sadness that her ancestors felt when they were told they must move from their home at Nett Lake to the White Earth Reservation to take allotments there.[35] In 1887, the United States government passed the Dawes Act, also known as the General Allotment Act. The primary purpose of this act was to break up communally owned tribal property and, therefore, facilitate the "civilization" of American Indians.[36] One of the incentives that provided solace to the Broker family was that they were promised that their allotments at White Earth would be theirs forever, and non-Indian Americans would not be allowed onto their land.[37] Some Anishinaabeg hoped that the individual land titles provided by the Dawes Act would better protect their lands from the insatiable Americans. For several reasons, Anishinaabeg from many different bands and reservations chose to move to White Earth, accepting their allotments there. Episcopal missionary Joseph Gilfillan commented that new residents came from "all parts of northern Minnesota and Wisconsin."[38]

> When the family arrived at White Earth, Oona noted the great variety of homes built by the people there, and observed that the homes generally reflected lifeways:
>
> After blueberry time Oona and her people reached a place with great numbers of lodges and Ojibway people. They knew it was White Earth. To Oona it seemed a mixed-up place, for there were many kinds of lodges—round lodges of mats and birch bark, lodges made of forest poles, lodges made of inner wood,

and lodges made of cloth. Many of the Ojibway wore the strangers' clothes and lived in the strange lodges.[39]

Broker tells a story that emphasizes the complex diversity that does not use simple divisions between "assimilationists" and "traditionals," which have often been used to characterize American Indians. Likewise, historian Melissa Meyer has examined the complex and dynamic interactions between various political factions of Anishinaabeg at White Earth near the turn of the twentieth century. She defines two primary political and cultural factions at White Earth during the late nineteenth century as "conservative" and "progressive," but argues that "conservative Anishinaabe bands located at a distance from fur trade outposts maintained a more subsistence-oriented way of life," while progressives "participated more fully in the market economy."[40] Additionally, she notes, "both groups had adapted to altered conditions from a foundation of continuity with past cultural constructs."[41] The conservative faction would eventually be known as "full-bloods" and the progressives as "mixed-bloods," but these labels were reflective of "culturally determined values," not biological or racial ancestry.[42]

Like many Anishinaabe families who moved to White Earth, Oona's family soon decided to make adaptations of their own. Broker demonstrates connection between the choice of home and lifestyle when she tells how Oona's family decided to build a new home made of lumber, rather than to continue to live in a wigwam. The family decided to make selected adaptations, accepting new ways that they saw as beneficial. Oona's mother said: "We cannot live forever in a bark lodge. They want to change us and I wish to do some of the things, make some of the changes."[43] In order to buy the materials needed to build their new home, Oona's father had to work for a lumber company. The decision to build the new home led to other changes. It was also at this time that it was decided that Oona and her sister would begin attending school: "Mother said that Oona and E-quay must go to the strangers' school and they must learn the new things."[44] Again we see the family engage in survivance by making selected adaptations to maintain their quality of life within a rapidly changing world. They were not victims, nor did they lose their identity or values during this challenging time.

At this point, the family elects to be baptized and begins learning Christian teachings. Oona is confused by some of what she is learning and seeks out her grandfather for guidance. She explains that she has been taught "Honor thy father and thy mother" and "Love thy neighbor as thyself" by the Christians.[45] Her grandfather explains that these teachings correspond with Anishinaabe practices. Oona further explains that the Christians say that they must forget their old beliefs and only believe the new teachings. Due to the similarity between the two belief systems, Oona is confused. Her grandfather explains that Christians do not know what Anishinaabe beliefs are, and wisely instructs her:

> Do not be ashamed of the good that we have taught and do not be ashamed of the good to be learned. Our way of life is changing and there is much we must accept. But let it be only the good. And we must always remember the old ways. We must pass them on to our children and grandchildren so they too will recognize the good in the new ways.[46]

Oona's grandfather emphasizes both the importance of the past and current actions in creating the future. He does not condemn or critique Christianity, but keeps a positive focus on incorporating what is good into Anishinaabe life.

The story continues, and Broker describes Oona's marriage and adaptation to European-American-style farming, noting that despite the dramatic changes, "it was a good life for Oona and the others."[47] Importantly, Broker takes time to specifically highlight a pattern of change within continuity by noting: "Through it all they kept the customs and beliefs. They continued the practices of the old life."[48] Using Oona as a model, Broker demonstrates that change in lifestyle does not mean that cultural values must change. Broker's charge to "remember the past and act accordingly" does not mean that Anishinaabeg should remain stagnant or resistant to change; instead it is a philosophy that adapts to the ever-changing dynamics of Anishinaabe life.

Broker's novel breathes life into the idea that adaptations were—and, I would argue, still are—necessary for survivance. She creates a narrative in which selected change does not equate with loss; instead, the family makes changes in order to continue being Anishinaabe. In fact, it is only by adapting to the new conditions while maintaining certain values, such as sharing, respect, giving thanks, and honoring elders, that the family is able to survive. The "philosophy of living" that can be taken from this story is that just as change and adaptation were necessary for Oona and her family, so too are such actions necessary for Anishinaabeg to continue to endure today. Like Broker's family, Anishinaabeg continue to find creative ways to adapt to the ever-changing world in which we live.

There are several important instances in *Night Flying Woman* where Broker illustrates that blood quantum did not correlate with identity or acceptance by the Anishinaabe community. One example is the integration of Oona's mother into the Anishinaabe community. Although Oona's mother, Wa-wi-e-cu-mig-go-gwe, was completely accepted within the Anishinaabe community, Oona had noticed a couple of nuanced differences she exhibited. After her mother passed on, Oona asked her paternal grandparents why her mother never spoke about her family or home. They informed her that her grandfather had found Wa-wi-e-cu-mig-go-gwe when he was out checking his snares. A child and another woman with her were dead. The family never questioned Wa-wi-e-cu-mig-go-gwe about her past; they fully accepted and integrated her into their community.[49] There were no questions about Wa-wi-e-cu-mig-go-gwe's identity. She was a fellow human being in need of help, and Oona's grandfather and the rest of the community took her in and made her a part of their family. This generous act demonstrates ideal behavior and the fluid boundaries of identity.[50] Broker's addition of this information about Oona's mother provides the reader with a concrete example of inclusion among the Anishinaabe. In addition, when describing Wa-wi-e-cu-mig-go-gwe in the beginning of the narrative, Broker identifies her as Ojibway, clearly asserting that Wa-wi-e-cu-mig-go-gwe was seen, and thought of herself, as Ojibway.[51] Here Broker is realizing her objective of instructing readers about the past and proper behavior; she is giving readers an ideal example to model. By creating an ideal past, Broker imagines a future in which identity is based upon actions and loyalties rather than race or pseudoscientific measures of blood.

Broker also directly addresses identity with the character Mary. Oona becomes very close friends with Mary, who Broker describes as being able to speak three languages (English, French, and Ojibwe) and having gray eyes and light skin. Yet, Broker does not describe Mary as either mixed-blood or part Ojibwe; rather, her identity is based on her actions.[52] Mary contributes to the family and community by watching over younger children, helping to pick chips for the morning fire, and carrying water from the pump.[53] Broker also notes: "Mary, who was new to the knowledge of the old ways, was now Grandmother's constant companion on her journeys into the forest."[54] Mary is not excluded or judged as lesser by Oona or other community members because she was not raised with "the knowledge of the old ways." Instead, Mary is respected for her efforts to learn as much as she can about those ways. Mary serves as a model for the reader because she worked to make herself part of the community through her actions. She creates her identity through respectful and reciprocal behavior and relationships.

Another instance that deals specifically with blood quantum and identity comes near the end of the story when Broker narrates a story about future generations. She states: "The children of Oona, E-quay, and Mary were Sa-gwa-de Anishinaabe, mixed bloods, but they were true in the spirit of the

Ojibway."[55] Broker acknowledges the diverse ancestry of the children, but highlights their cultural identity as Anishinaabe. These children are not less authentic, or "part Anishinaabe"; they are "true in the spirit of the Ojibway." Even though Broker mentions the children's "mixed" ancestry, she does not reduce it to simplistic and meaningless fractional measures. It is the spirit of these children that determines their identity, not the blood flowing through their veins. In the world that Broker constructs, it is actions that take center stage. I argue that blood quantum, or a racially based identity, is not part of the "philosophy of living" that will allow Anishinaabeg to "always people the earth." In fact, the use of blood quantum to determine tribal citizenship almost ensures that there will not always be Anishinaabeg.

In these instances, racial ancestry did not determine loyalties or cultural affiliations, nor did the community at large consider it especially meaningful. Although no one knew where Wa-wi-e-cu-mig-go-gwe was from, or her blood status, no one questioned Oona's authenticity or her place in the community; blood was never a consideration, and Oona's identity and place in the community was never challenged. Additionally, even though it was clear that the next generation of children were "mixed-blood," they were part of the community because of their actions and decisions as well as their familial connections. Taken together, these examples demonstrate Broker's desire to emphasize the traditional practice of inclusion. She illustrates that blood and/or race did not determine an individual's place in the community. People were not more or less Anishinaabe; they were simply Anishinaabe. By including these examples, Broker calls attention to the previous practices of the Anishinaabe and calls for an application of these practices in future generations. Broker's repeated focus on kinship suggests that family might be a starting point for considering how citizenship should be regulated today.

It is also important to note the absence of attention to blood quantum in *Night Flying Woman*. Family is the primary focus of the narrative. As already discussed, early in the narrative Broker says she will tell about her great-grandmother, "who is your grandmother five times removed."[56] By framing the story in this way, the reader becomes part of her family (as her grandchild) and she places herself in a position of authority as a grandmother. Broker ends the story by telling of a young girl named A-wa-sa-si who asks Oona to tell her the stories of the Anishinaabeg. A-wa-sa-si was also the name of the woman who named Oona and played a central role in her life. Giving the young girl the same name highlights a responsibility to the past as well as to the future. Oona is pleased by the girl's visit, and consequently, "she knew that the Ojibway ways would forever be known in future years."[57] The story ends with the cycle of telling beginning again for a new generation. The Anishinaabeg in this story are not lost; they adapt and endure by learning their history and acting accordingly. By publishing this story, which contains a "philosophy for living," Broker encourages and facilitates the survivance of the Anishinaabeg.

Broker honors readers by sharing stories of the past and instructions for the future. As White Earth prepares to hold a referendum vote on the ratified constitution, which requires lineal descent for citizenship, the strong and convincing message of family relationships and inclusion in *Night Flying Woman* can help individuals decide what is best for their families, communities, and nation as a whole. As part of my own effort to follow Broker's instructions, I wrote an article for *Anishinaabeg Today*, which is the newspaper for the White Earth Nation.[58] In that article, I shared the foundational principles from the text. I argued that as White Earth Anishinaabeg contemplate how citizenship should be regulated, we should look to our stories for instructions and guidance. In a very fundamental way, citizenship requirements answer the question "Who are we?" This is a deceptively easy question with no quick or easy resolution, but as Broker suggests, we must consider which choice will ensure that Anishinaabeg will always people the earth. We have to remember our responsibilities to both our ancestors and to future generations; learning about our past and acting accordingly is an act of survivance.

NOTES

1. Duane Champagne, "Remaking Tribal Constitutions: Meeting the Challenges of Tradition, Colonialism, and Globalization," in *American Indian Constitutional Reform and the Rebuilding of Native Nations*, ed. Eric D. Lemont (Austin: University of Texas Press, 2006), 11.

2. Erma J. Vizenor, "White Earth 2007 State of the Nation Address," *Anishinaabeg Today*, March 7, 2007, 10–14.

3. Ratified Constitution of the White Earth Nation.

4. Revised Constitution and Bylaws of the Minnesota Chippewa Tribe, Minnesota, Article 5: "Authorities of the Tribal Executive Committee," and Article 6: "Authorities of the Reservation Business Committees," November 23, 1963; Minnesota Chippewa Tribe official website, http://www.mnchippewatribe.org/excomandsub.htm (accessed August 16, 2009).

5. Jill Doerfler, *Fictions and Fractions: Reconciling Citizenship Regulations with Cultural Values among the White Earth Anishinaabeg* (Ph.D. diss., University of Minnesota, 2007), 94–122.

6. Doerfler, *Fictions and Fractions*, 94–122.

7. Ratified White Earth Constitution, chapter 2: Citizens of the White Earth Nation, Article 1.

8. I will be using the name Anishinaabe(g), but Broker uses the name "Ojibway." Both names are acceptable. My decision to use Anishinaabe(g) is based on personal preference.

9. Sherry Jacobson, "Across Texas 60,000 Babies of Noncitizens Get U.S. Birthright," *Dallas Morning News*, August 8, 2010, available at http://www .dallasnews.com/sharedcontent/dws/dn/latestnews/stories/080810dnmet babies.2be9a7e.html (accessed August 10, 2010). See also Julia Preston, "Citizenship from Birth is Challenged on the Right," *New York Times*, August 6, 2010, http://www.nytimes.com/2010/08/07/us/politics/07fourteenth.html ?_r=1&ref=fourteenth_amendment (accessed August 10, 2010).

10. Carol Goldberg, "Members Only: Designing Citizenship Requirements for Tribal Nations," in *American Indian Constitutional Reform and the Rebuilding of Native Nations*, ed. Eric D. Lemont (Austin: University of Texas Press, 2006), 107.

11. David E. Wilkins, *Documents of Native American Political Development, 1500s to 1933* (Oxford: Oxford University Press, 2009), 2.

12. For example, the Indian Reorganization Act (IRA) of 1934 brought significant changes to many Native nations. The IRA was also an important crossroads for tribal citizenship requirements. While the BIA officially recognized the inherent sovereignty of American Indian nations to define and regulate citizenship, in practice the bureau pushed tribes to enact racial requirements. Legal scholar L. Scott Gould has argued that the IRA "helped entrench race as an essential requirement for tribal membership." Scott L. Gould, "Mixing Bodies and Beliefs: The Predicament of Tribes," *Columbia Law Review* 101, no. 4 (May 2001): 720–21.

13. Scott Richard Lyons, *X-Marks: Native Signatures of Assent* (Minneapolis: University of Minnesota Press, 2010), 181.

14. Basil Johnston, *Ojibway Heritage* (1976; reprint, Lincoln: University of Nebraska Press, 1990), 7. Henry R. Schoolcraft, *The Hiawatha Legends* (reprint; AuTrain, MI: Avery Color Studios, 1984), 23–24.

15. In fact, as Maureen Konkle has noted in her groundbreaking work *Writing Indian Nations*, Anishinaabe writers produced and published the largest body of American Indian narratives during the first half of the nineteenth century. Konkle observes that Anishinaabe writers of the nineteenth century "make the same arguments that other Native writers make in the period: they write to counter misrepresentation, they reject the notion of inherent difference, they insist on Native authority for traditional knowledge, and they denounce European Americans' claims to know their own knowledge better than they

themselves do." Maureen Konkle, *Writing Indian Nations: Native Intellectuals and the Politics of Historiography, 1827–1863* (Chapel Hill: University of North Carolina Press, 2004), 162, quote at 166.

16. Gerald Vizenor, "Constitution of the White Earth Nation: Definitions of Selected Words," *Anishinaabeg Today*, September 2, 2009, 19.

17. Kimberly Blaeser, *Trailing You* (Greenfield Center, NY: Greenfield Review Press, 1994), 41–42.

18. Osage scholar Robert Warrior has recognized the significance of poetry in relation to intellectual sovereignty, writing: "Perhaps the greatest lesson of Indian poetry is that it has often shown us not only how tradition is able to live in new written forms, but that it does not have to dress up in beads and feathers in order to be powerful." Additionally, he writes, "Poetry has provided a vehicle for . . . resistance because of the way it can unsettle prevailing ideologies and give voice to what is not being spoken within a culture." Robert A. Warrior, *Tribal Secrets: Recovering American Indian Intellectual Traditions* (Minneapolis: University of Minnesota Press, 1994), 117.

19. Gerald Vizenor, *Manifest Manners: Postindian Warriors of Survivance* (Hanover, NH: Wesleyan University Press, 1994), 106.

20. Gerald Vizenor and A. Robert Lee, *Postindian Conversations* (Lincoln: University of Nebraska Press, 1999), 91.

21. Paul Spruhan, "A Legal History of Blood Quantum in Federal Indian Law to 1935," *South Dakota Law Review* 51, no. 1 (2006), available at Social Science Research Network http://ssrn.com/abstract=955032 (accessed April 16, 2007), 23–36.

22. Eva Marie Garroutte, *Real Indians: Identity and Survival in Native America* (Berkeley: University of California Press, 2003), 42.

23. Ignatia Broker, *Night Flying Woman: An Ojibway Narrative* (St. Paul: Minnesota Historical Society Press, 1983), 8, 33.

24. Ibid., 3.

25. Ibid., 7.

26. Ibid., 7.

27. Ibid., 8.

28. Ibid., 10–11.

29. Pauline Brunette Danforth, *Night Flying Woman: Sacred Stories of the Ojibway* (PhD diss., University of Minnesota, 2002), 7. The relationship between Broker and her character Oona is more complex than presented by Broker in the opening of the text. Danforth explains these intricacies and uses the text as a starting point for explaining Anishinaabe worldview, cultural practices, and spirituality in *Night Flying Woman: Sacred Stories of the Ojibway.*

30. Broker, *Night Flying Woman*, 8.

31. Johnston, *Ojibwe Heritage*, 7.

32. Broker, *Night Flying Woman*, 33.
33. Ibid., 33.
34. Ibid., 57.
35. Melissa Meyer gives an excellent account of the move to White Earth in *The White Earth Tragedy: Ethnicity and Dispossession at a Minnesota Anishinaabe Reservation, 1889–1920* (Lincoln: University of Nebraska Press, 1994), 56–65.
36. Sharon O'Brien, *American Indian Tribal Governments* (Norman: University of Oklahoma Press, 1989), 77; Meyer, *The White Earth Tragedy*, 52.
37. Broker, *Night Flying Woman*, 9–11, 63.
38. Meyer, *The White Earth Tragedy*, 48–55.
39. Broker, *Night Flying Woman*, 66.
40. Meyer, *The White Earth Tragedy*, 5.
41. Ibid., 5.
42. Ibid., 118–20, 180–83.
43. Broker, *Night Flying Woman*, 69.
44. Ibid., 70–71.
45. Ibid., 94.
46. Ibid., 94.
47. Ibid., 107.
48. Ibid., 107.
49. Ibid., 28–29, 105–6.
50. In *History of the Ojibway People*, Anishinaabe historian William Warren described the extensive adoption and intermarriage that occurred between the Anishinaabeg and the Dakota prior to the twentieth century. Warren told how after a period of warfare, the Anishinaabeg and Dakota "intermingled freely" on the St. Croix, where they camped together and intermarriages took place. In addition to creating relatives through intermarriage, the Anishinaabeg and Dakota adopted tribal members. Often during a period of peace, a Dakota and Anishinaabe would exchange presents and adopt each other. Those who had lost relations during the previous fighting sought to fill the void left by those who passed on, and members most often entered into this adoptive relationship. Adoptive ties were strong and meaningful. Warren noted many instances in which, during periods of warfare, adoptive relatives saved the lives of one another. This classic work gives some insight into Anishinaabe understandings of the ways in which "others" could be accepted and incorporated. Intermarriage and adoption were processes of merger and incorporation, and served to create large kinship networks and alliances. These fluid and flexible boundaries served Anishinaabeg well and were important survival strategies during periods of high death rate due to

warfare, disease, and decreased resources. During this time period, separation and exclusion would have not served Anishinaabe interests or contributed to their survivance. William Warren, *History of the Ojibway People* (reprint; St. Paul: Minnesota Historical Society Press, 1984), 164–65. See also Patricia Albers and Jeanne Kay, "Sharing the Land: A Study in American Indian Territoriality," in *A Cultural Geography of North American Indians*, ed. Thomas Ross and Tyrel Moore (Boulder, CO: Westview Press, 1987) for a discussion of intermarriage and identity among the Anishinaabe during the 1800s. In addition, nearly every story about Anishinaabe life in the late nineteenth and early twentieth centuries in Maggie Wilson's *Rainy River Lives* contains a story of adoption. Maggie Wilson, *Rainy River Lives: Stories by Maggie Wilson*, compiled, edited, and with an introduction by Sally Cole (Lincoln: University of Nebraska Press), 2009.

51. Broker, *Night Flying Woman*, 13.
52. It is worth noting that Broker does mention that Walter "had the blood of the voyageurs" and thus "knew many of the strange ways." She then immediately notes that he was "acceptable for he respected the Ojibway life." Broker, *Night Flying Woman*, 100–101.
53. Ibid., 86.
54. Ibid., 96.
55. Ibid., 113.
56. Ibid., 10.
57. Ibid., 131.
58. "'A Philosophy for Living': Ignatia Broker and Constitutional Reform," *Anishinaabeg Today: A Chronicle of the White Earth Band of Ojibwe* 14, no. 10 (White Earth, Minnesota, September 2, 2009), 2, 26.

A Perfect Copy
Indian Culture and Tribal Law

MATTHEW L. M. FLETCHER

LEECH LAKE OJIBWE NOVELIST AND LITERATURE CRITIC DAVID Treuer declared in his new book of literary criticism that "Native American fiction does not exist."[1] The *New York Times* described the book as "a kind of manifesto, which argues that Native American writing should be judged as literature, not as a cultural artifact, or as a means of revealing the mystical or sociological core of Indian life to non-Natives."[2] Treuer uses the trickster story "Wenebozho and the Smartberries"—in which the Anishinaabe trickster Wenebozho[3] tricks a not-so-smart Indian guy into eating small dried turds by calling them "smartberries"[4]—as the punch line to his argument focusing on Turtle Mountain Band Chippewa writer Louise Erdrich.[5] In short, Treuer alleges that American Indian novelists claiming to represent American Indian culture are frauds.

This paper reviews David Treuer's critique of Indian novelists in the context of Indian culture and tribal law. David Treuer's remarkable book of literary criticism offers a powerful critique of Native American literature—namely, that *there is no such thing*. Professor Treuer rejects three tenets of Native American literature: first, that "Native American literature contains within it links to culturally generated forms of storytelling";[6] second, that "Native American literature reflects the experience of Native Americans in the United States";[7] and third, "Native American literature acts out, by virtue of its cultural material, a tribally inflected, ancient form of 'postmodern' discourse."[8] Emphasizing the third point, Treuer argues that the novels of Louise Erdrich, for example, "are not made up of . . . Indian life. *Love Medicine* is created through a stunning array of literary techniques, sourced mostly from Western fiction. The real miracle is that with these foreign tools Erdrich convincingly suggests Ojibwe life."[9] Indian novelists like Erdrich, according to Treuer, are selling a "copy" of Native American life. And "we would never pay $43 million for a copy of Van Gogh, even if it were a perfect copy."[10] He compares works like James Welch's American Book Award–winning *Fools Crow* and Sherman Alexie's *Reservation Blues* to works by fakes, like *The Education of Little Tree*, by Forrest Carter, a virulent racist who wrote a sweet, but terribly inauthentic book about American Indians.[11]

The basis for Treuer's argument that "Native American fiction" does not exist—that good writing by American Indian authors that appears to bring to life the culture of American Indian people is not like that at all, but instead is just a very good copy of Indian culture—has a great deal of application to the debates over the use of tribal customary law in tribal courts. One goal of modern Indian tribal governments is to restore tribal customary law as an important piece of the legal infrastructure of Indian tribes in order to preserve the lifeways and law ways of Indian people, a critical part of preserving and advancing Indian cultures. Tribes and their judges recognize that the customary law of their ancestors is difficult to discover and apply; tribal customary law, for many tribal communities, exists only as a memory. Treuer's argument is that Indian writers invoke Indian culture as a "memory," not "reality"—or "the *longing for culture*, not its presence"[12]—and all of this is not authentic culture. Treuer's views on Indian literature have a great deal to say about the discovery and application of tribal law. Likewise, theorizing about tribal customary law provides an important counterweight to Treuer's thesis. This paper attempts to discuss and reconcile these competing views.

CULTURE AND THE LAW

Law and culture are inextricably intertwined. As Lawrence Rosen wrote, "Law does not exist in isolation. To understand how a culture is put together and operates, therefore, one cannot fail to consider law; to consider law, one cannot fail to see it as part of culture."[13] H.L.A. Hart's theory of primary and secondary rules has special import in any discussion of the relation between culture, literature, and the law.[14] The "primary rules" component of Professor Hart's work derives from a cultural framework—or as he termed it, "the idea of obligation."[15] "Primitive communities," Professor Hart theorized, were examples of societies that lived under primary rules of obligation, "where, though there are dissidents and malefactors, the majority live by the rules seen from the internal point of view."[16] These primary rules stem from the culture itself, or from the past.[17] The primary rules settle into what

Professor Hart referred to as "secondary rules," those legal rules that operate as "remedies" to the defects in primary rules that tend to make primary rules unenforceable and unworkable in the complexity of modern society.[18] These secondary rules offer certainty, flexibility, and efficiency to the primary rules.[19] In Ronald Dworkin's paraphrasing of Hart's model, "The combination of first-order standards imposing duties and second-order standards regulating the creation and identification of those first-order rules is a central feature of paradigmatic legal systems."[20] Or, put another way by legal anthropologist E. Adamson Hoebel, "All systems of law, whatever their content and unique dynamics, must have some essential elements in common. . . . We must have some idea of how a society works before we can have a full conception of what law is and how it works."[21] Justice Holmes's lectures "demonstrate[d] that the concept of liability [for example] as it occurs in both criminal law and the law of torts originates in a moral impulse and invokes a moral standard"[22]—that is, culture.

Like culture, law must be flexible. One of the defects Professor Hart identified in a society governed by primary rules is the "static" character of first-order rules.[23] Primary rules take a *slow* route to change—their growth from custom to rule and their eventual decay to anachronism.[24] Professor Hart's remedy for the static character of primary rules was for societies to adopt rules of change.[25] The unconscionability defense (allegedly borrowed by Karl Llewellyn's study of the Cheyenne Indians)[26] arose as a means to combat the formulism and harshness of common law contract doctrine.[27] Law's flexibility helps to ensure that law and culture remain consistent to the extent that law remains legitimate to the members of the community. To the extent that law and culture are not foursquare with each other (broadly speaking, of course), law is illegitimate.[28]

Consider a foreign visitor or an Indigenous community member living under the American legal regime, a problem in a legal system that does not take into consideration the values of the outsider. Ginnah Muhammad, a devout Muslim, wore a veil to court in a small claims case in Hamtramck, Michigan, where the judge threw out her case because she refused to remove the veil and he would not be able to see her face.[29] A federal district court took jurisdiction over a claim brought against a tribal community attempting to resolve internal disputes through traditional measures of temporary banishment or exclusion.[30] American laws derive from Anglo-American values as expressed in the original understanding of the Constitution or the Bill of Rights, or in the common law, or torts, or contracts, or criminal laws.

Ultimately, that systems of law codes enacted by legislatures and common law doctrines applied by judiciaries originate with a community's culture should be noncontroversial. Even the so-called "primitive" societies, Lévi-Strauss proved, had law:

> Given the crucial role that marriage rules play in the organization of human affairs, it follows that no society, including those of indigenous peoples and settlers, can be fairly characterized as being less rule-governed than any other. Thus, humans could never have lived in a state of nature as posited by Social Contract theorists, nor could any society exist that was "so low on the scale of social organization" as to be "incommensurate" with any other as supposed by *In re: Southern Rhodesia.*[31]

According to Professor Rosen, widely varying kinds of cultures have adopted doctrines of law that look suspiciously like unconscionability—for example, showing that even what anthropologists would have called "primitive" societies could generate rules that "civilized" societies could borrow.[32] The next section will demonstrate the general history of American Indian tribal law in the context of the history of federal-tribal relations. Under this relationship, the United States transformed law borrowing and sharing into a one-way street of imposition and dominance over Indian tribes.

THE EMERGENCE OF TRIBAL COURTS AND TRIBAL LAW

Tribal Law

Indian nations have always lived in accordance with their own laws and norms, but the intervention of Euro-American nations in the western hemisphere has all but destroyed the understanding of these rules. Many Indigenous laws and norms were incorporated into the languages and stories of Indian communities.[33] Stories and rules had meaning and relevance to Indian people so long as they were tied to a particular territory.[34] Colonization wiped much of that understanding away. The classic example is the so-called *Crow Dog* case, involving a political murder in Indian Country.[35] When the tribal community refused to execute the murderer and instead adopted a traditional punishment consistent with the community's needs, American Indian agents demanded a federal prosecution.[36] And when the Supreme Court held that federal courts had no jurisdiction in Indian Country (because it would be unfair to apply American "civilized" laws to "savage" Indians who would have no hope of understanding or complying with them),[37] the federal government enacted the Major Crimes Act,[38] extending federal criminal jurisdiction and American criminal law values into Indian Country.[39] Federal criminal justice values began to replace tribal justice systems.[40]

The United States further brought "justice" to Indian Country by enforcing law-and-order codes against Indian people.[41] The codes, enforced by "courts of Indian offenses," were intended to guarantee federal control over Indian people and eliminate tribal religious and cultural practices.[42] American boarding schools and religious missionaries, all funded and controlled by the United States, contributed to the destruction of tribal languages and religions.[43] The dispossession of Indian lands eradicated tribal learning as well by removing Indian people from their sacred places, away from where their cultural histories were tied.[44]

In 1934, Congress enacted the Indian Reorganization Act, which authorized Indian tribes to "reorganize" under the model of local and municipal governments.[45] While most of the benefits of the theory of reorganizing Indian tribes did not inure to the tribes until at least the 1970s for a variety of reasons,[46] after 1934, stated congressional policy tended to favor tribal government systems. The implementation of the act suffers from continuing federal bureaucratic control and intervention even to the present day, but the act serves as the critical governing document of the relationship between Indian tribes and the federal government. While the Bureau of Indian Affairs once mandated boilerplate tribal constitutions that limited tribal government authority and structure,[47] the bureau now grants broader leeway to tribes in determining their own constitutional foundation. While the bureau once retained all but complete control over tribal affairs by retaining secretarial veto power over all tribal government actions,[48] now tribal governments are freer to make their own laws with less bureau intervention.

Tribal Courts

Tribal courts and tribal common law have made an impressive comeback in the latter half of the twentieth century and beyond. Well over two hundred tribes now have a functioning tribal court system, and most of the remaining tribes are in the process of developing a tribal court system. And these tribal courts are not necessarily copies of state and federal courts. They follow their own court rules and tribal constitutions, statutes, and regulations. Outside of the criminal law context,[49] none of these decisions are reviewable on the merits by state or federal courts.[50] The final decision of the highest tribal court is lasting and complete.

Tribal court systems existed from the beginning of the Indian treaty period. The Cherokee Nation long has had a tribal court system from the Treaty of Hopewell period of the late 1700s to the Removal Era, and then again from the early 1840s until the United States terminated the nation.[51] The Bureau of Indian Affairs created Courts of Indian Offenses, later often referred to as CFR Courts, to dispense law-and-order rulings.[52] The courts were not indigenous in any way, as they were used by Indian agents to enforce the notorious law-and-order codes and stamp out Indian religion and culture.[53]

The emergence of tribal courts and tribal law in the latter half of the twentieth century is a result of a series of political and legal factors. In 1959, during the Termination Era, the Supreme Court decided *Williams v. Lee*,[54] which held that tribal courts have exclusive jurisdiction over cases arising in Indian Country where the defendant is a reservation Indian.[55] The Court explicitly recognized that tribes have the right to make their own laws and be governed by them.[56] In 1968, Congress enacted the Indian Civil Rights Act.[57] The act operated as a severe restriction (from Congress's point of view) of tribal sovereignty by requiring tribal governments to follow a series of restrictions on their authority—the so-called Indian Bill of Rights.[58] In 1978, the Supreme Court in *Santa Clara Pueblo v. Martinez* held that tribal courts could interpret the Indian Bill of Rights in accordance with tribal customs and traditions.[59] Just as important, the Court held that the civil rights protected in the Indian Civil Rights Act could be enforced against the tribe only in a tribal forum, such as a tribal court.[60] By in the 1990s, congressional policy favored the development and jurisdiction of tribal courts nationwide.[61]

The Problem of Tribal Customary Law

In the present era, tribal governments and tribal courts face an interesting dilemma: tribal legislatures are freer now than ever before to enact statutes, ordinances, and regulations that originate with Indian people and culture—or what I have referred to as "Indigenous legal constructs," for lack of a better term.[62] Tribal lawmakers can now reach back into tribal values, culture, customs, and traditions to make laws that are meaningful to the tribal community, that are local solutions to local problems. But these lawmakers often borrow large chunks of state, local, or federal law to fill up tribal code books.[63] In many instances, a major tribal statute constitutes of a few sentences indicating that the tribal government will follow state law in a particular field, such as probate law or commercial law.[64] The

Anglo-American cultural and legal values that shaped and informed the development of these statutes are brought unencumbered into tribal law without much consideration of their impacts. To be fair, in many of these instances, there are very good pragmatic reasons for importing state and federal law. Tribes under financial and time limitations might be required by a lender to adopt the Uniform Commercial Code, for example.[65] In many other instances, however, tribal lawmakers carefully consider and construct tribal statutes to meet critical tribal community needs with culturally relevant legal and political solutions. The rise of tribal statutes intending to protect cultural property is a great example.[66]

But all too often, tribal lawmakers take the easier route of borrowing Anglo-American legal constructs. Many of these statutes languish on the books, with the tribal community underutilizing them because they have little or no meaning or relevance to the community. Tribal government is, like all government, reactionary, meaning that tribal lawmakers have time only for reacting to issues and problems that arise. It is rare when tribal governments have the opportunity to act progressively, anticipating problems and enacting solutions to them. The wiggle room recognized under federal Indian law often goes unfilled. Perhaps part of the problem is that the very idea of lawmaking via legislation and rules promulgation is not Indigenous.

Concurrently, tribal courts face similar circumstances. Tribal judges have enormous discretion and opportunity to find, announce, and apply tribal customary and traditional law.[67] But only a few tribal courts take this opportunity on a consistent basis.[68] There are many factors that play into this, including the fact that litigants before tribal courts rarely make their arguments with reliance on tribal customary law. Moreover, tribal customary law is notoriously difficult to discover and understand by judges trained in Anglo-American law, even for those who are tribal members. Finally, tribal customary law often appears to have little to say about disputes in modern tribal communities.

In short, there is a dearth of customary and traditional law in modern tribal law. While traditional legal theory could offer numerous solutions to alleviating the crisis, American Indian literary criticism offers a different view.

A PERFECT COPY OF TRIBAL CUSTOMS

Professor Treuer's thesis has much to offer to the theory of the discovery and application of tribal customary law in tribal law and tribal jurisprudence.

One could roughly apply Treuer's framework on literature to tribal law, almost with a find-and-replace method. While there are limitations to this exercise, it is worth trying. Consider the three tenets that Treuer rejects.

Begin by contemplating "Native American literature does not contain within it links to culturally generated forms of storytelling," the first tenet reworded to conform to Treuer's point. Treuer's proof is Erdrich's *Love Medicine*, where all the Indian characters speak English (a "beautiful and terrible deficit"), and "the very structure of the stories they tell, and their contents, are not only modern, they are 'Western.'"[69] To put Treuer's critique another way, perhaps too glibly, is to say that there can be no "Native American novels" because Indian people living in the culture do not (did not) tell cultural stories in the form of a novel, let alone in English.

Consider Treuer's second tenet, that "Native American literature does not reflect the experience of Native Americans in the United States." Treuer argues that literary critics who treat Native American novels as "historical" documents have missed the point.[70] As the critical example, Treuer points to the assertion by one critic that James Welch's *Fools Crow*[71] is "the closest we will ever come in literature to an understanding of what life was like for a western Indian."[72] Treuer goes to a great deal of trouble to prove that *Fools Crow* is not historically accurate, nor could it be under any circumstances.[73]

Apply these tenets to tribal law and you have "Tribal law does not contain within it links to culturally generated forms of adjudication," and "Tribal law does not reflect the experience of Native Americans in the United States." These are both valid statements. Tribal legislation and jurisprudence often deviate in significant and substantive ways from Indian lifeways and law ways that Indian people living in the culture would not understand. Indian people prior to contact (and even for long after) did not resort to tribal courts to resolve disputes, nor did they often rely upon written prohibitions or restrictions on personal conduct, as exemplified by modern tribal codes. Indian people, with the possible exception of certain insular tribal communities, have been forced to move on from the customs and traditions of their ancestors. Tribal law does not and cannot recreate tribal history or culture perfectly. So far, we are foursquare with Professor Treuer.

Treuer's third tenet offers more difficulty: "Native American literature does not act out, by virtue of its cultural material, a tribally inflected, ancient form of 'postmodern' discourse." Treuer describes the meaning of this tenet, in part, this way: The novels of American Indians are not American Indian culture; instead, they are very good copies of American Indian culture. And the better the writer, the better the copy will be. Writers like Louise Erdrich, Leslie Silko, James Welch, and Sherman Alexie are very good at their craft (which involves using a westernized, Anglo-American set of literary tools), according to Treuer, and they use their skills to make the very best copies. But their work can never be part of Treuer's "cultural patrimony."[74] Treuer concludes, "Our written literature in English is responsive to a set of historical circumstances, inventive in its evasiveness, rich in its suggestive capabilities, but ultimately, it is not culture."[75]

Seen in this light, Treuer's third tenet offers an analogue to the status of modern tribal law, codes, and jurisprudence. Other than in limited enclaves such as the Navajo Nation, the Hopi Tribe, and other insular tribal communities where the first language spoken is tribal, the law of Indian tribes is in English. Tribal customary law and traditions as understood and lived by ancestors have been eroded by centuries of invasion, ethnocide, and grief. The tribal statutes enacted by modern tribal legislatures can be informed by tribal customary law, perhaps, but they cannot reproduce that law in the written form of the English language (let alone the legalese of Indian lawyers). The tribal courts can find, announce, and apply customary common law in their opinions (although they rarely do), but they cannot restore customary law to its place as the lifeway or law way of any tribal community. Tribal communities can attempt to circumvent the Anglo-American style of adversarial adjudication (an atrocity in small, insular communities)[76] through the development of alternative dispute-resolution mechanisms, such as pan-Indian-style peacemaker courts.[77] Like Treuer's novelists, the best that modern tribal governments can do is to make very good copies. Regardless of whether these legal structures are good copies of custom and tradition, or whether they involve radical changes away from Indigenous paradigms, these legal structures stand on their own as necessities in modern tribal life. And, as Treuer in the context of literature would say, these developments are important, even welcome.

But Professor Treuer goes further—he argues that these "very good copies" are not Indian culture at all. While singing the praises of the work of Erdrich, Welch, and others in the Indian literary canon, he also whispers fraud.[78] Would he also whisper fraud when confronted with modern tribal law?

RECONCILIATION . . . AND A CRITIQUE

So far, we have accessed the law of American Indians and the novels of American Indians as two parallel tracks. In my description of tribal law and in Professor Treuer's description of Native American literature, there are numerous parallels. First and foremost, both can never be anything more than copies of the real thing. Modern tribal law for the large majority of Indian tribes consists of the borrowing of Anglo-American legal constructs, language, and values by tribal communities. And while tribal courts and legislatures may intend to re-create tribal customary law in the context of these borrowed laws and rules, that attempt can never be complete—and certainly not in the context of the English language. There is no realistic chance of the complete restoration of the customs and traditions as they existed prior to first contact. The link between American Indian culture and tribal law will have to be made in the context of Anglo-American legal constructs and values.

Professor Treuer's analysis of Native American literature reaches a similar conclusion. American Indian novelists writing in English, using Western literary techniques, cannot hope to *be* culture, they can only hope to become a compelling reproduction of culture through the intense longing and desire for culture. But Treuer's reading goes further into a normative judgment about the novels of American Indian writers. He argues that American Indian novelists are committing a form of literary fraud by writing "Native American literature" when in fact they do not *live* in the culture and do not *speak* the language. Treuer's "cultural patrimony" is represented by someone like himself, who lives part of the year in Indian Country and is fluent in the language of his community.[79]

Professor Treuer bridged the gap between his work on the literature of American Indians and the paradox of tribal law and governance by asserting that the flaw in the novels of American Indian writers who do not speak the language also infects tribal government. He has recently written that tribal sovereignty as understood by tribal governments that conduct their business in English is "peculiar."[80] It stands to reason, given Treuer's stance on novels written in English by American Indian writers, that he views tribal government as a mere copy of traditional (and therefore ideal) tribal governance. Or, in other words, to take his argument to its logical conclusion, as he did with Sherman Alexie,[81] it is reasonable to assert that he views tribal government as a fraud as well.

The argument that tribal governments are frauds has a great deal of logical and rhetorical weight. Tribal governments tend to govern by majority rule, under the terms of governing documents (written mostly in English) that tend to put enormous political power into the hands of a few tribal members who have little or no inherent competence for the work they have been elected to do. Indian lawyers (some of them members of the community) have incredible persuasive authority to order tribal leaders around and to write the laws (again, in English) that cabin whatever traditional governance values remain. It is likely that no reservation Indian, or close relative or friend, has not been adversely impacted by a decision from one of these new-style tribal governments. Tribes are engaged in active disenrollment of tribal members based on strained readings of membership criteria (and some would say greed). Tribes fire qualified tribal members from tribal government jobs for arbitrary and capricious (read: political) reasons. Tribes engage in business development that will impact the environment. Tribes donate money to dirty state and federal politicians and lobbyists. David Treuer is not engaged in offering solutions to tribal governance problems, but his writings suggest that one solution would be a return to traditional governance, placing a premium on traditional tribal culture, where every word spoken is in the language, and every action taken is consistent with tradition and custom.

But this vision of American Indian culture is not one I am willing to buy. And frankly, it would appear, neither is Professor Treuer. This "cultural patrimony" is not my own and, in fact, is not anyone's. In this world, American Indian culture is static and rigid, unwilling and unable to grow and to preserve itself. It is Professor Hart's ancient society governed by primary rules, with no means to change. It is the same understanding of tribal culture that anti-Indian fishing and hunting opponents use when they assert that Indians should not be able to fish with modern boat and net technology, or hunt with modern weapons.[82] It is the same view of tribal culture that many non-Indians have; or, as Treuer writes, "Somewhere along the way—in the eighteenth century perhaps—Indians became associated with a very specific set of virtues."[83] Indian people took the goods they received from the French, English, and Americans in trade to make their own lives easier, leading anthropologists to argue that they were no longer Indians.[84] They made their own additions and subtractions from the culture.[85] Much of the history of the survival of Indian people and communities in the face of genocidal and assimilative American Indian law and policy can be framed this way: Sometimes Indian people traded away their traditional religion and language in order to remain in their homelands; sometimes Indian people traded their homelands away in order to retain their religion and language.[86] Flexible Indian communities with the intention of surviving by adapting had a better chance of avoiding extinction that those who did not adapt.[87] Moreover, the religions and languages did not disappear altogether; they went underground and are being resurrected to the extent possible. And Indian tribes continue to take every measure possible to restore their traditional territories to tribal membership. As a means of survival, Indian people appear to occupy what Richard White called a "middle ground" within American culture.[88]

Professor White's "middle ground" was both a territory and a cultural mixture that included much of the Great Lakes region during the seventeenth and eighteenth centuries, during a time when traditional tribal communities and French fur traders interacted and overlapped.[89] When the cultures first met, the "new people were crammed into existing categories in a mechanical way," with Indians classified as savages and the French classified as manitous.[90] Because neither side could accomplish their goals by force, "the middle ground grew according to the need of people to find a means, other than force, to gain the cooperation or consent of foreigners."[91] According to White, "the central and defining aspect of the middle ground was the willingness of those who created it to justify their own actions in terms of what they perceived to be their partner's cultural premises."[92] The two sides sought out aspects of "congruence" in their respective cultures for this purpose, sometimes leading to what outsiders consider "ludicrous" interpretations, but "any congruence, no matter how tenuous, can be put to work and take on a life of its own if it is accepted by both sides."[93] White's conclusion has powerful import for analyzing Treuer's theory of "cultural patrimony": "Cultural conventions do not have to be true to be effective any more than legal precedents do. They only have to be accepted."[94]

Treuer's view of his "cultural patrimony" compels him to question a tribal government conducting its official business using the language of the "conqueror"—English[95]—but his view exemplifies a fundamental naiveté about where tribal governments exist in the American political system.[96] Indian tribes are efficient and effective implementing agents of federal law and policy as they administer, for example, large federal housing, health care, road construction, law enforcement, education, and general administrative projects in accordance with complex federal spending regulations.[97] Tribal governments must be able to listen and speak to federal employees and officers, and to the congressional and executive branch leadership. Tribal governments had little choice in the face of physically dominant and oppressive American legal, political, and cultural attacks but to react to this process by adapting Anglo-American legal constructs. Some tribes have performed this ongoing task better than others. Every day, tribal leaders and Indian lawyers face down the federal government, state governments, county commissioners, school boards, waste management districts, and so on. Tribal leaders make decisions and tribal judges make law in this context. Failure to govern in this context is political death. It would be easy in the abstract to value "authenticity" above adaptation and to reject or disparage anything claiming to be authentic that does not square with some traditional Indian's "cultural patrimony."[98] It would be easy, but simply wrong. No community can survive by ignoring the outside world or through stubborn inflexibility. Of course, there are and will always be those in the federal government who will refuse to listen and speak to tribal governments. And there are and will always be Indian people who will refuse to listen and speak to the federal government. Both types of outsiders are tolerated by those in the "middle ground," but they are utterly ineffective in the modern version of the middle ground, where legitimate attempts at understanding and congruence are the currency of survival.

The "middle ground" also provides an analytical tool useful in responding to Treuer's critique of the literature written by American Indians. Treuer himself admits that he has never seen a novel written entirely in an American Indian language.[99] Treuer focuses on how the work of Erdrich et al. is interpreted by non-Indian literary critics, but he ignores how their work is interpreted (and enjoyed) by American Indians. And therein rests the fatal flaw of Treuer's critique of American Indian novels as culture—Treuer forgets how these writers speak to Indians. For the vast majority of American Indians who are members of Indian tribes and who live on or near Indian Country, the art of Erdrich, Alexie, Welch, Silko, and Treuer *is* the part of their culture that links reservation Indian people to urban Indians to non-Indians—the cultural "middle ground."[100] Indian people would not exist without this part of their culture. It is to be valued, not attacked for being inauthentic. Professor Treuer denies that the work of American Indian writers in English is "culture," but what else could it be? Indians do not stop being Indians because they cannot speak their language or recite the stories of their ancestors. If this were true, then genocide is all but complete. But writers like Louise Erdrich and Sherman Alexie and even David Treuer exemplify the viability, flexibility, and incredible staying power of American Indian people *and culture.*

CONCLUSION

There are many trickster tales told by the Anishinaabeg, most starring Wenebozho or Nanabozho. In one story,[101] Nanabozho and his family are starving.[102] After a series of failures in convincing (tricking) the woodpecker and muskrat spirits into being meals, Nanabozho convinces (tricks) several birds and kills them. He eats his fill, saves the rest for later, and takes a nap.

During the night, men approach. Nanabozho's buttocks warn him twice: "Wake up, Nanabozho. Men are coming."[103] Nanabozho ignores his buttocks and continues to sleep. When he awakens to find the remainder of his food stolen, he builds up his fire and burns his buttocks as punishment for their failure to warn him.

In arguing that "Native American literature" does not exist, Professor Treuer burns his own buttocks. While he asserts that he is trying to avoid a claim that the work of Erdrich, Welch, Silko, Alexie, and so on are inauthentic,[104] Treuer's argument, taken to its logical conclusion, denies the existence of *any* Indian culture. While perhaps Professor Treuer's literary critique is intended to create a normative distinction between the novels of writers like Erdrich and Alexie and his own, he puts the culture and art of all American Indians—and the law and politics of Indian tribes—in academic and intellectual jeopardy. Finally, the very existence and viability of modern tribal governments—despite all their flaws from all the borrowing and imposition of Anglo-American legal constructs—disproves the normative truth of Professor Treuer's theory. Indian people and Indian culture live on in new and changing forms every minute. Such is survival.

American Indians sitting around a campfire or a dinner table telling stories about the living and the dead, about history and the supernatural, once defined the rules by which people once lived. These stories functioned as an important link between culture and law. These stories were not, and could not be, a form of codified law—law that never changes. Circumstances change, people change, and even geographies change. And so the stories and cultures change, too. If the stories didn't change, then maybe the people wouldn't change. And then maybe the people wouldn't survive. The stories have to change, and often with those stories, the culture. And with those cultural changes, the law. And sometimes the new stories—and the new laws—will appear disingenuous to those who know the old stories—and the new laws. The study of the stories, old and new, must continue to keep tabs on how the culture changes.

Miigwetch.

NOTES

1. David Treuer, *Native American Fiction: A User's Manual* (Minneapolis: Graywolf Press, 2006), 191.

2. Dinitia Smith, "American Indian Writing, Seen through a New Lens," *New York Times*, August 19, 2006, B9.

3. Alternate spellings based on regional dialects include "Waynaboozhoo" (Edward Benton-Banai, *The Mishomis Book: The Voice of the Ojibwe* [Indian Country Press, 1979], 29); "Nanabush" (John Borrows, *Recovering Canada: The Resurgence of Indigenous Law* [Toronto: University of Toronto Press, 2002], 17); and "Nanabozho" ("Nanabozho," in *Ojibwa Narratives of Charles and Charlotte Kawbawgam and Jacques LePique, 1893–1895*, ed. Arthur P. Bourgeois [Detroit: Wayne State University Press, 1994]).

4. Treuer, *Native American Fiction*, 50–52 (quoting Rose Foss, "Why Wenaboozhoo Is So Smart," *Oshkaabewis Native Journal* 4 (1997): 33–34.

5. Ibid., 29–68 (criticizing Louise Erdrich, *Love Medicine* [1993]).

6. Ibid., 191.

7. Ibid., 192.

8. Ibid., 192.

9. Ibid., 67.

10. Ibid., 193.

11. Treuer, *Native American Fiction*, 77–105 (criticizing James Welch, *Fools Crow* [1986]); 164–86 (criticizing Sherman Alexie, *Reservation Blues* [1995]); also 164–77 (comparing *Reservation Blues* and *The Education of Little Tree*).

12. David Treuer, "Smartberries: Interpreting Erdrich's Love Medicine," *American Indian Culture & Research Journal* 29 (2005): 21, 35 (emphasis added).

13. Lawrence Rosen, *Law as Culture: An Invitation* (Princeton, NJ: Princeton University Press 2006), 5.

14. H.L.A. Hart, *The Concept of Law* (Oxford: Clarendon Press, 1961), 77–96.

15. Ibid., 79, 85 ("Rules are conceived and spoken of as imposing obligations when the general demand for conforming is insistent and the social pressure brought to bear upon those who deviate or threaten to deviate is great.")

16. Ibid., 89.

17. Martin Krygier, "Law as Tradition," *Law & Philosophy* 5 (1986): 237, 240 ("Every tradition is composed of elements drawn from the real or an imagined past."); 241 ("In every established legal system, the legal past is central to the legal present. Like all complex traditions, law records and preserves a composite of (frequently inconsistent) beliefs, opinions, values, decisions, myths, rituals, deposited over generations.").

18. Hart, *The Concept of Law*, 89–95.

19. Ibid., 91–93.

20. Ronald Dworkin, "Hart and the Concepts of Law," *Harvard Law Review Forum* 119 (2006): 95, 100.

21. E. Adamson Hoebel, *The Law of Primitive Man: A Study in Comparative Legal Dynamics* (Cambridge, MA: Harvard University Press, 1954), 5.

22. Elaine Scarry, *The Body in Pain: The Making and Unmaking of the World* (New York: Oxford University Press, 1985), 295 (citing Oliver Wendell Holmes, *The Common Law*, ed. Mark DeWolfe Howe [1881; Boston: Little, Brown and Co., 1963], 23, 25, 33).

23. Hart, *The Concept of Law*, 90.

24. Ibid., 90.

25. Ibid., 93.

26. Rosen, *Law as Culture*, 30.

27. E. Allan Farnsworth, *Contracts*, 4th ed. (New York: Aspen Publishers, 2004), § 4.28, 298. Cf. Roberto Mangabeira Unger, *The Critical Legal Studies Movement* (Cambridge, MA: Harvard University Press, 1986), 60–62.

28. Jerome E. Bickenbach, "Law and Morality," *Law & Philosophy* 8 (1989): 291, 292. Cf. Ronald Dworkin, *Is Democracy Possible Here? Principles for a New Democratic Debate* (Princeton, NJ: Princeton University Press, 2006), 94–98 (moral legitimacy of governments); Duncan Kennedy, *A Critique of Adjudication: Fin de siècle* (Cambridge, MA: Harvard University Press, 1997), 202–3 (legitimacy of decisions rendered in accordance with judicial ideologies).

29. Steven Lubet, "Veiled Truth," *American Lawyer*, March 1, 2007, available at http://www.law.com/jsp/tal/PubArticleTAL.jsp?hubtype=Inside&id=117257 0587864.

30. *Quair v. Sisco*, 359 F. Supp. 2d 948 (E.D. Cal. 2004); see also *Poodry v. Tonawanda Band of Seneca Indians*, 85 F.3d 874, 889 (2d Cir.) ("The respondents urged at oral argument that 'treason,' though a criminal act in our judicial system, is not necessarily 'criminal' in a traditional nation such as the Tonawanda Band. We doubt that this appeal to cultural relativism is relevant to our inquiry."), cert. denied, 519 U.S. 1041 (1996).

31. Michael Asch, "Lévi-Strauss and the Political: The Elementary Structures of Kinship and the Resolution of Relations between Indigenous People and Settler States," *Journal of the Royal Anthropology Institute* 11 (2005): 425, 434 (quoting *In re: Southern Rhodesia* [1919] A.C. 211 (Eng. P.C.).

32. Rosen, *Law as Culture*, 30–34 (noting the Cheyenne Indians and the nation of India as examples, not to mention the United States).

33. Karl N. Llewellyn and E. Adamson Hodel, *The Cheyenne Way: Conflict and Case Law in Primitive Jurisprudence* (1941; Norman: University of Oklahoma Press, 1983); Bruce G. Miller, *The Problem of Justice: Tradition and Law in the Coast Salish World* (Lincoln: University of Nebraska Press, 2000); Watson Smith and John M. Roberts, *Zuni Law: A Field of Values* (Cambridge, MA: Peabody Museum, Harvard University, 1954); Richard Posner, "A Theory of

Primitive Society, with Special Reference to Law," *Journal of Law and Economics* 23 (1980): 1.

34. E.g., Keith H. Basso, *Wisdom Sits in Places: Landscape and Language among the Western Apache* (Albuquerque: University of New Mexico Press, 1996), 37–70; Melissa L. Meyer, "We Can Not Get a Living as We Used To": Dispossession and the White Earth Anishinaabeg, 1889–1920," *American Historical Review* 96 (1991): 368.

35. *Ex parte Kan-gi-shun-ca (Crow Dog)*, 109 U.S. 556 (1883).

36. See Secretary of Interior, *Annual Report (1884)*, 9, reprinted in David H. Getches, Charles F. Wilkinson, and Robert A. Williams Jr., *Cases and Materials on Federal Indian Law*, 5th ed. (West Publishing, 2005), 157; Sidney L. Harring, "Crow Dog's Case: A Chapter in the Legal History of Tribal Sovereignty," *American Indian Law Review* 14 (1989): 191, 223.

37. *Kan-gi-shun-ca*, 109 U.S. at 405–06; cf. Robert A. Williams Jr., *Like a Loaded Weapon: The Rehnquist Court, Indian Rights, and the Legal History of Racism in America* (Minneapolis: University of Minnesota Press, 2005), 109 (showing how the Kan-gi-shun-ca Court reasoning was used later by then-Justice Rehnquist to divest Indian tribes of criminal jurisdiction over nonmembers in *Oliphant v. Suquamish Indian Tribe*, 435 U.S. 191, 210–11 (1978).

38. Act of March 3, 1885, ch. 341, 23 Stat. 385, codified as amended at 18 U.S.C. § 1153.

39. Russel Lawrence Barsh and James Youngblood Henderson, "Tribal Courts, the Model Code, and the Police Idea in American Indian Policy," *Law & Contemporary Problems* 40 (1976): 25, 26–49; Kevin K. Washburn, "Federal Criminal Law and Tribal Self-Determination," *North Carolina Law Review* 84 (2006): 779, 790–809.

40. Vine Deloria Jr. and Clifford M. Lytle, *American Indians, American Justice* (Austin: University of Texas Press, 1984), 110–16.

41. See Deloria and Lytle, *American Indians, American Justice*, 35, 113–16. See, e.g., *United States v. Clapox*, 35 F. 575 (D. Or. 1888) (upholding the regulations promulgated by the Secretary of Interior known as the "law and order codes").

42. See *Clapox*, 35 F. at 577 ("These 'courts of Indian offenses' are . . . educational and disciplinary instrumentalities, by which the government of the United States is endeavoring to improve and elevate the condition of these dependent tribes to whom it sustains the relation of guardian. In fact, the reservation itself is in the nature of a school, and the Indians are gathered there, under the charge of an agent, for the purpose of acquiring the habits, ideas, and aspirations which distinguish the civilized from the uncivilized man.").

43. See, e.g., J.D.C. Atkins, "The English Language in Indian Schools," reprinted in *Americanizing the American Indians: Writings by the "Friends of the Indian,"*

1800–1900, ed. Francis Paul Prucha, 197–206 (Cambridge, MA: Harvard University Press, 1973) (advocating for the replacement of Indian languages with English).

44. For histories of the dispossession of Indian lands, see Stuart Banner, *How the Indians Lost Their Land: Law and Power on the Frontier* (Cambridge, MA: Belknap/Harvard University Press, 2005); and Lindsay G. Robertson, *Conquest by Law: How the Discovery of America Dispossessed Indigenous Peoples of Their Lands* (Oxford and New York: Oxford University Press, 2005).

45. Wheeler-Howard Act (Indian Reorganization Act), 48 Stat. 984–988 (1934), codified as amended 25 U.S.C. § 461 et seq.

46. See, e.g., Felix S. Cohen, "The Erosion of Indian Rights, 1950–1953: A Case Study in Bureaucracy," *Yale Law Journal* 62 (1953): 348 (detailing the actions of the Bureau of Indian Affairs in stifling tribal governance development); "Comment: Tribal Self-Government and the Indian Reorganization Act of 1934," *Michigan Law Review* 70 (1972): 955.

47. See Timothy W. Joranko and Mark C. Van Norman, "Indian Self-Determination at Bay: Secretarial Authority to Disapprove Tribal Constitutional Amendments, *Gonzaga Law Review* 29 (1993–94): 81.

48. See, e.g., Reid Peyton Chambers and Monroe E. Price, "Regulating Sovereignty: Secretarial Discretion and the Leasing of Indian Lands," *Stanford Law Review* 26 (1974): 1061 (describing the secretary of Interior's control over the leasing of Indian lands).

49. See 25 U.S.C. § 1303 (extending the Great Writ to tribal criminal cases).

50. See *National Farmers Union Ins. Cos. v. Crow Tribe of Indians*, 471 U.S. 845 (1985).

51. See generally Rennard Strickland, *Fire and the Spirits: Cherokee Law from Clan to Court* (Norman: University of Oklahoma, 1975), 120–67.

52. See Christine Zuni, "Strengthening What Remains," *Kansas Journal of Law & Public Policy* 7 (1997): 17, 20.

53. Frank Pommersheim, *Braid of Feathers: American Indian Law and Contemporary Tribal Life* (Berkeley: University of California Press, 1995), 21 (describing how the federal government drove the "core of the culture . . . into a shadow existence").

54. 358 U.S. 217 (1959).

55. Pommersheim, *Braid of Feathers*, 223.

56. Ibid., 220 ("Essentially, absent governing Acts of Congress, the question has always been whether the state action infringed on the right of reservation Indians to make their own laws and be ruled by them.").

57. 25 U.S.C. § 1301 et seq.

58. 25 U.S.C. § 1302.

59. 436 U.S. 49, 71 (1978) ("Congress may also have considered that resolution of statutory issues under § 1302, and particularly those issues likely to arise in a civil context, will frequently depend on questions of tribal tradition and custom which tribal forums may be in a better position to evaluate than federal courts.").

60. 436 U.S. 49, 71 (1978).

61. See Matthew L. M. Fletcher, "The Supreme Court and Federal Indian Policy," *Nebraska Law Review* 85 (2006): 121, 147–50.

62. Matthew L. M. Fletcher, "Toward a Theory of Intertribal and Intratribal Common Law," *Houston Law Review* 43 (2006): 701, 720–21.

63. See Wenona T. Singel, "Cultural Sovereignty and Transplanted Law: Tensions in Indigenous Self-Rule," *Kansas Journal of Law & Public Policy* 15 (2006): 357, 359–60.

64. E.g., 9 Grand Traverse Band Code § 201(a) ("The Grand Traverse Band adopts the laws, codes, ordinances, and other instruments of the law of the State of Michigan to the extent these instruments, laws, codes, and ordinances do not conflict with appropriate federal law or Tribal codes, ordinances, and laws in force now or enacted in the future.").

65. See Singel, "Cultural Sovereignty and Transplanted Law," 360.

66. See generally Angela R. Riley, "'Straight Stealing': Toward an Indigenous System of Cultural Property Protection," *Washington Law Review* 80 (2005): 69.

67. See Matthew L. M. Fletcher, "Rethinking Customary Law in Tribal Court Jurisprudence," *Michigan Journal of Race and Law* 13 (2007): 57, 65-71.

68. See Steve Aycock, "Thoughts on Creating a Truly Tribal Jurisprudence," compiled in *Indigenous Justice Systems of North America*, 2nd Annual Indigenous Law Conference, Michigan State University College of Law, March 17–18, 2006 (on file with author).

69. Treuer, *Native American Fiction*, 66.

70. Ibid., 192 (quoting Cleanth Brooks and Robert Penn Warren, *Understanding Poetry: An Anthology for College Students* (New York: H. Holt and Co., 1938), iv.

71. James Welch, *Fools Crow* (New York: Penguin, 1986).

72. Treuer, *Native American Fiction*, 78 (quoting Dee Brown). This quotation appeared as a book-jacket blurb.

73. Ibid., 77–107.

74. Ibid., 198.

75. Ibid., 197.

76. See Gloria Valencia-Weber, "Tribal Courts: Custom and Innovative Law," *New Mexico Law Review* 24 (1994): 225, 250.

77. See Nancy A. Costello, "Walking Together in a Good Way: Indian Peacemaker Courts in Michigan," *University of Detroit Mercy Law Review* 76 (1999): 875.

78. To be clear, Professor Treuer mostly does not allege that the authors are committing fraud themselves, but that the literary critics that read and publicize these works through their scholarly papers and book-jacket blurbs commit a kind of fraud when they make the representation that the works of Erdrich, Welch et al. are a genuine expression of Indian culture. See, e.g., Treuer, *Native American Fiction*, 31 (Herth D. Sweet Wong); Treuer, *Native American Fiction*, 32 (Allan Chavkin). However, with his exposition of Forrest Gerard's known fraud, *The Education of Little Tree*, to Sherman Alexie's *Indian Killer*, Treuer all but screeches fraud. See Treuer, *Native American Fiction*, 159–89.

79. See, e.g., David Treuer, *The Translation of Dr. Appelles: A Love Story* (Minneapolis: Graywolf Press, 2006); David Treuer, *The Hiawatha* (New York: Picador, 1999); David Treuer, *Little* (New York: Picador, 1996).

80. David Treuer, "Jibwaa-ozhibii'igewin," *American Indian Quarterly* 30 (2006): 3, 7. The entire statement reads, "With few exceptions—the Southwest and some communities in Canada—our tribal communities are governed in English. Our tribal councils conduct business in English, write their by-laws and constitutions in English, and debate issues in English. Clearly our tribal languages do not influence tribal governance as such—even though we might be sovereign—it is a peculiar kind of sovereignty." Cf. Treuer, *Native American Fiction*, 199 (referring to "the mistake of the common loon (incidentally the chieftain clan among the Ojibwe) who answers his own call echoed back from the next lake over, and, unaware of the mistake, is urged to call again, and again—only to remain eternally thwarted.").

81. See Treuer, *Native American Fiction*, 159–89.

82. See, e.g., *State v. Gurnoe*, 192 N.W.2d 892, 899 (Wis. 1972) (holding that Indian treaty rights could only be exercised using the technology of Indian people at treaty times); cf. *United States v. Washington*, 384 F. Supp. 312, 362, 402 (W.D. Wash. 1974); Karen Ferguson, "Indian Fishing Rights: The Aftermath of the Fox Decision and the Year 2000," *American Indian Law Review* 23 (1998): 97, 145–46.

83. Treuer, *Native American Fiction*, 73.

84. See D'Arcy McNickle, *Native American Tribalism: Indian Survivals and Renewals*, rev. ed. (New York: Oxford University Press, 1973), 7–11.

85. See generally D'Arcy McNickle, *They Came Here First*, rev. ed. (New York: Harper and Row, 1975), 283 ("Indian societies did not disappear by assimilating to the dominant white culture, as predicted, but assimilated to themselves bits and pieces of the surrounding cultural environment. And they remained indubitably Indian, whether their constituents lived in a tight Indian community or commuted between the community and an urban job market.").

86. Compare, e.g., James A. Clifton, *The Pokagons, 1683–1983: Catholic Potawa-tomi Indians of the St. Joseph River Valley* (University Press of America, 1984) (Pokagon Band of Potawatomi Indians) with, e.g., James A. Clifton, *The Prairie People: Continuity and Change in Potawatomi Indian Culture* (Lawrence: University Press of Kansas, 1977) (Citizen Potawatomi and Prairie Band Potawatomi Nation).

87. See McNickle, *Native American Tribalism*, 4 ("Only the Indians seemed unwilling to accept oblivion as an appropriate final act for their role in the New World drama. Caught up in succeeding waves of devastating epidemics and border wars as settlement moved westward, the Indians retreated, protecting what they could, and managing to be at hand to fight another day when necessity required it. They lost, but were never defeated.").

88. Richard White, *The Middle Ground: Indians, Empires, and Republics in the Great Lakes Region, 1650–1815* (New York: Cambridge University Press, 1991), ix–x. Gerald Vizenor's theory of "survivance" is a tempting explanation as well, but not as satisfying, because it does not account as well for the meaning created by the mixture of these Indian and Anglo-American cultures, nor does it account for the endgame where Indian people returned to the status of the "exotic" or "other." See generally Gerald Vizenor, *Manifest Manners: Narratives on Postindian Survivance* (Hanover, NH: University Press of New England, 1994); Gerald Vizenor, "Native American Narratives: Resistance and Survivance," address at North Dakota State University, April 22, 2005. Cf. Malea Powell, "Rhetorics of Survivance: How American Indians Use Writing," *College Composition and Communication* 53 (2002): 396.

89. See generally White, *The Middle Ground*, 50–93.

90. Ibid., 51.

91. Ibid., 52.

92. Ibid., 52.

93. Ibid., 52–53.

94. Ibid., 53.

95. Cf. *Johnson v. M'Intosh*, 21 U.S. 543, 588 (1823).

96. See generally Alex Tallchief Skibine, "Redefining the Status of Indian Tribes within 'Our Federalism': Beyond the Dependency Paradigm," *Connecticut Law Review* 38 (2006): 667.

97. E.g., Native American Housing and Self-Determination Act, 25 U.S.C. §§ 4101 et seq.; Indian Self-Determination and Educational Assistance Act, 25 U.S.C. §§ 450a et seq. See generally *Cohen's Handbook of Federal Indian Law*, ed. Nell Jessup Newton et al. (LexisNexis, 2005), ch. 22 (describing federal government services for Indians).

98. Treuer, *Native American Fiction*, 193, 198.

99. See Treuer, "Jibwaa-ozhibii'igewin," 7.

100. See, e.g., Matthew L. M. Fletcher, "Looking to the East: The Stories of Modern Indian People and the Development of Tribal Law," *Seattle Journal for Social Justice* 5 (2006): 1, 18–19 (referencing the opening of Sherman Alexie's film *The Business of Fancydancing* at a small, independent movie theater on the Grand Traverse Band's reservation).

101. This story is sometimes referred to as "The Duck Dinner." Borrows, *Recovering Canada*, 46–54 (citing Richard M. Dorson, *Bloodstoppers and Bearwalkers* [Cambridge, MA: Harvard University Press, 1952], 49–50).

102. See "Nanabozho in a Time of Famine," in Bourgeois, ed., *Ojibwa Narratives*, 33–35.

103. Ibid., 35.

104. See Treuer, *Native American Fiction*, 193.

The Hydromythology of the Anishinaabeg

Will Mishipizhu Survive Climate Change, or Is He Creating It?

MELISSA K. NELSON

FOR ANISHINAABEG PEOPLE,[1] OUR STORIES GO BACK TO THE BEGIN-
ning of time with deep, endless roots. Yet our stories are also new and fresh
each time they are told. To be Anishinaabe is to know that stories can be
medicine and that they reveal fresh meanings for new times. This is a story
about the power of story and hydromythology. It looks at the Ojibwe mythical creature Mishipizhu, an underwater panther and powerful *manitou*. A
manitou is most easily and often translated to mean "spirit," but according to Ojibwe writer Basil Johnston, this is "the simplest of the abstract."[2]
For fluent Ojibwe language speakers, Johnston states, "Depending on the
context, they knew that in addition to spirit, the term also meant property,
essence, transcendental, mystical, muse, patron, and divine."[3]

Mishipizhu is a protector of natural resources and a mediator between
the water, land, and sky beings. "In his role as guardian of resources he is
immortal, reappearing to punish anyone who attempts to upset the balance of eco-social relations."[4] This essay examines Mishipizhu narratives
as critical Ojibwe hydromyths, and addresses my primary question, "Will
Mishipizhu survive climate change, or is he creating it?" I am conscious of
the polemics of this either/or question and pose it deliberately to flesh out
the extreme ends of a spectrum of possibilities. Related questions include:
Does Mishipizhu play a role in these ecologically tumultuous times? If so,
what? Is there an ancestral, moral understanding of Mishipizhu, and how
would this impact Anishinaabeg choices in response to climate change? I

suggest that Mishipizhu hydromyths can be used today to understand critical eco-cultural changes. I argue that Mishipizhu is a powerful metaphysical icon of the Ojibwe imagination, and that his active presence serves as an important indicator of traditional ecological knowledge about a moral landscape that supports cultural resilience.

Honoring what Ojibwe scholar Gerald Vizenor called "Trickster logic," I juxtapose and entertain two contrary positions regarding Mishipizhu and climate disruption. Trickster logic or "trickster consciousness" is "a tool of liberation from any form of linear, monologic style, and universalizing theory."[5] Employing this Ojibwe strategy of analysis, I examine two positions: One sees Mishipizhu as a victim of climate change. He is "collateral damage" in the ongoing Western war against the Native world and environment. The opposite position sees Mishipizhu as a *creator* of climate change. His power is beyond humans, and he is orchestrating these massive shifts as a way to renew and balance the peoples and systems of the earth. Just as many Native stories and oral cycles have no definitive beginnings or endings or "closure," this analysis examines contradictory points in the interpretation of the Anishinaabeg Mishipizhu hydromyth and invites readers to enter the watershed of Ojibwe imagination.

THE DOORWAY OF STORY

> *There's a story behind everything, every bush.*
>
> —DREW HAYDEN TAYLOR, *FUNNY YOU DON'T LOOK LIKE ONE—OBSERVATIONS FROM A BLUE-EYED OJIBWAY*

Story is one of the oldest ways to understand the world. Some may say it is the *only* way to do so. Stories provide windows into other realities, doorways into other worldviews. Narratives provide unique cultural lenses through which to envision the world. Within every human, every plant, every animal and object, there is a life story, and many other stories following: conception, birth, growth, maturity, aging, death, and rebirth. Like everything in life, stories have their own lives yet they never truly end; they are constantly renewed and reborn in each teller and context. And stories can also go dormant. They can lie fallow for decades or even centuries, buried in the land like winter seeds waiting for an ideal spring. When the conditions are right, the story seed can emerge with the signature of its origins, but with new shapes and colors given the latest conditions it finds life in.

The land has become a source of morals and
values that are rekindled each time a story is re-told.

—ENRIQUE SALMON, *EATING THE LANDSCAPE: AMERICAN*
INDIAN STORIES OF FOOD, IDENTITY, AND RESILIENCE

Stories can serve as cognitive maps to other states of consciousness. Storied landscapes are oral maps or storyscapes, animated and mobile narratives that travel through geographic places.[6] Storyscapes help us travel paths, ones we may never physically go on in our lives. Stories help us see farther and deeper than we can see on our own. As imagined geographies, stories reveal places and spaces never viscerally experienced. Storylines help us travel through metaphysical landscapes—mindscapes of adventure (scenarios, travel, explorations); mindscapes of emotion (longing, hope, fear, and resolution); mindscapes of instruction and ethical space (morals, values, beliefs, truths). These instructive vessels reveal moral landscapes that help us navigate social complexity and ecological unpredictability. As philosopher David Abram states, "Songs and stories carry much *more* than a set of instructions for moving through the terrain. While the topographic function of the songs is obviously important, the songs and stories also provide the codes of behavior for the community; they suggest, through multiple examples, how to act, or how *not* to act, in particular situations."[7] They provide intergenerational teachings about life's laws and purposes, according to that specific people's epistemological framework and indigenous territory. Storied landscapes, in a very real way, are moral landscapes. As I have heard from many native peoples, especially Rotumans and Hawaiians from the Pacific, "the land has eyes."[8] As we see stories in the land, the land sees what humans do. So stories can guide people in how to care for places. Indigenous stories, and perhaps all good ones really, combine adventure, emotion, and instruction in creative and enticing ways.

Lakes are books.

—LOUISE ERDRICH, *BOOKS AND ISLANDS IN OJIBWE COUNTRY*

Just as stories reveal imagined landscapes, natural landscapes comprise actual "text" and language to be translated, studied, and respected. As award-winning Ojibwe writer Louise Erdrich succinctly states it, the texture of land can be felt and read, and then hopefully understood. "You could think of the lakes as libraries," she says.[9] The texture of water is even more dynamic and mysterious to read, but it too can be observed, sensed, discerned. Okanagan writer Jeannette Armstrong claims, "The way we survived is to speak the language that the land offered us as its teachings."[10] Nature[11] or the "other-than-human"[12] or "more-than-human"[13] world tells us stories, and we also create stories for and about the other-than-human people of the world. I wonder, who among the Ojibwe today can read the stories of a lake?

As an Anishinaabe cultural ecologist, I am deeply interested in the relationships between place and memory, memory and identity, and imagination and health. I see place, memory, identity, and imagination as interwoven elements in the fabric of indigenous story and cultural health. Nurturing the story space between humans and other-than-humans means daring to walk outside of our own human creations to flirt with the mysteries and wonders of the other-than-human world.

HOLE IN THE SKY: RUPTURED STORY

Today, modern industrial society is insulated from the diversity of the earth. We are often enclosed within the trappings of our own human inventions. As a result, the reciprocal field of participatory story between humans and Nature has grown very thin, very weak—or we have simply stopped paying attention to it. For Indigenous peoples from oral cultures, we work hard to maintain, restore, and renew these stories of kinship with our other-than-human family, with all of the living beings and "extended relatives" of this created earth. This requires unmediated time spent alone in landscapes to refamiliarize ourselves with, and listen deeply to, the language of the land. This provides us with the opportunity to have visceral, hands-on, embodied experiences of a reality not made by human thought. Some have called these experiences a type of "ecoliteracy."[14] Yet in an increasingly human and machine-centered world with less and less "wild," natural places, these experiences are endangered. The rich stories that come from these experiences are fewer and fewer. Ethnobotanist Gary Nabhan calls this "the extinction of experience."[15] Humans in the developed worlds, including many Native Americans, have become quite "ecologically illiterate." Today, many tribal elders agree with this and feel that much has been lost in terms of the stories and teachings that come from the other-than-human world. The late Shoshone spiritual teacher Corbin Harney called this "the Nature way of life."[16]

Given the extinction of experience, pervasive ecological illiteracy, and the rupture in oral storytelling about the other-than-human world, what stories *have* survived? What stories stay strong? What stories go underground? What stories may I now be able to summon or dream? There is one story that comes from under the water. I have heard it for a long time. I heard it in my dreams, felt it in my flesh, saw it in a river, tasted it in a lake.

ANISHINAABEG HYDROMYTHOLOGY

This is a story about Mishipizhu. He is a Water spirit. Panther serpent. Horned snake. Underwater Lynx. Water Keeper. Lake Guardian. River Protector. Storm Maker. Child Taker. Copper Medicine Maker.

Being people of the Great Lakes and the Mississippi headwaters, Anishinaabeg people are water people.[17] There are many important traditional Anishinaabeg stories about the significance of water. According to traditional teachings, water or *niibi* is a primary sacred element in life and therefore must be cherished as an essential relative, elder, and teacher. Water is basic to human survival and it is also imbued with great meaning and supernatural power. Water *is* a manitou, and contains manitous.

Like other indigenous peoples around the world, the Anishinaabeg have distinct stories about different types of water bodies and the water spirits that dwell within them. One of our most important stories, the Creation of Turtle Island, starts when the world was nothing but water, and an earth diver (usually a muskrat) had to dive deep into the primal sea to find a bit of earth to place on Turtle's back. Another critical story in the history and identity of the Anishinaabeg is the migration story from the Eastern Seaboard to the Great Lakes that is said to have happened about one thousand years ago. It was the St. Lawrence River, Great Lakes, and the prophetic vision of the sacred *Megis* (cowry) shell that facilitated and consecrated that major migration westward. In some interpretations, this sacred migration protected Anishinaabeg from colonialism for many years: "It was prophesied that a light-skinned race would land on our shore and bring death and destruction to our people. After a great council, we started traveling westward, according to the prophecies, and followed the sign of a sacred vision along the way."[18]

The Ojibwe natural world is characterized by lakes and rivers—great and small—sloughs, creeks, ice and snow. Travel was traditionally done by birch-bark canoe along the immense waterways traversing Anishinaabe-akii

(Ojibwe homeland), from the Atlantic Ocean, through the Saint Lawrence Seaway, to the Great Lakes, and down the Mississippi River. The most sacred and important staple food, *manomin* (wild rice; literally "good grain"), is "the food that grows on water."[19] Another important food source, fish, comes from the waterways, along with medicinal plants used for healing. Likewise, the important healing drum of the Midewiwin Society (Grand Medicine Society) is the water drum. This special drum was usually made of basswood or cedar. "It was called *mitigwakik*, meaning "wooden vessel."[20] The water drum was and is strictly used as a medicine drum: "Its high pitched tone could carry great distances and characteristic sound informed one instantly that a medicine ceremony was in session."[21] The Ojibwe trace the original clans to a story that says they came out of the sea, and so our very social organization with the clan system has its origins in water. Those from the Fish Clan are generally the spiritual teachers and healers, and in some Ojibwe communities there is a *niibinaabi* clan or "water spirit" clan. Enrique Salmon explains, "As the people migrated, settled for a short while, and then migrated again, a library of traditional ecological knowledge (TEK) co-evolved with their increasingly complex social system of clans and societies."[22] So water is extremely important and revered by the Anishinaabeg—not only for its role in our ecological survival and social cohesion but for our very identity and cosmology. *Niibi* manitous, water spirits, are essential for an understanding of metaphysical realms, the fluidity of consciousness, and the ambivalence of power.

Due to this intimate immersion in waterscapes, Ojibwe have many teachings about water and the creatures, both tangible and intangible, that reside within water bodies. These teachings are encoded in the language. As Ojibwe writer and fluent language speaker David Treuer reinforces, "The Ojibwe language needed to be very precise when describing, especially weather phenomenon, in particular weather and water. In the Great Lakes region those are the two most important forces that are going to shape your life. So there are many, many words that deal with those concepts with a kind of precision that is astounding."[23] His brother Anton Treuer goes on to explain that water is more often used as a verb: water falling as mist, little droplets moving, hard rain pelting, rather than as a fixed noun. In the Ojibwe language, water is also referred to in terms of what it is doing in context, for example, what it looks and sounds like: what a wave looks like as it approaches the shore, what ice sounds like cracking.

The details of water movement are captured in the language, which is then communicated in stories. These narratives are often called myths and legends and are part of larger oral literatures. In the field of cultural anthropology and more specifically folklore, and in a lot of vernacular, the word "myth" often carries an undertone of quaint, primitive, false, and superstitious. There is often a pejorative connotation given to this word by anthropologists, historians, and other scholars. If not, then the word "myth" is sometimes overly romanticized as an idealized, static, or essentialized story. I am not using the word in either of these ways. Nor in the strange way these two positions are sometimes combined when "Native myths" are dumbed down, oversimplified, and reduced to caricatures. I am using it in an affirmative way to refer to the true oral (and written) narratives of the Ojibwe people that include the other-than-human world. What are often called "myths" are very old stories that have been passed on intergenerationally and are based on careful observation of natural cycles. They are actually part of what is often referred to as "geomythology,"[24] "narrative history," and "traditional history"[25] for indigenous peoples. Myths also include stories that may have not factually or historically occurred, but they carry profound truth and relevance as metaphors. Myths are often considered sacred by their people and therefore have religious dimensions. As such they contain sophisticated abstract knowledges about space, time, cosmology, cosmogony, medicine, and emotional, artistic, and spiritual states of consciousness.

The Anishinaabeg, like most Native nations, have an astounding library of oral literatures that constitute an immense imaginative mythology. One particular genre is what Gerald Vizenor called "pictomyth."[26] In *Summer in the Spring*, Vizenor states:

> The Anishinaabe drew pictures of their dream songs, visions, stories, and ideas on birchbark. The song pictures of the *midewiwin*, the religion of tribal healers, were incised on the soft inner bark of the birch. These scrolls of dream song pictures, or pictomyths, are sacred and heard only by members of the *midewiwin*, who believe that visions, songs, and the use of herbal medicine heal and sustain the human spirit.[27]

Pictomyths can also be generally interpreted as "picture writing," as in rock art, birch-bark scrolls, and other symbolic writing on stone, bark, hide, and bone. These are known as visual memory aids or mnemonic devices to visually symbolize complex mythical, historical, and ecological knowledge. The Ojibwe excelled at this type of oral/written communication. So much so that Louise Erdrich has a particularly "literary" interpretation of the meaning of "Ojibwe": "The meaning I like best of course is Ojibwe from the verb *ozhibii'ige*, which is 'to write.'"[28]

Many researchers, Native and non-Native, who have studied the oral literatures of indigenous peoples have categorized stories into different genres. One relatively new category useful for this essay is the term "hydro-mythology," and the more specific "ethnohydromythology"—the study of indigenous oral water myths. Hydromyths are oral narratives about the power of water that combine adventure, emotion, and instruction. Ojibwe hydromyths are imaginative ecosystems, and they contain a menagerie of creatures—familiar and strange; amphibious, reptilian, and mammalian; zoomorphic and supernatural. There are, of course, the important fish species of walleye, sturgeon, perch, pike, and bass, as well as river and lake animals like frogs and salamanders and turtles. There are also snakes and birds and insects that live on and around lakes and rivers. And *all* animals of course (including us), whether bear or wolf, hawk or lynx, dragonfly or hummingbird, depend on water for drinking. For the Ojibwe there are also the important unseen creatures of the water: mermaids, mermen, horned serpents and snakes, monsters, winged and finned creatures, and other water manitous. In numerous stories, both simple and complex, humorous and serious, these water creatures are discussed and narrated as key characters in Ojibwe life. But of all the amazing creatures, spirits, and energies that are known and honored in the hydromythology of the Ojibwe, it is probably Mishipizhu that garners the most respect and awe, because of his immense power and underwater mystery.

MISHIPIZHU: THE GREAT UNDERWATER PANTHER

Mishipizhu is a mythical creature who is painted on rocks, narrated in water stories, prayed to when crossing a lake, and offered gifts when harvesting *manomin* (wild rice). Etymologically, from Anishinaabemowin (Anishinaabe language) he is *Mishi, Misshe, Mici*—"great," "large," "big," and *Pizhu, Pissu, Peshu, Pijiu*—"lynx," "cat." He is the "Great Lynx." But he is unique in that he lives and travels through waterways, has a serpent tail and often antler horns. Some say he has scales made of copper. According to the American Museum of Natural History's exhibition on Mythic Sea Monsters, he has "a cat-like face, body and scales of a sea serpent, copper horns, spikes of energy radiating from his body, and lives at the bottom of lakes and rivers."[29] This Underwater Panther is known in the sacred stories and oral literatures of many North American Native nations—Arikara, Delaware, Cree, Dakota, Fox, Mandan-Hidatsa, Omaha, Potawatomi, and Ponca stories all describe this mysterious and powerful creature. Some minor details vary, but his basic form and function is the same. Around the Great Lakes, various rock art paintings depict him, and many early ethnographers recorded stories of him in the 1920s, 1950s, and 1960s.[30]

> The concept of the Underwater Panther seems to be very ancient in North America, and unmistakable carvings, pictographs, and other representations of the monster have been found in association with archaeological remains of Middle Woodland date. Several of the effigy mounds of Wisconsin are in the shape of this creature. Both the Underwater Panther and the Horned Serpent seem to be related to the Feathered Serpent of the Southwest, Mexico, and Middle America.[31]

Whether this Underwater Panther is linked to the universal archetype of the Cosmic Serpent is another interesting question, but out of the bounds of this essay.[32] The main point here being that this character is not just an Ojibwe phenomenon, but clearly taps into some collective human fear and imaginative reality of an underwater serpent creature. It has been argued that this iconographic association of serpents, water, and felines is a fertility symbol.[33] A unique aspect of the Ojibwe and other Algonkian groups in Northeastern North America is that this creature is an important hybrid of a horned serpent *and* a cat or lion *and* he provides a moral lens for water relations. All cultures have stories of underwater spirits and monsters. But I believe Mishipizhu is uniquely localized to the water landscapes and ecological knowledge of the Anishinaabeg, including other Northeastern Algonkian neighbors and relatives, like the Potawatomi and Fox, who share these stories. Ojibwe today continue to tell and retell stories of Mishipizhu. In Louise Erdrich's critically-acclaimed novel *Tracks*, she describes him and points to his dangerous power:

> He casts a shell necklace at your feet, weeps gleaming chips that harden into mica on your breasts. He holds you under. Then he takes the body of a lion, a fat brown worm, or a familiar man. He's made of gold. He's made of beach moss. He's a thing of dry foam, a thing of death by drowning, the death a Chippewa cannot survive.[34]

Mishipizhu, being the king of underwater spirits for the Ojibwe, is so powerful that his authority can be used for malevolence or compassion. "It is important to note that underwater spirits are often, but not always, malevolent."[35] His power is ambivalent, indeterminate; therefore Ojibwe must constantly be wary and cautious and make proper offerings for safety and long-term balance. "Although generally considered an evil creature, the Underwater Panther is greatly feared and respected by all of the groups having the creature in their pantheon. Among the Ojibwa and Potawatomi the monster is especially venerated by the members of the *Midewiwin* or Grand Medicine Society."[36] It is significant that the highest knowledge keepers of Ojibwe medicine revere Mishipizhu as a primary totem spirit. As religious studies scholar John Grim articulates,

> The many evil Manitou are not located in the earth or sky regions but in the cosmic waters that separate our flat-earth from the earth below us. The principal malevolent force, personified as Michibissy or Matchi Manitou, is a great underwater lion or feline being with horns and an encircling tail. Matchi Manitou not only assails the human order with disease, storms, and other intrusions but also takes possession of certain shamans, who then claim this Manitou as their patron spirit.[37]

But again, this "evil" is not stable or certain. Mishipizhu can also bestow great blessings, including health, safety, and healing for the Ojibwe. A Mishipizhu hydromyth shared in the classic work *Kitchi-Gami: Life among the Lake Superior Ojibway* (1860) illustrates this point. After a near-death encounter at the edge of a lake, a man, called an "enchanter," placated the "Water-King" with an offering:

> After the waters calmed down, the water-king emerged from the placid lake, in the form of a mighty serpent. The man asked the water-king, "Give me the recipe which will make me healthy, rich, and prosperous." The snake replied, "Dost thou see what I wear on my head, between my horns? Take it: it will serve thee. But one of thy children must be mine in return for it." The Indian saw between the horns of the water-king something red, like a fiery flower. He stretched out his trembling hand and seized it. It melted away in his finger into a powder, like the vermilion with which the Indians paint their faces. The Serpent then gave him further instructions.[38]

He instructed him to prepare some wood and place the red powder on the specially arranged pieces of wood.

> Then the water-king counted all the diseases and ills to which Indian humanity is exposed, and also all the wishes, desires, and passions, by which it is usually animated, and each time that the enchanter shook some powder on one of the

boards, the wicked water-spirit consecrated the powder, and named the illness which it would avert, or the good fortune it would bring.[39]

So, like our own human nature, but with more power, Mishipizhu can be benevolent and compassionate as well as harsh and wicked.

CLIMATE DISRUPTION AND ECOLOGICAL IMBALANCE

Given the profound and unprecedented ecological changes the world is experiencing right now, especially in relation to freshwater availability and climate change, it seems particularly important to understand how traditional water keepers like Ojibwe fishers and ricers maintain a reciprocal relationship with water bodies, and what role hydromyths may play in this effort. Given the growing water crisis exacerbated by climate change, lakes and rivers are drying up in some areas and being drowned with polluted waters in other areas. Icecaps are melting and changing the salinity of oceans and seas. Fish and other aquatic life are going extinct or becoming endangered due to exotic species, industrial poisons, dams, and other water diversions and negative human impacts. Fertile soils are being turned into deserts in some areas and creating massive erosion and mudslides in others. Native communities are challenged by these environmental impacts and health issues every day. Those Anishinaabeg who wish to maintain and revitalize traditional cultural practices and foodways such as fishing, hunting, wild-ricing; plant gathering by rivers and lakes for food, medicine, and craft; canoeing, and other activities, are already impacted by the growing water crisis. Sacred ceremonial practices are also significantly affected by polluted, desiccated, flooded, dammed, and diverted waterways.

All these impacts are being exacerbated by climate change. Rock art is flooded. Burials are exposed. Medicines stop growing where they've reliably grown before. Climate change—or "climate disruption," as Native restoration ecologist Dennis Martinez calls it; or "global weirding," as water ecologist Brock Dolman refers to it—is largely an issue of human-resource use exploitation patterns altering humans' relationship with water. The water cycle, after all, occurs through complex processes of evaporation and precipitation between earth water and sky water—from lakes, rivers, and oceans, to clouds to rain back to earth's water bodies. Water's ability to process heat and transform from earth liquid to sky gas back into liquid (rain) or solid (snow, ice, hail) again is extraordinary. The field of modern climatology studies this complex vertical layer between water bodies on the earth's surface and the sky (clouds, winds) in terms like "atmospheric boundary layers," "wind induced upwelling," "geostrophic currents," and "thermohaline circulation." This is also, according to traditional Anishinaabeg knowledge, the sacred domain of Mishipizhu, he who moderates and balances this powerful, transformative, and critical space that surrounds the earth and has protected life for the past 500 million years.[40]

For Anishinaabeg, Mishipizhu has always been a guardian of the waters and keeper of balance between the water spirits, land creatures, and sky beings. What is his role today given these human-induced changes in long-term climatic cycles? As the climate shifts and weather patterns are disrupted, there will be stronger Thunder Beings in some areas and less of them in others.[41] They will come at different times of the year and disrupt seasonal cycles. This is already happening, and wild-rice gatherers are finding that their lakes are flooded and the rice is stunted in some areas. Their lakes are dry, with no rice in others. Hunters are finding that moose, bear, and other animals are migrating farther and farther north because of the heat in the south. Other animals and birds, traditionally unknown to the Ojibwe, are migrating up from the hotter south. Increased temperatures also mean increased insects and diseases for some game animals like deer and moose. The temperature of the sky is heating up and changing the behavior, habitats, and health of land and water creatures. Mishipizhu has traditionally controlled the well-being of natural resources, especially fish and those others living in and around the waters.

In Ojibwe hydromythology, Mishipizhu has always been an enemy of the Thunder Beings. Today they are being aggravated and multiplied by what we call climate change. "His one enemy was the *Animikeeg* (the Thunderers); only those humans who dreamed of a Thunderer as a personal manido were empowered to survive Micipijiu's attacks when crossing a body of water."[42] Encoded within Ojibwe oral literature about Mishipizhu and *Animikeeg* are subtle and complex teachings about this important ecological association between water processes and sky dynamics, the very matrix that constitutes the "climate."

MISHIPIZHU THE VICTIM

This mythical creature may be a critical and endangered species of the Anishinaabeg imagination. This viewpoint sees Mishipizhu as a victim of colonization and its ensuing "monocultures of the mind"[43] and the destruction of sacred waterways. Mishipizhu, as an icon of a precolonial Ojibwe worldview and way of life, has been slowly erased and marginalized by cognitive imperialism and Western industrial thinking—the same thinking, I assert, that has caused our climate/ecological crisis. Mishipizhu is an indicator of Anishinaabeg traditional ecological knowledge, and as these Native ways of knowing have eroded with the "success" of Western assimilation, Mishipizhu has become a victim in the etymological sense of the word (from the Latin, "a living creature killed and offered as a sacrifice)."[44] The word "victim" was apparently first used in the 1650s, and then later described in 1718 as "a person oppressed by some power or situation." In this scenario, Mishipizhu is certainly a victim of the juggernaut of Western colonization. He is another creature on the list of endangered native species, a mythical creature vital to Anishinaabeg resilience and cognitive diversity generally.

This perspective is part of the growing genre of extinction narratives first romanticized with the "vanishing Indian" motif of the nineteenth century, and in vogue today due to growing ecological instability and a very real species extinction crisis. This crisis includes *Homo sapiens*, as some major scientists, such as paleoanthropologist Richard Leakey, currently place humans on this endangered species list.[45] Journalist, author, and lawyer Claire Hope Cummings shares: "You could fill a small library with works on climate change, oil spills, and species extinction. Now, get ready to fill a shelf or two with recent books and papers on why we neglect these crucial issues."[46] Accelerating rates of extinction for species, languages, and cultures are astonishing. Many species populations, the indicators of biological diversity, are a fraction of what they once were, even fifty years ago. For example, 97 percent of the old-growth coastal redwood trees have been cut down. One quarter of all mammal species face extinction in the next thirty years.[47] This list goes on and on. Despite efforts by many biologists, scientists, and ecologists to stop this extinction crisis, things keep getting worse. And there is an equally, if not more devastating crisis taking place with cultural diversity.

Ethnocide and genocide have always been a part of imperialism, colonialism, and political hegemony. Today it is still an "unintended consequence" of seemingly benign "economic development," such as soybean production in Brazil, energy exploration in Canada, or water privatization in Minnesota. So even though blatant colonialism has been minimized in North America, it still ravages many parts of the world. In North America we have more insidious and "normalized" forms of neocolonialism that affect Native American tribes and communities—economic globalization, stereotypes in the media, discrimination in education and healthcare, over-incarceration, and a host of other impacts and micro-aggressions that demonstrate ongoing racism toward, and erasure of, Native American diversity.

Colonial and neocolonial practices severely impact Native American lifeways. From the loss of ancestral lands, traditional foods, and Native languages and ceremonial rituals, many precolonial teachings have been erased. Many Native elders have said, "The health of a language indicates the health of the community."[48] According to the National Geographic Society's Enduring Voices Program, "every 14 days a language dies. By 2100, more than half of the more than 7,000 languages spoken on earth—many of them not yet recorded—may disappear, taking with them a wealth of knowledge about history, culture, the natural environment, and the human brain."[49] Language endangerment is a very real and serious problem and represents a loss of cognitive diversity and epistemological pluralism. At a federal hearing in 1992, linguist Michael Krauss supported the passing of the Native American Languages Act:

> At the rate things are going, of the present 155 languages (in the US), by the year 2000, 45 will be gone; by 2025, 60 more will be gone; and by 2050, 30 more—135 of 155 languages extinct. And will the remaining 20 too be on the road to extinction?[50]

Within this dystopian, apocalyptic extinction narrative (but, perhaps, realistic worldview), Mishipizhu will not survive climate change in the next twenty years. He is currently on the critical list of endangered species of the ethnosphere, that realm that some radical anthropologist like National Geographic explorer-in-residence Wade Davis describes as "the sum total of all thoughts and dreams, myths, ideas, inspirations, intuitions brought into being by the human imagination since the dawn of consciousness. The ethnosphere is humanity's great legacy. It's a symbol of all we are and all we can be as an astonishingly inquisitive species."[51]

What will be lost for the Anishinaabeg if the Mishipizhu hydromyth goes extinct and he no longer resides in the habitat of Ojibwe imagination? For what will he be sacrificed?

Some say that the Ojibwe and other Native peoples have gained from the benefits of Western modernism. This is certainly but partially true. I assert that one of the most pernicious guises of neocolonialism is the collective assumption that Western industrialism and economic globalization are "good for everyone." These capitalistic activities have given some Native Americans lower and middle-class jobs and, for some tribes, created successful businesses like Indian casinos and resorts, but they have also destroyed ancestral lands, poisoned sacred waters, increased health problems such as diabetes and cancer, and eliminated Native languages, thoughts, and practices. In this scenario, the Mishipizhu hydromyth is another victim of Western imperialism, a casualty of colonial success whose demise is a step toward a more monocultural and hegemonic world.

MISHIPIZHU THE REGENERATOR

The opposite position claims that Mishipizhu is actually one of the *causes* of climate change. According to many Indigenous teachings, when important manitous are not respected and properly treated, they will either go away or cause harm. Because of Mishipizhu's enormous power as a shape-shifting underwater lynx, he is creating water chaos for us two-legged humans (and unfortunately other creatures) because humans have forgotten how to revere and pay tribute to him. Floods, drownings, diseases, droughts—lack of fish, rice, water, medicine—these are all unintended negative consequences of humans' disrespect and desecration of Native waters and the unseen manitous that reside in them. Mishipizhu reminds us that there are real consequences to lack of respect for unseen powers and forgetting ancestral stories.

As has been prophesied in many stories, and witnessed and recorded by many Native groups over centuries and even millennia, when the ecological world gets significantly out of balance, major shifts occur.[52] Although often seen by humans as "disasters," these changes are ultimately healthy shifts to cleanse and renew ecosystems. Fire, for example, when not too intense, "cleans" the land of dead wood, debris, diseases, and increases soil fertility and seed germination. Climate change is, perhaps, simply part of a larger cycle of planetary change and eco-mythic regeneration. Here Mishipizhu is not a victim, but a creative destroyer and regenerator. He reminds us that we must acknowledge and revere *real* power, the power of the more-than-human world, which some people, like Ojibwe leader Winona LaDuke and Haudenosaunee chief Oren Lyons, refer to as natural law (as opposed to human law). This means paying tribute to the unseen manitous that dwell within Nature, including us. Anishinaabeg do this by feeding the unknowable but tangible realms of power between humans and other-than-human; between water and sky; between place and memory; between imagination and health. Ojibwe hydromyths embody these realms of meaning and provide instruction for how to respect these other-than-human powers. Out of our respect for these manitous, we express our gratitude for the gifts of life, and "feed" the lands and waters we live on with offerings. We praise fish with song, offer tobacco to river rapids, leave herbs at rock outcroppings, and share prayers in maple forests. But somewhere along the journey of assimilation, many of us stopped feeding the land and water. The other-than-human manitous, including Mishipizhu, have been neglected, ignored, and, some may say, abused. Mishipizhu's habitats have been poisoned, dammed, drained, and flooded with sewage. Many waterways are stagnant and need purging, cleansing, and regeneration. Consequently, Mishipizhu (in response to humans' destructive behavior) is creating climate disruption to renew the ecologies of Ojibwe homelands. He is taunting and agitating the Thunder Beings, so storms and rain come too soon, too much, or not at all. He is traveling through his underground waterways to evaporate fertile wet-lands, stunt vital medicines, and freeze wild-rice lakes. With his long copper tail, he is whipping up and disturbing the layers between earth and sky to disturb climatic patterns. This seemingly destructive behavior illustrates the ambivalent power of Mishipizhu, and places emphasis on what may appear to us as illogical and unnecessary cycles of eco-mythic regeneration.

CONCLUSION

At the beginning of this essay, I asked a question about Mishipizhu to learn more about his power as an entity and metaphor, and explore his relation-ship to the climate crisis. There is no clear or simple answer to my question "Will Mishipizhu survive climate change, or is he creating it?" Binary think-ing says we have two answers: (a) Mishipizhu will not survive, but some humans will (maybe for a while); and (b) Mishipizhu *will* survive because he is creating this climate chaos, but we won't. Can we entertain both pos-sibilities simultaneously and find, according to Trickster logic, a third or fourth option? This essay uses a koan-like question to examine the value of metaphor in Indigenous ways of knowing and relating to the other-than-human world. It points to the rich cognitive and imaginative realities of Anishinaabeg hydromythology, and how the continuation of these stories not only maintains Ojibwe identity and worldview but also may provide critical epistemological clues for how to creatively respond to the climate crisis affecting lands, waters, and peoples globally.

After reviewing these opposing possibilities, I wonder if there is a middle ground or another answer entirely, or perhaps there is a better question.

Why not just ask Mishipizhu himself and listen: "How shall we relate to water to protect and nurture it for future generations?" What would he say? What would I hear? When the Treuer brothers were asked on a National Public Radio program why Native Americans are losing their languages, they responded, "We are not losing our language, our language is losing us." Likewise, perhaps we are not losing Mishipizhu, he is losing us. It is our human responsibility, indeed perhaps one even vital to our cultural continuance, to keep these Ojibwe hydromyths and other narratives of moral ecologies alive. They remind us that "as Native people, we have known that to survive we had to create, re-create, produce, re-produce. In order to live we have to make our own mirrors."[53] We have the mirror of the other-than-human world that gives us beauty and humility; the mirror of our ancestral narratives that give us strength and longevity; the mirror of our imaginations that give us creative joy and cognitive agility. These mirrors nurture the place of story between humans and other-than-humans. They also, in some kaleidoscopic way, reflect the mirroring of the Water and Sky, Earth and Air, where climate roils and Mishipizhu travels. Today we are in dire need of good medicine stories, new myths of resilience for these unprecedented times. And now you've heard about Mishipizhu. He is just one example of the storied world of the Anishinaabeg. These stories illustrate the profound ecological ethics and values embedded in these narratives. They demonstrate their ability to increase humans' cognitive adaptability and to stretch our imaginative capacities so that we can generate new ways of thinking and being in the world.

NOTES

1. The Anishinaabeg nation is one of the largest in North America. We are part of the larger Algonquian language group. As dozens of independent but interrelated tribes on reservations and reserves, we cover five U.S. states and four Canadian provinces in the northeastern Great Lakes region. We are called by many different names: Anishinaabe is our traditional name for ourselves, and the "g" or "k" ending indicates plural. We are also known as the Ojibwe and Chippewa, also with alternative ending spellings. Sometimes we are also referred to as Salteaux and Soto in Canada.

2. See Basil Johnston, *The Manitous: The Spiritual World of the Ojibway* (St. Paul: Minnesota Historical Society Press, 2001), 2.

3. Johnston, *The Manitous*, 2.

4. Victoria Brehm, "Metamorphoses of an Ojibwa Manido," *American Litera-ture* 68, no. 4 (1996): 683–84.

5. See Kimberly Blaeser's *Gerald Vizenor: Writing in the Oral Tradition* (Nor-man: University of Oklahoma Press, 1996), 195; and Elvira Pulitano's *Toward a Native American Critical Theory* (Lincoln: University of Nebraska Press 2009), 164.

6. Richard Stoffle et. al., "Cultural Landscapes and Traditional Cultural Prop-erties: A Southern Paiute View of the Grand Canyon and Colorado River," *American Indian Quarterly* 21, no. 2 (1997): 235.

7. See David Abram, *The Spell of the Sensuous: Perception and Language in a More-Than-Human World* (New York: Pantheon 1996), 175.

8. See the award-winning indigenous film *The Land Has Eyes*, by Rotuman film-maker Vilsoni Hereniko: http://www.thelandhaseyes.org/.

9. Louise Erdrich, *Books and Islands in Ojibwe Country* (Washington, DC: National Geographic, 2003), 2.

10. See Jeannette Armstrong article, "I Stand with You against the Disorder," in *Yes! Magazine* November (2005).

11. Humans are part of nature, yet we often set ourselves apart, as if above, or different. This is a perennial question and philosophical debate that is not the subject of this paper. For more on these postmodern and ecocritical discussions about "the nature of nature," see *Reinventing Nature: Responses to Postmodern Deconstruction*, by Michael Soule and Gary Lease (Washington, DC: Island Press, 1995); *The Ecocriticism Reader*, by Cheryll Glotfelty and Harold Fromm (Athens: University of Georgia Press, 1996); *Sense of Place and Sense of Planet*, by Ursula Heise (New York: Oxford University Press, 2008). It is important to note that in this essay I am differentiating humans from nature by using the terms "other-than-human" and "more-than-human" discussed below.

12. A. Irving Hallowell coined this term in his landmark piece "Ojibwa Ontol-ogy, Behavior, and World View in *Culture in History: Essays in Honor of Paul Radin* (New York: Octagon Books, 1981), 17, to provide a more nuanced understanding of Ojibwe philosophy and epistemology, and to get away from the overused Western categories of "spirit" and "supernatural." As Graham Harvey has written, "Hallowell's coining of the term 'other-than-human persons' has not only been central to both previous points (worldviews and knowledges) but also enriched discussion of indigenous environmentalism, and notions of respect, sacrality, and power," in *Animism: Respecting the Living World* (New York: Columbia University Press 2006, 17).

13. See title of David Abram's book *The Spell of the Sensuous: Perception and Lan-guage in a More-Than-Human World* (New York: Pantheon, 1996).

14. The term was coined by environmental educator David Orr and physicist Fritjof Capra in the early 1990s. See David Orr's *Ecological Literacy: Education and the Transition to a Postmodern World* (Albany: SUNY Press, 1992).

15. Gary Paul Nabhan and Sarah St. Antoine, "The Loss of Flora and Fauna Story: The Extinction of Experience," in *The Biophilia Hypothesis*, ed. Kellert and Wilson (Washington, DC: Island Press, 1993).

16. Corbin Harney, *The Nature Way* (Reno: University of Nevada Press, 2009).

17. The great Anishinaabeg Nation covers five states in the United States and three provinces in Canada. They are known as Ojibwe/Ojibway in Canada and Chippewa in the U.S. They are one of the largest tribes in North America.

18. See Benton-Banai, *The Mishomis Book: The Voice of the Ojibway* (Minneapolis: University of Minnesota Press 1988), 94; and Thomas Peacock and Marlene Wisuri's *Ojibwe Waasa Inaabidaa: We Look in All Directions* (Minneapolis: Minnesota Historical Society, 2010), 25–27.

19. "Where the food grows on the water" is a common and important phrase for the Ojibwe, because, according to oral migration stories, it is what was told to the Ojibwe over a thousand years ago by a prophet who instructed our ancestors to leave the East Coast and migrate west because danger was coming from the east. See Winona LaDuke "Protecting the Culture and Genetics of Wild Rice," in Melissa Nelson's *Original Instructions—Indigenous Teachings for a Sustainable Future* (Rochester, VT: Bear & Company 2008), 207.

20. Thomas Vennum Jr., "The Ojibwa Dance Drum: Its History and Construction," *Smithsonian Folklife Studies*, no. 2 (1982): 41.

21. Ibid.

22. Enrique Salmon, *Eating the Landscape: American Indian Stories of Food, Identity, and Resilience* (Tucson: University of Arizona Press, 2012), 52.

23. "Letter Men: Brothers Fight for Ojibwe Language," National Public Radio *Fresh Air* program, April 22, 2008.

24. See D. B. Vitaliano's "Geomythology," *Journal of the Folklore Institute* 5, no. 1 (June 1968): 11; and Vine Deloria Jr.'s "Geomythology and the Indian Traditions," in *Red Earth, White Lies: The Myth of Scientific Fact* (Golden, CO: Fulcrum, 1997), 161.

25. This term was used by early Ojibwe writer George Copway (Kah-ge-ga-gah-bowh) in his 1850 classic book *The Traditional History and Characteristic Sketches of the Ojibway Nation* (Boston: Sanborn, Carter, Bazin & Co., 1887). The term "narrative history" was used by Ojibwe writer Gerald Vizenor in his *People Named the Chippewa: Narrative Histories* (Minneapolis: Minnesota University Press, 1984). The term "traditional history" is also used today by many anthropologists and archaeologists, such as Linda Cordell, School

for Advanced Research, Santa Fe, New Mexico; personal communication, October 30, 2010.

26. Gerald Vizenor in *Summer in the Spring: Anishinaabe Lyric Poems and Stories* (Norman: University of Oklahoma Press, 1993).

27. Ibid.

28. Erdrich, *Books and Islands in Ojibwe Country*, 10.

29. "Mythic Creatures: Dragons, Unicorns & Mermaids" exhibit, American Museum of Natural History, New York, May 2007–January 2008.

30. See Alanson Skinner's "The Mascoutens or Prairie Potawatomi Indians: Part I, Social Life and Ceremonies," *Bulletin*, Public Museum of the City of Milwaukee 6, no. 1 (1923): 1–262; James H. Howard's "When They Worship the Underwater Panther: A Prairie Potawatomi Bundle Ceremony," *Southwestern Journal of Anthropology* 16, no. 2 (Summer 1960).

31. James Howard, "When They Worship the Underwater Panther: A Prairie Potawatomi Bundle Ceremony," *Southwestern Journal of Anthropology* 16, no. 2 (Summer 1960): 217–24.

32. Serpent iconography is common among native groups in South, Central, and North America. But the plumed serpent of Meso-America appears to be quite distinct from the horned serpent of North America; see "Feathered, Horned, and Antlered Serpents: Mesoamerican Connections with the Southwest and Southeast," by Charles R. Cobb, Jeffrey Maymon, and Randall McGuire, in *Great Towns and Regional Polities in the Prehistoric American Southwest and Southeast*, ed. Jill Neitzel (Albuquerque: University of New Mexico Press, 1999), 177.

33. See note 35.

34. Louise Erdrich, *Tracks* (New York: Harper Collins, 1988), 11.

35. Amy Dahlstrom, "Warrior Powers from an Underwater Spirit: Cultural and Linguistic Aspects of an Illustrated Meskwaki Text," *Anthropological Linguistics* 45, no. 1 (Summer 2003): 2.

36. James H. Howard, "When They Worship the Underwater Panther: A Prairie Potawatomi Bundle Ceremony," *Southwestern Journal of Anthropology* 16, no. 2 (1960): 218.

37. See John A. Grim, *The Shamans: Patterns of Siberian and Ojibway Healing* (Norman: University of Oklahoma, 1983), 77–78.

38. See Johann Georg Kohl, *Kitchi-Gami: Life among the Lake Superior Ojibway* (1860; Minneapolis: Minnesota Historical Society Press, 1985), 424.

39. Ibid.

40. See "Cosmic Evolution" timeline and educational materials from the Wright Center for Science Education, Tufts University, http://www.tufts.edu/as/wright_center/cosmic_evolution/docs/splash.html.

41. According to many native traditions, including the Ojibwe, it is the Thunder Beings with their large wings, piercing eyes, and large beaks who create storms, thunder and lightning, and other major sky and climatic events.

42. See Victoria Brehm's "The Metamorpheses of an Ojibwa Manido," *American Literature* 68, no. 4 (1996): 680.

43. From Vandana Shiva's *Monocultures of the Mind: Perspectives on Biodiversity and Biotechnology* (London: Zed Books, 1993).

44. According to the *Online Etymology Dictionary*, http://www.etymonline.com/.

45. See Leakey interview in award-winning documentary feature film *Call of Life* (2010).

46. Claire Hope Cummings, The Whether Report, http://www.clairehope cummings.com/journalism.html.

47. According to United Nations, http://news.bbc.co.uk/.

48. From Dakota activist Germaine Tremmell, personal communication, 2006.

49. From http://travel.nationalgeographic.com/travel/enduring-voices/.

50. In Leanne Hinton and Kenneth Hale's *The Green Book of Language Revitalization in Practice* (San Diego and New York: Academic Press, 2001), 47.

51. "Wade Davis on Endangered Cultures," TED Talk 2003, http://www.ted.com/talks/wade_davis_on_endangered_cultures.html.

52. Native prophecies like those shared by the Hopi at the United Nations.

53. Marcie Rendon in *Nitaawichige: Selected Poetry and Prose by Four Anishinaabe Writers* (Duluth, MN: Poetry Harbor, 2002).

Eko-naanan Bagijigan

Stories as Resistance

ANISHINAABEG STORIES ARE A FORM OF RESISTANCE. AS STORIES illustrate worldview and guide how we interact with our world, Anishinaabe stories resist narratives of domination and subjugation that subsume Indigenous communities by providing an alternate way of understanding the world and relationships within Creation. At the same time, stories are not solely reactive creations, but expressions in the interest of the continuation and innovation of cultural and political traditions. They are acts of survival, innovation, and growth.

Kimberly Blaeser, in her essay "Wild Rice Rights: Gerald Vizenor and an Affiliation of Story," illuminates how Gerald Vizenor's use of story strategically resists historical and ongoing legal and colonial impositions. She outlines how we survive by stories, reminding us that children in Anishinaabeg tradition are not taught, they are storied. Stories are empowering methods of change and endurance, innovating our cultural and political lives as Anishinaabeg and human beings. Citing Vizenor's strategic and engaging style, Blaeser shows how stories construct an understanding of historical events as accounts of survivance and acts of resistance.

Heidi Kiiwetinepinesiik Stark proposes that resistance can occur when stories encounter stories. In her essay "Transforming the Trickster: Federal Indian Law Encounters Anishinaabe Diplomacy," Stark reminds us that stories have the power to heal and the power to destroy. She asserts that federal Indian law—which, she argues, is made up of creation stories of the nation-state—has transformed the trust relationship between Indigenous nations and the United States in dangerous ways that attempt to reduce Indigenous sovereignty. Yet, Stark posits that stories of Anishinaabe diplomacy may reveal an alternate way of being, one that resists the subordination of Indigenous peoples within state models.

With Anishinaabeg elder and storyteller Edna Manitowabi, Leanne Simpson's essay "Theorizing Resurgence from within Nishnaabeg Thought" demonstrates how Anishinaabeg stories resist containment and inspire individuals to think in culturally rich and diverse ways. Simpson and Manitowabi demonstrate how stories can serve to center the field in more favorable ways than postcolonial or critical theories that—while successful at revealing and interrogating colonialism—have failed to resonate with Indigenous peoples invested in revitalization and resurgence. They argue that stories can map a way out of and dismantle colonialism while also building "a renaissance of *mino-bimaadiziwin*." Like Blaeser and Stark, Manitowabi and Simpson remind us that we have the intellectual tools for resistance and rebuilding our communities and lives within stories.

Wild Rice Rights

Gerald Vizenor and an Affiliation of Story

KIMBERLY BLAESER

The tribal past lived as an event in visual memories and oratorical gestures;
woodland identities turned on dreams and visions.

—GERALD VIZENOR, *THE PEOPLE NAMED THE CHIPPEWA*

So once again a story sets out among us. You will see the story and where
it came from this time, but at other times the story comes from another
direction, waking all those who sleep in its narrative.

—GORDON HENRY, *THE LIGHT PEOPLE*

RICE RELATIVES

THE LIBRARY WHERE I WRITE THIS IS ROUGHLY 460 MILES AWAY FROM the reservation where I grew up—White Earth. My hometown in northern Minnesota today has a population of 1,161—down more than 250 people since I last lived there full-time. But for a weekend every fall, the three-block Main Street fills as the locals, plus farmers and residents of the lake regions and other small villages, gather to celebrate Wild Rice Days. The annual festival gets its name from the city's own—Mahnomen. In Anishinaabemowin, *mahnomen* or *manoomin* (as it is spelled in the current popular orthography) means wild rice. Many of the tribal people in the area, including my relatives

237

who live in and around White Earth, harvest wild rice each fall. For some, the rice crop still provides a significant part of their yearly income. In a region where the median household income is $32,725—roughly $23,000 less than the median household income for the state—the money provides a small bonus.

But if the significance of ricing centered solely around economics, I wouldn't be remembering and writing about it today. Like many of the seasonal activities of Anishinaabeg people, ricing forges relatedness—to family, to place, to tradition. We somehow claim and re-create these many layers of relatedness in our simple story acts:

My uncle Bill came visiting.
Sitting there by the fridge
three weeks ago in November.
Mother hunched on the company chair,
Muff by the toaster, Daddy in the middle,
and me perched on the stool.
Muff brought me a war club.
We passed it by the diamond willow handle
admiring it and making jokes.

Then Bill was talking ricing.
Naming his poling partner,
the lakes and rivers they paddled,
telling how long they stayed out,
how many pounds they harvested,
where they slept each night.
All those details
the husk around a kernel.
Do you ever just ache
for something
a sliver of beauty
so tightly encased?
Dance dance the rice.

They had to come home early
he said
their car so small
no room for another day
another canoe bottom full

they had to come home
while still he longed to go out.
Bend and pound the rice

Eighty-three this year,
he won't sell the rice.
Next season
he might not be able to go.
And him with so many
to support.
All us rice relatives.
Could he list us
like dependents
on his income tax?
Never once made enough
he laughs
to pay taxes.
Manoominike-giizis, ricing moon.

He ended the rice talk then
telling about a certain place
pretty place down by Mille Lacs.
It got dark early that day.
They had to turn back at the narrows
never got to rice the beds
beds they knew were just there
through the narrows
just there on the next lake.
"If I feel like I do now," he said,
"I'll go again."
Winnow with your every breath.[1]

The rice from that season is long used up, but the harvest of that telling feeds me still.

When I paddle the small rice beds near our family cabin on Farm Lake in the Boundary Waters Canoe Area Wilderness, the funnel of my strokes transport me. I think then of the relatives who over many generations, and on a host of Minnesota's lakes, swished through the wild oats. Their paddling and rhythmic pounding also loosened seeds upon the water. My ancestors, those scattered seed remnants—both forebears of these rice stalks.

I picture the old-time birch-bark canoes. These, too, have parted time as mine does. Now the slice of my paddle wells with a history that belies any Western telling. Like rice, story reseeds itself.

In my own experience, tribal telling involves a web of connectedness and a continuance. I claim a storied landscape. I say Indian people do not so much teach, but rather *story* their children. I include in my understanding the mythic, ceremonial, and casual stories, for these seldom if ever remain separate from one another. The range and reach of these vested words sustain us in vision.

Bill's everyday rice talk arose in a particular context. A particular tribal, political, and historical milieu. A context of family, community, and landscape. The Treaty of 1867. White Earth Reservation. Mississippi Band Bunkers and Antells. Naytahwaush and Twin Lakes. Rolling hills, hardwood forests, spring-fed lakes, white clay. Poverty and subsistence. This "placement" of his stories presupposes an understanding of much that remains unspoken. Yet the story "carries" this knowledge and builds upon it. Just as a fall breeze might sway the rice stalks, a telling wind blows through this spoken *Manidoo-noodin*. My Uncle Bill's story lists in time, leaning back in its telling to encompass his long history on the lakes, his parents' and grandparents' rice teachings, the longstanding tradition of harvest. Likewise it extends itself toward the seasons to come, the rice on the next bed, the next year, the poling partners *he* teaches, the ritual, the many-faceted harvest that includes us through his spoken images. My own retelling in the excerpt from "Passing Time" also gestures beyond itself. It consciously carries my uncle's story, and the larger tribal and historical context within this new poetic account. The speaker implicitly claims a connection, "affiliates" her/himself with that other storytelling moment. Thus in each telling, the confines of the temporal begin to dissolve.

Likewise, "story acts" can work to breach other barriers of perception. The rice relatives claimed in Bill's stories, for example, include not only his human "blood" family, but the rivers and lakes to which he travels, even the plants themselves. They embody a tribal idea of interrelatedness. The reach of ritual is also expanded as this account of harvest invests itself in the mundane details of the process—place names, paddling, poling, pounding—showing attentiveness as an end in itself. The palpable sustenance Bill draws from the act of ricing underscores a second "sustainable product." His story then gestures towards transformation, or moments of spiritual teachings.

As Native people, we often partake in a complex cycle of belonging in which the aesthetic sensibility—here, our awareness of ancestral acts, natural beauty, or the spirit of place—and the path to survival have been conjoined. The ceremonial and practical respect we pay to the land source also guarantees the continuance of community and the stability of food products. *We always leave a little behind.* Rice. Berries. Fish. Certain customs limit harvest or accomplish renewal. Seasonal practices like ricing become ritualized in song, story, or pattern. *Leave some for the animals. For the manidoog and little people.* These practices are then sustained or prescribed through the communal history of repetition. Many families still "plant" rice for later generations, deliberately reseeding the beds. Each generation takes up tasks tightly entwined with beliefs. The reciprocity involved in seasonal rituals is woven by the similar reciprocity of story. Just as our bodily labor is rewarded with physical and spiritual sustenance, our telling or retelling of story teaches appropriate process, enriches our experiences, and builds communal connections. When we ritualize appropriate action, we ritualize tribal continuance. When we invoke teachings and tell ourselves into communities, we build a genealogy of story.

STORIES OF SURVIVANCE

Perhaps no contemporary Anishinaabe writer so emphatically builds his vast and varied collection of publications around a central genealogy of story than does Gerald Vizenor, whose linked stories move across the genres and eras of his work. One particular serial retelling involves the wild-rice harvesting rights of the Minnesota Ojibwe peoples. Like my own story harvest, Vizenor's gathering of rice accounts incorporates several generations as he traces the connections between older stories, contemporary circumstances, and his own understanding of story. His affiliation with the story of Anishinaabe elder Charles Aubid becomes a means for further developing his sophisticated theoretical stance on *survivance*—the neologistic marriage between survival and resistance.[2]

Vizenor's biography itself offers a series of survivance stories. Vizenor first had to survive a childhood of foster homes, poverty, and loneliness, and then to resist the pull of truancy and delinquent acts. Yet something in his tribal inheritance coupled with this troubled background prepared him to lead a literal and linguistic resistance against the racism inherent in contemporary American society, and to center his work around liberation for Native peoples. Labeled "a trickster, contrary, muckraking political journalist and activist, poet, essayist, novelist, and teacher" by Choctaw scholar and writer Louis Owens, today Vizenor is recognized internationally as a writer and Native intellectual.[3] But in his years of emergence onto the literary scene, Vizenor's reputation in the Twin Cities region of Minnesota rested largely on his stature as a prickly activist, a thorn under the skin of the smooth machine of Minnesota politics, both tribal and mainstream. The long hours of his labor were given to community programs, then to local organizing. Vizenor's entrance into the literary scene came through the urgent need he felt to effect change; many of his early writings were political and social critiques of the status quo, indictments of individuals, institutions, and government policies. These various topical pieces Vizenor published as a freelance writer and then as a columnist for the *Minneapolis Tribune*. Throughout these early years, and even as he moved on in his literary career to collect these pieces in *Tribal Scenes and Ceremonies* and to release the books *The Everlasting Sky*, *Wordarrows*, and *Earthdivers*, Vizenor's work retained a balance between his theoretical or social analysis and the vested lives of the Anishinaabeg people. The stories of individuals, those he called the "*oshki anishinaabe*, the new people of the woodland"—Ted Mahto, John Buckanaga, Will Antell, Bonnie Wallace, Paulette Fairbanks, Michael Dane White, Clement Hudon Beaulieu, and a host of others—became the catalyst for his commentary on conditions and his various calls for change.[4] The early articles, editorials, profiles, and literary journalism display the grass-roots dedication of Gerald Vizenor to teach for change—for the small change or pittance that was paid in those days to journalists and in the interests of social change, with the motive to alter both ideas and conditions.

If we look at the rhetorical dynamics Vizenor displayed during his early work as a community activist and journalist, and trace the gradual transformation in his career and his writing as he moved into the college classroom and then onto the national and international scene, we find important continuities with these maiden writings and activities in the work that he continues to do in both his creative publications and his critical essays. Of particular interest is Vizenor's developing metalanguage and the linked stories (what I will call story affiliations) that inform his work throughout his career. From haiku to editorials, drama to novels—throughout his many literary transformations, Gerald Vizenor has retained the aura of a trickster teacher. A pause at the "traces" reveals the *agwaatese* or shadow presences of stories that have informed his survivance stance from the 1960s *Twin Citian* pieces through the 1998 *Fugitive Poses* and beyond. The story of the first White Earth newspaper, *The Progress*; the background and trial of convicted murderer James Thomas White Hawk; the unsolved murder of Vizenor's young father—these and other symbolic journalistic accounts recur or become recast in works of poetry, autobiography, and fiction over the years. Through the serial retellings, Vizenor works to construct an understanding of these historical events as tales of survival and acts of resistance. The storied remembrances become an important part of contemporary survivance.

My particular focus in this discussion is a 1968 column in the *Minneapolis Tribune*. The piece I've alluded to as the "wild rice rights" account continues to fuel retellings by Vizenor and illustrates the multiple and complex reincarnations of stories in his work. The original article, by then reporter Gerald Vizenor, was entitled "Ojibways Seek Right to 'Regulate' Rice on Wildlife Refuge" and first appeared on September 13, 1968. Thirty years later, in the 1998 *Fugitive Poses*, Vizenor was still working to develop the significance of the incident. Indeed, both pieces are themselves filled with imaginative depictions of individuals who purposefully invoke past figures and incidents in this clearly intergenerational drama. As we examine the survival of these linked stories in multiple retellings, we can trace the way Vizenor uses story to build a strategic resistance to historical and ongoing legal and colonial impositions. He employs stories of and for survivance. In reading Vizenor's work, we can clearly see the way he positions both storytelling and writing as political acts.

Over the years, his creative work has given voice to various beliefs about the nature and purpose of storytelling. He has also characterized his understanding of the function of the essay. A look at this combined theoretical framework proves helpful in understanding the strategic scaffolding Vizenor undertakes in the wild rice account(s). In one of his earliest publications, *Anishinabe Adisokan* from 1970, in which he collects comments on customs as well as mythic accounts, Vizenor works to distinguish Anishinaabeg story from what he presumes to be an ingrained Western aesthetic of storytelling. Note how these early comments write themselves against his idea of the already understood definitions of story, beginning as it does with a rejection of another understanding: "The tales of the *anishinaabe*," he writes, "*are not* an objective collection and interpretation of *facts*. Stories are a circle of dreams and oratorical gestures showing the meaning between the present and the past in the life of tribal people of the woodland" (my emphasis).[5] In a 2010 issue of the *Oskaabewis Native Journal* in which Red Lake Reservation elder and ceremonial leader Anna Gibbs shares stories and thoughts on Ojibwe life, her characterization of legend as "stories . . . [that] take you to a make-believe world where memories are shared" has important continuities with Vizenor's description of story. Both privilege the imaginative over the factual, but also suggest that traditional stories carry "meaning" or "truth." Gibbs, for example, notes, "They [legends] aren't supposed to be real, but sometimes they are a bridge to the truth."[6] Gibbs and Vizenor also both emphasize the connection stories forge with traditions or tribal past. Given Vizenor's foundational understanding of stories as a circle linking past and present, the implications in his telling (and interpretative "reading") of the Aubid wild-rice incident emerge clearly.

In addition to these relatively accessible statements on story, Vizenor has also developed more sophisticated theoretical language to explain his understanding of the way storytelling works in tribal societies. (We might characterize this as the political implications of story.) Most significant to this discussion is Vizenor's specialized use of the term "transmotion."[7] In the introduction to *Fugitive Poses*, where he talks about the new vocabulary of the volume, he explains, "Transmotion, that sense of native motion and an active presence, is *sui generis* sovereignty."[8] Ultimately, Vizenor builds a sense of transmotion as embodying tribal sovereignty through the imaginative and visionary links of story, tribal memory, and environmental knowledge. Specifically, he claims that "transmotion is motion and native memories," "performative transmotion is an ethical presence of nature, native stories, and natural reason," and "Native transmotion is an original natural union in the stories of emergence and migration that relate humans to an environment and to the spiritual and political significance of animals and other creations." Through transmotion, story can "reach," Vizenor claims, "to other contexts of action, resistance, dissent, and political controversy."[9]

Vizenor's own writing models these and other goals of tribal story. As author/storyteller, he often not only relates the story, but gestures towards an understanding of the medium, or suggests something about the proper use of the account. In the Vizenor canon, story and theory on story have long been interwoven. His narrators and fictional personae, for example, frequently dramatize the power of story. In the novel *Dead Voices*, we meet "the healers" who "touched an inner sound in their stories," and we learn of "stories that liberated shadows and the mind."[10] In his bicentennial novel *Heirs of Columbus*, Vizenor writes of "story energy" and "stories and humor" that become "the energy that heals."[11] His accounts of his personal experiences also comment on story. In *Wordarrows*, for example, he describes an encounter with an "old tribal woman in a vomit-stained shirt . . . telling stories in good time."[12] This incident he describes as "profound . . . one thing I have never gotten over."[13] Indeed, Vizenor's acknowledgment of the active power of ongoing story, even a sense of sovereignty in the transmotion of story, permeates his work. He writes stories about stories he has heard, about stories being told or retold, and about the function of storytelling in survival. In his canon of writings, stories are definitely not "dead voices." "The stories of survivance," he writes, "are an active presence."[14]

Various Native peoples see stories as dialogic agents of change. They may be used, for example, to teach proper behavior, or as a part of healing ceremonies. In this understanding of story, the listener/reader plays a significant role in the creative reality of story. As Simon Ortiz claims, "A story is not only told but is also listened to; it becomes whole in its expression and perception."[15] Vizenor, who resolutely resists stasis in general and the "static" definition of "Indian" in particular, aligns himself with this conception of *storying*. His playful characterization of the Anishinaabeg cultural hero, the trickster Naanabozho, as "a warrior on a coin that never lands twice on the same side" aptly demonstrates the vitality he attributes to Anishinaabeg story.[16] Also, like Leslie Silko, N. Scott Momaday, Tom King, Gordon Henry, and many other Indigenous writers, Vizenor understands literature and stories as involving both acts of connection and key acts of transformation.[17] From Proude Cedarfair in *Bearheart* to the urban Bagese in *Dead Voices*, Vizenor's Native characters are engaged in adaptation and change while still maintaining traditional perspectives. The acts of connection characteristic in Vizenor's writing may involve inheritance or forged cultural relationships— what Edward Said understood as "filiation" and "affiliation."[18] Story then becomes an important tool of, and conduit for, these "filial" connections as the contemporary teller "affiliates" with older tellers or stories and transforms these stories by applying them in new circumstances, or using them to carry knowledge, challenge conditions, or incite change.

Vizenor often uses mythic and contemporary story simultaneously or commingles the two, sometimes embedding the imaginative story in a nonfictional context (sometimes in a theoretical context, as I previously noted). Given this weaving of story and theory, the comments Vizenor makes on the essay and its relationship to liberation can inform our exploration of the blended genres and intentions of Vizenor's own critical writing. In a series of claims in *Fugitive Poses*, he characterizes the essay, saying: "The essay is resistance." "The essay is contention." "The essay is venture." "The essay is contingency."[19] Ultimately, he speaks of "the native essay" in particular, describing it as "a trace of survivance and sovereignty,"[20] once more linking the power and the practical or political usefulness of the literary. Hence, we find ourselves arriving again at an understanding of literature and stories as involving both acts of connection and acts of transformation.

A LITERARY SEVEN GENERATIONS

We see these theoretical stances embodied clearly in the aforementioned wild-rice pieces. Vizenor's return to the wild-rice regulation controversy thirty years after he wrote the original newspaper account in 1968, and his expansion of that story into the 1998 "Hearsay Sovereignty" in *Fugitive Poses*, evokes a literary seven-generations sensibility and enacts that textual gesture.[21] Vizenor essentially links the several story moments in a literary telescopic ring of relations, which extends and contracts as we view and re-view the relationships, our own vision shifting to discover past, contemporary, and even future significance(s). We can read the 1998 embodiment of these retro-story(ies) as indeed involving the ideas of, gestures toward, or performances of filiation and affiliation—as the awareness of inheritance and the self-conscious extension of our story relationships into and across new circumstances. Here, story indeed becomes resistance.

The original *Minneapolis Tribune* journalistic piece—a two-column, 600-word story—provides background on a debate over the government regulation of the wild-rice harvest on ceded tribal lands, and relates the events that take place in a September hearing at U.S. District Court in Minneapolis under the jurisdiction of Judge Miles Lord. The article sketches the points of debate, identifies the sides involved, provides some necessary history, underscores the significance of the courtroom event, and humanizes the account through descriptions, dialogue, and the inclusion of telling incidents. The focus for this newspaper piece was the concise presentation of vital facts. Even so, many of the details Vizenor selected and the statements he made suggested more than was declared at the time, or advertised their connection with other absent stories. For example, Vizenor mentions the ceding of Indian land in an 1855 treaty and the establishment of the Rice Lake Wildlife Refuge in 1935. The history and impact of these important events, though clearly significant to the present controversy, cannot be told in this limited space. Instead Vizenor's text gestures to the larger historical context, placing his current account within the continuum of intergenerational tribal story.

Vizenor's own storyteller voice and the kind of telling that will later blossom into "narrative history" also surfaces in several places, most clearly perhaps through the characterization of the witness Charles Aubid.[22] To his presentation of Aubid, an eighty-six-year-old Anishinaabe man who testifies partly through an interpreter, Vizenor brings his own awareness of trickster dynamics.[23] He elects to report two exchanges in particular that suggest Aubid's own sense of the comic and the ironic. In the second paragraph, he writes, "Charles Aubid sat in the witness chair and waved at U.S. District Court Judge Miles Lord when the judge attempted to show Aubid how he should raise his right hand when taking the oath." Then, near the end of the article, Vizenor describes a particularly telling moment. After Aubid has testified regarding a statement made years earlier by John Squirrel, in which Squirrel claimed the Anishinaabeg retained the right to regulate the rice harvest, a "hearsay" objection raised by the government attorney prompts this exchange between Judge Lord and Aubid:

> "Squirrel is dead," Lord told Aubid after Falvey objected to the testimony, "and you can't say what a dead man said."
>
> "Why should I believe what a white man says, when they don't believe what Squirrel said," Aubid replied through his interpreters.[24]

Although clearly ripe with political and philosophical implications, this suggestive scene from the courtroom is not developed in the 1968 article. Confined as he is to the journalistic form, Vizenor must content himself in that piece with astute selection and with the suggestive presentation of the rich elements of the drama. Development and interpretation will come later as the academic Vizenor affiliates himself with the story of that political moment in 1968, and with the stories that are themselves linked to Aubid's.

The Aubid incident populated Vizenor's own oral repertoire for years before he again explored it and its many threads of significance in the 1998 *Fugitive Poses* text.[25] Two-thirds of his way through a 200-plus page volume discussing historical, literary, and popular culture misrepresentations of Native peoples and a new understanding of the term "sovereignty," Vizenor turns to the wild-rice regulation controversy from thirty years earlier in a chapter on "Native Transmotion." The three-page account given in that volume is subtitled "Hearsay Sovereignty" and employs Vizenor's new critical metalanguage to address many of the issues unnamed in the early newspaper story. But even as the 1998 account abounds with evidence of alteration—in the telling, in the story connections, in the extrapolation of meanings, in the identified political impetus—it maintains its story af/filiations with the earlier printed version, as well as with the several interrelated oral story moments referenced in the texts.

The opening paragraphs, for example, illustrate both the links to the earlier account and the expansive temporal range of the text:

> Charles Aubid was a sworn witness in federal court that autumn more than thirty years ago; he raised his hand, heard the oath for the first time in *anishinaabemowin*,

the language of the *anishinaabe*, and then waved at the United States District Judge Miles Lord.

Aubid was a witness in a dispute with the federal government over the right to regulate the wild rice harvest on the Rice Lake National Wildlife Refuge near the East Lake Reservation in northern Minnesota.

The *anishinaabe* natives have harvested *manoomin*, wild rice, for more than three centuries. This nutritious native cereal, referred to as "fool's oats" by early explorers, is a trickster creation and sustenance to the *anishinaabe*; the traditional autumn harvest has been observed since the early fur trade in the territory. Today, *manoomin* is both a native tradition and a commodity.[26]

Here Vizenor acknowledges the time of the incident—"more than thirty years ago." He identifies the longstanding participation in the wild-ricing tradition—a harvest that has taken place "for more than three centuries" and "since the early fur trade." He also acknowledges the contemporary continuation of ricing—"Today, *manoomin* is both a native tradition and a commodity." We might also read in these statements an extension of the range to mythic time when Vizenor speaks of "trickster creation," and a gesture toward the future in the notion of ongoing "native tradition."

Here and in other sections of the piece, we can observe how the range of the text also expands linguistically, encompassing both the Ojibwe language and English, the written and the oral, as well elements from two specialized "languages"—the theoretical and the legal. In the original text, bilingualism is mentioned, but not embodied by textual gesture as it is here. Also in this account, Vizenor not only mentions the hearsay objection to Aubid's retelling of John Squirrel's exchange with government agents (as he had in the earlier newspaper account), but he expands the detail to include specific mention of the textual as well—when, for example, later in the piece Aubid is said to point "at legal books on the bench."[27] Vizenor also offers critical commentary on the courtroom scene, advancing his points through the use of theoretical vocabulary and his own variations on current theoretical terms. We see some of these elements in the expanded account of the hearsay controversy below:

Aubid, who was eighty-six years old at the time, testified in *anishinaabemowin* that he was present as a young man when the government agents told Old John Squirrel that the *anishinaabe* would always have control of the *manoomin* harvest. Aubid told the judge that there once was a document, but the *anishinaabe* always understood their rights in stories. . . . John Squirrel was there in memories, a storied presence, and he could have been heard by the court as a visual trace of a parol agreement.

Falvey, the federal attorney objected to the testimony, as he heard it in translation, as hearsay, and therefore not admissible as evidence. The judge agreed with the objection and explained to the witness that the court could not hear as evidence what a dead man said, only actual experiences of the witness.

"John Squirrel is dead," said Judge Miles Lord. "And you can't say what a dead man said." The judge waited for his words to be translated and then invited the witness to continue his story.

Aubid turned brusquely in the witness chair, bothered by what the judge said about John Squirrel. English was his second language, but he told stories in *anishinaabemowin*, the language of his visual memories and native sovenance. Aubid wore spectacles with thick lenses; he squinted and leaned into the line of sight, closer to the judge. He pointed at legal books on the bench and then shouted that those books contained the stories of dead white men.

"Why should I believe what a white man says, when you don't believe John Squirrel?" Aubid turned twice more in the witness chair and waited for the translation.

Judge Lord was deferentially amused by the analogy of native stories to court testimony, judicial decisions, precedent, and hearsay. "You've got me there," he said, and then considered the testimony of other *anishinaabe* witnesses.[28]

Among the key expansions in the account is Vizenor's pointed emphasis on the devaluation of the spoken in the legal scenario and, alternately, its merit in the tribal context in which Aubid is operating. In this 1998 version of the wild-rice regulation controversy, Vizenor underscores Aubid's perspective when he notes that "the *anishinaabe* had always understood their rights in stories," and he aligns himself with this Native perspective claiming John Squirrel's presence "in memories," as a "storied presence," and, most significantly, "as a visual trace of a parol agreement." In the language chosen for the latter phrase, Vizenor seems to construct the legal weight necessary for the Aubid/Squirrel account to become validated, as he claims not just the heard but the seen, the "visual trace," and when he employs the somewhat heightened or archaic term "parol" (for "spoken" or "that given orally") and the term "agreement," which implies a formal (legalistic) transaction. Vizenor has moved from the suggestive journalistic summary to engage in argument and critique through story.

In commentary to follow, Vizenor argues yet more strongly for the validity of the testimony, challenging the judge's ruling on the hearsay objection, when he explains, "Aubid named the storied *anishinaabe* as a presence, not an absence; as the virtual evidence, not as mere hearsay."[29] He goes on to claim Squirrel's presence "in stories," "in the memories of others," and as "an obviative presence as semantic evidence." Indeed, his interpretation suggests revision not only of the legal understanding of the virtual presence through story, but of the very grammar with which we acknowledge "person" in language, implying the addition of a "fourth person" presence in language: "That sense of presence, as sworn testimony in court, was the obviative, the fourth person in the poses of evidence."[30]

But Vizenor's arguments in regards to Aubid's testimony work to advance more than this single case. Ultimately he extends his claims beyond the specific controversy that gives rise to the testimony, and beyond the temporal moment represented in the courtroom. The following statements seem central to his understanding of the moment's larger significance:

> These stories and creases of native reason are evidence, a dialogic circle. John Squirrel is a virtual criterion of evidence in native sovenance; the stories of survivance and sovereignty.[31]

Note that the implications of the incident extend for Vizenor to three important elements in his representation of contemporary Native politics— sovenance, survivance, and sovereignty. Sovenance he characterizes as "a sense of presence in remembrance" (as opposed to a romanticized absence). Survivance he sometimes characterizes as "more than survival, more than endurance or mere response," and as "an active repudiation of dominance, tragedy, and victimry."[32] Sovereignty, of course, has become one of the catchwords in understanding the political clout of tribal nations, referring to their status as entities with the rights to govern themselves and to conduct foreign relations. Vizenor suggests that we see in the 1968 courtroom drama an example of transmotion, with implications for the larger national, perhaps global relations with Native nations.

My intent is not to debate the political realities of Native peoples, but rather to garner a way to read the texts, contexts, and intertextual relationships of the tellings Vizenor has undertaken. I suggest that his own texts throughout his career have entered the same "dialogic circle" of story he describes in the Squirrel/Aubid account. Charles Aubid gestures in story to the presence of Old John Squirrel and the long history of Anishinaabeg tradition in order to participate in an act of resistance in the courtroom and in the particular circumstances regarding the regulation of wild-rice harvesting. His storied testimony is, in Vizenor's terminology, an act of survivance—"active repudiation of dominance, tragedy, and victimry." The story Aubid tells moves into, and then within, the present. He places himself in the context of his filiations—the memory, knowledge, and traditions of wild-rice harvesting among generations of Anishinaabeg people—and he actively affiliates himself with the verbal authority of Old John Squirrel, with the oral transmission of story, and agreement to contest the curtailment of the inherent and legally acknowledged rights of the Anishinaabeg. The story becomes a vital agent in the present, in his act of resistance in the courtroom.

Vizenor, in his turn, in the serial retelling of the story, likewise invokes the historical filiations and invests himself in a relationship, an affiliation of story, with Aubid and, through Aubid, with Old John Squirrel, and beyond even that to the trickster tradition in Anishinaabeg storytelling. When he refers to the rice as "a trickster creation" and as "sustenance to the *anishinaabe*," his allusion is to the active presence of trickster stories, which, in their transmotion, continue to be life-sustaining. And, in his particular description of the demeanor of Aubid, who, the text tells us, "waves at United States District Judge Miles Lord," and later, of course, who is understood to reverse the direction of the hearsay objection by applying the same standard to dead white men, Vizenor by gesture also includes in his account "the storied presence" and "visual trace" of the Anishinaabeg trickster.

This act of storied survivance on Vizenor's part also involves current events never envisioned by the original storytellers or actors in the dramas of tribal survivance, and perhaps not envisioned by the younger Vizenor who first offered an account of the courtroom story and Aubid's testimony. The story in that first written accounting insinuated the legalistic tyranny under which the Minnesota Anishinaabeg struggled. Among the contemporary tyrannies against which Vizenor employs the *Fugitive Poses* story, for example, are those of the captured language and static representations of Indianness. The stories then always involve application in new circumstances, hence the *transmotion* of stories, the sense of "eternal return" with "difference." Today, Winona LaDuke might affiliate herself with that same story presence in her work to protect the *manoomin*, wild rice, against genetic modification.[33]

Vizenor's text speaks both filiations and affiliations in the Aubid story. He writes with a felt sense of history. The story itself took place more than thirty years before this account is given in *Fugitive Poses*, and the gestures in writing are to long-standing Native seasonal rituals of harvest—"the *anishinaabe* have harvested *manoomin* for more than three centuries"—as well as to the colonial production of treaties and the subsequent establishment of the wildlife refuge. The shadows of historical injustice enrich the story of contemporary struggle against tyranny through the text's subtle insinuations. For example, when Vizenor writes, "The federal attorney argued that . . . the natives in court were not elected to represent the interests of the reservation," he is writing within the presence of stories regarding the coercive establishment of treaties through the collection of signatures from individuals who were not recognized leaders of the nations whose land they signed away. The text is filled with such textured allusions.

Other ways the presence of this history is embodied, of course, are through the conscientious physical placement of the continuing activity of ricing—the virtual cartography—and through the use of the Anishinaabeg language both by those witnesses testifying in the court case and also by Vizenor in his text, by the affiliation of both with the language as cultural presence (not absence). The transmotion of tradition is likewise present in the author's acknowledgment of *manoomin* as both a "native tradition" and a "commodity." Here Vizenor uses the term "commodity" with its denotative meaning—rice is a product that the Anishinaabeg people harvest for sale. The tradition continues in an active adaptation to circumstance. The people participate in the present economy through the grace of the storied traditions of past generations surrounding the harvesting of *manoomin*—how to harvest, when to harvest, where, how to finish, how to protect the continuation of the crop through restraint and natural reseeding, etc. Vizenor does not write of an archival past, but of a present in which the stories embody transmotion: "a sense of sovereignty, an ethical relationship with nature, 'native motion and an active presence.'" "*Today, manoomin* is both a native tradition and a commodity" (my emphasis).

So the essay Vizenor writes about survivance and transmotion, represented in the story of Charles Aubid's act of resistance against the government, then undertakes another act of resistance. Itself "a trace of survivance and sovereignty," the 1998 wild-rice rights piece sets up opposition to the very grammar that underpins the colonial mentality, challenges the language of domination, and seeks to liberate the contemporary Anishinaabeg from the "fugitive poses" of Native peoples.

SEED BANKS

Like the Aubid story, many of Vizenor's early pieces have arisen from a particular set of historical circumstances and had their first life as reportage or journalistic political responses. Also, like the Aubid story, they have continued to resonate with new implications as Vizenor's own life has evolved, and as the cultural and intellectual issues of the day have swung like story on the mad tale of changing circumstances. My interest is in both the original stance represented in many of these pieces—a stance that sometimes could only be vaguely hinted at because of the purpose, form, and audience of their original production—and in the serial lives of the stories and the sometimes changing, sometimes progressive development of their political intentions. Among these stories, I include not only those normally acknowledged as "factual," but also the mythic and as well as those "true" tribal and family stories that have likewise had a vital felt presence over the years in various texts.

The list might include such accounts as Naanabozho and the evil gambler, which has served as the metaphoric framework for several of Vizenor's fictional works, as well as for his telling of his father's death in an unsolved urban crime. His writings on his AIM (American Indian Movement) encounters, the development of works in various genres on the historical Ishi, his accounts of the killing of a red squirrel, his accounts of his Beaulieu ancestors' struggle to establish the White Earth newspaper *The Progress*, and a host of other stories he has cast and recast over the decades demonstrate the vitality Vizenor finds in "old" stories and the progressive revelations his af/filiation with them has brought.

If, as Vizenor claims, we survive by stories, his own writing career is the best illustration of this, as his serial retelling with slight variations of a cache of stories serves as metaphor and map in many changing circumstances. A trickster-teacher, he tracks the eternal return of stories for ever-new applications in the interests of justice and survival.

When I investigate the Native seed banks that seek to preserve Indigenous varieties of tribal foods like wild rice, I think also of the vast "story banks" that preserve Anishinaabeg beliefs and tradition. Just as each traditional seasonal activity in the Anishinaabeg yearly cycle necessarily involves both doing and telling, likewise each storytelling is both harvest and reseeding. As my Uncle Bill understood instinctively, telling stories is also planting stories. Rice kernels fall back upon the fall waters, sink slowly again to the soft silt. Stories, too, must seek fruitful grounds, settle, arise again in new voice. We only continue by the grace of these spirit acts. Somewhere there is intersection between the motion of stories, the motions of life, and the mobile centers of meaning. The intersection, of course, is momentary, disappearing on the breath of each spoken *Diibaajimowin-nodin*.

NOTES

1. Kimberly Blaeser, "Passing Time," *Absentee Indians & Other Poems* (East Lansing: Michigan State University Press, 2002), 21–22.

2. "Survivance" has also been understood by some scholars as a blending of survival and endurance.

3. Louis Owens, "Afterword[0]," in Gerald Vizenor, *Bearheart: The Heirship Chronicles* (Minneapolis: University of Minnesota Press, 1990), 252.

4. Gerald Vizenor, *The Everlasting Sky: New Voices from the People Named the Chippewa* (New York: Crowell-Collier Press, 1972), ix.

5. In the same section, Vizenor also rejects what he perceives as the expectation of Native stories when he writes: "Many modern listeners would like to hear the original authorized historical and cultural legends of the *anishinabe* past for easy memory and analysis. But the stories of the past only show the humor and compassion of the present" (np).

6. Anna Gibbs, "Once upon a Legend," *Oshkaabewis Native Journal* 7, no. 2 (Spring 2010): 21.

7. Vizenor characterizes and explores the workings of transmotion throughout *Fugitive Poses: Native American Scenes of Absence and Presence* (Lincoln: University of Nebraska Press, 1998). See especially 181–85.

8. Vizenor, *Fugitive Poses: Native American Indian Scenes of Absence and Presence* (Lincoln: University of Nebraska Press, 1998), 15.

9. Ibid., 182–183.

10. Gerald Vizenor, *Dead Voices: Natural Agonies in the Word Wars* (Norman: University of Oklahoma Press, 1992), 127, 16.

11. Gerald Vizenor, *The Heirs of Columbus* (Hanover: Wesleyan University Press, 1991), 164.

12. Gerald Vizenor, *Wordarrows: Indians and Whites in the New Fur Trade* (Minneapolis: University of Minnesota Press, 1978), 5.

13. Personal interview with Gerald Vizenor, May 27–29, 1987. This series of interviews was conducted at the University of California—Berkeley. All of the formal sessions were tape-recorded and later transcribed.

14. Vizenor, *Fugitive Poses*, 15.

15. Simon Ortiz, "Always the Stories: A Brief History and Thoughts on My Writing," in *Coyote Was Here: Essays on Contemporary Native American Literary and Political Mobilization*, ed. Bo Schöler (Aarhus, Denmark: SEKLOS/University of Aarhus, 1984), 57.

16. Gerald Vizenor, *The Trickster of Liberty: Tribal Heirs to a Wild Baronage* (Minneapolis: University of Minnesota Press, 1998), xviii.

17. See, for example, Thomas King's *The Truth about Stories: A Native Narrative* (Minneapolis: University of Minnesota Press, 2003), in which he closes each chapter with this remonstrance: "Don't say in the years to come that you would have lived your life differently if only you had heard this story. You heard it now" (29, 60, 89, etc.).

18. Said's use of the terms has been compared this way: "'Filiation' as its etymology implies, denotes natural ties, belonging, and conformity to received traditions; by contrast, 'affiliation' signifies distance, a worldly self-situating response to the dominant culture, in short, critical consciousness" (E. San Juan Jr., "Edward Said's Affiliations: Secular Humanism and Marxism," *Atlantic Studies* 3, no. 1 (2006): 43). I believe both play a role in Vizenor's work, but he understands "filiation" much as Gilles Deleuze interprets time—as "eternal return" with "difference." In Vizenor the "received traditions" mentioned as part of filiation are not static, but part of what he calls the "transmotion" of stories.

19. Gerald Vizenor, *Fugitive Poses*, 23–24.

20. Ibid., 23.

21. I refer here to the belief held by various tribal nations that the wisdom of contemporary decisions should be evaluated by taking into account seven generations in the past and seven generations in the future.

22. Vizenor has used imaginative techniques usually associated with fiction in rendering historical story. Examples of this method can be seen throughout his work, but most particularly in the book *The People Named the Chippewa: Narrative Histories* (Minneapolis: University of Minnesota Press, 1984), in which he also discusses the weaknesses of traditional historiography. For a short analysis of his work in this area, see my comments in Blaeser, *Gerald Vizenor: Writing in the Oral Tradition* (Norman: University of Oklahoma Press, 1996), especially pages 82–99.

23. Here I suggest that Vizenor characterizes Aubid's demeanor and actions as marked by the humor and anarchical energy often attributed to Naanabozho, the Anishinaabeg trickster. For discussion of the Native American trickster figure and Vizenor's particular understanding of, and use of, trickster in his writing, see Blaeser, *Gerald Vizenor: Writing in the Oral Tradition*, especially pages 136–63.

24. Gerald Vizenor, "Ojibwe Seek Right to Regulate Rice on Wildlife Refuge," *Minneapolis Tribune*, September 13, 1968, 24.

25. This author has had the pleasure of hearing both public and private retellings of the incident in various circumstances and contexts since my acquaintance with Gerald Vizenor began in 1985.

26. Vizenor, "Hearsay Sovereignty," in *Fugitive Poses*, 167.

27. Ibid., 168.

28. Ibid., 168.

29. Ibid., 169.

30. Common usage includes first person (I, we), second person (you), and third person (he, she, they). We also commonly note case, such as objective, nominative, etc.

31. Vizenor, "Hearsay Sovereignty," in *Fugitive Poses*, 169.
32. Vizenor, *Fugitive Poses*, 15.
33. See the White Earth Land Recovery website for an update or link to information on LaDuke's work to prevent contamination of wild rice by genetic modification.

RESOURCES

Blaeser, Kimberly. *Absentee Indians & Other Poems.* East Lansing: Michigan State University Press, 2002.

———. Gerald Vizenor: *Writing in the Oral Tradition.* Norman: University of Oklahoma Press, 1996.

Deleuze, Gilles, with Félix Guattari. *What Is Philosophy?* New York: Columbia University Press, 1994.

Gibbs, Anna. "Once upon a Legend." *Oshkaabewis Native Journal* 7, no. 2 (Spring 2010): 21.

King, Thomas. *The Truth about Stories: A Native Narrative.* Minneapolis: University of Minnesota Press, 2003.

Ortiz, Simon. "Always the Stories: A Brief History and Thoughts on My Writing." *Coyote Was Here: Essays on Contemporary Native American Literary and Political Mobilization,* ed. Bo Schöler, 57–69. Aarhus, Denmark: SEKLOS/University of Aarhus, 1984.

Owens, Louis. "Afterword." In Gerald Vizenor, *Bearheart: The Heirship Chronicles.* Minneapolis: University of Minnesota Press, 1990.

Said, Edward. *The World, the Text and the Critic.* Cambridge, MA: Harvard University Press, 1983.

San Juan, E., Jr. "Edward Said's Affiliations: Secular Humanism and Marxism." *Atlantic Studies* 3, no. 1 (2006): 43–61.

Vizenor, Gerald. *Anishinaabe Adisokan.* Minneapolis: Nodin Press, 1970.

———. *Dead Voices: Natural Agonies in the Word Wars.* Norman: University of Oklahoma Press, 1992.

———. *Earthdivers: Tribal Narratives on Mixed Descent.* Minneapolis: University of Minnesota Press, 1981.

———. *The Everlasting Sky: New Voices from the People Named the Chippewa.* New York: Crowell-Collier Press, 1972.

———. *Fugitive Poses: Native American Indian Scenes of Absence and Presence.* Lincoln: University of Nebraska Press, 1998.

———. *The Heirs of Columbus.* Hanover, NH: Wesleyan University Press, 1991.

———. "Ojibwe Seek Right to Regulate Rice on Wildlife Refuge." *Minneapolis Tribune*, September 13, 1968, 24.

———. *The People Named the Chippewa: Narrative Histories.* Minneapolis: University of Minnesota Press, 1984.

———. *Tribal Scenes and Ceremonies.* Minneapolis: Nodin Press, 1976.

———. *The Trickster of Liberty: Tribal Heirs to a Wild Baronage.* Minneapolis: University of Minnesota Press, 1998.

———. *Wordarrows: Indians and Whites in the New Fur Trade.* Minneapolis: University of Minnesota Press, 1978.

Transforming the Trickster

Federal Indian Law Encounters Anishinaabe Diplomacy

HEIDI KIIWETINEPINESIIK STARK

Stories are wondrous things. And they are dangerous.

—THOMAS KING, *THE TRUTH ABOUT STORIES*

KING REMINDS US THAT STORIES HAVE POWER. THEY ARE BOTH WON-drous and dangerous. Federal Indian law contains many of the creation stories of the nation-state. These stories have proven dangerous, having the power to (re)imagine the legal universe, (re)create the nation-state, and (re)structure Indigenous-state relations. The creation stories of the state have transformed the legal landscape and left Indigenous peoples in a constant state of flux as they seek to challenge and reconfigure the law to make space for themselves. But what happens when creation stories of the state, codified in federal Indian law, encounter stories of Anishinaabe diplomacy?

Stories are transformative and have the power to either heal or injure, to create or destroy. This power is perhaps most clearly elucidated in federal Indian law, where the trickster has been diligently at work reconfiguring the legal landscape. This is evident in the recent Supreme Court rendering of the trust doctrine in *U.S. v. Jicarilla Apache Nation* (2011).[1] Justice Alito continues a long tradition of legal magic that began with the original creation stories of the state espoused in the Marshall trilogy. After an analysis of the courts, I turn my attention to the critical question raised above: what would the trust relationship look like, what kinds of alternative relationships would be unearthed if the creation stories of the state were met with stories of Anishinaabe diplomacy?

David Wilkins and K. Tsianina Lomawaima find that "common to many, but not all, definitions of 'trust' is the notion of federal *responsibility* to *protect or enhance* tribal assets (including fiscal, natural, human, and cultural resources) through policy decisions and management actions" (emphasis original).[2] This trust relationship was initially born out of treaty pledges to live in peace and act in good faith, memorialized explicitly in treaty articles of protection.[3] Thus, I look to the 1846 treaty negotiations between the United Nation of Pottawatomie, Odaawa, and Ojibwe with the United States to illustrate the myriad ways in which the trust relationship was expressed by Anishinaabe leaders. This story of Anishinaabe diplomacy demonstrates that the real power of stories is in their ability to transform relationships. Stories lie in wait, ready to not only serve as the center for the field of Anishinaabeg Studies but also to guide us in our interactions with one another.

THE TRANSFORMATIVE POWER OF STORIES

Stories shape how we see and interact with the world. They lend insight into the ways in which we see our communities, as well as how we see ourselves within these communities. The power of stories is found in their ability to outline and clarify the connections people have to their place, their people, and their history. Indigenous stories outline relationships—the relationships we have to one another, and the relationship we have to self. N. Bruce Duthu has said:

> Our oral tradition encompasses diverse stories, but within them are recurrent themes, chief among them the idea of relationships. Stories carry us through time and reveal our relationships to our historical selves, to others around us, and to the natural and supernatural world. The meanings attached to these stories, like the relationships they explore, are dynamic, increasingly complex, and often surprising.[4]

Stories are how we make sense of the world. It is chiefly for this reason that stories can so aptly serve as the center for the field of Anishinaabeg Studies. They function as road maps, guiding us towards exploration, discovery, and meaning. As Anishinaabe scholar Gerald Vizenor reminds us, "You can't understand the world without telling a story."[5]

There are a multitude of stories among the Anishinaabeg, contained in various forms, that all work toward to same end: to provide meaning to the world we live in, teach us how to relate to one another, and help us understand our place in creation. Lessard et al. remind us that "We come into existence . . . as embodied beings, processing the partial fragments of sensory experience (sounds, images, smells, touches), sorting them into patterns of consequence, patterns of meaning. Narrative—or 'story'—is one of the primary vehicles through which we sort, arrange, and produce those patterns."[6] It is through lived experiences, through interaction with all of creation that we come to produce the stories that serve to aid us in making sense of the world.

For the Anishinaabeg, some of our earliest interactions with creation are contained in narratives about Nenabozho.[7] His interactions with the various places and peoples of creation contain a variety of lessons for the listener, who is required to expand his or her perceptions when confronted with stories of a main character whose motivations are inherently contradictory—sometimes selfless and sometimes self-interested. Nenaboozhoo's seemingly contradictory behaviors promote underlying values and principles, yet each listener is encouraged to make sense of the story for himself and to infer meaning that will be applicable to his own behaviors, actions, and relationships with creation.[8]

The trickster is a transformative figure.[9] Nenabozho, in his interactions with creation, transformed the landscape, and his actions had varied impacts on those he encountered. Nenabozho narratives often contain insights into how animals came to attain certain physical attributes or markers. For example, when Nenabozho took the form of a rabbit to steal fire, he was marked by this action.[10] Nenabozho's actions affected all hares from that day forward, as their white fur would become brown in the summer as a result of their ancestor's act of carrying fire on his back.[11] In addition, Nenabozho stories explain how the land and earth's beings came to be, reinforcing an understanding of how our own actions and engagements create lasting impact.

Stories detail relationships. They teach us how to conduct ourselves and how to make sense of our actions vis-à-vis one another.[12] Julie Cruikshank found that "such narratives depict humans, animals, and other nonhuman beings engaged in an astonishing variety of activities and committed to mutually sustaining relationships that ensure the continuing well-being of the world."[13] Stories, in teaching us how to relate to one another, can also be understood as law. Law, of course, is an important organizing force within virtually all societies. "However," Anishinaabe legal scholar John Borrows notes, "there are many definitions and disagreements about what constitutes law. . . . Its effect can simultaneously produce peace and chaos, depending in whose name it is administrated and from whose perspective it is processed."[14] And yet law plays an important role in each person's life, as it seeks to guide how we should relate to and interact with one another. Stories are emphatically a source of law, as they lay out critical principles for how Anishinaabeg order their world.

In addition, stories are alive—in regard to both the spirit within stories and the ongoing creation and recreation of story.[15] The creation of story did not cease at a particular moment for Anishinaabeg. Our ongoing interaction with creation—in all her forms—continues to generate stories that teach us how to be in the world. This cannot only be seen in contemporary oral storytelling, but also in the prolific writings of Anishinaabeg. From *Drawing Out Law*, where Borrows is informed by dream and personal relationships, to Gerald Vizenor's litany of work demonstrating that the trickster is alive and well, stories continue to work on and within the people. Indeed, I am telling you a story now—a story about how story encounters story.

What constitutes story, however, evades definition and containment. As Leslie Marmon Silko reminds us, "Many individual words have their own stories. So when one is telling a story and one is using words to tell the story, each word that one is speaking has a story of its own too."[16] As a single word is capable of carrying many stories, once it is uttered into the air or onto the page, it is imbued with a life force—just as Anishinaabeg were when the Creator blew the breath of life into the first human.[17] Because words have power, and thus stories—as a collection of words—have power, we are cautioned about how we may use them. As Thomas King writes, "A story told one way could cure, that same story told another way could injure."[18] The wondrous and dangerous character of stories, their ability to injure or to heal, is perhaps most clearly seen in the legal narratives that constitute federal Indian law in the United States.

LAW AS STORY: CREATION STORIES OF THE NATION-STATE

There is a rich body of scholarship that calls for us to seriously consider how narratives, whether encoded in law or circulated throughout dominant society and embedded in the national consciousness, shape and inform how we understand ourselves and relate to others. Just as creation stories provide the Anishinaabeg with a sense of belonging and outline their relationships to their place, citizenry, and nation, U.S. law and the national narratives that inform law and policy function as the creation stories of the nation-state.[19] Patricia Tuitt notes:

> No sovereign entity exists without an accompanying set of narratives surrounding its emergence. It is through stories of settlement, conquest, exploration, and discovery that distinctive nations, peoples, and communities are constructed. Although such narratives are embedded in a variety of cultural forms, few of these are equal in weight to the narration of the processes in which an entity acquires legal shape and status.[20]

Stories, of course, may be "real" or "imagined" in the Western understanding. They are always open to contestation and represent a particular view. These stories (often thought of as histories) transcend time, as the state pulls on real and imagined narratives of the past to inform and legitimate the present.[21] Bain Attwood echoes this sentiment:

> In the case of settler societies, colonizers have found it necessary to persuade others as well as themselves that the land they have appropriated as their basis is rightfully theirs. This is done in large part through the formulation of legal stories of one kind or another, since the law plays a crucial role in creating boundaries between what is deemed to be legitimate and what is not.[22]

Yet, as Lumbee legal scholar Robert Williams Jr. reminds us, these creation stories of the state, which discount or utterly deny Indigenous narratives and are contingent on the erasure or absorption of Indigenous peoples into the state, have rendered law a loaded weapon. He contends that seminal nineteenth-century federal Indian law decisions remain *ready for the hand* of current justices who continue to employ these narratives as a means to deny Native peoples their political rights.[23] The danger of law in narrating the creation stories of the state is echoed by Jacinta Ruru. Though focusing on New Zealand, her findings also fit in the United States. She argues, "Law was used as a tool to endorse a new narrative of nationhood—a country founded and settled by the British." She goes on to say that "Europeans consciously used law as a means to create and define themselves in relation to the new realm they had entered, imposing their world view and legitimating their existence on these lands."[24]

Like the stories that give it meaning, law is neither fixed nor static. It is always transforming. Law, like the trickster, can have an altering impact on those it interacts with. As Greg Sarris remind us, stories "can work to oppress or to liberate, to confuse or to enlighten."[25] Law as story, in the United States, has frequently worked to oppress Indigenous peoples and transform Indigenous narratives by subjugating their stories within the nation-state, sometimes to the point of defining Indigenous rights out of existence. This can be seen in the litany of U.S. Supreme Court decisions that manipulate and reconfigure the meaning of "protection," which is interpreted often as the trust relationship, in order to contain and limit tribal sovereignty.[26]

In June 2011 the high court took on the trickster persona, stretching and contorting the trust doctrine in *U.S. v. Jicarilla Apache Nation* to a degree that practically drained it of any vitality.[27] The case centered on whether the federal government could claim attorney-client privilege in withholding information from a tribe involving the government's management of money that it holds in trust. In a 7–1 decision, the majority contorted the origins and definitions of trust. Justice Alito, writing for the majority, said, "When the tribe cannot identify a specific, applicable, trust-creating statute or regulation that the Government violated, . . . neither the Government's control over Indian assets nor common-law trust principles matter. The Government assumes Indian trust responsibilities only to the extent it expressly accepts those responsibilities by statute."[28]

Alito contended that "while one purpose of the Indian trust relationship is to benefit the tribe, the Government has its own independent interest in the implementation of federal Indian policy."[29] Indeed, the Court acknowledged unapologetically that "the Government has often structured the trust relationship to pursue its own policy goals."[30] But perhaps the ultimate sleight of hand, in true trickster fashion, occurred when the justices dramatically repositioned the origins of the trust relationship—not as emerging from the diplomatic accords where the United States jointly agreed to be protective allies of Native nations, but instead claiming it was a direct byproduct of congressional plenary power.[31] This is the ultimate trickster narrative, with the United States wielding virtually absolute power over all things Indigenous. Indeed, the twin doctrine of discovery and plenary power are comparable to flood narratives.[32] They are incredibly pernicious and can destroy existing worlds. But they also contain unlimited abilities for the nation-state to imagine and create itself anew. In its re-creation through legal doctrines, the United States grants itself the power to drown out any memory of its diplomatic arrangements and commitments to Native nations. These creation stories allow the state to disregard earlier recognitions of Native sovereignty and political authority in favor of narratives that posit that tribal sovereignty is limited when Native nations accept the "protection" of the state. In fact, the Court relies on this narrative frequently to subjugate earlier stories of "trust."

Alito cited one narrative after another to demonstrate the Court's continued ability to manipulate and reconfigure trust, tribal sovereignty, and plenary authority. The Court first gestured toward *Merrion v. Jicarilla Apache Tribe*, where the Court had previously argued that "The United States retains plenary authority to divest the tribes of any attributes of sovereignty."[33] The Court then looked to *U.S. v. Wheeler* to determine that "Congress has plenary authority to legislate for the Indian tribes in all matters, including their form of government."[34] Resorting to one of the original creation stories of plenary power, *Lone Wolf v. Hitchcock*, to assert supreme authority, the Court then wrote, "Plenary authority over the tribal relations of the Indians has been exercised by Congress from the beginning, and the power has always been deemed a political one, not subject to be controlled by the judicial department of the government."[35] In *Jicarilla* we see clearly how the creation stories of the state, as articulated by the judicial branch, are most dangerous. They oppress and injure.

Like the trickster, stories can distract just as much as they can enlighten. The federal courts have been particularly successful in distracting us from our own stories by instead putting on a magic show, full of fancy tricks that distract the audience by posing endless riddles so they will be unable to see the sleight of hand that enables the justices to pull a quarter out from behind one's ear. Like magic, the courts have used narratives to enable the state to slip between the real and the imagined, to legitimate their claims by saying they are so. As one scholar puts it, "Law is one of the many narrative forms that generate material truth out of discursive fictions."[36] These stories of the state disorientate and misguide the listener as they traverse the legal landscape.[37]

The state has found itself caught in its own riddle, lost in a maze that purports to administer justice and act with morality while imagining its sovereign authority is contingent on the suppression of Indigenous sovereignty. Chief Justice John Marshall first posed the national riddle in 1823 when he utilized his legal imagination to reduce Indigenous land title to "a mere right of occupancy."[38] In 1831 he again performed the trick of transforming Native nations from self-governing and independent nations to "domestic-dependent" nations.[39] In both cases, the chief justice carried out unnecessary tricks that sought to disguise the larger questions of federation that the Court had to contend with.

Like any story, once it was told, there was no way to recall it. As Leslie Marmon Silko reminds us in *Ceremony*, recounting a contest among witches that escalates out of control and threatens destruction and despair for all, stories cannot be undone. The witches plead, "Take it back. Call that story back. But the witch just shook its head . . . *It's already turned loose. It's already coming. It can't be called back.*"[40] Marshall, like the other witches, sought in a later ruling to call back this creation of "discovery" and "conquest" that had subjugated Indigenous rights and lands within the supreme authority of the state. In his 1832 decision *Worcester v. Georgia*, he denied that discovery stripped Native peoples of their land title, and instead sought to recognize Indigenous sovereignty and trust responsibilities outlined in their treaty relations. He recognized that the Cherokees' national character had not been diminished by having placed themselves under the protection of the United States. Rather, he said that "the very fact of repeated treaties with them recognizes it; and the settled doctrine of the law of nations is, that a weaker power does not surrender its independence—its rights to self government by associating with a stronger, and taking its protection."[41] But these competing and overlapping opinions, collectively referred to as the Marshall trilogy, swirled around a legal universe, allowing the courts to gaze in any direction necessary to support their particular desires.

Subsequent Court decisions have been able to utilize the Marshall trilogy to narrate countless stories that, though sometimes upholding it, frequently legitimate the denial or erasure of tribal sovereignty. While *Johnson v. McIntosh* (1823) allowed for the territorial subordination of Native peoples through narratives of "discovery," other creation stories of the state came to legitimate the jurisdictional absorption of Native peoples. In *U.S. v. Kagama* (1886) the Court asserted that Native nations "are communities dependent on the United States." Congress, therefore, had the plenary authority to pass legislation that would position Native peoples as subjects of the state because "the power of the General Government over these remnants of a race once powerful, now weak and diminished in numbers, is necessary to their protection, as well as to the safety of those among whom they dwell."[42] In order to "lawfully" abrogate treaties, the courts reconfigured "protection" as "dependency" and declared that Congress had authority, "in respect to the care and protection of the Indians," to dispose of tribal lands.[43]

Indeed, when states' rights had been sufficiently subsumed under federal power, the courts would sometimes dismiss their earlier, more historically grounded stories, such as *Worcester*, that expressly precluded states from exercising their laws over Indigenous peoples, to instead allow for a rise in states' rights in their dealings with Native nations. Protection became a national narrative the courts could utilize to erode tribal sovereignty. For example, the courts denied tribal jurisdiction over non-Indians in *Oliphant v. Suquamish* (1978) because, the Court argued, that would have been "inconsistent with their status" as dependent nations. Rehnquist declared:

Indian tribes do retain elements of "quasi-sovereign" authority after ceding their lands to the United States and announcing their dependence on the Federal Government. But the tribe's retained powers are not such that they are limited only by specific restrictions in treaties or congressional enactments. As the Court of Appeals recognized, Indian tribes are prohibited from exercising both those powers of autonomous states that are expressly terminated by Congress *and* those powers *"inconsistent with their status."*[44]

The courts have frequently reconfigured their trust responsibility to tribes, conflating *protection* with *dependency*, and dependency with limited or "quasi" sovereignty. In the same way Nenabozho stories demonstrate the impacts our actions have on creation—detailing how the land came to take its current shape, or outlining particular encounters that explain animal features—Supreme Court justices' engagement and interaction with the trust doctrine in general, and notions of protection in particular, continue to reshape the legal landscape that Native nations must contend with. The courts have erected theoretical mountains that often prove difficult to pass, and have carved great divides between the legal world espoused in *Worcester* and the one most recently outlined in *Jicarilla*.

Yet, the legal landscape breathed into life in *Worcester* was no less dangerous and full of obstacles than the legal landscape we now find ourselves contained within. While *Worcester* recognized that a nation's sovereignty was in no way diminished or limited by bringing itself under the protection of another, it was still a world that had to contend with narratives that were incapable of reconciling Indigenous nations as separate sovereigns, connected through alliance and treaty, while having retained political autonomy and self-determination. Previous stories of discovery and conquest, circulated in dominant discourse and given legal force in *Johnson*, were contingent on the subjugation of Indigenous peoples and their lands. These stories were alive and could not be called back.

STORY ENCOUNTERS STORY:
IMAGINING AN ALTERNATE RELATIONSHIP

As the nation-state imagined itself, it did so to the exclusion of Indigenous story. Instead the United States took up the act of creating and controlling stories of Indigenous peoples—stories that contained the limited possibilities of either erasure or absorption into the state. But what would happen if these creation stories of the state encountered Anishinaabe stories of diplomacy? Gordon Christie, in his study of sovereignty and indigeneity in the Arctic, examines how words and stories function, and suggests a path for how Indigenous peoples "can usefully meet stories with stories, words with words."[45]

Christie argues that "sovereignty" has served to define a state-controlled political agenda in the Arctic. State notions of sovereignty have precluded any consideration of Indigenous stories that unearth alternate ways of relating to one another. Christie cautions Indigenous peoples to reconsider attempts to reshape and transform the stories of the state from within, warning that we may lose sight of another form of resistance available: "resistance that meets story with story."[46] Christie believes that the form of resistance that meets story with story illuminates other possibilities to the sovereignty model—possibilities that imagine other ways of relating to one another. He notes that "Questions about how people might interact with one another and the land and sea around did not trace back to first-order questions about which body had the rightful authority to make decisions in this context. First-order questions would be about *how* one might act—they were about the appropriateness of the action in question, not who might be appropriately positioned to decide how to act."[47]

Stories transform; they reveal new possibilities. They look to the past to inform our present and provide direction for the future. Stories told by Anishinaabe leaders—their diplomatic speeches in their treaty negotiations with the United States—illuminate alternate ways of being, a path for mutually beneficial partnerships that focus on questions of how one might act, instead of keeping us contained within a narrative that has exclusively centered on the question of who has the authority to act.

DIPLOMACY AS STORY: ANISHINAABE
TREATY EXPRESSIONS OF TRUST

Throughout their treaties, the Anishinaabeg told stories of nations partnered in trust. It was in these encounters that the trust doctrine was initially imagined and breathed into life. The trust doctrine, or fiduciary relationship, has been foundational to federal Indian law and is possibly the clearest expression of a continued relationship based on mutual respect. The treaty record surrounding the aforementioned 1846 treaty between the United Nation of Ojibwe, Odawa, and Potawatomi, and the United States perhaps best illustrates the myriad ways trust and protection were expressed throughout the treaty era. The United Nation had engaged in five treaties with the United States prior to this 1846 accord. In their 1833 treaty at Chicago with the United States, the United Nation had ceded some five million acres in Illinois and Wisconsin and were removed to lands in Iowa. In November 1845, chiefs from the United Nation delegation went to Washington to meet with the President of the United States. They wanted to learn about the previous treaty annuities they had yet to obtain, as well as receive word from the President regarding a treaty proposed to their people a few months earlier. The President had approached the United Nation, through Major Harvey, to propose their removal to lands west of the Southern Potawatomi. The United Nation had refused this offer and instead sent back a written "talk" regarding the terms under which they would remove.

In order to urge removal, the United States declared that they would provide protection for the United Nation. Treaty commissioners claimed that removal would allow the President to protect the Anishinaabeg from white settlers. In response, the Anishinaabeg expressed their understanding of the trust relationship between themselves and the President, outlined and promised in earlier treaties. Anishinaabe leaders stated, "You say the whites are crowding on us. This is not our fault. We suppose our Great Father has power to make his white children respect his promises and he has already assured us that we shall not be forced to remove from our lands. Why then should we fear our White neighbors?"[48] The Anishinaabeg understood protection as the President's promise to safeguard them from American citizens—that the President pledged to make American citizens respect the nation's treaty promises.

In addition, the United Nation understood this trust to entail their protection from state interference. The Anishinaabeg asserted, "You say 'the state of Iowa is about extending her laws' over us. We are not alarmed at this. We are told there is no such state, and cannot be, unless our Great Father creates it. Surely he would never do this to break his word with his red children."[49] The Anishinaabeg expressly interpreted state interference as a violation of their treaty. They reminded the commissioner of this, stating, "If any other government be created over us, it will be a violation of our treaty. We protest against this. We want to hold our lands as they were guaranteed to us."[50] Protection was not understood as a diminishment of their national character, but instead as a safeguard against treaty violations and violators.

The U.S treaty commissioners also argued that removal would ensure their protection from the Dakota. The Anishinaabeg recounted their previous treaties to demonstrate the various applications of protection, and explicitly noted that these agreements with the United States were renewed several times. At the Treaty of Prairie du Chien in 1825, in which the Anishinaabeg and Dakota agreed to maintain peace, the United States had committed to help uphold this treaty by offering protection against anyone who sought to break it. The Anishinaabeg recalled this and later agreements, stating, "Did not our Great Father promise at Chicago to protect us against the Sioux? Did he not send Maj. Cummins to our country four years ago to renew the promises? Did he not send Dragoons for two years? Why then cannot he protect us? He has done it once; why cannot he do it again? Or why did he withdraw that protection if not to force us from our lands?"[51]

The United Nation reminded the commissioner that if the President rescinded his protection, then they would be forced to neglect their treaty responsibility to maintain peace with the Dakota. They warned, "Our Great Father told us not to fight with them, and we did as he told us. But if the Sioux murder our people, we will tell our young men to dig up the hatchet."[52] Thus, protection entailed the commitment to previous treaty promises. The President, throughout numerous treaties, extended protection to the Anishinaabeg: protection from American citizens who often sought to settle within Anishinaabe territories; from state interference as they attempted to extend their laws over Anishinaabeg; as well as protection from any party to the treaty that threatened to disrupt their pledge of peace. Protection, therefore, necessitated a relationship of trust.

The Anishinaabeg, in their recitation of their trust relationship with the President, echoed these principles in concrete terms. Anishinaabe leaders reiterated the words of President James Polk, who had met with the United Nation during their month-long stay in Washington. "He said to our Interpreter '. . . I am the friend of the red man, and all within our territory shall have full and entire justice done to them so far as I have the power to do so. Tell the [Pottawatomie] Chiefs that they must banish all fears of being forced from the lands they now occupy: these lands were made theirs by treaty and they shall be protected in their peaceable possession.'"[53] President Polk, as reiterated by the Anishinaabeg, had also stated:

> Tell them, also that every promise made to them by my predecessors shall be [?] carried in to effect. . . . whatever promise was made to them by their Great Father shall be *with good faith* and great pleasure redeemed by me now. It is my determination to carry out, in letter and spirit, every treaty stipulation made between our Government and the Indians within our borders. Justice shall be done to them, and I trust to secure the confidence and affection of all our red brethren in such effectual manner as shall forever keep the tomahawk buried

between them and our people. Tell them again that we never had any intention of driving them from the lands they now occupy.[54] (emphasis mine)

President Polk nonetheless linked these statements with his promotion for their removal, stating, "If they decide to exchange them for other lands better adapted to their habits and wants, we will gratify them if we can agree upon the terms. But they must be perfectly satisfied with the change: they shall never be forced to it." Regardless of the President's desire to remove the United Nation, this account by the Anishinaabeg illustrates how they understood their trust relationship with the President of the United States. The President promised respect for the United Nation and ensured justice. He declared he would protect their treaty-guaranteed lands and renewed previous treaty promises in good faith.

The treaty record illuminates an Anishinaabe understanding of the trust relationship: protection from U.S. citizens, from state interference, and from parties that seek to disrupt treaty commitments. These pledges were made in good faith, necessitating a relationship of trust.

CONCLUSION: TRANSFORMING TRUST

This story told by Anishinaabeg leaders at their treaty negotiations provides an alternate way of imagining the trust doctrine as a trust *relationship*. How the Anishinaabeg engaged others in their diplomatic accords was deeply informed by the stories that signified what it meant to be Anishinaabe. These stories outline how we should relate to one another. This alternate way of being neither requires the subjugation of Indigenous peoples and their rights within the state, nor does it threaten an extinction of the nation-state—a fear that often closes off alternative stories. The nation-state will be altered, changed, as the land and the animals have been, because that is the power of story. But like all stories, this one contains the power to heal as much as it threatens to destroy. Indeed, this story poses danger to notions of supreme authority that are currently rooted in state sovereignty. However it can also provide a path for reconciliation.

Reconciliation is a loaded term and contains many stories of continued subjugation under the cloak of liberalism. I am not arguing that this story provides a path for reconciliation between Indigenous peoples and the state. Indeed, that narrative of reconciliation often promises liberation while still operating as oppression. We must be careful of these seemingly progressive models because, as Johnny Mack notes, they threaten to ultimately absorb "the indigenous story into this larger narrative of imperialism."[55] Instead, this term is appropriate in that this story can aid the state in reconciling its own creation stories, narratives of morality and justice that coalesce and collide with stories of continued imperialism, dangerously chipping away at the legal landscape until there may be nothing left. Tools for liberation, capable of untangling the riddles within national narratives, lie in wait, just as federal Indian law lies about like a loaded weapon. These tools for transformation are stories. It is now up to us to decide whether to utilize them to destroy or to build. As Thomas King reminds us, "Don't say in the years to come that you would have lived your life differently if only you had heard this story. You've heard it now."[56]

NOTES

1. 131 S. Ct. 2313.
2. David E. Wilkins and K. Tsianina Lomawaima, *Uneven Ground: American Indian Sovereignty and Federal Law* (Norman: University of Oklahoma Press, 2001), 65.
3. See Rebecca Tsosie and Wallace Coffey, "Rethinking the Tribal Sovereignty Doctrine: Cultural Sovereignty and the Collective Future of Indian Nations," *Stanford Law and Policy Review* 12, no. 2 (2001): 204.
4. N. Bruce Duthu, "Incorporative Discourse in Federal Indian Law: Negotiating Tribal Sovereignty through the Lens of Native American Literature," *Harvard Human Rights Journal* 13 (Spring 2000): 141–42.
5. Laura Coltelli, *Winged Words: American Indian Writers Speak*, American Indian Lives (Lincoln: University of Nebraska Press, 1990), 156.
6. Hester Lessard, Rebecca Johnson, and Jeremy Webber, "Stories, Communities, and Their Contested Meanings," in *Storied Communities: Narratives of Contact and Arrival in Constituting Political Community*, ed. Hester Lessard, Rebecca Johnson, and Jeremy Webber (Vancouver: UBC Press, 2011), 7.
7. Nenabozho, often referred to as *original man*, is the central character (trickster) in many Anishinaabe *aadizookaanan* (stories or legends). He is also referred to as Wenabozho. These spellings come from John Nichols and Earl Nyholm, *A Concise Dictionary of Minnesota Ojibwe* (Minneapolis: University of Minnesota Press, 1995), 118.
8. Basil Johnston, *Ojibwe Heritage*, 122–23.

9. Jo-Ann Archibald, *Indigenous Storywork: Educating the Heart, Mind, Body, and Spirit* (Vancouver: UBC Press, 2008), 5.

10. Truman Michelson, ed., and William Jones, comp., *Ojibwa Texts*, ed. Franz Boas, 2 vols., Publications of the American Ethnological Society (Leiden: E. J. Brill, Ltd., 1917), vol. 7, pt. 1, p. 7.

11. For additional analysis of this story, see Heidi Kiiwetinepinesiik Stark, "Marked by Fire: Anishinaabe Articulations of Nationhood in Treaty-Making with the United States and Canada." *American Indian Quarterly* 36, no.2 (2012): 119–149

12. See, for example, Heidi Kiiwetinepinesiik Stark, "Respect, Responsibility, and Renewal: The Foundations of Anishinaabe Treaty Making with the United States and Canada," *American Indian Culture and Research Journal* 34, no. 2 (2010): 145–164.

13. Julie Cruikshank, *The Social Life of Stories: Narrative and Knowledge in the Yukon Territory* (Lincoln: University of Nebraska Press, 1998), xii.

14. John Borrows, *Canada's Indigenous Constitution* (Toronto: University of Toronto Press, 2010), 7.

15. See John Borrows, *Recovering Canada: The Resurgence of Indigenous Law* (Toronto: University of Toronto Press, 2002); Borrows, *Drawing Out Law: A Spirit's Guide* (Toronto: University of Toronto Press, 2010); Borrows, *Canada's Indigenous Constitution* (Toronto: University of Toronto Press, 2010).

16. Leslie Marmon Silko, *Yellow Woman and a Beauty of the Spirit: Essays on Native American Life Today* (New York: Simon and Schuster, 1996), 50.

17. Edward Benton-Banai, *The Mishomis Book: The Voice of the Ojibway* (St. Paul, MN: Red School House, 1988).

18. Thomas King, *The Truth about Stories: A Native Narrative* (Minneapolis: University of Minnesota Press, 2005), 92.

19. See Lessard, Johnson, and Webber, "Stories, Communities, and Their Contested Meanings."

20. Patricia Tuitt, "Narratives of Origins and the Emergence of the European Union," in *Storied Communities: Narratives of Contact and Arrival in Constituting Political Community*, ed. Hester Lessard, Rebecca Johnson, and Jeremy Webber (Vancouver: UBC Press, 2011), 229.

21. Lessard, Johnson, and Webber, "Stories, Communities, and Their Contested Meanings," 8.

22. Bain Attwood, "The Batman Legend: Remembering and Forgetting the History of Possession and Dispossession," in *Storied Communities: Narratives of Contact and Arrival in Constituting Political Community*, ed. Hester Lessard, Rebecca Johnson, and Jeremy Webber (Vancouver: UBC Press, 2011), 190.

23. Robert A. Williams, *Like a Loaded Weapon: The Rehnquist Court, Indian Rights, and The Legal History of Racism in America*, Indigenous Americas (Minneapolis: University of Minnesota Press, 2005).

24. Jacinta Ruru, "Layered Narratives in Site-Specific 'Wild' Places," in *Storied Communities: Narratives of Contact and Arrival in Constituting Political Community*, ed. Hester Lessard, Rebecca Johnson, and Jeremy Webber (Vancouver: UBC Press, 2011), 216.

25. Greg Sarris, *Keeping Slug Woman Alive: A Holistic Approach to American Indian Texts* (Berkeley: University of California Press, 1993), 4.

26. For a detailed analysis of how the U.S. Supreme Court has defined and limited tribal sovereignty, see David E. Wilkins, *American Indian Sovereignty and the U.S. Supreme Court: The Masking of Justice* (Austin: University of Texas Press, 1997).

27. *U.S. v. Jicarilla Apache Nation*, 131 S. Ct. 2313 (June 13, 2011).

28. *U.S. v. Jicarilla Apache Nation*, 131 S. Ct. 2325 (June 13, 2011).

29. *U.S. v. Jicarilla Apache Nation*, 131 S. Ct. 2327 (June 13, 2011).

30. *U.S. v. Jicarilla Apache Nation*, 131 S. Ct. 2324 (June 13, 2011).

31. Thank you to David E. Wilkins for sharing this point that the Court in this case positioned trust as coming from plenary power.

32. For detailed explanation of the doctrine of discovery, the trust relationship, and plenary power, see Wilkins and Lomawaima, *Uneven Ground: American Indian Sovereignty and Federal Law.*

33. *Merrion v. Jicarilla Apache Tribe*, 455 U.S. 130 (1982).

34. *U.S. v Wheeler*, 435 U.S. 313 (1978).

35. *Lone Wolf v. Hitchcock*, 187 U.S. 533 (1903).

36. Audrey Macklin, "Historicizing Narratives of Arrival: The Other Indian Other," in *Storied Communities: Narratives of Contact and Arrival in Constituting Political Community*, ed. Hester Lessard, Rebecca Johnson, and Jeremy Webber (Vancouver: UBC Press, 2011), 40.

37. As Julie Cruikshank reminds us, "The question of which versions are 'correct' may be less interesting than what each story reveals about the cultural values of its narrator." She argues that neither written nor oral history can merely be sifted for facts, and that combining the two does not provide the "real story." Instead, Cruikshank finds that these sources serve as windows into how the past is constructed and discussed. How, when, and in which context stories are told is as telling of the people as the stories themselves. See Julie Cruikshank, "Discovery of Gold on the Klondike: Perspectives from Oral Tradition," in *Reading Beyond Words: Contexts for Native History*, ed. Jennifer S. H. Brown and Elizabeth Vibert (Toronto: Broadview Press, 1996), 433. Also see Cruikshank, *The Social Life of Stories: Narrative and Knowledge in the*

Yukon Territory. Also see Keith H. Basso, *Wisdom Sits in Places: Landscape and Language among the Western Apache* (Albuquerque: University of New Mexico Press, 1996).

38. *Johnson v. McIntosh*, 21 U.S. (8 Wheat) 543 (1823).
39. *Cherokee Nation v. Georgia*, 30 U.S. 1 (1831).
40. Leslie Marmon Silko, *Ceremony* (New York: Fire Keepers/Quality Paperback Book Club, 1994), 138.
41. *Worcester v. Georgia*, 31 U.A. (6 Pet.) 515 (1832), at 560–61.
42. *U.S. v. Kagama*, 118 U.S. 375 (1886), 384.
43. *Lone Wolf v. Hitchcock*, 187 U.S. 553 (1903), 221.
44. *Oliphant v. Suquamish Indian Tribe*, 435 U.S. 191 (1978), 208.
45. Gordon Christie, "Indigeneity and Sovereignty in Canada's Far North: The Arctic and Inuit Sovereignty," *South Atlantic Quarterly* 110, no. 2 (Spring 2011): 330.
46. Ibid., 338.
47. Ibid., 341.
48. *Ratified Treaty No. 247, Documents Relating to the Negotiation of the Treaty of June 5 and 17, 1846, with the Chippewa, Ottawa, and Potawatomi Indians*, Documents Relating to the Negotiation of Ratified and Unratified Treaties with Various Tribes of Indians, 1801–69, National Archives Microfilm Publications, Record Group 75, Microcopy no. T-494, Roll 4:F308, Records of the Bureau of Indian Affairs, National Archives and Records Services, Washington, DC [hereafter NAMP RG 75, M T-494 Roll 4:F308].
49. Ibid.
50. Ibid.
51. *Ratified Treaty No. 247, Documents Relating to the Negotiation of the Treaty of June 5 and 17, 1846, with the Chippewa, Ottawa, and Potawatomi Indians*, NAMP RG 75, M T-494 Roll 4:F309.
52. Ibid.
53. *Ratified Treaty No. 247, Documents Relating to the Negotiation of the Treaty of June 5 and 17, 1846, with the Chippewa, Ottawa, and Potawatomi Indians*, NAMP RG 75, M T-494 Roll 4:F311.
54. Ratified Treaty No. 247 Documents Relating to the Negotiation of the Treaty of June 5 and 17, 1846, with the Chippewa, Ottawa, and Potawatomi Indians, NAMP RG 75, M T-494 Roll 4:F309.
55. Johnny Mack, "Hoquotist: Reorienting through Storied Practice," in *Storied Communities: Narratives of Contact and Arrival in Constituting Political Community*, ed. Hester Lessard, Rebecca Johnson, and Jeremy Webber (Vancouver: UBC Press, 2011).
56. King, *The Truth about Stories: A Native Narrative*, 29.

RESOURCES

Legal Documents

Cherokee Nation v. Georgia, 30 U.S. 1 (1831).

Johnson v. McIntosh, 21 U.S. (8 Wheat) 543 (1823).

Lone Wolf v. Hitchcock, 187 U.S. 553 (1903).

Merrion v. Jicarilla Apache Tribe, 455 U.S. 130 (1982).

Oliphant v. Suquamish Indian Tribe, 435 U.S. 191 (1978).

U.S. v. Jicarilla Apache Nation, 131 S. Ct. 2313 (June 13, 2011).

U.S. v. Kagama, 118 U.S. 375 (1886).

U.S. v Wheeler, 435 U.S. 313 (1978).

Worcester v. Georgia, 31 U.A. (6 Pet.) 515 (1832).

Ratified Treaty No. 247, Documents Relating to the Negotiation of the Treaty of June 5 and 17, 1846, with the Chippewa, Ottawa, and Potawatomi Indians. Documents Relating to the Negotiation of Ratified and Unratified Treaties with Various Tribes of Indians, 1801–69, National Archives Microfilm Publications, Record Group 75, Microcopy no. T-494, Roll 4:F308. Records of the Bureau of Indian Affairs, National Archives and Records Services, Washington, DC.

Archibald, Jo-Ann. *Indigenous Storywork: Educating the Heart, Mind, Body, and Spirit.* Vancouver: UBC Press, 2008.

Attwood, Bain. "The Batman Legend: Remembering and Forgetting the History of Possession and Dispossession." In *Storied Communities: Narratives of Contact and Arrival in Constituting Political Community*, ed. Hester Lessard, Rebecca Johnson, and Jeremy Webber, 189–210. Vancouver: UBC Press, 2011.

Basso, Keith H. *Wisdom Sits in Places: Landscape and Language among the Western Apache.* Albuquerque: University of New Mexico Press, 1996.

Benton-Banai, Edward. *The Mishomis Book: The Voice of the Ojibway.* St. Paul, MN: Red School House, 1988.

Borrows, John. *Canada's Indigenous Constitution.* Toronto: University of Toronto Press, 2010.

———. *Drawing out Law: A Spirit's Guide.* Toronto: University of Toronto Press, 2010.

———. *Recovering Canada: The Resurgence of Indigenous Law.* Toronto: University of Toronto Press, 2002.

Christie, Gordon. "Indigeneity and Sovereignty in Canada's Far North: The Arctic and Inuit Sovereignty." *South Atlantic Quarterly* 110, no. 2 (Spring 2011): 329–46.

Coltelli, Laura. *Winged Words: American Indian Writers Speak.* American Indian Lives. Lincoln: University of Nebraska Press, 1990.

Cruikshank, Julie. "Discovery of Gold on the Klondike: Perspectives from Oral Tradition." In *Reading beyond Words: Contexts for Native History,* ed. Jennifer S. H. Brown and Elizabeth Vibert, 433–59. Toronto: Broadview Press, 1996.

———. *The Social Life of Stories: Narrative and Knowledge in the Yukon Territory.* Lincoln: University of Nebraska Press, 1998.

Duthu, N. Bruce. "Incorporative Discourse in Federal Indian Law: Negotiating Tribal Sovereignty through the Lens of Native American Literature." *Harvard Human Rights Journal* 13 (Spring 2000): 141–89.

Johnston, Basil. *Ojibwe Heritage.* Lincoln: Bison Books/University of Nebraska Press, 1990.

King, Thomas. *The Truth about Stories: A Native Narrative.* Minneapolis: University of Minnesota Press, 2005.

Lessard, Hester, Rebecca Johnson, and Jeremy Webber. "Stories, Communities, and Their Contested Meanings." In *Storied Communities: Narratives of Contact and Arrival in Constituting Political Community,* ed. Hester Lessard, Rebecca Johnson, and Jeremy Webber, 5–25. Vancouver: UBC Press, 2011.

Mack, Johnny. "Hoquotist: Reorienting through Storied Practice." In *Storied Communities: Narratives of Contact and Arrival in Constituting Political Community,* ed. Hester Lessard, Rebecca Johnson, and Jeremy Webber, 287–307. Vancouver: UBC Press, 2011.

Macklin, Audrey. "Historicizing Narratives of Arrival: The Other Indian Other." In *Storied Communities: Narratives of Contact and Arrival in Constituting Political Community,* ed. Hester Lessard, Rebecca Johnson, and Jeremy Webber, 40–67. Vancouver: UBC Press, 2011.

Michelson, Truman, ed., and William Jones, comp. *Ojibwa Texts.* Edited by Franz Boas. 2 vols. Publications of the American Ethnological Society, vol. 7, pt. 1. Leiden, Netherlands: E. J. Brill Ltd., 1917.

Nichols, John, and Earl Nyholm. *A Concise Dictionary of Minnesota Ojibwe.* Minneapolis: University of Minnesota Press, 1995.

Ruru, Jacinta. "Layered Narratives in Site-Specific 'Wild' Places." In *Storied Communities: Narratives of Contact and Arrival in Constituting Political Community,* ed. Hester Lessard, Rebecca Johnson, and Jeremy Webber, 211–26. Vancouver: UBC Press, 2011.

Sarris, Greg. *Keeping Slug Woman Alive: A Holistic Approach to American Indian Texts.* Berkeley: University of California Press, 1993.

Silko, Leslie Marmon. *Ceremony.* New York: Fire Keepers/Quality Paperback Book Club, 1994.

———. *Yellow Woman and a Beauty of the Spirit: Essays on Native American Life Today.* New York: Simon and Schuster, 1996.

Stark, Heidi Kiiwetinepinesiik. "Respect, Responsibility, and Renewal: The Foundations of Anishinaabe Treaty Making with the United States and Canada." *American Indian Culture and Research Journal* 34, no. 2 (2010): 145–64.

Tsosie, Rebecca, and Wallace Coffey. "Rethinking the Tribal Sovereignty Doctrine: Cultural Sovereignty and the Collective Future of Indian Nations." *Stanford Law and Policy Review* 12, no. 2 (2001): 191–221.

Tuitt, Patricia. "Narratives of Origins and the Emergence of the European Union." In *Storied Communities: Narratives of Contact and Arrival in Constituting Political Community*, ed. Hester Lessard, Rebecca Johnson, and Jeremy Webber, 229–44. Vancouver: UBC Press, 2011.

Wilkins, David E. *American Indian Sovereignty and the U.S. Supreme Court: The Masking of Justice.* Austin: University of Texas Press, 1997.

Wilkins, David E., and K. Tsianina Lomawaima. *Uneven Ground: American Indian Sovereignty and Federal Law.* Norman: University of Oklahoma Press, 2001.

Williams, Robert A. *Like a Loaded Weapon: The Rehnquist Court, Indian Rights, and the Legal History of Racism in America.* Indigenous Americas. Minneapolis: University of Minnesota Press, 2005.

Theorizing Resurgence from within Nishnaabeg Thought

LEANNE BETASAMOSAKE SIMPSON
WITH EDNA MANITOWABI

ONE OF THE MOST CRUCIAL TASKS PRESENTLY FACING INDIGENOUS nations is the continued creation of individuals and assemblages of people who can think in culturally inherent ways. By this, I mean ways that reflect the diversity of thought within our broader cosmologies, those very ancient ways that are inherently counter to the influences of colonial hegemony. I believe we need intellectuals who can think within the conceptual meanings of the language, who are intrinsically connected to place and territory, who exist in the world as an embodiment of contemporary expressions of our ancient stories and traditions, and who illuminate *mino bimaadiziwin* in all aspects of their lives.

Western theory, whether based in postcolonial, critical, or even libera-tory strains of thought, has been exceptional at diagnosing, revealing, and even interrogating colonialism; and many would argue that this body of theory holds the greatest promise for shifting the Canadian politic, because it speaks to that audience in a language they can understand, if not hear. Yet Western theories of liberation have for the most part failed to resonate with the vast majority of Indigenous peoples, scholars, or artists. In particular, Western-based social movement theory has failed to recognize the broader contextualizations of resistance within Indigenous thought, while also ignoring the contestation of colonialism as a starting point. While I believe liberatory theory and politics are always valuable, Indigenous thought has the ability to resonate with Indigenous peoples of all ages.[1] It not only maps a way out of colonial thinking by confirming Indigenous lifeways or alter-native ways of being in the world. Ultimately Indigenous theory seeks to dismantle colonialism while simultaneously building a renaissance of *mino bimaadiziwin*. What if this was our collective focus?

Part of being Indigenous in the twenty-first century is that regardless of where or how we have grown up, we've all been bathed in a vat of cognitive imperialism, perpetuating the idea that Indigenous peoples were not, and are not, thinking peoples—an insidious mechanism to promote neo-assimilation and obfuscate the historic atrocities of colonialism.[2] In both subtle and overt ways, the current generation of Indigenous peoples has been repeatedly told that individually we are stupid, and that collectively our nations were and are void of higher thought. This is reinforced when the academic industrial complex—often propped up by Indian and Northern Affairs Canada (INAC)—promotes colonizing education for our children and youth as the solution to dispossession, poverty, violence, and a lack of self-determination in our lives. Cognitive imperialism also rears its ugly head in every discipline every time a student is told that there is no literature or no thinking available on any given topic from within Indigenous intellectual traditions.

Our elders and knowledge holders have always put great emphasis on *how* things are done. This reinforces the idea that it is our own tools, strategies, values, processes, and intellect that are going to build our new house. While theoretically we have debated whether Audre Lourde's statement "The master's tools can dismantle the master's house" is correct, I am interested in a different question. I am not so concerned with how we dismantle the master's house—that is, which sets of theories we use to critique colonialism—but I am very concerned with how we (re)build our own house, or our own houses. I have spent enough time taking down the master's house, and now I want most of my energy to go into visioning and building our new house.

For me, this discussion begins with our creation stories, because these stories set the "theoretical framework," or give us the ontological context from within which we can interpret other stories, teachings, and experiences.[3] These stories and their Nishnaabeg context are extremely important to our way of being, and they are told and retold in our communities throughout one's life. Our children first start to learn Nishnaabeg thought and theory through these *Aandisokaanan* very early in their lives.[4] As they travel through the Four Hills of Life,[5] these teachings deepen and resonate in different ways. Benton-Banai writes:

> And so, Anishinaabe can see that if he knows his creation story, if she knows her creation story, they know also how all of life moves. They can know how life

comes to be. All of life is a creative process that began in this original way and continues in the same way in all aspects of our life. In all places and all facets of creation, and creative activity, these seven stages are reflected.[6]

Our elders tell us that everything we need to know is encoded in the structure, content, and context of these stories, and the relationships, ethics and responsibilities required to *be* our own creation story. In my own life, I did not fully understand this story until I became pregnant with my first child. My elder Edna Manitowabi guided me through my pregnancy, revealing the responsibilities that go along with bringing forth new life, with nurturing that life with my own sacred water, my thoughts, my emotions, my breath, and my own creative power. In doing so, Edna breathed into me a new way of seeing the world and of being in it. So for me, this is the only place to begin.

GWIINMAAGEMI GDI-DBAAJIMOWINAANIN: WE TELL STORIES

Cree scholar, poet, and visual artist Neal McLeod has written extensively about the importance of storytelling in his book *Cree Narrative Memory: From Treaties to Contemporary Times.* Neal writes that the process of storytelling within Cree traditions requires storytellers to remember the ancient stories that made their ancestors "the people they were," and that this requires a remembering of language. He also emphasizes that storytellers have a responsibility to the future to imagine a social space that is just, and where Cree narratives will flourish.[7] Storytelling is at its core decolonizing, because it is a process of remembering, visioning, and creating a just reality where Nishnaabeg live as both *Nishnaabeg* and *peoples.* Storytelling then becomes a lens through which we can envision our way out of cognitive imperialism, where we can create models and mirrors where none existed, and where we can experience the spaces of freedom and justice. Storytelling becomes a space where we can escape the gaze and the cage of the empire, even if it is just for a few minutes.

Oral storytelling becomes an even more important vehicle for the creation of free cognitive spaces, because the physical act of gathering a group of people together within our territories reinforces the web of relationships that stitch our communities together. The storyteller then has to work with emergence and flux, developing a unique relationship with the audience based entirely on context and relationships. Who is in the audience? Where are they from? Which clans are present? What age groups? What challenges are individuals, families, and communities going through? What personal gifts does the audience bring with them? What emotions do people bring? Which moon are we in? This context provides the storyteller with information s/he uses to decide what to tell, and how to tell it, to gain both individual meaning and collective resonance. The relationship between those present becomes dynamic, with the storyteller adjusting their "performance"[8] based on the reactions and presence of the audience. The lines between storyteller and audience become blurred as individuals make non-verbal (and sometimes verbal) contributions to the collective event. The "performance," whether a song, a dance, or a spoken-word story, becomes then an individual and collective experience, with the goal of lifting the burden of colonialism by visioning new realities.

While this is now also accomplished by Indigenous artists through the written word, spoken word, theater, performance art, visual art, music and rap, film and video, it is most powerful in terms of transformation in its original cultural context because that context places dynamic relationships at the core. When mediated through print or recording devices, these relationships become either reduced (technology that limits interactivity) or unilateral (as in print, film, or video, when the creator cannot respond to the reaction of the audience). Then the process, to me, loses some of its transformative power because it is no longer emergent.

Storytelling is an important process for visioning, imagining, critiquing the social space around us, and ultimately challenging the colonial norms that our daily lives are fraught with. In a similar way, dreams and visions propel resurgence because they provide Nishnaabeg with both knowledge from the spiritual world and processes for realizing those visions. Dreams and visions provide glimpses of decolonized spaces and transformed realities that we have collectively yet to imagine.

This is a thread that runs through this entire book, but begins here with the consideration of a creation story. There are several different creation stories within Nishnaabeg cosmology, and these stories are epics in and of themselves, often taking several hours or even days to tell. It is not ethically appropriate for me to tell these stories here, since these stories are traditionally told by elders who carry these responsibilities during ceremony or under certain circumstances. They are not widely shared. However, sketches of these stories have been printed by some of those elders themselves.[9] Relying on these published versions, and versions I have heard told in workshops and elders conferences (so in public *not* ceremonial contexts), I wish to bring attention to four tenets of the story that directly relate to the role of intellectual pursuits and theory in relation to resurgence; and I want to reclaim the context for interpretation of these teachings. One print version of this story is by Eddie Benton-Banai and is known as the Seven Fires of Ojibway Creation.[10] The following version was told to me by Edna Manitowabi, and she spent a lot of time explaining this story in the context of her own life and in the context of her work with our young women. It is printed here with her permission.

GRANDMOTHER TEACHINGS BY EDNA MANITOWABI

My name is Asinykwe and I am a relative of Mkwa, the Bear.[11] I am from Wiiwemikong, Mnidoo Minising. My father was Gaazongii (John Mnidoo Abi). My mother was Naakwegiizigokwe (Mary Louise Trudeau),[12] and she was a relative of Jijak (Crane). My mother lost nine children to residential school. I was the last to go. I went searching for these teachings as a way of recovering from this loss.

Dreamtime has always been a great teacher for me. I see my dreams as guides or mentors, as the Grandfathers and Grandmothers giving me direction in my life. Dreams are how my own spirit guides me through my life. In the mid-1970s, a dream led me to ceremonies and to the Little Boy water drum. When I first heard the sound of the Little Boy and felt his incredible vibration quivering through every cell and every fiber of my being, I knew I had come home, because I had dreamed of that Little Boy long before then.

I vividly recall the way the Little Boy was dressed the first time I saw him. He wore a headband with Seven Teaching Stones on his head. These symbolize the Seven Fires or the Seven Stages. I have tried to live my life according to these teachings, especially now as I move into my senior years. The time has come for me as a Grandmother, a teacher, and a Great-Grandmother to pass these on to the next generation of women. I have taken up this work and these responsibilities, and now I must remember these teachings, wear them, and pass them on to the younger generation of women who are now coming into that power time as a new woman spirit.

For a number of years now, I have had the honor and the privilege of preparing our young girls as they move into womanhood, and for helping young women, Mothers and Aunties who want to change their lives and have new understandings as Oshki-Nishnaabekwe[13] and as Ogichitaa.[14] These are not easy transitions to make. As a Grandmother, I try to help young women understand what is happening to them when their Grandmother comes to visit for the first time.[15] It is important that we as Grandmothers, Mothers, and Aunties come together as women to help and support these young women. This is particularly important now as our Mother the Earth is going through her own cleansing. We reflect this cleansing when we renew ourselves with these teachings, ceremonies, fasting, and our rites of passage. We need to pass on the teachings of the sacredness of the water that sustains us, the air that we breathe, and the fire within us, so that our next generation of women have an understanding of what is happening to them during this powerful transition. Through these teachings they will then come to understand the Earth as their Mother. Through these teachings, they will then come to understand the Earth as themselves.

They will understand her seasons, her moods and her cycles.
They will understand that she is the Mother to all of Creation.
They will understand that she takes care of herself.
They will see that she is beautiful, sacred and that she was created first.
They will know that she holds a special place in our hearts because she is our
  Mother.
They will understand that our people connect to this land as their Mother.

We need to help our young people maintain this relationship and these teachings, because that connection is the umbilical bond to all of Creation.

When our young women understand this, they will understand their own seasons, cycles, and moods. They will understand that they are sacred and beautiful. They will understand that they must take care of themselves, and that they are the mothers to generations yet to be born.

We do this for our young women so they will be guided by our Mother's wisdom and so they will model themselves after this Earth. So they might grow up to be good and kind compassionate Anishinaabekwewag. So they might know how to look after their children and their grandchildren. So that together, we might be a strong nation again. That is my dream. That is why I keep working. We do this work because we love our children. This is my purpose in life as a Grandmother and a Great-Grandmother. This is my purpose in life as a Kobaade.[16]

In the beginning, before the beginning, there was only darkness and emptiness. In this cold, dark vastness there was a sound, a sound like the shaking of seeds in a gourd. Then there was one thought, the first thought. The thought of the Great Mystery, Creator, Gzhwe Mnidoo.[17]

Gzhwe Mnidoo's thoughts went out into the darkness. S/he knew s/he had to create a place for these thoughts, so Gzhwe Mnidoo created a circle in that darkness, and within that circle s/he made a fire. At the center of the circle was the heartbeat of the Creator.

In the beginning, the first thought was the pulse and rhythm of Gzhwe Mnidoo. The thoughts and the heartbeat went out into the vastness. The thoughts and the vibrational sound of the heartbeat created the star world, the sky, and the universe. The Creator's first thought combined with the first heartbeat became the First Fire of Creation.

Within that great circle of the universe came another circle when Gzhwe Mnidoo made a fire creating light in that darkness. This is Creator's Second Fire, Giizis, the Sun. Within that great circle was the partner to the Giizis, our Grandmother the Moon. Dibiki-Giizis is the nighttime sun who would give us light in our darkness—the duality of all was created.

Grandmother Moon is the Grand woman of the universe, was given to govern the cycles. The seasons would renew all the life that would be created. The partnership of night and day was established, and this was the Third Fire of Creation. All of this was set into motion with the four sacred directions, and in doing so movement was created, the Fourth Fire of Creation.

Gzhwe Mnidoo then called on the beneshiinyak (birds) of every color, song, size, and shape. Gzhwe Mnidoo put all of the thoughts and creative energy into seeds and asked the beneshiinyak to spread the seeds. Those seeds carried all of the creative energy, all of the thoughts and the potential for all of life. This was the Fifth Fire of Creation.

Then Gzhwe Mnidoo made a place for those seeds to go. S/he made the most beautiful Woman, who we know as our Mother the Earth. Three times, Gzhwe Mnidoo tried. On the fourth try, s/he made our beautiful, round Earth. Gzhwe Mnidoo gave her a heart from the First Fire and placed it at the very core of her being. The very first woman created was a woman with a heart, with emotion, and it was a woman with a heart that would give birth to all of Creation.

Gzhwe Mnidoo looked upon Creation, the incredible beauty of the Earth, the waterways, the lakes and streams, the rivers. Her Life Blood flowing below and above the ground. These are the very waters of life that feed and nourish all of life, all of Creation. Her veins and her lifeblood, her bloodlines give life to all that Gzhwe Mnidoo had made. In all of that we would always know that we are joined together as one. We have the same Mother. We would always know she was created first, the first woman with a heart. When Creator finished Creation, Gzhwe Mnidoo gave it to her. You are the Creator now; you will create life and renew it. This is why these teachings are so important to our young women— when we bring forth new life they are reenacting this story.

When the seeds had been scattered on the face of the Earth, Gzhwe Mnidoo saw the beauty of her and how everything moved in harmony and in balance.

Gzhwe Mnidoo saw how everything was full and so complete, and Creator was filled with great joy. Gzhwe Mnidoo was filled with tears at this great joy, and they fell to the Earth, nourishing the land and the seeds mated to the soil.

And so from her breast, from her, came all that there is, and all that there will be; the winged of the air, the swimmers, the four legged, the flowers, the plants, the crawlers, the trees, and the seas that moved across the land. Upon her bosom reigned peace and happiness for ages and ages, and this was the Sixth Fire of Creation.

Original Man was the last to be created. Gzhwe Mnidoo wanted one who would reflect her/his thoughts, and so from the first woman s/he took four parts of her body—soil, air, water, and fire—and molded a being, a vessel. Gzhwe Mnidoo blew his/her own spirit breath into the being and gave him her/his own thoughts, and these thoughts were so vast that they spilled out of his head into his entire body. Gzhwe Mnidoo touched Original Man's breast, causing his heart to beat in harmony with the rhythm of the universe and with Gzhwe Mnidoo.

Gzhwe Mnidoo then lowered him down to the Earth so that he might also be a child of the great Mother. It is in that and with great kindness and humility, with the utmost gentleness, that Anishinaabe touched and met his Mother. This is the Seventh Fire of Creation.

This story is important for young women to know because they re-create this story in pregnancy. When we create new life, it is an extension of ourselves, just as Original Man was an extension of Gzhwe Mnidoo. In the same way, our thoughts, our breath, and our heartbeat pulse in the new life they carry in our sacred waters.

OUR THEORY IS PERSONAL

A theory in its most basic form is simply an explanation for why we do the things we do.[18] When we think of theory in this way, the *Aandisokaanan* and our language encode our theories, and we express those theories in both the *Dibaajimowinan*[19] and our ways of being in the world. I have come to understand the *Dibaajimowinan* as echoing the *Aandisokaanan*. Our personal creation stories, our lives, mirror and reflect the Seven Fires of Creation.

The starting point within Indigenous theoretical frameworks, then, is different from that within Western theories: the spiritual world is alive and influential, colonialism is contested, and storytelling, or "narrative imagination," is a tool to vision other existences outside of the current ones by critiquing and analyzing the current state of affairs, but also by dreaming and visioning other realities.[20] The responsibility for finding meaning within these *Aandisokaanan* lies within individual Nishnaabeg, and this is communicated through our *Dibaajimowinan*. Every Nishnaabeg has our own personal stories or narratives that communicate their personal truths, learning, histories, and insights. *Dibaajimowinan* in this sense are personal opportunities to create. Our elders consider creation stories to be of paramount importance because they provide the ontological and epistemological framework to interpret other *Aandisokaanan* and *Dibaajimowinan* in a culturally inherent way. It is critical, then, that these stories themselves are interpreted in a culturally inherent way, rather than through the obfuscated lens of imperial thought, because they are foundational, and they serve to build meaning into the other stories.

The first insight into Nishnaabeg theoretical foundations I would like to explore occurs in the Seventh Fire of Creation, after Gzhwe Mnidoo[21] has dreamed the physical world through the first Six Fires. The First Fire created the universe through the union of the first thought (intellectual knowledge) with the first heartbeat (heart knowledge or emotion, truth). In the Second Fire, Gzhwe Mnidoo created the first fire and the Four Directions. In the Third Fire, duality exists for the first time. The Fourth Fire brings movement. By combining duality and movement, Gzhwe Mnidoo encapsulated his thoughts into seeds (the Fifth Fire), and the Sixth Fire was the creation of the first woman as a mother, the earth, so those seeds would have somewhere to go.

Gzhwe Mnidoo next created the first beings, but it took a very, very long time. S/he wanted to create the most beautiful beings possible. So Gzhwe Mnidoo dreamed. Gzhwe Mnidoo visioned. Gzhwe Mnidoo took time, tried some things out. S/he was careful and persistent, and finally, after a good length of time, Gzhwe Mnidoo lowered the first being, ever so gently, to earth. Nishna is our verb for "being lowered." Reclaiming the context of this story means that rather than saying or thinking that Gzhwe Mnidoo lowered an abstract "first person" to the earth, if I am a woman, I say or think Gzhwe Mnidoo lowered "the first woman to the earth."[22]

That first being was the most beautiful thing Gzhwe Mnidoo had ever seen, and Gzhwe Mnidoo's heart swelled with love. Again, our elders teach us that this most beautiful, perfect, lovely being was not just any "First Person," but that it was me, or you. We are taught to insert ourselves into the story. Gzhwe Mnidoo created the most beautiful, perfect person possible, and that most beautiful, perfect person was me, Betasamosake.[23] What does this tell us about Nishnaabeg thought?

It is personal.

We were created out of love.

That the love of Gzhwe Mnidoo is unconditional, complete, and that s/he loves us the way we are, without judgment.

By inserting ourselves into these stories, we assume responsibilities—responsibilities that are not necessarily bestowed upon us by the collective, but that we take on according to our own gifts, abilities, and affiliations. Nishnaabeg theory has to be learned in the context of our own personal lives, in an emotional, physical, spiritual, and intellectual way. Every time I tell my children this story, or they hear this part of it in ceremony, their faces light up. It reaffirms that they are good, and beautiful, and perfect the way they are. Every time I have shared this part of our creation story with Indigenous students, their faces light up as well. When interpreted this way, our stories draw individuals into the resurgence narrative on their own terms and in accordance with their own names, clan affiliations, and gifts. For just a moment, they are complete in the absence of want—decolonizing one moment at a time. Indigenous thought can only be learned through the personal; this is because our greatest influence is on ourselves, and because living in a good way is an incredible disruption of the colonial metanarrative in and of itself. In a system requiring presence, the only way to learn is to live and demonstrate those teachings through a personal embodiment of *mino bimaadiziwin*. As Edna said in her creation story, we *wear* our teachings.

EMBODIED KNOWLEDGE, UNLIMITED INTELLIGENCE

The next part of the story, after Gzhwe Mnidoo has lowered me to the earth, tells us that Gzhwe Mnidoo put her/his right hand to my forehead and s/he transferred all of Gzhwe Mnidoo's thoughts into me. There were so many that the thoughts couldn't just stay in my head; they spilled into every part of my being and filled up my whole body. Gzhwe Mnidoo's knowledge was so immense from creating the world that it took all of my being to embody it.[24]

This tells us that in order to access knowledge from a Nishnaabeg perspective, we have to engage our entire bodies: our physical beings, emotional self, our spiritual energy, and our intellect. Our methodologies, our lifeways must reflect those components of our being and the integration of those four components into a whole. This gives rise to our "research methodologies," our ways of knowing, our processes for living in the world.[25]

It also tells us that there is no limit to Indigenous intellect. Gzhwe Mnidoo dreamed our world into existence. S/he dreamed us into existence, demonstrating that the process of creation—visioning, making, doing—is the most powerful process in the universe. My creation story tells me that collectively we have the intellect and creative power to regenerate our cultures, languages, and nations. My creation story tells me another world is possible, and that I have the tools to vision it and bring it into reality. I can't think of a more powerful narrative.

All of the knowledge that Gzhwe Mnidoo possessed from making every aspect of creation was transferred to us. We can access this vast body of knowledge through our cultures by singing, dancing, fasting, dreaming, visioning, participating in ceremony, apprenticing with elders, practicing our lifeways and living our knowledge by watching, listening, and reflecting in a good way. Ultimately we access this knowledge through the quality of our relationships, and the personalized contexts we collectively create. The meaning comes from the context and the process, not the content.[26] In another way, Sákéj Youngblood Henderson says the meaning comes from the performance of our culture.[27] Gerald Vizenor says the meaning is in the telling and in the presence, our individual and collective presence—Creation as presence.[28] We are all saying the same thing. The performance of our "theories" and thought is how we collectivize meaning. This is important because our collective truths as a nation and as a culture are continuously generated from those individual truths we carry around inside ourselves. Our collective truths exist in a nest of individual diversity.

A little while later in the story, Original Man—or in my case, Betasamosake—goes searching for answers about both the meaning of life and the meaning of her own existence. She finds that for every question she has, Gzhwe Mnidoo has created a story with the answers. She finds that it is her responsibility to discover those stories and seek out the answers. This is our journey through resurgence. This is our responsibility. We are each responsible for finding our own meanings, for shifting those meanings through time and space, for coming to our own meaningful way of being in the world. We are each responsible for being present in our own lives and engaged in our own realities.

Interpreting creation stories within a culturally inherent framework provides several insights into Nishnaabeg thought. First, it is highly personal. All Nishnaabeg people are theorists in the sense that they hold responsibilities to make meaning for their own creation and their own lives. This happens in the context of Nishnaabeg knowledge, their name, their clan, their community, their own personal gifts and attributes, and their own life experience. Theory is collectivized through the telling of our stories and the performance of our ceremonies. We begin to teach our children theory immediately, and they begin to teach us theory immediately. In part because they are fresh from the spiritual world, with a purity of heart and mind that is difficult to find in adults, but also because they tell it like it is, unaware of whether that is considered "appropriate" or not.

In terms of resurgence, our creation stories tell us that collectively and intellectually we have access to all of the knowledge we need to untangle ourselves from the near destruction we are draped in, because Gzhwe Mnidoo transferred all of her/his thoughts into our full bodies. It tells us that each of us must live in a good and balanced way—physically, intellectual, emotionally, and spiritually—in order to access this knowledge. For me, it took participating in my own creation story and the creation stories of my children through the ceremonies of pregnancy, birth, and mothering that enabled me to understand the deeper meanings of these theories. These ceremonies in my life were profoundly transformative in all aspects of my being, and yet it took seven years to be able to articulate these meanings from within *debwewin*, meaning truth.

NOTES

This chapter originally appeared in *Dancing on Our Turtle's Back: Stories of Nishnaabeg Re-Creation, Resurgence, and a New Emergence* (Winnipeg: Arbeiter Ring, 2011).

1. The term "Indigenous theory" or "Indigenous thought" is problematic because it reinforces an artificial division between thought and embodiment. For Indigenous peoples, thought is fully integrated into living, being, and performance of our traditions. For a more detailed discussion, see Sákéj Youngblood Henderson's *First Nations Jurisprudence and Aboriginal Rights* (Saskatoon, SK: Native Law Centre, 2006). "Indigenous theory" is lived, not just discussed and actualized in the intellectual realm. I have attempted to use terms from Nishnaabemowin where appropriate.

2. Sákéj Youngblood Henderson, "Postcolonial Ghost Dancing: Diagnosing European Colonialism," in *Reclaiming Indigenous Voice and Vision*, ed. Marie Battiste (Vancouver: UBC Press, 2000), 57–77.

3. I have carefully considered the ethical issues around this discussion, and I decided to frame this chapter around published versions (both oral, in the form of public talks and written) of these stories by reputable Nishnaabeg

elders. This means that what is available to widely share is a small fraction of these stories and their meanings. Full understanding only occurs after several years of learning these stories in appropriate oral contexts under the guidance of elders. I have heard the telling of various versions and parts of this creation story over the past fifteen years from a variety of sources, including Robin Greene-ba, Edna Manitowabi, and Doug Williams. Most recently, Jim Dumont told a similar version to the one I am using for my purposes here at the Elders Conference at Trent University in Peterborough, Ontario, on February 20, 2010. I have also heard Nishnaabeg educator Nicole Bell retell several aspects of these stories in our local language nest, Wii-Kendimiing Nishnaabemowin Saswaansing. I have relied on these oral versions for the purposes of this book, but they are also similar to Benton-Banai's telling in *The Mishomis Book: The Voice of the Ojibway* (St. Paul, MN: Indian Country Press, 1979).

4. *Aandisokaanan* are traditional, sacred stories. See Wendy Makoons Geniusz, *Our Knowledge Is Not Primitive: Decolonizing Botanical Anishinaabe Teachings* (Syracuse, NY: Syracuse University Press, Syracuse NY, 2009), 12.

5. There are both Four Hill and Seven Hill versions of this concept in Nishnaabeg philosophy.

6. N. Bell, E. Conroy, K. Wheatley et al., "Anishinaabe Creation Story," in *The Ways of Knowing Guide* (Toronto: Ways of Knowing Partnership Turtle Island Conservation, Toronto Zoo, 2010), 32, available online at http://torontozoo .travel/pdfs/tic/Stewardship_Guide.pdf. The story present in *The Ways of Knowing Guide* is based on the teachings of the Seven Fires of Creation by Edward Benton-Banai, rendered as a poem entitled "The Seven Fires of the Ojibway Nation," originally published in *The Sounding Voice* (St. Paul, MN: Indian Country Press, 1978), and found in Pamela Williamson and John Roberts, *First Nations Peoples*, 2nd ed. (Toronto: Emond Montgomery, 2004), 20.

7. Neal McLeod, *Cree Narrative Memory: From Treaties to Contemporary Times* (Saskatoon, SK: Purich Press, 2007), 100.

8. I use this term in the sense of presence and engagement, rather than a performance that is aimed at entertaining the audience.

9. Basil Johnston, Edward Benton-Banai, Doug Williams, Jim Dumont, Edna Manitowabi, Thomas Peacock, and Marlene Wisuri, who have published these tenets in print form, digital form, or have discussed these tenets in oral forms in public. Following their lead, I do not discuss our creation story further than the boundary they have established.

10. N. Bell, E. Conroy, K. Wheatley et al., "Anishinaabe Creation Story," 25. The story present in *The Ways of Knowing Guide* is based on the Teachings

of the Seven Fires of Creation by Edward Benton-Banai, rendered as a poem entitled "The Seven Fires of the Ojibway Nation," originally published in *The Sounding Voice* (Indian Country Press, 1978), and also found in print in Williamson and Roberts, *First Nations Peoples*, 17–20.

11. This was written by Edna Manitowabi and is printed here with her permission, March 18, 2011, Peterborough, Ontario.

12. *Asinykwe* means "Rock Woman." Wiiwemikong refers to Wikwemikong Unceded Indian Reserve. Mnidoo Minising or "Spirit Island" is the Nishnaabeg name for Manitoulin Island, Ontario. *Gaazongii* means Grizzly Bear. *Naakwegiizigokwe* means Half-Day Women.

13. *Oshki-Nishnaabekwe* means "New Woman."

14. *Ogichitaa* is a "sacred or holy woman."

15. This is a reference to a visit by Nokomis Giizis, Grandmother Moon, and is a way of talking about a young woman's first menstrual cycle.

16. *Kobaade* means great-grandmother and refers to making a link from one generation to another. We are not to keep the teachings, but to pass them on.

17. There is no gender associated with Gzhwe Mnidoo, and it can be translated as life force, life essence, Creator, the Great Mystery, or "that which we do not understand."

18. I am using the word *theory* here to mean entities, explanations, and engagements that bring about meaning to both the individual and the collective.

19. *Dibaajimowinan* are personal stories, teachings, ordinary stories, narratives, and histories. See Wendy Makoons Geniusz, *Our Knowledge Is Not Primitive: Decolonizing Botanical Anishinaabe Teachings* (Syracuse, NY: Syracuse University Press, 2009), 12. It is my understanding that there is not a uniform boundary between the two, or that different elders and different regions have specific teachings and protocols around which stories are considered sacred, and which are personal stories, teachings, ordinary stories, narratives, and histories. There is a relationship between the *Aandisokaanan* and *Dibaajimowinan* that to me is like an echo, not a dichotomy.

20. Neal McLeod, *Cree Narrative Memory: From Treaties to Contemporary Times* (Saskatoon, SK: Purich Press, 2007), 98.

21. Doug Williams noted that while the terms "God" or "Creator" might invoke feelings of fear, punishment, or authority, Gzhwe Mnidoo invokes feelings of awe, warmth, love, total acceptance, and protection. Gzhwe Mnidoo is the one who can see you and accepts you completely. Waawshkigaamagki (Curve Lake First Nation), July 15, 2010.

22. This teaching was reaffirmed to me by Jim Dumont, Elders Conference, Trent University, Peterborough, Ontario, February 20, 2010; and Edna Manitoba, Guest Lecture INDG 2601, Trent University, September 23, 2010.

23. Ibid.

24. Ibid.

25. It is my understanding through many conversations with Edna Manitowabi that the story of Original Man and his trip around the earth visiting all aspects of Creation reveals many of our Nishnaabeg ways of knowing. Original Man is our first teacher, or first researcher. Original Man learns about the world by engaging with it. He learns by visiting, observing, reflecting, naming, singing, dancing, listening, learning-by-doing, experimentation, consulting with elders, storytelling, and by engaging in ceremony. For a print version of this story, "Original Man Walks the Earth," see pages 6–12 in Edward Benton-Banai, *The Mishomis Book: The Voice of the Ojibway* (Hayward, WI: Indian Country Communications, 1988). Also see Leanne Simpson, "Advancing an Indigenist Agenda: Promoting Indigenous Intellectual Traditions in Research," in *Sacred Landscapes*, ed. Jill Oakes, Rick Riewe, Rachel ten Bruggencate, and Ainsly Cogswell (Winnipeg: Aboriginal Issues Press, University of Manitoba, 2009), 141–54.

26. Leanne Simpson, "The Construction of Traditional Ecological Knowledge: Issues, Implications and Insights" (Ph.D. diss., University of Manitoba, 1999).

27. Sákéj Youngblood Henderson, *First Nations Jurisprudence and Aboriginal Rights* (Saskatoon, SK: Native Law Centre, 2006).

28. Gerald Vizenor and Robert Houle, Pine Tree Lecture, Trent University, Peterborough, Ontario, February 23, 2010; and Gerald Vizenor, *Fugitive Poses: Native American Indian Scenes of Absence and Presence* (Lincoln: University of Nebraska Press, 1998).

Eko-ingodwaasi Bagijigan

Stories as Reclamation

ANISHINAABEG STORIES CLAIM OUR LIVES, ASSERT PRESENCE, AND ensure the continuation of our communities as active contributors to humanity and all of Creation. They honor the past, recognize the present, and provide visions for the future—all of which engage the struggle of being Anishinaabeg in an ever-changing world. Just as Anishinaabeg have encountered the challenges and beauties of existence in the past, Anishinaabeg storytellers from all walks of life are using the critical tools of the present to engage their futures. They are centering our critical paths and guiding our paths—providing gifts for future Anishinaabeg to inherit.

David Stirrup, in his essay "*Aadizookewininiwag* and the Visual Arts: Stories as Process and Principle in Twenty-first Century Anishinaabeg Painting" explores the interconnected relationship between art and story, between the visual and verbal. He shows how innovative Anishinaabe artists Andrea Carlson, Star Wallowing Bull, and Jim Denomie are revising, revisioning, reimagining, and reconceptualizing stories, histories, and contexts. Stirrup argues that story and art are processes and spaces for participation, critical engagement, and beginnings rather than endpoints. Anishinaabe art, understood as a process and appreciated as stories, reclaims representation and aesthetic/intellectual sovereignty.

Dylan Miner, in "Stories as *Mshkiki*: Reflections on the Healing and Migratory Practices of Minwaajimo" focuses on the themes of migration and *mshkiki* (medicine). Drawing upon tribalography and the Seven Teachings to construct his essay, Miner forms a narrative that migrates home and works toward decolonization. He discusses the ways in which certain aesthetics within storytelling have profound cleansing and healing capabilities. He also emphasizes the importance and need to include stories of urban Anishinaabeg. Integrating his own experiences with those of Anishinaabe ethnologist Keewaydinoquay Peschel and Odawa activist Pun Plamondon, Miner demonstrates how stories engage diverse forms of expression, heal wounds from colonization, and form critical connections that promote interdependence and create beauty.

In "Horizon Lines, Medicine Painting, and Moose Calling: The Visual/Performative Storytelling of Three Anishinaabeg Artists," Molly McGlennen explores the visual and performative forms of story carried out by contemporary Anishinaabeg artists George Morrison, Norval Morrisseau, and Rebecca Belmore. McGlennen argues that contemporary art "can be viewed as a vibrant continuation, adaptation, and creative expression of traditional modes of storytelling that helped (and still help) Anishinaabeg understand the world around them and how to 'be' in that world." Examining the intellectual, political, and spiritual roles of art within Anishinaabeg communities, McGlennen examines how artistic expression is storied expression that can teach us about the power of meditating and contemplative forms of knowledge production, the connection between creativity and spirituality, and how to politicize movements that disrupt colonization, trauma, and violence.

Aadizookewininiwag and the Visual Arts

Story as Process and Principle in Twenty-First Century Anishinaabeg Painting

DAVID STIRRUP

*In old times, the artists were the keepers of memory,
the recorders of events, the markmakers of prayers, and
the shamen who brought the unseen world into view.*

—JAUNE QUICK-TO-SEE SMITH

*Discourse, theory, cognizance, and the transference of knowledge are
parts of a creative, oratorical, dramatic process through which our
narrative history and story—oratory—were crafted, understood,
and transferred systemically, both locally and nationally.*

—LEE MARACLE

Seeing is mandatory; conclusions are optional.

—GERALD MCMASTER

In his preface to *Narrative Chance*, Anishinaabe writer Gerald Vizenor asserts that "Native American stories are told and heard in motion, imagined and read over and over on a landscape that is never seen at once."[1] The natural imagery, ubiquitous in Vizenor's writing, is literal—"words are heard in winter rivers," he continues; "crows are written on the poplars"—but, with its emphasis on the visual, on the ocular, and on the explicit relationship he describes between telling, hearing, imagining, and seeing, that imagery refers also to the represented landscape. Whether we see the word "landscape" in formal European terms as a compositional descriptor, burdened with colonial connotations; or more simply as the literal canvas itself, the artistic "ground"; or more fully as the complex terrain—the histories, conversations, legacies—with which and in which the artist engages, we, as viewers, tend rarely to see that landscape all at once, as a singular "event." Rather, I argue here, we are invited into a discursive space in which the artist is always already participating in a dynamic exchange, revising and revisioning, reimagining and reconceptualizing those selfsame stories, histories, and contexts.

This essay will explore the vitality of the relationship between art and story, visual and verbal, in contemporary Anishinaabe art.[2] I will argue that story, as represented by three examples of painting (as) story, can be understood as process rather than product. As such, story is intrinsic to the ongoing circulation and construction of meaning between audience, painter/writer/teller, text, and source. It is that circulation—in which stories, works of art, and so on exist not as products or artifacts, but as participants and spaces for participation—that constitutes the ground of knowledge of Anishinaabeg Studies and enables discourse around questions of responsibility, personhood, community, and sovereignty. Looking specifically at the ways in which three contemporary artists—Andrea Carlson, Star Wallowing Bull, and Jim Denomie[3]—both use and create stories as major components of the complex layering of their "landscape" aesthetic, I will explore how their narrative forms resist easy classification according to art-historical conventions (though I will refer to them as landscapes here) and confront questions of representation and aesthetic/intellectual sovereignty.

I will show how all three draw from different elements of Native narrative arts to form interpretive containers for the consideration of objects, ideas, and stories, engaging among other things in "the crucial social and aesthetic project of establishing Indigenous sovereignty, or collective agency, over representational practices."[4] Carlson, for instance, calls directly on the genii loci of Anishinaabeg stories, while Denomie invokes Plains ledger art (absorbing non-Native art and photography of the American West in the process), and Wallowing Bull uses a whole range of traditional patterns and forms from different Indigenous traditions, alongside the dream/vision as source. All three create spaces that, while realistic in one sense, are also dreamlike—imaginative, recuperative spaces where stories and histories, loaded objects and inferences are folded into the discursive field of *story* as established by the aforementioned aesthetic ground. In considering paintings in these terms, I seek to understand story not as a codified or definitive category, but as a method of engagement, a means of relaying, participating in, generating, and understanding experience.

The relationship between image and word/story in Anishinaabeg artistic traditions is ancient. This connection, in numerous forms, persists, from the pictographic knowledge recorded in petroglyphs and birch-bark scrolls, for example, and in contemporary quill and bead work, through the work of the Professional National Indian Artists Inc.,[5] and successive artists such as Blake Debassige and Leland Bell, Rene Meshake, Ahmoo Angeconeb, David Beaucage Johnson, and David Bradley, to name a few. This indicative sample is interested in practice—particularly the established relationships between Anishinaabeg heritage, story, and painting. With this legacy in mind, I will argue that an emphasis on story and storying is essential to understanding the sophisticated referential fields of the paintings under consideration here—as they engage in dialogue with all sorts of stories and songs, moments in history and movements through time, the intensely personal (dream and vision) and transformative, the humorous and ironic/disjunctive, and other paintings and painters. In doing so, in their combinations of the tribal specific, the intimate, and the cross-cultural exchange, each artist creates a distinct visual language that is both representative and generative of its own discourse. I will examine how the viewer's interaction with these paintings *as* narrative implicitly encourages ethical engagement of the nature and importance of story—whether it be personal anecdote, cultural myth, or historical narrative—in the carrying, shaping, and ordering of knowledge. That focus not just on image but on storied image enables the artists to interrogate received ideas about being and belonging; to collapse the corrupt binary of pre- and postcolonial; to engage with strategies of decolonization through a shared visual language that absorbs, without becoming absorbed by, a wide range of cultural and historical references; and to reassert storied knowledge as the central mechanism for understanding and negotiating both personal and communal-historical experience.

STORY

The proliferation of Native writers coming to prominence since the late 1960s has brought new focus—outside Native communities—to the primacy and legacy of story, challenging the long-standing tendency to market Native "myths and legends" as facile, if fabulistic, children's stories, and resisting the comprehension (in every sense) of anthropological taxonomies. Successive generations of Indigenous intellectuals have urgently demonstrated the power and valence of language and, in turn, of story to constitute the conditions of and for its reception: "[The storyteller] creates the storytelling experience and himself and his audience in the process."[6] According to Leslie Marmon Silko, this storied becoming describes a continuum, in that "Whatever the event or the subject, the ancient [Pueblo peoples] perceived the world and themselves within that world as part of an ancient, continuous story composed of innumerable bundles of other stories."[7] Silko and others describe story, frequently repeated across tribal-cultural boundaries, as a complex system or network of open and active participation,[8] as a process through which knowledge is both carried and developed, and as a key principle of Indigenous experience. "When I say 'storytelling,'" notes Silko,

> I don't just mean sitting down and telling a once-upon-a-time kind of story. I mean a whole way of seeing yourself, the people around you, your life in the bigger context, . . . in terms of what has gone on before, what's happened to other people.[9]

Far more simply, "The truth about stories," emphasizes Thomas King, "is that that's all we are."[10]

Much of the emphasis on story in conventional Native literary criticism has tended to seek ways of tying Native writing to what is loosely and often pejoratively called the oral tradition. Increasingly, however, scholars seek to avoid the reductive mechanism of situating writers narrowly according to inherited tradition;[11] rather, the story of written literature is itself understood as a part of that wider phenomenon of story that encompasses education, entertainment, philosophy, spirit, and ethics. Its history is as old as the knowledge it carries; the intellectual traditions manifest in the written literatures of the past few decades join the narratives disseminated "in the 'oral tradition,' pictography, codices, wampum, drums, rock, earth, and sand for centuries."[12]

If the academic treatment of Native storied traditions, then, had tended to concentrate on the content and value of individual stories, finding some redress in the move by Indigenous intellectuals away from symbols and tropes to questions of power and vitality, this essay depends on a simpler, no less profound value: "Stories continue to be the predominant vessels in which Anishinaabeg knowledge is carried."[13] Acknowledging this means considering how the invocation and examination of storied contexts in narrative painting (including those contexts generated in and by non-Native cultural institutions) permits the reappraisal, even reshaping of "known history" and, in turn, ethical engagement with alternative frames of reference. As Heath Justice notes of literary study, "The work of the . . . scholar has profound ethical implications. . . . Stories are what we *do*, as much as what we *are*. . . . The stories told both *by* and *about* Indian people are vital to the processes of peoplehood."[14] The carriage of knowledge through and in story means, ultimately, that story both *is* and *does*; in other words, stories both communicate (meaning, ideas, values, and so on) *and* create the conditions by which those ideas and values can be understood and applied. To put it another way, "'story' lives in its application to changing contexts."[15]

As the tiny sample here suggests, numerous voices within and without the academy speak of the vitality of Native story precisely as a robust and deeply intellectual pursuit of the theoretical and philosophical questions too often incarcerated in the multiple "isms" and disciplines around which European educative systems revolve. Indigenous storied traditions openly and actively challenge this stasis. Sinclair quotes Lee Maracle:

> "There is a story in every line of theory. The difference between us and European (predominantly white male) scholars is that we admit this, and present theory through story. We differ in the presentation of theory, not in our capacity to theorize."[16]

The explicit assumption that theory and story are not only mutually informing/constituting (serving to "humanize theory by fusing humanity's need for common direction—theory—with story")[17] points to the processual nature of storytelling, implicit in the discursive arena in which story participates:

> Stories are the lifeblood between storyteller, community, and universe—how they relate, how they interact, how they change as a result. This interconnectivity is a fruitful space that is as full of perspectives, creativity, and growth as it is full of controversy, polemics, and politics.[18]

That change, the vitality of the ever-unfolding, ever-developing nature of stories, of theories, is key. Story is not conclusion; is not autotelic artifact, discrete from the things it describes and/or speaks to. As Acoma Pueblo poet Simon Ortiz describes, "Stories are a form of process art, even ritual art, which confirms the 'act' of storyteller and listeners participating in the wonderful experience of creating their existence."[19] Story, then, is the principle by which knowledge is both carried and tested, a "fruitful space" in which, and through which, processes of becoming, of relating, of conversing, and of knowing proceed.

JOURNEY

Each of the paintings under consideration here references a journey of sorts: this includes, in Carlson's case, a journey to the British Museum, London; in Denomie's, a figurative journey to the American West in narrative and art; and in Wallowing Bull's, a metaphorical dream-journey to the meeting point of perception and imagination. Each of these presents journey as story and, in doing so, draws on numerous more or less explicit and more or less "complete" (hi)stories. In contrast to the pejorative sense of the word "story" in European discourses—as that which is always apart from, or teetering on the edge of "fact," or that which simply connotes plot or anecdote—*story* in Anishinaabeg Studies suggests a multivalent and dynamic field. The relationship between story and travel may be seen, then, as a way of understanding that dynamism, illustrating the processual nature of story. We can readily understand journeying, the passage, itself as literal process and, importantly, the narrating of a journey as multiply referential. Each journey narrative enfolds the representation and reenactment of the original event, the new event of its recounting, and the numerous unpredictable outcomes of its recounting as it touches the common and divergent experiences of its audience.

In "Sacred Journey Cycles: Pilgrimage as Re-Turning and Re-Telling in American Indigenous Literatures," for instance, Kim Blaeser notes that "In . . . journey literature, the creation of a storied context becomes an ever more complex process as the layers of re-speaking and re-enacting themselves multiply."[20] In that same essay, discussing a poem by Simon Ortiz, Blaeser asserts that "in the literal, and in the literary journey which recounts it, the passage finds meaning in continuance, simple going on, the process of the journey, the process of being."[21] If, as Blaeser implies, we understand the literal and literary journeys (the "passage" as both movement and section of text) to be two inflections of the same thing, *story* immediately takes on a multidimensional aspect, encapsulating not just the event and the narrative representation of that event, but the continuous event of its reception and evolution as it is 'heard' (or in our case viewed), retold/recalled, and re-imagined. Blaeser's emphasis on *process* ascribes to story not so much a firstness in a linear sense as it does an ever-evolving, ever-unfolding praxis. *Story* is paradigmatic, then, both recounting and enactment, subject matter and methodology: the archetypal hermeneutic circle.

ART

Andrea Carlson's 2007 painting *Vaster Empire* ironically undermines the strategies and assumptions of imperial/colonial histories and re-presents its subject matter as an Anishinaabe storied landscape. The painting, one of a series that uses elements of Anishinaabeg winter stories as its ground, is a large, four-paneled piece in oil, acrylic, ink, colored pencil, and graphite on paper. Large, slightly overlapping circles, horizonlike—as if land is looming, or multiple suns are rising and setting—two of them echoing the eyes of two skulls beneath them, hover above a seascape with stylized mythical creatures in lower right and left corners. Against this, five key elements, or objects, float, unfixed but for the rays or power lines emanating from the eyes and horns of two of the creatures to the two largest objects.

These elements, the two skulls, face each other: above the skull on the left hangs a Victorian "jewel," a Grade 5 Grand Star badge once awarded by the Primrose League.[22] A white primrose in its center is encircled by the motto "Imperium et Libertas" (Empire and Freedom), two interlocking stars, a further four primroses, and a royal crown. Above that, on the right of the painting, floats a button with a figure at its center, with the slogan "Join the Polly Anna Club and Be Glad" around its edge. In the lower center of the painting, a further double circle contains the words "We hold a vaster Empire than has been." The core referents of these various elements are, at face value, relatively clear. The skull on the left of the painting is a quartz crystal skull, one of a number held in museum and private collections throughout the world, and believed, erroneously, to have been carved by ancient Mexica (Aztec) artisans. Acquired by the British Museum in the 1890s, it is, scientists believe, likely to have been carved in Europe sometime in the late nineteenth century. The skull on the right, wearing a "crown" of bronze, is known as the "Deal Warrior," an Iron Age skeleton with grave items excavated and exhumed at a tiny cemetery in Deal, southeast England.[23]

The badges above their heads, both inverted so that the viewer has to read them upside-down, refer respectively to British imperial history and to the Pollyanna story first conceived by Eleanor Porter in 1913—a deeply ironic, if apparently anomalous reference to the orphan Pollyanna Whittier's ineluctable optimism in the face of adversity. Anomalous though it may be, the four objects—the two skulls and the two badges—are all located in the collections of the British Museum, London. The motto "We hold a vaster Empire than has been," meanwhile, is a line from Sir Lewis Morris's "A Song of Empire," written in 1887 to commemorate Queen Victoria's Golden Jubilee.[24] The badge, button, and motto seem collectively to speak ironically, subversively even, to the arrogant optimism of the British Empire, particularly as it is represented in Morris's poem:

> Let all men know it, England shall be great!
> We hold a vaster Empire than has been!
> Nigh half the race of man is subject to our Queen!
> Nigh half the wide, wide earth is ours in fee!
> And where her rule comes all are free.[25]

Against this, of course, the optimism implied by the Pollyanna button, and the "Glad Club" it advertises, even more ironically reflects on those distant "free" subjects of England's dominion who survive and continue in (and despite) the imperial wake. These various elements of the painting, then, each of which carries with it its own narrative nexus, are collected here by Carlson within a narrativized landscape that draws principally on Ojibwe cosmology and on a seascape intended to connote flux. This is no static still life, but rather a dramatic, dynamic interchange.

The artist herself says of her paintings:

> My interests in objects relate to the story of an object, and how objects are utilized as surrogates for cultural exchange. The objects and texts represented in my work are displayed hovering like holy icons, floating and centered on the page. As these objects dangle over the seashore like a carrot, the shore rises up, itself fluid, all-consuming and assimilating as the earth takes back and buries it's [*sic*] histories. Waterways are historically a conduit of trade, interaction, and conflict and are cited in the work for their role in aiding the fluidity and continual change of culture.[26]

That waterway, here, connotes the various levels of exchange within the painting: from the Anishinaabeg *Adizookaan* juxtaposed with the "formal" histories of the museumified objects; through the literal and figurative dialogue between the two skulls (with their *human* histories and shared artifact status); to the compositional relationship between the inverted badges and the other circular motifs. The two skulls speak explicitly of change, invoking empire (the Mexican and early Spanish as well as the Victorian British empires in the crystal skull, and the Celtic settlement and Roman Imperial period in the Deal Warrior); the economic, military, and political histories in which they are implicit; and of course the passages of the artifacts themselves to the museum, in various ways fueling the often parallel appetite for exotica and drive to discovery of the colonial world. The stories they carry in the painting are, of course, intricately tied to these histories; yet their new context here engenders new stories, from the artist's own discovery of them in the museum collection, to associations with NAGPRA, surely unavoidable in any situation in which grave remains and Native agency are linked. Then we have the Victorian badge, emblem of empire, of the exporting of values. Crownlike atop the crystal skull's forehead, the inverted badge is subtly aligned with the Pollyanna button, a more recent and reverse export from an ex-colony; both are representative of culture as artifact and outlook (for where, if not the United States, is optimism a more prevalent national trait?).

More importantly, all four objects comment on the ways in which these stories are commonly "told." Carlson notes that "Museums are the self-nominated stewards charged with telling the stories of cultural objects." Unpacking those contexts and systems of representation, through a process of re-representation, the painting retells those stories, demanding far more of the viewer-participant in the process. The object speaks to the mythologization of the various spheres in which the colonial power moved; it challenges the viewer to dismiss the storied context of the background as any less real or present than the objects themselves, and it re-places those objects in a way that draws out the possibilities of their histories as opposed to imposing an interpreted narrative on them. What Lucy Lippard says of Flathead artist Jaune Quick-to-See Smith is equally applicable to Carlson here:

> Lippard notes that the pictorial is, simultaneously, textual. Quick-to-See Smith writes, *It's not copying what's there, it's writing about it.* Her art is not mimetic reproduction, but a quasi-textual response, a reciprocation, yielding.[27]

How that text is read, the next layer of exchange between painting and viewer, depends on prior knowledge and subject position—whether it becomes a personal exchange between artist and community member, or another form of cultural exchange between painting and viewer in a small London gallery[28]—but that, of course, is all part of the process.

The stories both implicitly and explicitly present in this painting mushroom down from the visible surface, which, like the audible tale, is only ever a small part of the wider connective tissue. The painting, then, both yields its stories and demonstrates the wider process in which those stories take their part, calling viewer and viewer knowledge into play in their synthesis, recalling the numerous contexts and relationships in which these objects have existed, and with which the viewer implicitly engages. Their combination here, in turn, speaks to another story of empire and representation, this time in the form of the painting itself. Karen Ohnesorge, writing about what Quick-to-see Smith herself calls her "narrative landscapes" (paintings that combine "assemblages of images and texts with the land as their unifying point of reference"), notes that "she and her peers combine image and text to interrogate the genre of landscape painting as a stage for fantasies of racialized white manifest destiny . . . [drawing] on Native sources for language and iconography."[29] If, then, the painting deals with another kind of story—the story of European art, particularly its representational impositions on non-European cultures—it also undermines the power of that story:

> Traugott says, "Native Americans can salvage parts of the dominating culture—as well as of their own culture—to further their own identity . . . for both modernist and postmodernist goals" as well as "to expand the meaning of nativeness in the contradictory context of contemporary society."[30]

In Carlson's painting, these various stories and their associations—of the European "primitive," of the ravenous trade routes of colonization, and so on—are folded by that "moltenous shore" into the storied imagery of Anishinaabe *Adizookaanag*; the question of context becomes, then, an image of artistic sovereignty.

Jim Denomie's *Edward Curtis, Paparazzi—Black Hills Golf and Country Club* (2007)[31] is, at first sight, a far more direct painting than *Vaster Empire*. Similarly ironic—though more obviously humorous—it draws on two very different representational traditions in the production of its narrative, critiquing those traditions and, like *Vaster Empire*, drawing a history of colonial intervention into a Native context through a process of generic subversion. Like Carlson's painting, however, the result is not a deterministic anti- or postcolonial statement. Rather, it demands of its viewers the effort to make sense of its historical and aesthetic allusions in order to understand its comment on, and contribution to, those questions of representation and narrative tradition.

Rebecca Dallinger writes:

> Infusing his sense of tradition with his perceptions of contemporary Native life, [Denomie] tells stories through his paintings, weaving the themes of his life to create a painting which comments on the political, social, personal and cultural issues concerning modern Native nations.[32]

Again, though, the "story" here provides no simple, single narrative thread, but rather several overlapping stories and archives that once more draw attention to the processual nature of active participation in the storied moment. Going a step further than Dallinger's analysis, Denomie's painting directly engages with what Lee Maracle defines as the "art" of study, itself the object of storymaking and telling, namely, "to question the direction from which looking occurs, or to ponder the motive for seeing and study-ing, [without which] study becomes reactive, reproductive, and colonial."[33] Breaking open the reactive, reproductive, and colonial cycle is, in many senses, the effect—possibly even the intent—of Denomie's piece, challeng-ing perspective and juxtaposing narratives in such a way as to question and subsequently reorient the "direction from which looking occurs."

In a scene vaguely reminiscent of a George Catlin landscape,[34] a small herd of bison run across a semi-arid plain, pursued by four warriors on horseback. In the distance, the Black Hills of the title span the horizon, while in the lower right-hand corner, almost in line with the viewer's per-spective of the scene, a motorcycle-riding Edward Curtis follows on, camera at the ready. Secondary detail, subtle but clear, is equally humorous. Among the bison run a scattering of chickens; to the right of the painting we realize the chase is passing the 10th hole of the titular golf club; centrally, at the very top of the painting, a hot air balloon floats, implying the painting's fourth, though unseen, perspective (the third being that of the horseback warriors, two of whom, in looking at the bison, also look back at us). Two of the warriors appear to carry golf clubs, while a third, the only one "shoot-ing" in the direction of the largest buffalo, seems if anything to have shot the startled chicken on its nearside flank; either he is a terrible shot or, as is suggested by the other elements of the painting, Denomie is forcing us to question what we see in terms of what we expect of such a scene.

I have already mentioned Catlin; the other clear non-Native art reference of course is to the aforementioned Curtis, photographer of the "vanishing Indian," whose voluminous *The North American Indian* was produced in the early twentieth century. Both allusions—the painter who traveled the American West in the early nineteenth century to record what he saw as tribal remnants, and his "successor" who did the same with a camera one hundred years later—are made more ironic by the literal depiction of the double chase. As the buffalo are chased on horseback, so the hunters are chased by motorbike, with Curtis's reinvention as a paparazzo adding to the humor. The will to "capture" what is elusive—nature, the light, the past, change, the masked layers of the American palimpsest—is effectively communicated there.

That elusiveness in turn is checked by the painting's *allusive* qualities, which are forcefully rendered: commodification, objectification, fetishization, and the continued incarceration of Indigenous lands and bodies. Aptly represented by the three key touristic emblems in the painting—the Catlin/Curtis cultural tourism, the hot-air balloon ride over the Black Hills, and the Black Hills Golf and Country Club—these scenes refer explicitly to ways in which Native lands and the peoples who inhabit them have been appropriated and despoiled. They do so implicitly as well. That an Anishinaabe artist chooses to render a Plains scene set in the Black Hills of South Dakota/Wyoming speaks clearly to the presence of that range of mountains in spiritual and historical terms, and to the dominance of such imagery in popular culture. Who can forget that *Pahá Sápa* were the subject of a hunt for a more immediate form of gold than tourism in the 1870s? Or that another kind of "Indian hunter" than Curtis, no less famous, would be at the center of the consequential routing of Plains tribes and the death of that man—George Armstrong Custer—at the Little Bighorn in 1876?

In simple terms, Denomie raises some of the major events that affected Indian Country in the nineteenth century, engages through them some of America's grandest narratives (the vanishing Indian, General Custer, the commercial imperative of land settlement, the lure of gold, the Western), and in turn draws these into some key issues of the twentieth/twenty-first centuries (the golf club and continued land-claim struggles), and re-presents this whole as a parody of the two principal Indian documenters of the nineteenth and twentieth centuries.

But it doesn't stop there. Denomie makes one further allusion through the general composition and choice of figures he employs in his painting. This is most clearly demonstrated in the horses to left and right of the composition—blue horses, highly evocative of the blue horses that run through the work of ledger artists. Most famously generated in incarceration at Fort Marion in 1874 (though the form developed from earlier Plains painting traditions and continues to the present), ledger art was a narrative form rooted in the tradition of pictorially documenting exploits on the battlefield, the hunting ground, and so on. Importantly, many ledger artists also documented elements of the changing world around them. While several contemporary artists—George Flett, Smith—render ledger art and elements of ledger art more literally, this evocation in Denomie's painting serves to draw those various threads of narrative/history into a specific aesthetic frame, which is in turn derived from the storied traditions—including the pictorial methods of recording and documenting stories and histories both representationally and as mnemonic "scripts"—of Indigenous peoples.

Like Carlson, then, Denomie brings into play a number of elements significant to questions of cultural and colonial exchange, reinterpreting the "myths" of one culture through the interpretive frame of another. The waterway as trade route in Carlson's painting, and the plains as *terra nullius* in Denomie's, available throughout U.S. history for the comprehension of speculators, documenters, and artists alike, stand in ironic tension with the notion of art/story as commodity itself, a further strand in this multiple tale. Both artists effectively narrate the journey that that exchange becomes, drawing it in (remember Carlson's assimilative seascape) to scenes that resonate with stories that conflict, compete, collide, and coalesce. If Blaeser's sense of the journey-story as process has purchase with regard to painting, it is surely in this resonance, where the "creation of a storied context becomes an ever more complex process as the layers of re-speaking and re-enacting themselves multiply."[35] And, as viewers, "in seeing ourselves through story, we become part of the journey."[36] Whether we are in the hot air balloon, literally (in every sense) surveying the scene; on the bike with Curtis; in the gallery looking in, or the hunt looking out, we can't help but participate in the process of re-looking, rethinking, and reimagining the world depicted.

Star Wallowing Bull's *Black Elk's Little Sandman* (2002)[37] takes a similar approach to very different, but no less striking material. The "exchange" in his painting is illustrated in an intensely vibrant mosaic of what can only be described as icons. Crowded with figures, patterns, and other images, the picture is bewildering in scope, mesmerizing in its range of colors. If we take its iconography literally, the image of Black Elk, Oglala Lakota elder, standing pipe in hand in the center of a circle that dominates the upper center of the picture,[38] suggests we are looking at (or are perhaps being induced to see) a vision or dreamscape. Immediately below Black Elk is a caricature of Wallowing Bull himself, a puzzled look on his face and a question mark hovering above his head. Staring straight back at us, and standing, in fact, upon the head of a creature, its horns and eyes visible, the caricature seems to reflect the initial state of the viewer, puzzlement emanating back and forth, placing the artist's searching or questioning consciousness at the heart of the picture. This is further dramatized where a jagged line cuts the painting in half. Above the line the imagery is generally comedic, light, colorful, celebratory; below, it becomes dark and brooding, the stuff and substance of nightmares. This bifurcation—a clear split, although, of course, the painting's balance is only achieved by the relationship of the two halves—is clearly exemplified by the juxtaposition of a butterfly at top center and an owl, *gookooko'oo*, an omen, at bottom center.

While the caricature of Wallowing Bull expresses a sense of bewilderment, rather than clarity per se, it reflects an aspect of the storier's role:

> Mythmakers, storiers, are present to bear witness, see, and understand the subject under study, and serve as adjuncts to the process, so that they may story up each round of discourse in a way that governs the new conduct required to grow from the new knowledge discovered.[39]

Drawing heavily, too, on images reminiscent of Native art—totem poles, beadwork, pictographic images, and so on—Wallowing Bull places his painting in a dual narrative context. Firstly, that of the mnemonic and pictographic archive so intricately bound up with the oral traditions of different nations—the "writing systems" that accompany storied heritage—and secondly, the various media and histories he invokes. In the chaos of *Black Elk's Little Sandman*, there is both a response to the miasma of popular culture and an assimilation of largely discordant images from Native and non-Native, high- and lowbrow sources. If the painting does not necessarily order these images, it is precisely because they exist in tension, and it is in the sharing—just as Black Elk shared his childhood vision with his elders—and its concomitant exchange that they might begin to coalesce.

Like both paintings discussed above, there are clear elements of ironic appropriation, of liberating objects from their contexts and reinvesting them with alternative stories. In this regard, an image of Yoda in feathered headdress and buckskin at the top (left) of the painting, and the subject from Norwegian painter Edvard Munch's *The Scream* (1893) in flaming headdress and buckskin attire at the bottom (left) have the biggest impact as key images from film and art. In the image of Yoda, American cinema is invoked with a story that itself draws from Greek myth, alongside the history of European/ Scandinavian art with a painting that is both incredibly well known and utterly immediate. Both speak, no doubt, personally to and about Wallowing Bull, but they will also have significant resonance for a very wide audience, most of whom will either be tickled or disturbed by the artist's iconoclasm.

In contrast, center left of the picture, an image of the twin towers of the World Trade Center against a U.S. flag is a hugely poignant element, though not without significant freight added by the context of their placement, set alongside a small image of a figure wearing traditional attire. Elsewhere, images of a knight in shining armor, a *Tyrannosaurus rex*, and Darth Maul seem both incongruous and yet entirely appropriate additions to the totemic and stylized Native imagery that surrounds them. All three speak to different kinds of codes and behaviors, of power and strength, of ancient stories and popular contemporary mythmaking. Similarly, the range of masks apparent in the picture, particularly the dramatic masks of comedy and tragedy, attest to the performative nature of this interaction, the ritualized nature of the exchange. While that exchange will come out differently for every viewer, since the magic of the painting is its incredible variety, with different elements coming to the fore at every viewing, at its most basic level it is constructed from images and stories that in turn inflect one another to construct a new image, or series of images, and a new story. Whether that story be one of the artist's own experience, or more generally of contemporary Native experience, or more universal than that even, it speaks directly to the principle and process of story as not just informing and reflecting experience, but becoming experience itself—seeing/hearing is mandatory, as McMaster puts it; conclusions are optional. Or indeed personal. Or subject to further influences beyond the scope of the story or painting; and sometimes simply not possible at all. But what the painting draws out and forces its viewer to deliberate on is the range of modes of communication, forms of visual and verbal expression, on which we rely to order and understand ourselves as individuals and our place in the world.

Of the three pictures, *Black Elk's Little Sandman* appears most clearly to illustrate the notion of storytelling as process suggested here.

> Every deliberation leads to discovery, new relationships, new directions, and, of course, new story because we build on what we have not heard or said before. Once the new thought is understood, then the storiers, the mythmakers, the poets, and the dramatists conjure story in a way that will assist the whole in establishing a relationship to the new.[40]

Beginning at the center with the subjective consciousness of the artist himself, awakening through the imagination, dream, or vision, the stories unfold discretely and yet in overlapping patterns that speak to their fundamental connectedness. Absorbing and assimilating a diverse range of imagery, the painting doesn't solve the puzzle, it poses it, becoming a stage in the process of synthesizing elements of a larger narrative. All three of these paintings demand that we look, and we look again—just as Native scholars who write about story demand that we listen, and then we listen again. Neither painting nor story is endpoint—the paintings do not rewrite or resolve any of the problematic narratives or complex questions they invoke; rather, they open them up to reflection. They do not, as has been so often argued for Native literatures, simply bridge the cultural divide; in a clearer sense, they expose it, actively working through the processes of representation by and in which Native stories and Euro-American histories are disseminated and differentiated, evidence of the decolonizing methodologies of artistic sovereignty. Examining the intense focus on story, therefore, can also open up the structural boundaries of academic study, the imposed limitations on social and institutional movement (between, say, the secular/sacred, or the community/academy), and the imagined division of physical, spiritual, and intellectual experience.

Story cuts across disciplinary as well as formal and methodological boundaries, providing both model (archetype) and source for the intellectual, ethical-political, and aesthetic parameters of Anishinaabeg Studies, and enables effective communication within and between different communities and audiences. Whether through displacing objects from their contexts, or rendering familiar scenes and motifs unfamiliar, by creating new relationships between objects through juxtaposition, and constructing new narratives through setting and composition, each of the three painters considered here engages the storied contexts of the images/objects they depict and takes various different signifiers and contexts of Anishinaabe story and pan-Native storytelling as primary ground for their painting. Both illustrating *and* enacting story-as-process becomes a means of addressing and reorienting experience—in these specific cases by vividly rendering the bordering of cultural and colonial exchange as, principally, a Native story, circulating outwards from an Anishinaabeg center.

NOTES

1. Gerald Vizenor, *Narrative Chance: Postmodern Discourse on Native American Indian Literatures* (1989; Norman: University of Oklahoma Press, 1993), xiii.
2. It must be made clear that the exegetical gestures here are made primarily about questions of form and imagery relating to popular and museum culture. I do not presume either the knowledge or the authority to speak of the

specifics of the relationships any of these painters hold to Anishinaabeg stories in particular.

3. Specifically Carlson's *Vaster Empire* (2007), Wallowing Bull's *Black Elk's Little Sandman* (2002), and Denomie's *Edward Curtis, Paparazzi—Black Hills Golf and Country Club* (2007).

4. Karen Ohnesorge, "Uneasy Terrain: Image, Text, Landscape, and Contemporary Indigenous Artists in the United States," *AIQ* 32, no. 1: 43.

5. Among whom Norval Morrisseau is perhaps most famous, whose highly recognizable images drew heavily on pictographs and petroglyphs, and whose aesthetic was significantly informed by his spirituality.

6. N. Scott Momaday, *The Man Made of Words: Essays, Stories, Passages* (New York: St. Martin's Griffin, 1998), 3.

7. Leslie Marmon Silko, *Yellow Woman and a Beauty of the Spirit: Essays on Native American Life Today* (New York and London: Simon & Schuster, 1996), 30–31.

8. Whether teller or audience, the simple point is that "authority" rests with the story itself, less so with its bearer.

9. Kim Barnes, "Leslie Marmon Silko Interview," *Journal of Ethnic Studies* 3: 86.

10. Thomas King, *The Truth about Stories: A Native Narrative* (Minneapolis: University of Minnesota Press, 2003), 2.

11. There has been a somewhat problematic tendency, particularly in literary criticism, to equate writing with a more advanced state than the oral tradition, but then to qualify the cultural authenticity of poets and novelists by declaring them "modern-day storytellers." While this is true in a general sense, it tends to elide the importance of the living verbal arts and traditions that continue unabated both formally and informally, and also to assume that Native written literature's primary value resides only in its proximity to "pure" cultural forms. This would seem at worst an essentialist, and at best a static interpretation of both spoken and written literatures.

12. Niigonwedom James Sinclair, "Trickster Reflections: Part I," in *Troubling Tricksters: Revisioning Critical Conversations*, ed. Deanna Reder and Linda M. Morra (Waterloo, ON: Wilfrid Laurier University Press, 2010), 37.

13. Ibid., 22.

14. Daniel Heath Justice, *Our Fire Survives the Storm: A Cherokee Literary History* (Minneapolis and London: University of Minnesota Press, 2006), 206–7.

15. David L. Moore. "Rough Knowledge and Radical Understanding: Sacred Silence in American Indian Literatures," *AIQ* 21, no. 4 (1997): 646.

16. Lee Maracle, "Oratory on Oratory," in *Trans.Can.Lit: Resituating the Study of Canadian Literature*, ed. Smaro Kamboureli and Roy Miki (Waterloo, ON: Wilfrid Laurier University Press, 2007), 49.

17. Maracle, qtd. in Judith Leggatt, "Native Writing, Academic Theory: Post-Colonialism across the Cultural Divide," in *Is Canada Postcolonial? Unsettling Canadian Literature*, ed. Laura Moss (Waterloo, ON: Wilfrid Laurier University Press, 2003), 120.

18. Sinclair, "Trickster Reflections: Part I," 45.

19. Simon Ortiz, Review of *Coyote Tales from the Indian Pueblos*, by Evelyn Dahl Reed, and *The Other Side of Nowhere: Contemporary Coyote Tales*, by Peter Blue Cloud, *AIQ* 16, no. 4: 600.

20. Kimberly Blaeser, "Sacred Journey Cycles: Pilgrimage as Re-Turning and Re-Telling in American Indigenous Literatures," *Religion & Literature* 35, nos. 2–3: 86.

21. Ibid., 94.

22. The Primrose League was established in honor of Benjamin Disraeli to disseminate conservative principles throughout the British Empire.

23. I presently live within a quarter of a mile of the cemetery in which the "Deal Warrior" was found, a coincidental reminder of the dynamic network of stories tied up with objects—including this painting itself. The range of personal stories (particularly of walking my children to school through that cemetery), local "legends," and historical narratives of national and wider import that the skull unlocks is extensive. Deal itself is a mile downshore from the site at which Julius Caesar is supposed to have landed in 55 B.C. Although that first invasion was unsuccessful, it heralded the ascendancy of the Roman Empire in Britain, a fact tied up in a personal anecdote that possibly expands the irony of the painting's subject matter even further!

24. This line was also printed on a commemorative Canadian two-cent stamp, "Xmas 1898." It depicts a map of the world with Britain's colonial territories highlighted, including some territories that were not actually British! http://en.wikipedia.org/wiki/File:Stamp_Canada_1898_2c_Xmas_blue.jpg.

25. Lewis Morris, *The Works of Sir Lewis Morris* (London: Kegan Paul, 1904), rpt. at http://www.archive.org/stream/worksofsirlewism00morruoft/worksof sirlewism00morruoft_djvu.txt (last accessed August 2, 2010), 483.

26. Andrea Carlson website, http://mikinaak.com/ (last accessed August 2, 2010).

27. Ohnesorge, "Uneasy Terrain," 56.

28. I first saw this painting, along with work by Frank Big Bear and Star Wallowing Bull, at the October Gallery in London (in association with the Bockley Gallery) in an exhibition entitled *Oshki-Bawaajige (New Dreaming)*, 13 September–27 October 2007.

29. Jaune Quick-to-See Smith, "Star Wallowing Bull: Born with a Gift" (2009), Star Wallowing Bull, http://starwallowingbull.blogspot.com/ (accessed March 21, 2010), 44.

30. Ohnesorge, "Uneasy Terrain," 53.

31. Oil on canvas.
32. Rebecca Dallinger, "Anishinabe Artist's Work Transcends Romantic Native Images," *The Circle*, June 30, 1995; *HighBeam Research*, August 3, 2010, at http://www.highbeam.com.
33. Maracle, "Oratory on Oratory," 57.
34. "Buffalo Hunt, Chase" being one example vaguely echoed in the phrasing of Denomie's title too. See http://www.britannica.com/EBchecked/topic/99958/George-Catlin.
35. Blaeser, "Sacred Journey Cycles," 86.
36. Maracle, "Oratory on Oratory," 59.
37. Prismacolor pencil on paper.
38. The circle appears to be part of a necklace or other adornment.
39. Maracle, "Oratory on Oratory," 57.
40. Ibid., 58.

RESOURCES

Abbott, Lawrence. "Contemporary Native Art: A Bibliography." *American Indian Quarterly* 18, no. 3 (1994): 383–403.

Barnes, Kim. "Leslie Marmon Silko Interview." *Journal of Ethnic Studies* 3 (1986): 83–105.

Blaeser, Kimberly. "Sacred Journey Cycles: Pilgrimage as Re-Turning and Re-Telling in American Indigenous Literatures." *Religion & Literature* 35, nos. 2–3 (2003): 83–104.

Carlson, Andrea. Artist's website. http://mikinaak.com/ (last accessed August 2, 2010).

Dallinger, Rebecca. "Anishinabe Artist's Work Transcends Romantic Native Images." *The Circle*, June 30, 1995. HighBeam Research: http://www.highbeam .com (accessed August 3, 2010).

Justice, Daniel Heath. *Our Fire Survives the Storm: A Cherokee Literary History.* Minneapolis and London: University of Minnesota Press, 2006.

King, Thomas. *The Truth about Stories: A Native Narrative.* Minneapolis: University of Minnesota Press, 2003.

Leggatt, Judith. "Native Writing, Academic Theory: Post-Colonialism across the Cultural Divide." In *Is Canada Postcolonial? Unsettling Canadian Literature*, ed. Laura Moss, 111–26. Waterloo, ON: Wilfrid Laurier University Press, 2003.

Maracle, Lee. "Oratory on Oratory." In *Trans.Can.Lit: Resituating the Study of Canadian Literature*, ed. Smaro Kamboureli and Roy Miki, 55–70. Waterloo, ON: Wilfrid Laurier University Press, 2007.

Momaday, N. Scott. *The Man Made of Words: Essays, Stories, Passages.* New York: St. Martin's Griffin, 1998.

Moore, David L. "Rough Knowledge and Radical Understanding: Sacred Silence in American Indian Literatures." *American Indian Quarterly* 21, no. 4 (1997): 633–62.

Morris, Lewis. *The Works of Sir Lewis Morris.* London: Kegan Paul, 1904. Rpt. at http://www.archive.org/stream/worksofsirlewism00morruoft/worksofsirlewism00morruoft_djvu.txt (last accessed August 2, 2010).

Ohnesorge, Karen. "Uneasy Terrain: Image, Text, Landscape, and Contemporary Indigenous Artists in the United States." *American Indian Quarterly* 32, no. 1 (2008): 43–68.

Ortiz, Simon. Review of *Coyote Tales from the Indian Pueblos,* by Evelyn Dahl Reed, and *The Other Side of Nowhere: Contemporary Coyote Tales,* by Peter Blue Cloud. *American Indian Quarterly* 16, no. 4 (1992): 598–600.

Sanchez, Georgiana Valoyce. "Indigenous Voices: Following Ancient Trade Routes—World Symposium and Storytelling Festival." *News from Native California* 22, no. 4 (2009): 6–7, 38–39.

Silko, Leslie Marmon. *Yellow Woman and a Beauty of the Spirit: Essays on Native American Life Today.* New York and London: Simon & Schuster, 1996.

Sinclair, Niigonwedom James. "Trickster Reflections: Part I." In *Troubling Tricksters: Revisioning Critical Conversations,* ed. Deanna Reder and Linda M. Morra, 21–58. Waterloo, ON: Wilfrid Laurier University Press, 2010.

Smith, Jaune Quick-to-See. "Star Wallowing Bull: Born with a Gift." Star Wallowing Bull, 2009. http://starwallowingbull.blogspot.com/ (accessed March 21, 2010).

Vizenor, Gerald. "George Morrison: Anishinaabe Expressionist Artist." *American Indian Quarterly* 30, nos. 3–4 (2006): 646–60.

———. *Narrative Chance: Postmodern Discourse on Native American Indian Literatures.* 1989; Norman: University of Oklahoma Press, 1993.

Stories as *Mshkiki*
Reflections on the Healing and Migratory Practices of Minwaajimo

DYLAN A. T. MINER

DABASENDIZOWIN (HUMILITY): LEARNING TO SPEAK

AT THE MOMENT OF INCEPTION, HUMANS GAINED THE ABILITY TO speak. As a parent, I still recall the moment when my daughters uttered their first words in reference to the world around them. Much like birth itself, speech emerged, from my daughters as well as within our Indigenous communities, as a sacred act that connects human beings with non–human beings through dialogic conversations. According to the biblical tradition, "In the beginning was the Word." The Anishinaabeg, as original inhabitants of Turtle Island, are no different in this regard, with Anishinaabemowin communication being the preferred mode of storytelling, with Nanabozho being born with the gift of speech.[1] Due to continued colonial policies, however, many Anishinaabeg have been forcefully de-tongued.[2] In response to this violent linguicide, both storytelling and everyday communication frequently operate as an English-dominant domain, with Anishinaabemowin appearing as a specter of Indigenous cultural specificity.

As a Michif person, I am unfortunately generations removed from personal and familial fluency in our language.[3] I nonetheless maintain a keen interest in the reclamation of Indigenous languages and their respective epistemologies as a particular modality to begin healing from the atrocious and ongoing wounds of colonial encroachment and hegemonic assimilation. By returning to our stories of the past—that is, returning to the "word"—we may construct both a solid present and future. It is for this reason that I begin telling you the following story, couched in the guise of an academic essay.

In this manner, this story–essay migrates through the work of two Michigan-born Anishinaabeg writers, Keewaydinoquay Peschel and Lawrence "Pun" Plamondon, as well as reflecting upon my own experiences sharing tea, *scon*,[4] stories, and laughter with a group of Anishinaabemowin-speaking elders. By focusing on these non-reservation, Michigan-specific stories, I hope to offer a humble Michif contribution to this important anthology, *Centering Anishinaabeg Studies*. I do this by demonstrating the centrality of urbanization and the importance of urban (and lesser-known) voices within the development of a nuanced Anishinaabeg Studies. I will focus on two primary themes: migration and *mshkiki* (medicine). In this fashion, I am interested in the medicinal or healing nature of stories as a form of earth-based strength that allows diasporic, and in some cases de-tribalized, Anishinaabeg to heal the personal, familial, and communal wounds of colonialism.

In the introduction to the 2005 edition of Frances Densmore's classic *Strength of the Earth*, Anishinaabe historian Brenda Child (Red Lake) writes:

> In *Ojibwemowin*, our language, the term for medicine is *mashkiki*, or "strength of the earth." Medicine people approached plant and medicinal knowledge in a meticulously systematic way, according to Frances Densmore, always emphasizing "experiment and study." Like artists in their work, they were masterful observers of the natural world. They knew the exact time to harvest a multiplicity of plants, many of which had the most ephemeral season. . . . Their work sustained the Ojibwe goal of *mino bimaddizi* [the philosophy of a good life].[5]

Like the *mshkikikwe* or *mshkikiwinini*, the artist and storyteller observe the world around them in ephemeral ways that create meaning from an otherwise unintelligible existence.

I have structured this essay in seven brief sections, referencing the prominence of the number seven within Anishinaabeg teachings. In this fashion, I evoke the seven sacred grandfathers' teachings, as well as the seven sacred stops in the migration narrative from the Eastern Seaboard into present-day Anishinaabewaki. Each of the seven sections, being a brief vignette or snapshot, migrates through the healing power of stories. By applying *storywork*, as Jo-Ann Archibald (Sto:lo) calls the process of Indigenous storytelling labor, I offer this essay as a humble *mshkiki* or *michin* (the Michif word for medicine) in the growing discourse on Anishinaabeg literature and Indigenous stories more generally.[6] With the centrality of seven, I evoke storytelling as a way to migrate home.

Anishinaabe storyteller and writer Basil Johnston (Nawash Unceded First Nation) noted in *Ojibway Ceremonies*:

> We were given speech by the Great Spirit to foster goodwill among ourselves, and to commune with the spirits. It has both a practical and a spiritual end. It is a sacred act. . . . In order to inspire trust we must attend to our elders, who have urged us to listen and to talk—but to be as gentle in our speech as the balm of the south wind.[7]

Through the gentle act of speaking, a humanizing process that colonial regimes have each attempted to violently deny, Native peoples have been able to maintain intrapersonal communication in their respective aboriginal languages. Not only have these languages allowed Native interlocutors to speak to their peers and elders, Indigenous languages have also facilitated cross-cultural interchange with other tribal peoples, as well as with relations in the animal, plant, and spirit worlds.

Unfortunately, as White Earth elder Joe Auginaush so prophetically noticed, "We're not losing our language, our language is losing us."[8] Due to a variety of factors, not the least of which include boarding school, urbanization, and the need for wage labor, Anishinaabemowin fluency is decreasing at exponential rates across Anishinaabewaki. This trend is not limited to Anishinaabeg communities in the Great Lakes region; Indigenous languages are becoming threatened on a global scale.[9] Thankfully, alongside Cree and Inuktitut, Anishinaabemowin maintains a large enough base of speakers to prevent its imminent death. For urban Indian youth and for children of mixed descent, however, language fluency is quite uncommon, which has calamitous implications for psychological and cultural well-being. With this in mind, the multifaceted stories and experiences of the Anishinaabeg are central to understanding the diversity of experiences in Anishinaabewaki.

The art of storytelling has profound cleansing and healing capabilities that may help diminish the painful effects of this ongoing colonial process of being de-tongued.[10] Since having our tongues literally or figuratively removed is only one of the many scars that Native peoples must perpetually bear, Anishinaabe citizens often internalize the blame for this systematic linguicide, disregarding the practicality of both telling *stories* and speaking *the language* in the process.

Thankfully, both Anishinaabeg elders and youth are attending to this issue in Great Lakes communities, both reservation and urban. In metropolitan Lansing, the urban Indian community to which I presently belong, projects such as the Indigenous Youth Empowerment Program directly combat language attrition through culturally specific, intergenerational pedagogies and programs.[11] In this community, like many across Turtle Island, we have numerous fluent language speakers who have amassed profound knowledge that they are more than willing to share. It is up to us, the younger generations, to mine this immense cultural resource, borrowing a colonial metaphor.[12]

While local activities demonstrate the omnipresent need to conduct language-based programming and activities, this essay, "Stories as *Mshkiki*," discusses ways that both fluent Anishinaabemowin speakers and monolingual Anglophone storytellers use the craft of conversation and dialogue, which operates within a storytelling tradition to heal the wound of historic, contemporary, and future de-tongueings.

NIBWAAKAAWIN (WISDOM):
TELLING STORIES AND TRIBALOGRAPHIES

Paramount to any speech act is its ability to transcend the particularities of that specific act and communicate in a way that transfers meaning in excess of its most basic literal signification. In this way, speech must evoke within the listener a sense of empathy with the speaker, and commence an awareness of community among all those involved. Storytelling, as a unique mode of communication, does exactly this: it establishes a community of shared experiences and memories. Speech, as the basis of transmitting memory, serves communal needs in a way that fulfills the reciprocal desires of all parties involved, both teller and listener. For many Anishinaabeg, the presumptions of fiction, a narrative genre whose efficacy we could spend time debating, seem irrelevant in relation to the raw power and emotional strength embedded in autobiographies and oral histories—literary genres that have been inadequately addressed within Native literary studies. When discussing its ability to challenge and critique, Robert Warrior writes in *The People and the Word: Reading Native Nonfiction*:

> Nonfiction writing is particularly well suited to this purpose as it typically has allowed Native authors to speak more directly to the situations and conditions Native people face than fiction or poetry has.[13]

While Indigenous literary genres do not easily distinguish between the *truthfulness* of nonfiction and the *imagined* qualities of fiction, I am nonetheless drawn to the powerful way that telling one's own story enables both the storyteller and listener/reader to migrate through a variety of constructed situations in a way that empowers the storyteller to possess their community's history and to construct its parameters in an ethical and healing fashion. It is in this manner that I interrogate Anishinaabe storytelling as a way to demonstrate the medicinal qualities of their autobiographic "stories." As such, to center Anishinaabeg Studies, I follow in the established intellectual tradition of writing a tribalography, an interdisciplinary literary genre generated by Choctaw writer Leanne Howe. In her essay establishing a tribalography for the White Earth Chippewa reserve, Jill Doerfler states that her work "is a tribalography—not completely fiction or history but a story that draws on the past, present, and future; documents and imagination; [and] the spaces between reality and rumors of memory."[14] Weaving together personal stories of individual and collective pasts, both Native nonfiction and tribalography initiate healing by uncovering otherwise hidden truths—truths that transcend the concepts of Western temporality.

I follow the ideas of Michif writer Maria Campbell, acclaimed author of *Halfbreed*, who, in reference to her own labor as an author, maintains that

> I don't think of myself as a writer. My work is in the community. Writing is just one of the tools that I use in my work as an organizer. . . . I get quite embarrassed when I have to speak from the view of a writer, because I really don't know what that is. I know what a storyteller is. A storyteller is a community healer and teacher.[15]

By integrating brief moments of my own autobiography into this narrative, I hopefully show the multifarious ways that storytelling and healing are interconnected, within ourselves and within our respective communities. Moreover, through this process we likewise link the histories of Anishinaabeg and Michif peoples, a relationship that I will explain.

As Indigenous elders have informed us since time immemorial, the process of orally transferring community histories from one generation to the next is crucial to any community's capacity to self-determine in the face of sustained colonial and capitalist attrition. Orality, as well as writing serve at the core of Anishinaabe ontology and the development of Ojibwa, Ottawa, and Potawatomi epistemologies.

Maori intellectual Linda Tuhiwai Smith argues that storytelling is one of twenty-five Indigenous projects rooted in decolonial methodologies; Archibald makes similar claims in *Indigenous Storywork*.[16] Basil Johnston argues that "it is in story, fable, legend, and myth that fundamental understandings, insights, and attitudes toward life and human conduct, character, and quality in their diverse forms are embodied and passed on."[17] Engaging the process of storytelling, as a medicinal practice tied to the *strength of the earth*, helps Indigenous peoples combat the omnipotent horrors of colonialism, and therefore serves as an anticolonial and liberatory device. By doing so, we center ourselves and our communities and, in turn, better focus the study and development of Anishinaabewaki and her people.

ZAAGI'IDIWIN (LOVE): KEEWAYDINOQUAY PESCHEL, ACADEMIC *MSHKIKIKWE*

In a period when few Native people went to university, Keewaydinoquay Margaret Peschel was schooled in both traditional Anishinaabeg and Western educational systems. Born in Northern Michigan in 1918, she studied at the University of Michigan (U of M) before gaining her bachelor's degree from Central Michigan University (CMU) at the age of twenty-six. From this period onward, Keewaydinoquay spent the rest of her life as both student and teacher, earning a master's degree from Wayne State University in 1953, with an additional master's in ethnobotany awarded in 1977 from CMU. Peschel subsequently enrolled in doctoral studies at U of M, followed by a period of teaching Indigenous philosophy at the University of Wisconsin-Milwaukee.[18] According to the editor of her autobiography, Lee Boisvert, Keewaydinoquay "is the only person of her time who we know studied both traditional Ojibway and western medicines."[19] Keewaydinoquay was at the vanguard of a developing sector of Indigenous intellectuals trained in both Native and settler knowledge systems.[20]

Impressively, unlike many of today's Native intellectuals who commonly publish exclusively in academic venues, Keewaydinoquay labored outside the tenure system, and as such published not only community-oriented texts in accessible English (including Anishinaabemowin whenever needed), but also within esteemed academic publishing venues, such as her 1978 *Puhpohwee for the People: A Narrative Account of Some Uses of Fungi among the Ahnishinaubeg* for the Botanical Museum of Harvard. *Puhpohwee for the People* is a nuanced and important discussion of Anishinaabeg ethnomycology (the study of fungi).

Her thoughtful writing and ability to merge Anishinaabe storytelling with Western academic writing is a hallmark of her work. In "The Girl Who Was Raised by the Owls," she commences the essay with a challenge to

Western notions of the "real" and its correlation with knowledge. According to Keewaydinoquay, "For those who seek wisdom, it is best to understand early that matters in this life are not always what they seem."[21] By evoking traditional stories and knowledges, she draws from an established body of Indigenous literature as the core to direct her academic work. In this way, she believes that "We must allow the Blessed spirits to guide us so we are enabled to understand such things, to rise above worldly pettiness, and to accomplish our intended True Purpose."[22]

Keewaydinoquay's well-tuned capacity to traverse equally within academic settings and customary Anishinaabeg environments is fitting for the material she covers and the manner in which she writes. This dialectic between maintaining community knowledge and the economic necessity to work within mainstream institutions is one many Native leaders and intellectuals constantly confront in their work. The unique power of Keewaydinoquay's complex positionality materialized for me during the summer of 2010, while writing this essay during a residency at the National Museum of the American Indian (NMAI) in Washington, D.C.

Following a few days at NMAI, I spent time in the National Anthropological Archives (NAA), where I came across a series of folders in Ruth Landes's personal papers that included material by and about Keewaydinoquay.[23] Landes, a Manhattan-born anthropologist, conducted extensive fieldwork in Anishinaabeg communities in Minnesota and Ontario during the 1930s, publishing her findings as *Ojibwa Sociology* (1937), *Ojibwa Woman* (1938), and *Ojibwa Religion and the Midewiwin* (1965).[24]

Within Landes's papers, I encountered the very real way that Keewaydinoquay was interacting with both academic and tribal communities, my very charge while conducting research in Washington, D.C. Included in a "national" archive composed of anthropological notebooks, writings, and visual documentation of Native treaty delegates from the nineteenth century, Keewaydinoquay's specter-like presence highlighted the dilemma of participating in mainstream academic discourses, while, as Beatrice Medicine argues, "remaining Native."[25] Keewaydinoquay's work does just that: it speaks to both Anishinaabeg and non-Native audiences.

The complexity within Keewaydinoquay's intellectual life is discussed in one source:

> She was the subject of a fair amount of controversy, much of it stemming from her willingness to teach those of other than native backgrounds. She started doing this at a time when native people had just secured their abilities to openly practice traditional ceremonial rites and religious observances.[26]

As a form of twentieth-first-century moccasin telegraph, this citation is telling in its recognition of the complex nature of Indigenous intellectual labor. Whatever disciplines Native intellectuals choose, we frequently do so in an attempt to create careers as working within mainstream disciplines in ways that are applicable to both non-Native academic and Indigenous audiences.

As I incorporated this profound serendipity into this essay, I was moved by the way that, even after walking into the Spirit-world in 1999, Keewaydinoquay, as an elder and scholar, continues to teach from the other world. Her profound love of learning and teaching, as well as her ability to heal the breaches of colonialism, transcend the earthly and spiritual worlds that maintain Anishinaabeg knowledge.

MANAAJI'IDIWIN (RESPECT): PUN PLAMONDON, ANTI-COLONIAL STORYTELLER

Unlike the work of Keewaydinoquay, who was intimately engaged in Anishinaabeg *mshiki* and mycological practices, Pun Plamondon's medicinal qualities developed in his unique ability to narrate his own personal homeward migration. In fact, Plamondon is nearly epic in his confrontation with capitalism and colonialism. While Keewaydinoquay was known for "sharing that in all healthy relationships reciprocity is involved," Plamondon's approach to healing progressed from his explosive and destructive youth to his eventual role as a sought-after storyteller.[27] An Odawa activist and storyteller, Plamondon spent time during the 1960s on the FBI's Most Wanted list, as well as helped found the White Panthers, an anti-racist hippie counterpart to the Black Panther Party. Throughout all of this, Plamondon was central in dismantling Richard Nixon's warmongering presidency, a theme he discusses in his storytelling.[28]

As a child in Northern Michigan, Plamondon was physically and culturally alienated from his Anishinaabeg relations, an experience shared by many urban Anishinaabeg. Born in a state psychiatric hospital in Traverse City, Plamondon was adopted by non-Native parents and raised outside Anishinaabeg tradition. In *Lost from the Ottawa*, Plamondon recounts his birth outside tradition:

> For a thousand years the tradition has been the same: shortly after the birth of a child, the father gathers the placenta and buries it in the yard near the home, maybe out back near the old oak. This is done so the child will always know where her home is and the spot where her home is and the spot where she is

connected to the earth. Later, when the umbilical cord dries and falls off the baby, the father makes a special leather pouch and places the cord inside. . . . None of this happened at my birth. Instead, in 1945, I was conceived and born in the State Mental Hospital in Traverse City, Michigan. My father was a 52-year-old half-blood Ottawa suffering from chronic alcoholism. My mother was a 39-year-old mixed-blood Ojibway woman diagnosed with syphilis. And so the circle begins.

By migrating home through stories, Plamondon completed the circle left open by colonial removal. Storytelling centers Plamondon.

Following a stint organizing Latino farm workers, Plamondon moved to southeast Michigan and took part in Ann Arbor–Detroit social movements. During the 1960s, he was accused (and later acquitted) of bombing a clandestine CIA office in Ann Arbor. Momentarily fleeing to postcolonial Algeria, Plamondon returned to the United States only to enter a period of prolonged alcoholism and psychological desperation. As he recalls, "Beer made me feel good"—a sentiment shared by all too many Native peoples.[29] To combat this self-medicated amnesia, Plamondon immersed himself in traditional Anishinaabeg ways of living, eventually finding storytelling as a potent *mshkiki* that helped him re-center his life. Through storytelling, Plamondon finally migrated home as an Anishinaabe person.

Plamondon's healing is significant. Following decades of alcohol/drug abuse, Plamondon needed to come home. He did so through ceremony, the healing ceremony of storytelling. As Plamondon stated in 2006, "I can't talk about getting sober without talking about returning to the Ottawa, and I can't talk about returning to the Ottawa without talking about getting sober 'cause they happened at the same time and they had to happen at the same time."[30] He continues:

> The white people didn't even want me. And I couldn't talk about quitting alcohol without returning to the Ottawa because the Ottawa was connected to the spirituality that I needed to have. But once I got sober and returned to the Ottawa I became a valuable member of my Ottawa community . . . reconnecting with the Ottawa, I found the traditional spirituality of the Ottawa, and I was welcomed because I was of value.[31]

Disappointed with the state of Indian Country today, Plamondon envisions the world in a radical dialectic. Again, Plamondon states:

> The history of the world is made up of two kinds of stories. One is the story of people who struggle against oppression, exploitation, and repression. They

generally win, or else the story isn't over yet. We don't know if they're gonna win. But then there's another story of people who hope they're gonna wait it out. They think that their lives ain't too bad, and that's where we're at today.[32]

Instead of acquiescing to the demands of settler regimes, Plamondon tells stories, including his own, because, in his own words, "the history of struggle against oppression and against government is significant and important."[33]

Lost from the Ottawa, Plamondon's autobiography, remains firmly committed to the revolutionary politics of his youth. Unlike many ex-radicals whose writings later in life contradict the radicalism of their youth, Plamondon's 2006 interview indicates that he is steadfast in his ongoing critique of both colonialism and capitalism. Plamondon's journey home terminates without any easily marked conclusion. While engaging the ways of the ancestors to help serve the role once fulfilled by alcohol, *Lost from the Ottawa* leaves the present and future entirely unresolved. Recognizing the actual human qualities of his life, as opposed to the constructed ones of mainstream cinema, Plamondon's resolve and healing commence in their incommensurability. Instead, he acknowledges that his contribution to tribalography "ain't no Hollywood story."[34] The *mshkiki* that powers Plamondon's writing is located not in his attempt to gloss over the rawness of life, but in the direct ways that he confronts life, in all of its horrific and *wendigo*-like moments. As an elder, his stories begin to touch upon the emotions and realities of urban Anishinaabeg who, through colonial forces, deal with the everyday effects of settler colonialism.

ZOONGIDE'IWIN (COURAGE): VISITS FROM WIKWEMIKONG

The final group of storytellers that enter this narrative are a group of Anishinaabemowin-speaking elders who meet on a semi-regular basis for intergenerational conversation over tea.[35] Throughout these conversations, we share stories, we listen, we laugh, we drink tea, we eat.[36] From these stories, we have presented at conferences, walked through the woods recording traditional ecological knowledge, and generally enjoyed visiting. After a few sessions, the Elders' Night became less about recording oral histories and more about the process of visiting with one another. What emerged from these conversations was the fact that *visiting*, as a quintessential component of maintaining community ties, has all but disappeared within urban Indian communities. Just stopping by someone's house, especially unexpected, allowed for relationships to develop between and among different generations. Through visiting, the elders informally instructed us in a way that formal educational structures do not facilitate. Around a kitchen table, authentic learning emerged.

Paramount to these conversations is Anishinaabemowin, both speaking the language and discussing the ways that it informs their ways of being. At a recent dinner attended by aboriginal elders from Australia, Nunavut, and North America, Alphonse Pitawanakwat (Wikwemikong) stated that "for a time, the [Western] educated ones left the language behind, but now they are coming back."[37] Whether migrating home or coming back to Anishinaabemowin, we still have much to learn. It is through stories that this pedagogy takes place. Manitoulin Island, the location where Lansing's elders primarily come from, plays an important role in Anishinaabe culture and the maintenance of language.

Following prophecy, the Anishinaabeg left Waabanakiing, Land of the Dawn, and began traveling down the St. Lawrence River and into the Great Lakes. Along the way, their journey was marked by a series of turtle-shaped islands, markers in the landscape that helped delineate their historico-geographical migration. Following respites at Mooniyaang (present-day Montreal), Wayaanag-gakaabikaa (Niagara Falls), and near present-day Detroit, the Anishinaabeg came across the largest freshwater island in the world, Manidoo Minis, or Manitoulin Island. This fourth stopping point, translated as Spirit Island, became an important cultural center, one highlighted today in the work of contemporary cultural organizations such as the Ojibwe Cultural Foundation on the M'Chigeeng (West Bay) reserve, as well as the profound cultural work being created on the island and by diasporic Anishinaabeg with roots on the island.

Margo Little, herself born on the island, writes that Manitoulin Island serves as a creative vessel:

> Manitoulin Island evolved into a remarkable crucible of creativity. The image of a crucible is apt because it suggests that something valuable and lasting can often be salvaged from experiences of prolonged anguish and privation. In essence, a crucible signifies that a struggle has been very difficult, but the results are a refining or reinforcement of a particular outlook or design. . . . It is clear that the island, a vessel forged by its own volatile and molten history, gave birth to a contingent of talented individuals as resourceful and stalwart as the land itself.[38]

Named a "crucible of creativity," Manitoulin has a significant place in the history of Indigenous arts, particularly the Woodland School of Painters, with many prominent artists coming from the island, among them Daphne Odjig and Carl Beam. The rich cultural heritage and ongoing linguistic preservation are contained in stories shared by elders from Manitoulin who, due to the economic necessities of capitalism, found themselves working in automobile factories in Lansing, Michigan.

The first arrivals came to Mid-Michigan from Manitoulin Island in the late 1950s, through a series of chain migrations. Elders revealed in our conversations that many initially went to Toronto, Chicago, Detroit, and Minneapolis, before eventually allowing roots to grow in Mid-Michigan. Most elders left the island in their late teens, returning frequently to Manitoulin, but living permanently outside the island. With many working-class men fighting in Vietnam during the 1950s and 1960s, recruiters for the auto industry began actively seeking out Native workers. Stories were told of recruiters coming to the reserve to entice workers to move south. The automotive industry served as a significant pull factor for people like the ex–fur traders in my family who left the bush to migrate south across the U.S.-Canada border to work in the city.

Relations with Michigan Anishinaabeg were not always ideal, with obvious social differences between Anglophone Anishinaabeg and Anishinaabemowin speakers. In our visiting, the elders shared their experiences working on the line for months before discovering another coworker was Anishinaabeg. Since many Michigan Anishinaabeg are not fluent in the language, initial conflicts existed between those fluent in Anishinaabemowin and those who were monolingual English speakers. These stories, even when about social conflict, preserve a level of humor throughout.

We could say that the oral exchanges uphold the specter of humor, a concept that many literary and cultural scholars have noted. When discussing the relationship between humor and healing in the work of Jim Northrup (Fond de Lac), White Earth Anishinaabe intellectual Lawrence W. Gross writes that humor allows Anishinaabe communities and their citizens to deal with the effects of what in his earlier work he begins to call "postapocalypse stress syndrome."[39] Because of the mass deforestation that transpired across the Great Lakes in the late nineteenth and early twentieth centuries, intergenerational trauma has developed based on the apocalyptic nature of this ecological destruction. Humor facilitates dealing with this trauma. Located throughout Anishinaabe writing and storytelling, Gross recognizes that

> The sacred stories of the people often involve slapstick and anal humor. These are the types of stories the Anishinaabeg embrace and that keep them coming

back for more. Because the humor of the Anishinaabeg is so closely bound to the storytelling tradition, any discussion of humor within the culture must include a consideration of storytelling.[40]

When visiting with elders, grossities are common, with sexual puns likewise frequent. In most cases, the jokes are told among the elders, with subsequent English translations occurring immediately afterwards. For non-Anishinaabemowin speakers, the English translations commonly miss the raw hilariousness of the initial joke. Through translation, Gross notes that "a native speaker will get the joke, while a non-native speaker will be left in the dark."[41] Even though my Anishinaabemowin-learning collaborators and I may find the situations humorous and frequently laugh, we nonetheless lack the language fluency to fully locate the hilarity of the untranslated joking.

Even when jokes are not fully understood, this cross-border, intergenerational visiting reclaims familial and tribal relationships severed by the geopolitics of capitalist nation-states. The relationship between Anishinaabeg from the other side of the Medicine Line and their cousins in Michigan is a long one. Sandy Wabigjig (Wikwemikong) attempts to find her paternal ancestors by tracing the lineage of her grandfather, Joseph Wabegijig, chief of Wikwemikong. In her story, she traces the profound migratory stories connecting the Anishinaabeg in Michigan and on Manitoulin, a story that also touches on my own family's history in Penetanguishene and Drummond Island. Wabigjig concludes her essay by acknowledging that

> Many of the Odawa relocated to Manitoulin Island after the War of 1812, the Removal period of 1830's, and after the Michigan Treaty of 1836. The residents of Wikwemikong are part of a collective history of trade, alliances and wars, removal from traditional homelands and many other hardships, but we are also a part of a resurgence of our history, spirituality and culture . . . we remain forever connected as we move forward in the wheel of life.[42]

By migrating home, and then sharing their stories, these elders are moving our communities forward through the quotidian act of sharing stories.

GWAYAKWAADIZIWIN (HONESTY): MIGRATING HOME

Each of the preceding vignettes, and the stories they reference, intimate the very real impact that migrations, be they geographic, intellectual, or cultural, have on Indigenous people. It is not insignificant that Kimberly

Blaeser's collection of Anishinaabeg writing is aptly titled *Stories Migrating Home*. In the introduction, Blaeser writes:

> Story power has always been a vital part of native lives. Indian people don't really instruct their children; they story them. That is, not only tell them stories but encourage them to hear and see the stories of the world around them, admonish them to remember the stories, and inspire them to create and discover their own stories.[43]

My inability to tell stories, in many ways, is an example of the colonial detongueings that have been rampant across Turtle Island. My desire to decolonize my mode of thinking relates to my interest in learning Indigenous languages and storytelling practices. To decolonize, one must migrate home through stories. Through this story-essay, I have returned home. These stories, as a form of strengthening the earth, serve as cartographic devices that lead us through the landscape of an ever-urbanizing Anishinaabewaki.

According to Anishinaabe-Lakota scholar Patrick LeBeau, "The Ojibwa people have a rich oral history and pictorial tradition regarding their origins and migration."[44] He continues:

> The tale of this journey over thousands of miles many hundreds of years ago is vivid and full of myths of good and evil spirits. . . . While written in the symbology of mythology, the maps of the ancient migration of the Ojibwa have identifiable reference points to the modern landscape.[45]

The symbology of migration, although embedded in the landscape, is likewise inherent when our stories migrate home.

As a Great Lakes Michif person, with familial roots in Michif, Cree, Anishinaabeg, and settler communities around the Great Lakes and in western Canada, Anishinaabeg stories are intimately woven into my individual and communal ontology. Allow me to share two brief stories, experiences that have recently cemented the reciprocity between Michif ontologies and Anishinaabeg ways of being, ones that touch upon issues of migration, healing, and telling our own collective stories. As Michif writer and activist Maria Campbell maintains, this retelling of Indigenous stories has become a type of "one small medicine," in many ways an understatement of the tangible healing capacity embedded in Native stories.[46]

The first instance occurred during a conference I helped organize on direct action within Indigenous and immigrant communities. As part of these events, Pun Plamondon spoke eloquently about his experiences as a 1960s radical, and his eventual migration home to become a tribal councilman and Ottawa elder.[47] During his provocative explication, Plamondon discussed how his family was involved in the fur trade in Northern Michigan. In the nineteenth century, Plamondon's family disregarded geopolitical boundaries and relocated with a group of Anishinaabeg (and Michif) families to Drummond Island, a British stronghold located between Michigan's Upper Peninsula and Lake Huron's Manitoulin and Cockburn Islands.

During this period, Drummond Island was an easily accessible yet isolated location, one that possessed a British fort and therefore allowed certain Native communities access to trade goods. Through subsequent treaty negotiations between the United States and Britain, Drummond Island, unlike the neighboring Manitoulin and Cockburn Islands, came under U.S. jurisdiction following the Treaty of Ghent, forcing a diaspora of independent Anishinaabeg and Michif peoples to migrate across the newly established international boundary line in 1828.[48] These aboriginal migrants moved to escape the violent realities of American expansionism, with treaty negotiations having ominous implications for Indigenous sovereignties on both sides of the U.S.-Canada border.

Discussing the Treaty of Detroit (1855), Anishinaabe legal scholar Matthew L. M. Fletcher (Grand Traverse Band) notes that "the terms of the treaty were disastrous to the Michigan Anishinaabek and forced some significant, unplanned, and yet incremental changes to tribal government structures."[49] Communities responded to these political shifts in diverse ways. During the period of extensive treaty negotiations between Indigenous and colonial governments, Plamondon's family, like my own, left Drummond Island for land located in the Georgian Bay, just across the U.S.-Canada border.[50] Once across the Medicine Line, aboriginal migrants became legally defined as Indian, Halfbreed, or White under the jurisdiction of the British colonial state, a humorous yet painful reality of how colonial governments (at times) control Indigenous legal identities.[51]

As Anishinaabe historian Karl Hele (Garden River First Nation) writes about the Michif and Anishinaabeg of the Sault Borderlands, treaty negotiators

> refused to cede to demands made by Ojibwa chiefs, specifically Nebenagoching, for the inclusion of their relations, the Métis. . . . Failing to achieve their inclusion, the chiefs permitted the Métis to join the bands. As such, ties formed over years of intermarriage allowed many families—Bell, Biron, Boissonneault, Larose, and Cadotte—to join either Garden River or Batchewana bands.[52]

While Plamondon's Anishinaabeg descendants came to be defined as "Indians," mine, on the other hand, were entered into the 1901 Canadian Census as either "French Breeds" or simply as "French," a story common in the Michif diaspora.[53] How my family—the Brissettes, Miners, and L'Hirondelles—saw themselves ethnically is not entirely clear. Significantly, many in their community of Penetanguishene, Ontario, filed a petition in 1840 demanding access to the same rights granted to the Anishinaabeg and "Halfbreeds" in Sault Ste. Marie. Although my family did not sign this document, many of their kin did, individuals and families with whom they traveled the expanses of the Great Lakes and Rupert's Land. What remains apparent, however, are the Indigenous cultural practices that my family maintained—ones my grandfather shared with me.

As family history tells it—as does the written history of Carling Township, Ontario—my great-great-grandmother was known for her ability to create a medicine from *la rasinn nwyar* (black root), as well as her skills in baking oatmeal cookies.[54] Likewise, her amazing skill as a beadworker parallels the material culture housed in priceless museum collections. Grandma Miner's beaded bag rivals those at NMAI or the Museum of Civilization in Ottawa. Regardless of the 1901 Census's ability to define my family as French Breeds, prior to my family's urban migration to Detroit, the Miners continued to practice the "ways of the country," those aboriginal lifeways that directly connect our experiences with those of our cousins, the Anishinaabeg. Stripped of sovereignty until the 1982 Constitution Act in Canada, Michif people evoked storytelling as the primary linkage to maintaining a communal sense of indigeneity.

What amazed and saddened me about my stay at NMAI was that of the over 800,000 items in the collection, there are a mere three shelves identified as "Métis," with all but a few items being contemporarily collected from the Michif community at Saint-Laurent, Manitoba.[55] While this museological conundrum of misclassifying Michif cultural artefacts was identified in 1985 by Ted Brasser, it nonetheless horrified me that in a museum intended to be a space for Native peoples, little Michif history is included.[56] What I did find, however, was that throughout Cree and Anishinaabeg collections (which are housed separately as Chippewa/Ojibwe, Odawa, and Potawatomi) there were hundreds of items that are potentially Michif. This, in fact, illuminates the extreme difficulty of trying to understand Métisness in a society where kinship remains the key to indigeneity.

What strikes me about shared Michif and First Nations archival holdings, besides the basic excitement of seeing items that our communities created over the past one-and-a-half centuries, is the realization that Anishinaabeg,

Cree, and Michif (hi)stories are so intimately linked. In fact, our stories are, if not the same, thoroughly intertwined. When discussing the history of the Michif in Sakitawak—what is known in French and English as Île à la Crosse, Saskatchewan—Michif historian Brenda Macdougall uses the Cree concept of *wahkootowin* to describe how Michif society relates to both land and other tribal peoples. For Macdougall,

> What makes the northwest truly compelling is that it is home to one of the oldest, most culturally homogenous Metis communities in western Canada, a community of people who grounded themselves in the lands of their Cree and Dene grandmothers by adhering to a way of being embodied in the protocols of *wahkootowin*. . . . This worldview, wahkootowin, is predicated upon a specific aboriginal notion and definition of family as a broadly conceived sense of relatedness with all beings, human and non-human, living and dead, physical and spiritual.[57]

In this fashion, Michif ontology, in the Great Lakes as in Saskatchewan, is fundamentally Indigenous in orientation. As such, Michif stories become irreconcilably intertwined with Anishinaabeg stories.

While disappointed to not see more Michif collections at NMAI, it struck me that by identifying Michif materials as either Anishinaabeg or Cree forced me to metaphorically speak with my cousins. This is, I believe, exactly where the objects belong, as do the Michif as an Indigenous people. When searching for Michif history at the Smithsonian, I migrated home to objects and stories of my Cree and Anishinaabeg relations. As Michif, we may not have the same personal connection to tribal land bases and the Anishinaabeg clan systems that our enrolled or status relations do, but we nonetheless remain cousins. Stories, including the brief stories I share in this essay, serve as the *strength of the earth*, an Anishinaabe earth that is shared by Michif relations.

DEBWEWIN (TRUTH): SHARING STORIES

As Linda Tuhiwai Smith writes in *Decolonizing Methodologies*, storytelling

> [has] become an integral part of all indigenous research. Each individual story is powerful. But the point of the stories is not that they simply tell a story, or tell a story simply. These stories contribute to a collective story in which every indigenous person has a place.[58]

Stories take many forms: from the writing of university-trained Anishinaabeg ethnologists, like Keewaydinoquay Peschel, to the revolutionary activism of Pun Plamondon; from the bilingual Anishinaabemowin-English conversations with fluent elders over cups of cedar tea and Lake Superior whitefish, to my narratives based on my experience in Western institutions. In addition to these multivalent literary migrations, stories are also found in our quotidian experiences as Native peoples, and in the quillwork-turned-beaded that our grandmothers have been making since time immemorial.

Stories of migratory healing connect with the medicinal qualities of *mshkiki* at disparate times and in random geographies. Each of these experiences confronts the never-ending effects of colonialism in a way that begins to heal generations of linguicide and intellectual ethnocide. By reclaiming our own stories and locating them within our own sovereignty, these narratives are the *mshkiki* we so intimately long for and so desperately need.

NOTES

While written exclusively by the author, the idea for this essay emerged because of conversations I have had with multiple Indigenous community members. Although any errors or intellectual irregularities are solely my own, its origin is in a collaborative project based on conversations at a Lansing kitchen table over cups of cedar tea. Many thanks, and possible authorial credit should be extended, in alphabetical order, to Doug Debassige, Don Lyons, Alphonse Pitawanakwat, George Roy, Ahz Teeple, and James West, as well as occasional participants Janis Fairbanks and Adam Haviland, among others.

1. Basil Johnston, *The Manitous: Spiritual World of the Ojibway* (Minneapolis: Minnesota Historical Society, 1987).

2. Gloria Anzaldúa, *Borderlands/La Frontera: The New Mestiza* (San Francisco: Aunt Lute Books, 1987). Chicana poet Gloria Anzaldúa develops this concept extensively in relation to colonialism along the U.S.-Mexico border.

3. Throughout this essay, I will use the term *Michif* in place of the more common *Métis*.

4. Some would call this baked good *bannock*.

5. Brenda Child, in Frances Densmore, *Strength of the Earth: The Classic Guide to Ojibwe Uses of Native Plants* (Minneapolis: Minnesota Historical Society, 2005), vi. The book was originally published, without Child's introduction, as "Uses of Plants by the Chippewa Indians," extracted from *Forty-fourth*

Annual Reports of the Bureau of American Ethnology (Washington, DC: Government Printing Office, 1928).

6. Jo-Ann Archibald, *Indigenous Storywork: Educating the Heart, Mind, Body, and Spirit* (Vancouver: University of British Columbia, 2008).

7. Basil Johnston, *Ojibway Ceremonies* (Lincoln: University of Nebraska Press, 1990), 107.

8. Joe Auginaush, in Anton Treuer, *Living Our Language: Ojibwe Tales and Oral Histories* (Minneapolis: Minnesota Historical Society, 2005), 5.

9. David Crystal, *Language Death* (Cambridge: Cambridge University Press, 2000). Linguist David Crystal notes that of the approximately 6,700 global languages, 96 percent of these languages are spoken by a mere 4 percent of the world's population. Crystal continues by writing that in Canada between 1981 and 1996, "for every 100 people with an indigenous mother-tongue, the number whose home language was most often an indigenous language declined from 76 to 65." The same study also found that Canada's fifty Indigenous languages each suffered significant erosion during this short fifteen-year period, with only three languages having enough fluent speakers to escape the threat of long-term extinction.

10. Anzaldúa, *Borderlands/La Frontera*.

11. The Indigenous Youth Empowerment Program is generally known by the acronym IYEP and is a coalition of youth, elders, and Native professionals. It is co-coordinated by Ashley Harding (Diné), Dr. Estrella Torrez (Chicana), and Becky Bebamikawe-Roy (Anishinaabe).

12. While elders are inherently *teachers*, many within metropolitan Lansing are quite literally teachers, instructing the Anishinaabemowin language courses at Saginaw Chippewa Tribal College (George Roy), University of Michigan (Alphonse Pitawanakwat), and Michigan State University (Helen Roy). Their pedagogies, like their stories, become *mshkiki* in a healing and sacred way.

13. Robert Warrior, *The People and the Word: Reading Native Nonfiction* (Minneapolis: University of Minnesota, 2005), xxi.

14. Jill Doerfler, "An Anishinaabe Tribalography: Investigating and Interweaving Conceptions of Identity during the 1910s on the White Earth Reservation," *American Indian Quarterly* 33, no. 3 (2009): 295.

15. Janet Witalec and Sharon Malinowski, eds., *Smoke Rising: The Native American Literary Companion* (Detroit: Visible Ink, 1995), 103.

16. See Linda Tuhiwai Smith, *Decolonizing Methodologies: Research and Indigenous People* (London: Zed Books, 1999). Also, see Jo-Ann Archibald, *Indigenous Storywork*.

17. Johnston, *Ojibway Ceremonies*; Basil Johnston, *Ojibway Heritage* (Lincoln: University of Nebraska Press, 1990), 7.

18. For nearly seven years during the 1920s and 1930s, Keewaydinoquay also apprenticed with *mishkikikwe* Nodjimakwe.

19. Lee Boisvert, in Keewaydinoquay, *Stories from My Youth* (Ann Arbor: University of Michigan Press, 2006), xiv. While we can likely name others who studied within both educational structures, think of figures schooled in Catholic and secular boarding schools—individuals like William W. Warren, who wrote an important Ojibway history during the late nineteenth century.

20. William W. Warren, *History of the Ojibway People*, 2nd ed. (1885; Minneapolis: Minnesota Historical Society, 2009).

21. Keewaydinoquay, "The Girl Who Was Raised by the Owls," *Square One* (Spring/Summer 1985): 59. A photocopy of this item is located in Ruth Landes Papers, National Anthropological Archives. Apprenticing for six years with Nojimakwe, a *mshkikwe* or herbalist, from 1925 to 1931, Keewaydinoquay applies these Anishinaabe learnings to her own teachings, ones we may all access through the written word.

22. Ibid., 59.

23. Ruth S. Landes (1908–1991), Papers, National Anthropological Archives and Human Studies Film Archive, Smithsonian Institution.

24. Like other non-Native anthropologists of the early twentieth century, Landes's writings are both eminently important, yet undoubtedly contained by the restraints of mid-twentieth-century anthropological assumptions about indigeneity.

25. Beatrice Medicine, *Learning to Be an Anthropologist and Remaining "Native"* (Urbana and Chicago: University of Illinois Press, 2001).

26. Wikipedia entry on Keewaydinoquay Margaret Peschel (accessed September 1, 2010).

27. Keewaydinoquay, *Stories from My Youth*, 168.

28. Ann Larabee, "Interview with Lawrence Robert 'Pun' Plamondon," *Journal for the Study of Radicalism* 1, no. 1 (2006): 111–27.

29. Pun Plamondon, *Lost from the Ottawa: The Story of a Journey Back* (Cloverdale, MI: Plamondon Inc., 2004), 23.

30. Larabee, "Interview with Lawrence Robert 'Pun' Plamondon," 123.

31. Ibid.

32. Ibid.

33. Ibid., 111.

34. Plamondon, *Lost from the Ottawa*, 346.

35. This project is generally known as the Nkwejong Project, or simply Elders' Night.

36. In Spring 2009, alongside Anishinaabeg activists Don Lyons (Leech Lake Ojibwe) and Allard (Ahz) Teeple Jr. (Bay Mills Ojibwe), we established an

oral-history project for elders in the Lansing metropolitan area. As personal friends and graduate students at Michigan State University, the three of us devised a way to create a summer course, with me as faculty, in which we would lay the foundation for an urban Anishinaabeg oral-history project in Michigan. While tribal nations have been adept at funding community histories, urban Indian stories are less frequently told. In Michigan, little is written about urban Indians.

In locations like Lansing, Anishinaabe history remains strong and vibrant, although little is known by either Native or non-Native community members about its specificity. The year before commencing Nkwejong, Lyons and Teeple had developed an internationalist-indigenist network in Michigan by working with the Aboriginal Australian Traditional Knowledge Revival Pathways (TKRP). From this visit in 2008, Lyons facilitated a delegation of Aboriginal Australians to tour Great Lakes Anishinaabeg communities, including urban communities in Lansing, Detroit, and Bawaating (Sault Ste. Marie), as well as tribal nations: Bay Mills Indian Community, Saginaw Chippewa Indian Tribe, Pokagon Band of Potawatomi, Grand Traverse Band of Ottawa and Chippewa, Little Traverse Band of Odawa, and Chippewas of Nawash Unceded First Nation, among others. TKRP, as both an organization and working methodology, incorporates digital technologies to record Indigenous ecological knowledge. Don Lyons, Ahz Teeple, and Bucko Teeple (Ahz's uncle) established an autonomous Great Lakes affiliate of TKWP aptly named Anishinaabeg Traditional Knowledge Revival Pathways (ATKRP). Since ATKRP works primarily in the realm of ecology, we were particularly interested in focusing on language issues and community histories—tribalographies, if you will.

37. This dinner was a special event where we honored invited guests Tim Knox, a Gamilaraay ecologist from Australia, and Jimmy Manning, an Inuk artist from Kiingait (Cape Dorset), Nunavut. They were both in the area as part of an Indigenous Peoples event.

38. Margo Little, "Manitoulin: Crucible of Creativity," in *Witness: A Selected Proceedings of Witness, A Symposium on the Woodland School of Painters*, ed. Bonnie Devine (Ottawa: Aboriginal Curatorial Collective, 2007).

39. Lawrence W. Gross, "The Comic Vision of Anishinaabe Culture and Religion," *American Indian Quarterly* 26 (Summer 2003): 436–59.

40. Lawrence W. Gross, "Humor and Healing in the Nonfiction Works of Jim Northrup," *Wicazo Sa Review* (Spring 2009): 70.

41. Lawrence W. Gross, "Silence as the Root of American Indian Humour: Further Meditations on the Comic Vision of Anishinaabe Culture and Religion," *American Indian Culture and Research Journal* 31, no. 2 (2007): 70.

42. Sandy Wabigjig, "In the Spirit of Our Ancestors: Who We Are and Where We Come From," in *Witness: A Selected Proceedings of Witness, A Symposium on the Woodland School of Painters*, ed. Bonnie Devine (Ottawa: Aboriginal Curatorial Collective, 2007).

43. Kimberly Blaeser, *Stories Migrating Home* (Bemidji, MN: Loonfeather Press, 1999), 1.

44. Patrick LeBeau, *Rethinking Michigan Indian History* (East Lansing: Michigan State University Press, 2005), 198.

45. Ibid.

46. Maria Campbell, "One Small Medicine," interview by Susan Gingell, *Essays on Canadian Writing* 83 (2004): 188–205.

47. If you know Pun, then you know that he does not speak "eloquently." Rather, at times he is quite blunt. In this way, I take liberties through interpreting his storytelling. This is, after all, a tribalography that allows for such creative tribal historiography.

48. A. C. Osborne, *The Migration of Voyageurs from Drummond Island to Penetanguishene in 1828*, vol. 3 (Toronto: Ontario Historical Society, 1901).

49. Matthew L. M. Fletcher, "Race and American Indian Tribal Nationhood," Michigan State University College of Law Legal Studies Research Paper 08–11 (2010), 20. Available online at http://ssrn.com/abstract=1620603 (accessed October 1, 2010).

50. For my family's migration, see Osborne, *The Migration of Voyageurs*, vol. 3.

51. "French Breed" (FB) or "Half Breed" (HB) was the manner in which the 1901 Census identified Michif people in the Georgian Bay region of Ontario. Sometimes, "French" (F) was also employed.

52. Karl S. Hele, "Manipulating Identity: The Sault Borderlands Métis and Colonial Intervention," in *The Long Journey of a Forgotten People: Métis Identities and Family Histories*, ed. Ute Lischke and David T. McNab (Waterloo, ON: Wilfrid Laurier University Press, 2007): 178.

53. 1901 Census of Canada.

54. See "Early Days in Carling Township," undated local history publication (Parry Sound, ON); *A Pictorial History of Carling Township* (Parry Sound, ON: Carling History and Heritage Committee, n.d.); and Osborne, *The Migration of Voyageurs*, vol. 3.

55. The Michif community of Saint-Laurent, Manitoba, was one of eight North American Indigenous communities chosen to tell their own histories for *Our Lives: Contemporary Life and Identity*. As part of this permanent exhibition, the National Museum of the American Indian collected materials that were not exhibited and are now in the museum's archive.

56. Ted Brasser, "In Search of Métis Art," in *The New Peoples: Being and Becoming Métis in North America*, ed. Jacqueline Peterson and Jennifer S. H. Brown (Manitoba: University of Manitoba Press, 1985), 221–30.

57. Brenda Macdougall, *One of the Family: Metis Culture in Nineteenth-Century Northwestern Saskatchewan* (Vancouver: University of British Columbia, 2010), 3.

58. Linda Tuhiwai Smith, *Decolonizing Methodologies: Research and Indigenous Peoples* (New York: Zed Books, 1999), 144.

Horizon Lines, Medicine Painting, and Moose Calling

The Visual/Performative Storytelling of Three Anishinaabeg Artists

MOLLY MCGLENNEN

WHERE AND HOW DO WE FIND STORY?

IN HER COLLECTION OF NARRATIVES *PORTAGE LAKE: MEMORIES OF AN Ojibwe Childhood*, Anishinaabe elder Maude Kegg relays a story entitled "Canoe." Her student and editor John Nichols transcribes and translates "Canoe" as follows:

> I can barely remember long ago—I don't know how big I was—going down to the shore. There was a canoe there so I got in it. I must have climbed down to the far end. I don't remember much.
>
> When I took a look, the boat was far out and I heard some ladies, maybe three or four of them, my grandmother and my aunt, two of my aunts, running toward me, crying as they came, some of them running right into the water, and so I got scared.
>
> I remember that I was scared. I must have jumped. Then I remember looking at fish of all different colors. They were sunfish. Sometimes they came real close and looked at me. That's all I have remembered. I must have been picked up out of the water.[1]

I have always found this story fascinating because while on the surface it seems simple enough, a story of a young girl rescued from the water, underneath breathes a world luminous, mysterious, and provocative. And through this richness, I learn several things at once. It is a cautionary tale: Don't get into a canoe by yourself, especially into the end sticking out into the water as that might launch you from the shore, and be especially cautious if you're young and inexperienced at handling a canoe. It is also a story of Anishinaabe kinship and gender: Kegg's aunties and grandma come running and hollering for her when they notice, almost immediately, she's in trouble; Kegg is part of a community where she is being watched, noticed, cared for, and loved by a network of women, specifically. It is a story of observance and respect for the water (the lakes) and the fish that, as we know, have traditionally fed and continue to feed Ojibwe people. It is also a story about beauty and a meditation on spirit. Finally, it is an incomplete story as she twice iterates how she doesn't "remember much" or "that's all [she has] remembered."

When I read this story, I imagine Kegg speaking it in Anishinaabemowin. I imagine Nichols recording it, maybe retelling it to someone. I imagine myself and my family on any one of many canoe trips, looking for places to fish, or for a cool place to land then jump in the water. I imagine ancestors of mine ricing from their canoes. I "picture" this story infinitely. I could draw or paint or perform these imaginings, and the work would be a sort of shorthand for Kegg's story, for my stories, for what will become my daughter's stories, I hope. In this way, could not those imaginings rendered as art (drawn, painted, performed, and so on) also be stories themselves?

Historically, the Anishinaabeg used pictures to relay stories and cultural information. According to Anishinaabe scholar Ben Burgess, the Midewiwin traditionally used and currently continue to use pictographs to relate teachings; however, not a Midewiwin member himself, Burgess says that only initiated *Mide* have access to the scrolls, as far as he knows.[23] Anishinaabe scholar Anton Treuer affirms that "the Ojibwe still use scrolls in religious rituals."[4] In many ways, this method of relaying knowledge suggests particular forms of Anishinaabe cultural production. Thus, the artwork (painting, sculpting, drawing, performance, etc.) of Anishinaabe people in the twentieth and twenty-first centuries can be viewed as a vibrant continuation, adaptation, and creative expression of those traditional modes of storytelling that helped (and still help) Anishinaabeg understand the world around them and how to "be" in that world.

For this paper, I will look at specific pieces by three Anishinaabe artists, George Morrison (Grand Portage Reservation), Norval Morrisseau (Sand Point Reserve), and Rebecca Belmore (Lac Seul First Nation) as a way to examine the intellectual, spiritual, and political roles their artwork plays in Anishinaabe communities, and the ways in which their artwork, read as Anishinaabe-produced texts, convey and trouble notions of Indigenous presence and ways of being through the storied knowledge found within their creative work. Though disparate in its era and mode of expression, the artwork of Morrison, Morrisseau, and Belmore works from and out of Anishinaabe intellectual and aesthetic traditions. And by understanding this trajectory more clearly, we begin to see not only how Anishinaabeg Studies broadens definitions and uses of "texts," but also underscores the primary role stories serve in relating and illuminating the world around us.

BEFORE THE ART: CENTERING STORY

In *Ojibwe Heritage*, Anishinaabe scholar Basil Johnston explains to his readers that in writing his book, "it is one way of perpetuating and enhancing the bequest of our [Anishinaabeg] forefathers" and "it is the hope that . . . Ojibwe speaking peoples . . . will be a little better understood."[5] Although Johnston's initial intent for his book was a sort of textbook of truthful but general information about Ojibwe peoples, I view *Ojibwe Heritage* as a helpful guide for my understanding of Anishinaabe stories and their purpose in people's lives. Johnston reminds us that

> It is in story, fable, legend, and myth that fundamental understandings, insights, and attitudes toward life and human conduct, character, and quality in their diverse forms are embodied and passed on. But it is *not enough* to listen to or to read or to understand the truths contained in stories; according to the elders the truths must be lived out and become part of the being of a person. The search for truth and wisdom ought to lead to fulfillment of man and woman."[6]

Johnston, an Ojibwe elder himself, teaches us here that to identify as Anishinaabe and to live as an Anishinaabe is not only to listen to and know the stories, but also to live out the truths found within the stories. Moreover, he reminds us that "living out" the truths is a process of becoming over time; thus, centering our stories in our lives means creating our being in conjunction with a community of people who share and have helped shape a specific body of knowledge. Centering our stories also means subscribing to particular modes of learning that the stories themselves intimate, such as the accrual of deepened knowledge over long periods of time, or the power in learning through observation and meditation, or the evolution of traditions articulated in story built *on* the communal knowledge of those who have gone before us, and built *for* those who are yet to be born.

One of the ways this idea of centering stories plays out in our day-to-day lives is the individual attempt to decolonize our way of being, intellectualizing, and forming community, no matter where we reside. If we are to take what Johnston lays out for us and put it into practice, what does that mean in our everyday life and the lives of our families and communities? Linda Tuhiwai Smith in *Decolonizing Methodologies* (as well as several other theorists who came before her, concerned with the decolonization of colonized peoples, e.g., Frantz Fanon) asserts the primary significance of centering the concerns and worldviews of the colonized, and breaking free from imitating the colonizer as a means toward decolonization. Tuhiwai Smith also reminds us of the limits of the anthropologization of Indigenous communities as privileged forms of knowledge production, the outsider's intentions "justified as being for the 'good of mankind.'" Tuhiwai Smith says, "Research of this nature *on* indigenous peoples is still justified by the ends rather than the means,"[7] and we can certainly understand "ends" to be the justification for oppression, forced removal, attacks on sovereignty, and a whole slew of other markers of imperialism. We can also deepen and reinterpret "the means" as a form of centering Indigenous knowledge and cultural production, and in the case of my argument here, Anishinaabe creative expression.

When we examine the means of centering Ojibwe stories in our lives as a path to better understanding the world around us, we begin to see that those means produce ways to combat those unjust political, intellectual, and spiritual corners in which we may find ourselves and/or our communities. Johnston's text reminds us of Anishinaabe modes of learning and knowledge production as he describes the origins and character of the Ojibwe Midewiwin Society. By relaying the story of the first medicine man and woman, Johnston articulates how knowledge was (and is) procured and passed on within the Medicine Society.[8] But this story, acting as a sort of direction-finding source for how Ojibwe attempt to live the "good life," is in a lot of ways its own compass for pointing Anishinaabeg to the stories that not only help define them, but help guide them. The story of the young man Odaemin, the first medicine man, teaches Ojibwe modes of learning: that the power to learn comes through observation (as when Odaemin watches which animals eat which plants), and that knowledge is gained through retreat and meditation (as when Odaemin withdrew from the community to seek out and attain his curative powers). In addition, while Johnston teaches us through this story what constitutes healing and living a good life for a medicine person, he also connects the Midewiwin lifestyle to the Anishinaabeg in general when he says, "Wherever the Anish-nabeg established their villages and homes, they too commemorated the gift of knowledge annually in ritual [as the Midewiwin did]."[9] I believe we can take this as a lesson about how central intellectualism (knowledge-seeking) exists in Anishinaabe life, and how closely related teaching, learning, and spiritual life are. We must commemorate and celebrate the medicine found in the stories.

Additionally, Anishinaabe scholar Lawrence Gross reminds us through his reading of several texts containing studies of Anishinaabe myth that the stories teach the proper conduct for human life, how to carry out various relationships, and how to form alliances.[10] Through the story of the Earth Diver, Gross reminds us of the concept of *Bimaadiziwin* ("live well"), which teaches Anishinaabeg how to live with and in the landscape of their home-land, how to live as balanced people in a layered cosmos, and how to respect all life forms. In the end, Gross reminds us that "bimaadiziwin . . . does not exist as a definite body of law. Instead, it is left up to the individual to develop an understanding of bimaadiziwin through careful attention to the teaching *wherever it can be found.*"[11]

If we are to "live out" our stories, as Johnston reminds us; if we are to center our ways of perceiving and interpreting the world around us on our own terms, as Tuhiwai Smith suggests; if we have the ability to recognize our stories in various forms coming from various places, as Gross puts forth, it seems reasonable in our attempt toward building the field of Anishinaabeg Studies that various forms of cultural expression—both creative and critical, theoretical and material, expressed and written, imaged and textual—are valid and enduring forms of storytelling. Moreover, if we are to move from the inside out in our critical study of Anishinaabeg-authored story, we must honor those Anishinaabe elders who have already set the "mnemonic pegs" out before us, as Mi'kmaq scholar Stephen Augustine suggests,[12] so we may then pass through these markers to new, deepened, and collective ways of understanding the original values of the Anishinaabeg.

STORIED CONNECTIONS TO ARTISTIC EXPRESSION

It seems safe to say that artistic expression in all of its forms comes from an artist's intense and extensive amount of observation, introspection, and mindfulness toward the thinking through of a problem or idea. In a way, this imaginative enterprise is a sort of science—perhaps not one based on objective "evidence," but one of deep contemplation and examination of the world around him or her. In his preface to *Honour Earth Mother*, Basil Johnston explains:

> North American Indians were as keen observers as the scientists of today. But, unlike modern scientists who conduct their research indoors, North American Indians conducted their studies in the natural setting of the earth under natural conditions. Nor did they limit their reports to fact and data. They went beyond that. They used fact and data as bases for stories that exemplified something of human nature and conduct to be imitated or spurned.[13]

Though Johnston is not referencing artistic endeavors per se, Johnston's point is still helpful in understanding how Indigenous people acquired (and perhaps continue to acquire) bodies of knowledge, as well as how we might go about "reading" and understanding Anishinaabe wisdom. Conveying and absorbing knowledge (fact, data, information in any form) endures through the vehicle of story.

This relates to the way I read the three Anishinaabe artists' work, in that I'm attempting to understand each "piece" (drawing, painting, or performance) as a story. It also relates to the way I contextualize my critique of centering this mode of learning and knowledge production in relationship to Anishinaabeg Studies. Being attentive to George Morrison's work teaches us the power of meditating and contemplative forms of knowledge production. Only by being in, interacting with, and observing a place over a long period of time does an individual or his/her collective community come to "know" a place.[14] Being attentive to Norval Morrisseau's work teaches us about the connection between creativity and spirituality. Often working from birch bark and utilizing Cree syllabics, Morrisseau aspires to "transform his visions into tangible forms of expression" as a spiritual being;[15] in this way we are reminded that artistic expression is also sacred expression. Being attentive to Rebecca Belmore's work teaches us that by centering Indigenous concerns and ways of being, communities of people can work to politicize movements to foil the courses of colonization or trauma or violence with compassionate but unyielding creative energy.

From these Anishinaabeg artists, we learn that artistic expression is storied expression. The process involves the artist observing, struggling with, and engaging with the world around him or her, and then thinking through that observation, struggle, and engagement only to release it into the world, as a storyteller would, in some new and deepened and aesthetic way.

THREE ANISHINAABE ARTIST-STORYTELLERS

George Morrison (1919–2000)

Labeled as an abstract expressionist by the larger art world, George Morrison bases his "Horizon Series" (a series lasting from the 1960s into the 1990s) on his visioning of a sacred place for the Anishinaabe—Lake Superior, near Morrison's home on the Grand Portage reservation. As a vital artist of the Modernist age, Morrison has garnered a considerable amount of study and scholarship; most scholars, both Native and non-Native, conclude that Morrison is "a major American artist and Indian artist at the same time."[16] Some scholars see the literal likeness of Morrison's work to Anishinaabe cultural expression, as when art historian Truman Lowe suggests that Morrison's drawn designs *To Edge of Lines All Around* and *Landscape* "resemble woven basketry or birchbark abstractions."[17] Other scholars, like Anishinaabe author Gerald Vizenor, view his work on a continuum of Anishinaabe storytellers:

> The Anishinaabe painted and incised subjective, surreal pictures on wood and stone. Many centuries later, similar images were renewed on spiritual scrolls, beaded patterns on clothes, ceremonial objects, and in contemporary art. Surely the ancient pictures are atavistic expressions, the intuitive course of nature on a mythic horizon."[18]

Vizenor suggests that Morrison captures storied expression through his art via Lake Superior's horizon line; even so, Vizenor also suggests that Morrison does not render the literal horizon, but uses the line as an anchor to tap into the subconscious, the dreams, the spaces that house those memories of who the Anishinaabe were and who they are, much as stories do.

Perhaps understanding Morrison's series along this Anishinaabe artistic trajectory, Vizenor also notes that Morrison "created an elusive shimmer of endless space, the color and eternal motion of nature. The horizons he painted were inspired by nature and lightened by his watch and visual memories of Lake Superior near the Grand Portage reservation in Minnesota."[19] It is documented in several places how much Morrison was drawn to the shore of Lake Superior: Morrison himself has said,

> One of the notions in my imagination was to capture the infinite variations and changes of moods that pass over the lake at different times. I am fascinated with ambiguity, change of mood and color, the sense of sound and movement above and below the horizon line. Therein lies some of the mystery of the paintings:

the transmutation, through choosing and manipulating the pigment, that becomes the substance of art.[20]

Morrison's use of the artistic "trope" of the horizon between the sky and water locates the viewer in a particular storied landscape. Morrison does not abstract a literal representation of a specific landscape, but rather (like a good storyteller, perhaps) illuminates the transformations emanating from a particular place at a particular time; thus, in *Awakening, Time Edge Rising, Red Rock Variation: Lake Superior Landscape* (1990), for instance, a dynamic sunrise over Lake Superior reveals a transmutational understanding of horizon.

In many ways, Morrison "writes" a story of deep meditation and observation, which locates and dislodges storehouses of knowledge found in and around the lake. In *Awakening*, with its pastel colors, shaded and shadowed haze of lines that sink down the canvas from the faint horizon line, we as participants in this storied experience come to know in some ways the atmosphere of sunrise over Lake Superior, those interstitial or liminal moments only known through extended contemplation and acute studying of place. Morrison's *Awakening* becomes a teaching story, a storied pedagogy that relays ways of being attentive to and present in the world. As story, the piece enriches one's understanding of living a mindful life, one that is connected to revelatory experience with Anishinaabe landscape that supersedes mere reflection on it. And for those who now live in other parts of the world away from "home," it reminds them who they are. *Awakenings* and other Horizon Series pieces are also cartographic stories.

David Martinez's (Gila River Pima) essay "Along the Horizon a World Appears: George Morrison and the Pursuit of an American Indian Esthetic" works to construct the link between Anishinaabe oral and dream traditions and Morrison's abstract series. Positioning our understanding of the horizon line as the "ultimate organizer of place,"[21] Martinez shows how our "knowing body" holds within it a sophisticated and ancient science unto its own, which allows humans to search, locate, orientate, and find direction. Morrison, Martinez tells us, returned to Minnesota from New York to the shores of Lake Superior, to his home he called Red Rock, where his Horizon Series would emerge, because "it is *being here* from which our knowledge and understanding of a place truly derives."[22] Martinez explains that this emergence, located in and orientated through the horizon, comes from "his imagination, which is really . . . a connection to his 'subconscious.' The result of this technique, which is probably better described as a lifestyle, are paintings that incite an immediate effect, free of the burdens of narrative."[23] He quotes Morrison as saying, "You didn't have to look for a [literal] story in the picture. You could look at an abstraction and have an immediate reaction.[24] I argue here that Morrison's pieces in the series are not representations of the horizon line on Lake Superior, nor are they literal ("worded") narratives about it; they do not, in fact, stand in for or represent Anishinaabe culture either. *Awakenings* and other pieces in the series invigorate and perpetuate Ojibwe storytelling because to "react" to Morrison's work is to be invited into a particular way of seeing a specific place that is very special, significant, and spiritually meaningful to the Anishinaabe people. And in this way, the viewer's reaction or interaction with the pieces make up the storied experience of the work.

Morrison's horizon pieces—though not relayed orally, as Kegg's story "Canoe," for instance—emit some of the same types of information. They story the contemplative knowledge that only comes through deep and prolonged meditation and mindfulness. His pieces are a sort of "living out" of the truths found in Anishinaabe philosophies, as his creative expression comes from a contemplative and revelatory relationship with Lake Superior, the body of water that Anishinaabe stories denote as a spiritual home for the people.

Norval Morrisseau (1932–2007)

Norval Morrisseau's work is heavily influenced by birch-bark scrolls, which traditionally recorded Anishinaabe history, *Mide* knowledge, and songs; thus, Morrisseau (labeled as the creator of the art movement known as the Woodland School or Medicine Painting)[25] works to express sacred Anishinaabe stories, sites, and philosophies. A seminal figure of Modern Art, Morrisseau produced an immense oeuvre. In addition, his complicated life story and the conflicting scholarship on the ties between shamanism and his art as well as Morrisseau's own tense feelings over revealing Ojibwe stories through his art all urges me to greatly limit the scope of my examination of Morrisseau in order to engage more deeply with his work as story. I hope to do this by looking at one of his paintings, *Observations of the Astral World*, that (like most of his work) clearly identifies his style and highlights the connection between traditional and contemporary storytelling modes. Ultimately, I hope this will allow us to stretch the concept of story, as it has been traditionally categorized as "written versus oral," to include non-orthographized and nonverbalized communications of story. Like the pictographs on traditional birch-bark scrolls and petroglyphs that dot the Anishinaabe landscape, his work is a form of storytelling that, in

Morrisseau's own words, correlates to ancient traditions: "That was where I started to paint. My grandfather showed me how to do interpretations of the shaman beliefs on birchbark."[26]

Observations of the Astral World conveys an Anishinaabe story of being in the world. This enormous painting, approximately 8 feet by 17 feet, renders figures nearly life-size and presents itself in mural fashion, which makes it almost impossible to take it in all at once. Like a story, it unfolds, whether the viewer moves left to right or from the center outward, or in any other direction. Equally as interesting, the story/painting is one of observation, as human, animal, and spirit figures convene to gaze, and as earth, sky, and water intertwine as part of this viewing. As a form of Anishinaabe ontology, the story/painting is also one of shared experience, as all figures and elements are linked by the continuous black lines, the quintessential markers of Morrisseau's work.

There is no obvious reference point toward which the humans, spirits, and some animals appear to be gazing; likewise, a night sky with stars and planets is not rendered literally either. One yellow circle in the middle could be taken for the sun, but it is filled with fish. The two larger circles on either side could be taken for earth and sky. But much of this is skewed, off-scale, as fish teem in what would be the sky, as birds congregate on the ground and become extensions of the vine, or flowers, stems, and leaves, instead of perching on them. All figures are connected by the bold black lines that characterize the Anishinaabe School; the lines "delineate flat fields of bright colour and the use of 'spirit' or 'power' lines that emanate from, surround, and join figures."[27] In what has been termed an "x-ray form of representation of people and animals," "the interiors of living beings are shown with a stylized skeletal structure, often embellished with linear design elements and sometimes incorporating an interior animal or spirit being."[28] The effect of this "style" or patterning on the viewer/listener is that one may read and understand the images and their story in dimensional ways, a means in which the spiritual landscape of the world is as marked and imperative as the physical landscape.

Interpreting the story/painting this way, we understand observation as not only a communally shared means of knowledge production but also a spiritually charged enterprise. An artist who has been described as melding "ancient knowledge with a form of contemporary expression," Morrisseau "relied solely on his inner vision."[29] Like many of Morrisseau's paintings, *Observations of the Astral World* teaches us about modes of learning and modes of being in the Anishinaabe world. This world, however, is not one that exists in a bubble, as if Anishinaabe people aren't affected to varying degrees by colonialism and the greater globalized planet. But perhaps in some ways Morrisseau (painting this immense piece in the early 1990s) is reminding us of our beginnings, as well as our interconnections to other people. The title suggests ideas of theosophy and reverence towards other planes of existence and other worlds, but the story the painting renders establishes a world defined by Anishinaabe culture, including schools of fish, a wolf, and what could be taken for a turtle. In many ways, *Observations* exists as a story that teaches tolerance (for other forms of knowledge), humility (as humans are not dominant over other beings), and patience (as all appear to be invested in the study and wonder of that which cannot always be explained). Like Kegg's story and like Morrison's horizon lines, *Observations* presents a valuable story of how *to be* in the world.

Rebecca Belmore (1960–)

A contemporary performance and installation artist, Rebecca Belmore seeks to envision Indigenous presence on a global scale by centering Anishinaabe culture as a decolonizing lens for her work. In "Performing Power," Jolene Rickard (Tuscarora) describes Belmore's sound performance entitled *Ayumee-aawach Oomama-mowan: Speaking to Their Mother* (1991–92) as giving "voice to aboriginal people across Canada. Constructed as a giant megaphone, reminiscent of birch-bark cones used for moose calling in northern Ontario, this piece opened up a space for aboriginal people to speak and be heard. It created a site for the recognition of the historical erasure of aboriginal voices, and empowered aboriginal people to speak and be heard."[30] I'd like to look at this sound performance piece (which now sits as a permanent display at NMAI in Washington) as a means to link Belmore's work to the decolonizing and politicizing aspects of Anishinaabe storytelling.

This very deliberate piece is actually a means for spontaneous and uncensored speech. Cree/Blackfoot artist and scholar Gerald McMaster describes *Ayumee-aawach Oomama-mowan* as a dynamic communal event, a mobile performance-installation that toured across Canada to ten different sites, involving Indigenous people from across Indian country, spanning several months:

> In the performance, several people speak into the attached microphone, their voices amplified by the megaphone . . . Belmore created an opportunity for everyone to speak to the universe without prejudice, fear, or embarrassment, because at the moment of enunciation everything and everybody . . . witness

the address. . . . Her insistence that the event take place outdoors carries with it the idea of inclusiveness—everybody and everything participates. . . . What she helps create is a sacred time, a liturgical moment, where every responsible action is subject to everybody and everything. As traditional spiritual beliefs indicate, there are key times of the year for large formal performance gatherings but none for personal enunciations.[31]

Created in part in reaction to the Oka Crisis in 1990,[32] Belmore's installation satirizes the traditional tools of the anthropologist and ethnographer—the gramophone, phonograph, and microphone, instruments of recording and nailing down information in some assumed permanency; in turn, the installation becomes "a flashpoint of protest and storytelling in the wake . . . of the crisis."[33] Additionally, this large wooden megaphone (seven feet long and six feet wide) releases or projects the words of those who would be subjects or informants outward and recontextualizes the relationship between binaries of informant/expert, victim/oppressor, and oral/written; as a result, it reconstitutes our understanding of storytelling as a form of knowledge production.

The installation allows people the opportunity to share stories, memories, frustrations, and concerns through which their voices echo out towards the landscape of whatever space of contention they are inhabiting at the time. For most Native people, the Oka Crisis signified the long history of silencing Indigenous people's voices and concerns and the stamping out of their rights to self-determination. Through Belmore drawing our attention to the various and vibrant forms of "recording voices" and narrative forums, a community of Indigenous people actualize the subversion of the very tools that have chipped away at the autonomy of Native people. Belmore does this by drawing on, and complicating in some ways, traditional Anishinaabe forms of communication, namely, moose calling through birch-bark cones.

In a talk she gave at the Global Feminisms Forum at the Elizabeth A. Sackler Center for Feminist Art, Belmore explained that her art is a way to use her body to "address history, the immediate, the political," and that because she uses her body in most of her performance pieces, the pieces are "deeply personal."[34] In this way, she creates a powerful forum to speak out against injustice and violence done against Indigenous people. In *Ayumee-aawach Oomama-mowan*, Belmore and communities of people through personal, kinesthetic, and evocative means communicate their rights as Indigenous people, and their land rights as members of sovereign tribal nations. In this political act of subversion, the communicating is no longer controlled by the social scientist outsider, but by activist-citizens themselves. And because the voices are amplified by the cone, each person's words—in both Indigenous and colonial languages—are put out into the world to reverberate and live on, as opposed to being nailed down on paper or tape. This performative installation, allowing many Native people to speak up and speak out against injustice,[35] thrives on the continuum of Anishinaabe traditional storytelling.

WOVEN REFLECTIONS

Indeed, each artist deserves much more attention to his or her work than I have been able to offer here. Each artist's work spans multiple decades and has broken artistic ground in various ways and forums. So, in this way, let this essay also stand as an invitation for more scholars to take on projects involving Morrison, Morrisseau, or Belmore. I hope that I have shown, however, that it is not enough to only study their work in relationship to Modernism, Abstract Expressionism, or contemporary performance art—labels of Western art movements and schools (though each artist is indeed an astounding force within and beyond each respective classification). Instead, I hope I demonstrate the relationship between each artist's work and Anishinaabeg Studies, and in turn unearth Anishinaabe modes of storytelling that score and augment core Anishinaabe values in the twenty-first century.

In addition, it is *not* my intention to say that my very short examinations of each artist's work are the only readings of, or lessons from, the pieces; rather, it is my purpose to center Anishinaabe receptivity in order to better learn from what is presented to us through the work. Through the art of Morrison, Morrisseau, and Belmore, we learn in much the same way as we learn from our community's stories, and like those teachings, we come to a deeper understanding the more we come into contact with them. In the preface to *Original Instructions: Indigenous Teachings for a Sustainable Future*, Anishinaabe scholar Melissa Nelson posits, "Indigenous forms of education are usually based on storytelling," and she goes on to say that no matter how they take shape ("origin legends and history, famous speeches and epic poems, songs, the teachings of spirit mentors, instructions for ceremony and ritual, observations of worlds, and storehouses of ethno-ecological knowledge"),[36]

> Stories often live in many dimensions, with meanings that reach from the ordinary to the divine, from the "before worlds" to the present. Stories are possessed with such power that they have survived for generations despite attempts at repression and assimilation. Native American storytelling is an invaluable

cross-cultural continuum that has no beginning and no end. All cultures can learn and be enriched by Native storytelling.[37]

Morrison's *Awakenings*, Morrisseau's *Observations*, and Belmore's *Ayumee-aawach Oomama-mowan* are not *only* Anishinaabe stories, but they are indeed Anishinaabe stories. Just as Morrison indigenized/Anishinaabe-ized modernist sensibilities and expectations of mid to late twentieth-century art, so too did he stand as an "elusive visionary"[38] and an abstract expressionist painter without racial categories that defined himself and his art. Similarly, just as Morrisseau admired the surrealists and primitivists of the Modernist era, he forged an entirely new and decidedly Indigenous/Anishinaabe form of art. Finally, just as Belmore has been at "the forefront of artistic multimedia projects"[39] for the last twenty years, her permanence ironically may lie with her overt attention to Indigenous/Anishinaabe cultures and issues. And yet, *Awakenings*, *Observations*, and *Ayumee-aawach Oomama-mowan* each add to the body of knowledge that continually grows out of a unique cultural landscape that has been nurtured for generations. When we center these artists as storytellers, we begin to complicate and broaden the burgeoning field of Anishinaabeg Studies—as one that seeks cross-cultural dialogues and connections at the same time it delves into its own storehouse of knowledge by making that antiquity relevant in the lives of Anishinaabeg today.

NOTES

1. Maude Kegg, *Portage Lake: Memories of an Ojibwe Childhood* (Edmonton: University of Alberta Press, 1991), 41.
2. Benjamin Burgess, personal correspondence, July 15, 2010.
3. For more information on how Burgess understands and articulates the Mide-wiwin Medicine Society's use of stories, see his powerful essay "Elaboration Therapy in the Midewiwin and Gerald Vizenor's *The Heirs of Columbus*," in *SAIL* 18, no. 1 (2006). In the essay, Burgess explains his personal relationship to the Midewiwin, and he argues how stories can house spirits and heal, and thus, how the healer has the ability to elaborate on the story.
4. Treuer, a fluent Ojibwe speaker, relayed to me the following about the delicate nature of divulging such information about the Midewiwin: "I only hesitate to say more because the real substance of what we do with the scrolls and legends and songs is divulged to people as part of their initiations into our sacred societies. To remove the information from its proper place and context is to

give people permission to walk around their elders and circumvent traditional protocol for what usually amounts to anthropological discovery rather than survival of the cultural form."

5. Basil Johnston, *Ojibway Heritage* (Toronto: McClelland and Stewart, 1976), 7.

6. Ibid., 7 (italics mine).

7. Linda Tuhiwai Smith, *Decolonizing Methodologies: Research and Indigenous Peoples* (Dunedin: University of Otago Press, 1999), 24.

8. For a more complete story and historical context, see Basil Johnston's *Ojibway Heritage*, 80–93.

9. Johnston, *Ojibway Heritage*, 83.

10. Lawrence Gross, "The Comic Vision of Anishinaabe Culture and Religion," *American Indian Quarterly* 26, no. 3 (2002): 436–59.

11. Qtd. from Lawrence Gross, "*Bimaadiziwin*, or the 'Good Life,' as a Unifying Concept of Anishinaabe Religion," *American Indian Culture and Research Journal* 26, no. 1 (2002): 19 (italics mine).

12. Stephen Augustine, "Preface: Oral History and Oral Traditions," in *Aboriginal Oral Traditions: Theory, Practice, Ethics*, ed. Renée Hulan and Renate Eigenbrod (Halifax: Fernwood Publishing, 2008), 2.

13. Basil Johnston, *Honour Earth Mother* (Lincoln: University of Nebraska Press, 2003), xxi.

14. For this concept of knowing a place through deep and prolonged observation, I look to Vine Deloria Jr.'s teachings in his chapter "Reflection and Revelation: Knowing Land, Places, and Ourselves," from his book *For This Land: Writings on Religion in America* (New York: Routledge, 1999). In this essay, Deloria argues the difference between being reflective about a place or landscape and being revelatory—differences that Europeans, as visitors to the North American continent, experience in contrast to Indigenous Americans. He says, "Revelatory places are known only through the experience of prolonged occupation of land, and they cannot be set aside because of the aesthetic or emotional appeal of a particular place. . . . Tribal histories, for the most part, are land-centered. That is to say, every feature of a landscape has stories attached to it" (252). Deloria goes on to argue that because of Native people's storied connections to particular places/landscapes over a prolonged period of time, individual groups of Indigenous peoples feel the responsibility of a "moral title" to that place.

15. Greg Hill, "Norval Morrisseau: Shaman Artist," in *Norval Morrisseau: Shaman Artist*, ed. Greg Hill (Ottawa: National Gallery of Canada, 2006), 16.

16. Richard West, "Foreword: The Art of Contradiction," in *Native Modernism: The Art of George Morrison and Allan Houser*, ed. Truman Lowe (Seattle: University of Washington Press, 2004), 8.

17. Lowe, Truman, "Introduction: The Emergence of Native Modernism," in *Native Modernism: The Art of George Morrison and Allan Houser*, ed. Truman Lowe, 10–37 (Seattle: University of Washington Press, 2004), 29.

18. Gerald Vizenor, "George Morrison: Anishinaabe Expressionist Artist," *American Indian Quarterly* 30, nos. 3–4 (2006): 649.

19. Ibid., 646.

20. George Morrison, *Turning the Feather Around: My Life in Art* (St. Paul: Minnesota Historical Society Press, 1998), 170–71.

21. David Martinez, "Along the Horizon a World Appears: George Morrison and the Pursuit of an American Indian Esthetic," in *American Indian Thought*, ed. Anne Waters (Malden and Oxford: Blackwell Publishing, 2004), 258.

22. Ibid., 258.

23. Ibid., 257.

24. Ibid., 257.

25. Morrisseau is credited and renowned as the founder of the Woodland School, which is now more often referred to as the Anishinaabe School of painting. It is also referred to as "Legend Painting" or "Medicine Painting."

26. Ruth B. Phillips, "Morrisseau's 'Entrance': Negotiating Primitivism, Modernism, and Anishinaabe Tradition," in *Norval Morrisseau: Shaman Artist*, ed. Greg Hill (Ottawa: National Gallery of Canada, 2006), 53. Art historians, anthropologists, and Morrisseau himself have made conflicting conclusions as to his initiation into the Medicine Society. Ruth Phillips highlights this controversy: "In the nineteenth and early twentieth centuries much of the ritual practice of Great Lakes shamans had become concentrated in the Midewiwin Society, whose members recorded their oral traditions, esoteric knowledge and complex rituals of initiation by incising pictographic symbols on birchbark panels and scrolls. Although government agents and missionaries had worked steadily to suppress the Midewiwin and other forms of Indigenous spirituality since the mid-nineteenth century, the Society nevertheless remained active in parts of northwestern Ontario and Manitoba through the thirties and forties. According to [Selwyn] Dewdney, who conducted extensive fieldwork in central Canada during the fifties and sixties, the Midewiwin was not active in the Lake Nipigon area during Morrisseau's youth. However, Morrisseau's grandfather and other traditionalists in the community from whom he sought knowledge must have been familiar with Midewiwin beliefs, practices, and visual traditions, and it is very likely that some still owned birchbark scrolls. Morrisseau's own statements on this subject are contradictory. . . . Next to the question, 'Did Grandfather draw pictures for him?' Dewdney wrote down Morrisseau's answer as, 'No.' Yet in an autobiographical essay published in 1979, Morrisseau wrote that his grandfather had taught him the pictographic tradition" (52).

27. Hill, "Norval Morrisseau: Shaman Artist," 13.

28. Ibid., 13.

29. Ibid., 14.

30. Jolene Rickard, "Rebecca Belmore: Performing Power," in exhibition catalogue *Rebecca Belmore Fountain*, Kamloops Art Gallery, Morris and Helen Art Gallery, University of British Columbia, 2006, 69.

31. Gerald McMaster, "Living on Reservation X," in *Reservation X: The Power of Place in Aboriginal Contemporary Art*, ed. Gerald McMaster (Seattle: University of Washington Press, 1998), 28.

32. The Oka Crisis (as it came to be known) arose from a land dispute between the town of Oka, Quebec, and the Kanesatake Mohawk. Lasting 78 days, the Mohawk and allied Indigenous people constructed several key barricades to try and prevent the expansion of a golf course that was to be built on traditional Mohawk land, which included ancestral graves. The standoff has come to symbolize one of the key moments in recent history that exhibits the might of Indigenous solidarity and sovereignty-building.

33. Sophie McCall, "Amplified Voices: Rebecca Belmore's Reinvention of Recording Technologies in the Transmission of Aboriginal Oral Traditions," in *Aboriginal Oral Traditions: Theory, Practice, Ethics*, ed. Renée Hulan and Renate Eigenbrod (Halifax: Fernwood Publishing, 2008), 110.

34. Rebecca Belmore, Lecture, Global Feminisms Forum at the Elizabeth A. Sackler Center for Feminist Art, March 23–25, 2007.

35. Rebecca Belmore, "On the Fightin' Side of Me," interview with Lori Blondeau and Lynne Bell, *Fuse* 28, no. 1 (2005): 31.

36. Melissa Nelson, "Introduction: Lighting the Sun of Our Future—How These Teachings Can Provide Illumination," in *Original Instructions: Indigenous Teachings for a Sustainable Future*, ed. Melissa Nelson (Rochester, VT: Bear & Company, 2008), 5.

37. Nelson, "Introduction," 5.

38. Vizenor, "George Morrison," 649.

39. Viviane Gray, "A Culture of Art: Profiles of Contemporary First Nations Women Artists," 273, in *Restoring the Balance: First Nations Women, Community, and Culture*, ed. Valaskakis, Stout, and Guimond (Manitoba: University of Manitoba Press, 2009), 273.

RESOURCES

Augustine, Stephen. "Preface: Oral History and Oral Traditions." In *Aboriginal Oral Traditions: Theory, Practice, Ethics*, ed. Renée Hulan and Renate Eigenbrod, 1–5. Halifax: Fernwood Publishing, 2008.

Belmore, Rebecca. Lecture. Global Feminisms Forum at the Elizabeth A. Sackler Center for Feminist Art, March 23–25, 2007.

———. "On the Fightin' Side of Me." Interview with Lori Blondeau and Lynne Bell. *Fuse* 28, no. 1 (2005): 25–33.

Burgess, Benjamin. "Elaboration Therapy in the Midewiwin and Gerald Vizenor's *The Heirs of Columbus*." *Studies in American Indian Literatures* 18, no. 1 (2006): 22–38.

———. Personal correspondence, July 15, 2010.

Deloria, Vine, Jr. "Reflection and Revelation: Knowing Land, Places, and Ourselves." In *For This Land: Writings on Religion in America*, 250–60. New York: Routledge, 1999.

Gray, Viviane. "A Culture of Art: Profiles of Contemporary First Nations Women Artists." In *Restoring the Balance: First Nations Women, Community, and Culture*, ed. Gail Guthrie Valaskakis, Madeleine Dion Stout, and Eric Guimond, 267–81. Winnipeg: University of Manitoba Press, 2009.

Gross, Lawrence. "*Bimaadiziwin*, or the 'Good Life,' as a Unifying Concept of Anishinaabe Religion." *American Indian Culture and Research Journal* 26, no. 1 (2002): 15–32.

———. "The Comic Vision of Anishinaabe Culture and Religion." *American Indian Quarterly* 26, no. 3 (2002): 436–59.

Hill, Greg. "Norval Morrisseau: Shaman Artist." In *Norval Morrisseau: Shaman Artist*, ed. Greg Hill, 13–41. Ottawa: National Gallery of Canada, 2006.

Johnston, Basil. *Honour Earth Mother*. Lincoln: University of Nebraska Press, 2003.

———. *Ojibway Heritage*. Toronto: McClelland and Stewart, 1976.

Kegg, Maude. *Portage Lake: Memories of an Ojibwe Childhood*. Edmonton: University of Alberta Press, 1991.

Lowe, Truman. "Introduction: The Emergence of Native Modernism." In *Native Modernism: The Art of George Morrison and Allan Houser*, ed. Truman Lowe, 10–37. Seattle: University of Washington Press, 2004.

Martinez, David. "Along the Horizon a World Appears: George Morrison and the Pursuit of an American Indian Esthetic." In *American Indian Thought*, ed. Anne Waters, 256–62. Malden, MA, and Oxford: Blackwell Publishing Ltd., 2004.

McCall, Sophie. "Amplified Voices: Rebecca Belmore's Reinvention of Recording Technologies in the Transmission of Aboriginal Oral Traditions." In *Aboriginal Oral Traditions: Theory, Practice, Ethics*, ed. Renée Hulan and Renate Eigenbrod, 99–112. Halifax: Fernwood Publishing, 2008.

McMaster, Gerald. "Living on Reservation X." In *Reservation X: The Power of Place in Aboriginal Contemporary Art*, ed. Gerald McMaster, 19–30. Seattle: University of Washington Press, 1998.

Morrison, George. *Turning the Feather Around: My Life in Art.* St. Paul: Minnesota Historical Society Press, 1998.

Nelson, Melissa. "Introduction: Lighting the Sun of Our Future—How These Teachings Can Provide Illumination." In *Original Instructions: Indigenous Teachings for a Sustainable Future,* ed. Melissa Nelson, 1–19. Rochester, VT: Bear & Company, 2008.

Phillips, Ruth B. "Morrisseau's 'Entrance': Negotiating Primitivism, Modernism, and Anishinaabe Tradition." In *Norval Morrisseau: Shaman Artist,* ed. Greg Hill, 42–77. Ottawa: National Gallery of Canada, 2006.

Rickard, Jolene. "Rebecca Belmore: Performing Power." In exhibition catalogue *Rebecca Belmore Fountain,* 68–76. Kamloops Art Gallery, Morris and Helen Art Gallery, University of British Columbia, Canadian Pavilion, Venice Biennale, 2006.

Treuer, Anton. Personal correspondence, September 28, 2010.

Tuhiwai Smith, Linda. *Decolonizing Methodologies: Research and Indigenous Peoples.* Dunedin, New Zealand: Otago University Press, 1999.

Vizenor, Gerald. "George Morrison: Anishinaabe Expressionist Artist." *American Indian Quarterly* 30, nos. 3–4 (2006): 646–60.

West, Richard. "Foreword: The Art of Contradiction." In *Native Modernism: The Art of George Morrison and Allan Houser,* ed. Truman Lowe, 6–9. Seattle: University of Washington Press, 2004.

Eko-niizhwaasi Bagijigan
Stories as Reflections

FINALLY, STORIES REFLECT ANISHINAABEG LIVES. THEY ENCOURAGE Anishinaabeg to turn inward and devise visions that can live in the world, changing themselves, their communities, and the rest of Creation as a result. Stories provide the basis in which Anishinaabeg Studies is a tribally specific field while at the same time a global one. Stories embody partnerships between the corporeal and incorporeal world too, transporting speakers, writers, listeners, and thinkers across planes of existence. They are reflections of a dynamic culture within humanity.

Brock Pitawanakwat opens the concluding section of this anthology by providing much-needed critical reflection about the field of Anishinaabeg Studies and the potential of stories to serve as a center. He outlines how stories can both reveal the world around us and provoke us to consider how it can be transformed. His essay "Anishinaabeg Studies: Creative, Critical, Ethical, and Reflexive" posits that stories can allow Anishinaabeg Studies to escape the fate of educational institutions with scholarship that purports to be rooted in Indigenous knowledge and epistemologies, but fails to locate and utilize non-assimilative forms of education. Pitawanakwat concludes that story "may well be the most appropriate pedagogical tool and heuristic device for learning and teaching what it means to be Anishinaabe." Considering stories as a center may enable Anishinaabeg Studies to remain continually self-reflexive, responsible, and empowering.

Keith Richotte Jr., in "Telling All of Our Stories: Reorienting the Legal and Political Events of the Anishinaabeg," asks us to always consider the myriad question "What is story?" He interweaves this question throughout his essay to mirror a critical framework, establishing that history is a continually unfolding story. Richotte argues that re-envisioning tribal histories as stories is imperative to finding cogent solutions to the political and legal quandaries facing Indigenous nations today. Modeling a potential solution, Richotte re-narrates history in an effort to escape the threats of mummification posed by traditional Western historical accounts. When reconstituted as story, these narratives regain pliability and vitality, and Richotte posits that they can begin to participate in and contribute to contemporary society.

Our final essay comes from our youngest contributor. Lindsay Keegitah Borrows illustrates how stories are reflections of our homes; they remind us where we have come from, illuminate our paths, and can bring us back when we need to return. Throughout her essay "On the Road Home: Stories and Reflections from Neyaashiinigiming," Borrows reminds us that stories can provide glimpses into the Anishinaabeg world and provide reflections of ourselves, our communities, and our lands. She states that they allow us to reflect on the past and make it our own. This story transports the listener/reader to past times and connects us to places we have yet to traverse, deepening our connections with the beings we know and the beings we have yet to encounter. Borrows's essay serves as a conclusion to this anthology; her story is a call to act in harmony and is an encouragement to Anishinaabeg and non-Anishinaabeg to always engage in interpretive participation. As this collection reflects, when centered through story, Anishinaabeg Studies encourages harmony, relationships of respect and responsibility, and meaningful practices, in the hope of promoting good and healthy lives.

Anishinaabeg Studies
Creative, Critical, Ethical, and Reflexive

BROCK PITAWANAKWAT

THIS ESSAY EXPLORES THE TRANSFORMATIVE POTENTIAL OF ANISHI-naabeg Studies as it takes root in North American educational institutions. The present anthology gathers together several interpretations of Anishinaabeg Studies that unite around their collective engagement with the concept of "story." To better understand this topic from an Anishinaabe perspective, I turn to one of my favorite storytellers, who demonstrates how Anishinaabe stories can make sense of the world while also revealing how to transform it. In November 2008, Basil Johnston accepted my interview request about his extensive work developing Anishinaabemowin learning and teaching resources. He began by explaining how stories are central to his scholarship and teaching of Indigenous literature.

I teach Native literature, the meaning of stories, but often I find it objectionable that our stories are regarded as children's stories by universities and by Natives themselves because they don't know enough about stories as they reflect our way of looking at human beings and conduct. One story that has had a great impact upon me reflects the way the Anishinaubaeg look on the way we perceive things. It's a story about perception and it goes like this:

A trapper had been up north on a trapline all winter. At the end of the trapping season he came dragging his toboggan which was bogged down with a load of pelts. He took this to the Hudson's Bay Company, brought all the pelts inside and while the factor was evaluating the pelts, this Anishinaubae guy, Indian guy, stood looking directly ahead of him. But being an Indian guy, he had peripheral

363

vision and he could see out of the corner of his eye. And he noticed out of the corner of his eye a guy looking at him in the window. The guy was looking at him in the same way he was. And he started to seethe and boil—angry with this guy in the window. And after a little while he turned directly to this image and gave him a dirty look and the guy did the same thing in return. Shook his fist at him. The guy did the same thing. He poked the factor on the shoulder and said, "who's that ugly looking son of a bitch over there, he's making me mad. I'm going to go out there and beat the hell out of him." So the factor said, "what guy?" "That guy over there in the window." "Well that's not a window, that's a mirror. And that's you. Come on." So the factor conducted this Indian guy over to the window and said, "Look, look, look that's you." This guy continued to look at this thing. The factor said, "Smile, smile, smile." The trapper smiled, "My god he's pretty damn good looking. Have to be Anishinaubae." He said, "I'm going to buy it." "I can't sell you that, but I can sell you a small one." So after the business of evaluating the furs and entering the credit this guy had earned with his pelts was entered into this ledger, the trapper bought all the stuff that his wife would need; flour, salt pork, sugar and maybe lard, all the basics. And the last article to go into the last potato bag was this little flat package wrapped in brown paper and tied with a store string. . . .

When the guy got home his wife chased him outside to go cut some wood. He went out. The wife took the packets out of these potato bags and the last little packet was this flat package. She shook it, put it to her nose and then she undid, unwrapped, folded back the wrappers and looked in it. She saw a woman looking at her. God she screamed and she started to cry. Her mother, who was upstairs, came running down, "Aaniin eyaayin?" "What's the matter with you?" "Oh mama, he's found another woman ahahahah." So the old lady took that thing, "Aaniin tagiiyeyan? What's the matter with you, she's old, she's all wrinkled, she's got no teeth."

Now that is about perception and what we see is not what is. What you see is an image in a mirror. You don't see the inside of that person. In the same way you see a person in reality, that's all you see. And you make a judgment immediately whether that guy is good or bad. You can't see into his spirit, into his heart and our people knew that. So they came up with a story and similar stories and it goes into, you know, our understanding of identity. Who are you? And the question they ask themselves is who am I?

Johnston illustrates the importance of identity in his story and its interpretation. Identity questions will also be, by definition, at the core of Anishinaabeg Studies. Who is Anishinaabe? What constitutes Anishinaabeg

Studies? In our interview, Johnston explains what the "mirror" story can teach us about identity and how it guides our goals and sense of purpose. Johnston also described how Anishinaabeg grapple with existential and identity questions.

> And I think you know, all the way through life this is what we ask ourselves, who am I? Am I what I would like to be? Am I what I think I would like to be? Or am I what I should be? If I fall short then how can I be what I ought to be? But that story that I related to you, it's very simple. It's funny but it represents a reality and you know, people are puzzled by it. "What does it mean?" And there's a lot more depth to Native stories like that, than people assume them to be.
>
> So it's a story that I tell often to begin a class and what you hear, what you perceive and how you communicate what you think you saw. And so it has something to do with the idea of truth, truth in the West European sense is absolute. Not so among the Anishinaubaeg, it's only the highest degree of accuracy, because you perceive certain things and what you see is different from another person. The more accurate your perception is, and the more fluent you are in language, the more accuracy you'll convey. And so to us, although there is no such thing as absolute truth, there is the highest degree of accuracy and this is what I follow. And I remember Sam Osawamick saying to me, I'd tell him what I understood. He'd never say you were wrong. You don't say that. What he said was, "Bkaan so genii ngiizhiiminik gzhemindoo jinzidminaa" you know the Great Mystery has given me a different understanding. And probably because his command of Anishinaubae language is greater than mine, his perception was more accurate. But because of that you don't find fault with another person's perception.

I had originally sought out Basil Johnston to better understand how Anishinaabeg are organizing to revitalize Anishinaabemowin. When I asked him about the best practices of Anishinaabemowin revitalization, he praised the efforts of Sagamok First Nation and a dedicated group of educators who have established a language-immersion primary school. Johnston has been involved in curriculum development, and he describes the importance of Anishinaabe stories within the new immersion curriculum. Johnston also links story as the cultural core of Anishinaabeg and an expression of our relationship to the land.

> They've got some really outstanding people who are heading that program so one of the things that I've been doing with them is writing stories. Ten stories for Grade 1, ten for Grade 2, all the way up to Grade 8 so that by the time they finish grades in elementary school they should have eighty stories. That's not

too heavy a burden. That's one story a month. So by the time the youngsters are finished elementary school, they'll have a fairly good understanding of the way in which we think, and how we perceive things and how we interpret things.

Finding relationships is how our ancestors learned things and how they taught things. You didn't go into a classroom and read books. You went out in the field and you saw, what you call specimens in museums, in real life doing real things and where these creatures live and the relationships they had with one another, and with plants and with birds and with animals and with the weather. So they call that I think today holistic learning, holistic teaching. But you've got to get out there. We have a word in our language, Aki-noomaage, the earth teaching and this is what Red Jacket pointed out to the missionaries in 1805 who attempted to get the Six Nations to renounce the long house religion and adopt civilization. Red Jacket, one of the things he said was, "To you He has given the book, to us He has given the mountains and the rivers and the valleys, has given us the land." I don't know if it was him or somebody else who said, I think it was a Dakota, "If all the books were eaten up by moths then you have nothing to read, you still have the land." And you'd have to start learning all over again.

There are a lot of things to teach and re-teach our people. In the stories one of the values that comes out, one of the very first lessons for kids was to espouse selflessness, to share, based on the assumption that we are all born with a consciousness of self. You know, me, me, me. And that's the source of all ill will, ill deeds. If you can diminish that and replace it by selflessness and sharing and in order to do that you have to instill the principle, walk in balance or live in harmony. We didn't need West Europeans, or missionaries to come along and tell us that. We knew that already. It was there. So, you know, I think the kind of life that our ancestors led demanded that they get to know themselves and it's the land that tells you that. And that brings out the best in you.

Johnston emphasizes the value of stories as the ideal medium to convey Anishinaabe values in terms of relationships to our history, land, and language. Regardless of its core concept or paradigm, Anishinaabe knowledge faces challenges if it is delivered in Western education systems and their institutions. Many Anishinaabeg academics have spent decades challenging the colonial narratives that Europeans brought the gifts of civilization and enlightenment to a dark continent. Johnston laments the way that universities have portrayed Anishinaabeg.

I think universities have also been at fault in this. Anthropologists have represented us as a people who've cared only for survival and they've imposed on us, and on others, on schools, the notion that our heritage consisted of nothing more than social organization, hunting and fishing, food preparation, transportation, dwellings. "Oh, that's all they got." So it's discouraging.

Anishinaabeg Studies can limit the homogenizing aspects of "Indigenous" or "Native" studies by shifting the focus from the dichotomy between Indigenous and settler, or Native and newcomer. Colonization is not, never has been, nor ever will be, the defining experience of Anishinaabeg. Anishinaabeg and their dedicated field of academic study deserve a potential pathway past the obsession with European contact and its fallout. Anishinaabeg Studies has an added benefit beyond general Indigenous studies because it offers cultural, historical, linguistic, and spiritual specificity. Even while acknowledging our internal diversity, Anishinaabeg are recognized as a confederacy of Indigenous nations with a common heritage.

Although it is increasingly common for them to host certain ceremonies and cultural performances, educational institutions remain a crucial site of contestation for Indigenous self-determination.[1] Education can be highly assimilative when it lacks Indigenous wisdom to mentor younger generations of staff and students. Onondaga chief Oren Lyons explains why a strong sense of identity is necessary to survive a university education.

> If you are not secure in your identity, when you go to university you become whatever the university is. It is important to have pride in your own heritage. Know who you are first. Know your nation, your history, your clan and family. Even if you learn all you can in school, it's only half of what you already have.[2]

Academic credentials are rarely granted to Indigenous knowledge keepers, which thereby excludes the vast majority from teaching and writing. Johnston identifies a significant limitation in efforts to indigenize or, even more awkwardly, "Anishinaabe-ize" the academy in the following passage of *Ojibway Ceremonies*, which reveals why this limitation complicates the integration of Anishinaabe spirituality with the mainstream education systems in North America. "To understand the origin and nature of life, existence, and death, the Ojibway speaking peoples conducted inquiries within the soul-spirit that was the very depth of their being. Through dream or vision quest they elicited revelation—knowledge that they then commemorated and perpetuated in story and re-enacted in ritual."[3] A complication arises because the manner in which such inquiries were made by Anishinaabeg were intensely private. Revealing a vision could only be done with a respected elder or medicine person, or else its power would be lost; not even close family members were told a vision's details.[4] In a university setting, full disclosure is a standard requirement of our scholarship. How then can Anishinaabeg protect the sanctity of their individual visions? Greater Anishinaabe autonomy in higher education would be necessary before such spiritual inquiries can be treated with the required respect.

In the meantime, Anishinaabeg look elsewhere for the appropriate spiritual guidance to understand the ontological questions posed by Johnston. Anishinaabe scholar Duane Champagne advocates that "students should not go to university to learn about the central values and institutions of their cultures. Their communities are better places to gain close knowledge about their specific tribal history and culture."[5] Although Champagne's community solution is ideal, many Indigenous individuals arrive in schools without the necessary armor of identity, nation, history, clan, and family. Education was intended to erase Anishinaabe identity markers and inculcate American and Canadian values. The boarding or residential schools attempted to erase Indigenous spirituality and replace it with Christianity. Their impact has been a terrible legacy that is well documented in the academic literature. Even in the post–boarding school era, secularization often clashes with Indigenous understandings of interconnection between the physical, spiritual, emotional, and intellectual aspects of being. Attempts to fill the resultant void have led to a widespread ceremonial and spiritual revitalization among Indigenous peoples; however, this spiritual revitalization has been sporadic and incomplete.

The future of Anishinaabe education draws upon the old knowledge processes and systems that North American governments have worked so hard to suppress. Johnston describes how information was traditionally transmitted differently. Children learned, but they were not taught in the manner of mainstream education today.

> To foster individuality and self-growth children and youth were encouraged to draw their own inferences from the stories. No attempt was made to impose upon them views. The learner learned according to his capacity, intellectually and physically. Some learned quickly and broadly; others more slowly and with narrower scope. Each according to his gifts. . . . But when the time came, testings were severe.[6]

Another respected Anishinaabe author and elder contrasts Anishinaabe education with the authoritarian mainstream education system in Canada. Wilfred Pelletier believes that traditional values conflict with those inherent in the education system. "In an Indian community people who speak out, for example, or who are aggressively competitive are regarded with silent disapproval. That's why I doubt that there'll ever be any great numbers of successful Indian students."[7] He offers a simple but drastic solution: "I am opposed to schools and schooling. I keep saying in public that we should burn the schools . . . I know that schools stand in the way of life and learning."[8] Pelletier's anarchistic critique of mainstream education compares it to an artificial dam designed to channel people's energy and discipline them into submission.[9]

> Now I think that school, like all schools, was like a dam built across the natural flow of childhood. That river of youthful energy was forcibly channelled into the school and what you had to learn, more than any other thing, was submission—to allow the energy that belonged only to you to be controlled and directed by someone else. When you stepped into the school you were confronted by a boss adult . . . you were trapped between the teacher and a wall of abstraction.[10]

Pelletier characterizes Western ways as obsessive about "achievement, the realization of goals and objectives," and singles out higher education for inculcating these competitive values.

> It is significant that this is called an educative rather than a learning system. It is productive of specialists, experts in hairline disciplines. Its effect is narrowing rather than broadening. It suppresses consciousness. Specialists suffer from restricted vision. Their "discipline" forces them to see the world through a porthole, but they are under the delusion that what they see is all of it. So it isn't surprising that they feel deficient, less than whole, unhealthy. Nor is it surprising that they tend to feel their world is falling apart. Those people are scared stiff. They're driven to achieve, driven to hold their disintegrating world together, driven to make it come together.[11]

Pelletier's scathing critique suggests that efforts to indigenize the academy may be misguided. Can we expect non-Indigenous institutions such as schools and universities to provide us with "inquiries into the soul-spirit that [is] the very depth of their being?"[12] I believe such spiritual inquiries will be difficult until Indigenous self-determination has been more fully realized in education.

Although difficulties can be expected in mainstream institutions, even Indigenous-controlled universities have failed to demonstrate respect for Indigenous ways. Cree/Saulteaux Indigenous Studies professor Blair

Stonechild identifies First Nations University of Canada (FNUniv),[13] a former flagship of Indigenous higher education, as in many respects a colonized and, some would argue, a colonizing institution. Métis activist and scholar Howard Adams blasted FNUniv for socializing Indigenous peoples to capitalism and cultural assimilation.[14] According to Adams, "[FNUniv] courses indoctrinate Native students to conservative middle class ideologies. They are oriented toward creating an Aboriginal bourgeoisie to act as a bridge to the impoverished masses to help control and oppress them."[15]

Another concern is the marginalization of Indigenous languages in what is supposed to be an Indigenous institution. Basil Johnston explains the importance of Indigenous languages to Indigenous knowledge:

> Language is crucial. If scholars are to increase their knowledge and if they are to add depth and width to their studies, they must study a Native language. It is not enough to know a few words or even some phrases. . . . Without a knowledge of the language, scholars can never take for granted the accuracy of an interpretation . . . let alone a single word.[16]

Respect for Indigenous knowledge and Indigenous epistemologies must also be applied to Indigenous institutions of higher learning. Indigenous education suffers in the absence of Indigenous languages and philosophies. FNUniv is perhaps more dangerously assimilative than mainstream programs because uncritical staff and students believe its label. FNUniv is administered and governed as a mainstream university. Its programs, with the sole exception of the language courses, are delivered entirely in English. An improvement would be an independent tribal college that is networked to share resources and develop graduate programs—similar to the Okanagan Nation's Enowkin Centre, or the Treaty 6 Cree Nation's Blue Quills First Nations College.

Nation-based institutions will be the next step to overcome the institutional default of settler languages and institutional practices that occur in mainstream and even pan-Indigenous university programs. One example is already under development with the Shingwauk Kinoomaage Gamig in Sault Ste. Marie, Ontario, which offers degree programs in Anishinaabe Studies and Anishinaabemowin.

Nation-based tribal colleges can also bring higher education one significant step closer to local communities. The spiritual equivalent to nation-based tribal colleges already exists in the various Midewiwin lodges of the Anishinaabeg.

The Anishnabi have the Midewewin Lodge (Midé), a society of medicine people who are responsible for preserving Anishnabi philosophy and ceremonies. To become a full member of this lodge one must be of strong moral character (as judged by other medicine people) and undergo years of difficult training and study. All of this learning is done in the Anishnabi language, and all Anishnabi people, although most are not privileged to sit in the Midé, learn from these indigenous philosophers.[17]

If "story" should become the core concept of Anishinaabeg Studies, perhaps an appropriate paradigm would be the "Peoplehood Matrix." The Peoplehood Matrix was a proposed paradigm for Native American studies that identifies four aspects: ceremonies, land, language, and sacred history. Holm, Pearson, and Chavis critique the lack of a "central paradigm" and express concern that this complicates American Indian Studies' status as an independent discipline.[18] The authors adopt Cherokee scholar Robert Thomas's universal matrix for all Indigenous peoples and suggest it "could serve as the primary theoretical underpinning of indigenous peoples studies."[19] The authors believe that each component need not be "authentic," as English has replaced some Indigenous languages, such as that of the Lumbees.[20] They also believe that by reconceptualizing sovereignty according to peoplehood, it legitimizes peoples and delegitimizes states as sovereign entities.[21] Holm et al. believe that their model is useful for applied research and offer the following example:

> For example, linguistic studies are extremely important to the preservation of a group's identity, but what can linguistic studies do beyond writing grammar books, compiling a complete dictionary, creating a pedagogy for teaching the language, or making tapes of Native speakers? Does the creation of these projects open up new areas of study or, from a practical point of view, effectively end scholarly inquiry? The answer to those questions lies in emphasizing the linkages between language, place, ceremony, and history. Practically anyone can learn a Native language, but without understanding of its intricacies and its nuances in terms of preserving and passing along the knowledge of the people who speak it, the language is rendered useless. Language is not primary, it is simply an equal part of the matrix.[22]

This Peoplehood paradigm for Anishinaabeg Studies offers four branches: land, language, sacred history, and spirituality. Story represents a form of expression that can be interwoven through each of these four branches. The Peoplehood Matrix focuses on Anishinaabeg, the people, and prioritizes the four branches without privileging any single form of cultural expression: art, literature, or music. Looking at ourselves through the Peoplehood paradigm can also guide our scholarship. I will offer one example from my research on Anishinaabemowin: our Anishinaabe language. Anishinaabemowin is inter-woven throughout this anthology that posits story as a center for Anishinaabeg Studies. A culturally and linguistically rooted understanding of story for Anishinaabeg might include Johnston's description of *debwewin*—truth, but in a sense that is contextual and personal. In English, story can connote falsehood, rumor, or spin, whereas Anishinaabemowin is more specific in its types of stories. By using our own language, we can add specificity to the word "story": *dibaajmowin* (a personal account) or *aadsookaan* (a sacred story). An understanding of Anishinaabe values that includes a commitment to truth promotes an integrity and honesty lacking in English. It also explains why "story" may well be the most appropriate pedagogical tool and heuristic device for learning and teaching what it means to be Anishinaabe.

My hope for a deep commitment to *debwewin*—especially truths that are painful to confront—is exemplified in a story shared by my grandmother about her experiences at residential school. Like any colonized people, Anishinaabeg have stories of both collaboration with and resistance to the colonizer. Our resistance narratives stoke Anishinaabe nationalism and patriotism that counter the deep demoralization of cultural, intellectual, physical, and spiritual genocide. Reconciliation with our past requires that Anishinaabeg be able to draw upon more stories than those that focus only on colonization. Resistance narratives support cultural pride, but deserve to be tempered with critical self-reflection on the many ways that Anishinaabeg have collaborated in unjust relations. One of the most painful examples was a story my grandmother shared shortly before her death in 1996. I was doing an oral history assignment for an Indian Studies course when I asked about her time as a student at the Indian Residential School in Spanish, Ontario. I was stunned when she stated that the only abuse she remembered at the school was by other students. Part of the Indian Residential School legacy that remains largely unspoken is that many harms were committed by our own people against each other, often when both perpetrator and victim were still young children. How do we handle such stories?

Historian Eric Hobsbawm has cautioned scholars about the risk of writing for a particular ethnic or national audience, because of the temptation to "produce work that can be of use to our own people or cause."

We will no doubt be tempted to interpret our findings in the way most favour-able to the cause. We may be tempted to abstain from enquiring into topics likely to throw unfavourable light on it. It is not surprising that historians hostile to communism were considerably more likely to research into forced labour in the USSR than historians sympathetic to it. We may even be tempted to remain silent about unfavourable evidence, if we happen to discover it, though hardly with a good scholarly conscience.[23]

Hobsbawm's challenge for Anishinaabeg Studies is for its participants to maintain a self-reflexive and critical approach that upholds sacred commitments to honesty and truth while also remaining open to an honest and respectful engagement with non-Anishinaabe knowledge and knowledge keepers. Hobsbawm offers the example of his own people, part of Europe's Jewish diaspora, to advocate a universal concept of history that acknowledges the holism of the Peoplehood paradigm, but in the broader context of humanity. Ideally, Anishinaabeg Studies can extend this broader context beyond humanity to include all of Creation. Adhering to core Anishinaabe values may help inoculate Anishinaabeg Studies from degrading itself to becoming an Indigenous equivalent of a corporate-sponsored think tank that obfuscates issues, such as environmental contamination caused by certain industries, instead of illuminating them. Commitments to core Anishinaabe values of wisdom, love, respect, bravery, honesty, humility, and truth would best contend with the moral implications of privileging narratives of resistance over those of collaboration or oppression. One of the flaws of our systems of higher education is a tendency to decouple awareness of injustice from the responsibility to challenge injustice.

> Students learn that it is sufficient only to learn about injustice and ecological deterioration without having to do much about them, which is to say, the lesson of hypocrisy. They hear the vital signs of the planet are in decline without learning to question the de facto energy, food, materials and waste policies of the very institution that presumes to induct them into responsible adulthood. Four years of consciousness-raising proceeds without connection to these remedies close at hand.[24]

Correcting this systemic flaw requires Indigenous intellectuals who are also willing to be activists. However, as Stohlo writer Lee Maracle describes, many Indigenous scholars have lost any appetite for confronting colonization.

> We found that intellectuals preferred the truth with its clothes on. They preferred polite discussion about abstract ideas and not the challenge that characterized our old ways. They preferred peace—at any price—to the inevitable

consequences of social resistance. They feared the wrath of the State. The rage of backlash from white folk terrified the intelligentsia . . . divorced from their communities, alienated from their culture, they preferred distorted recognition by white liberal supporters rather than the mass movement of Native youth.[25]

Maracle reserves high praise for Indigenous intellectuals who are rooted in their communities.

> On the other side of the split are those people, young and old, from the Okanagan, the Gitksan-Wet'suwet'en, Iroquoian, Ojibway and Cree nations, who base their politics in their own history and their own law. There are intellectuals among them who did not lose themselves in the settlers' universities. Such intellectuals are precious gems in a sea of mis-education. They are a tremendous source of inspiration and empowerment. . . . The translators of the knowledge of our grandmothers must be well versed in their own language and in the language of the English people. And they must possess a deep sense of loyalty to our people.[26]

Fortunately, there are Anishinaabeg activists and scholars who have maintained community connections and relevance. Anishinaabe activist and scholar Pat Ningewance Nadeau is an ideal example. Through her artwork and her language textbooks, Ningewance exemplifies the latter of both types of Indigenous intellectuals sought by Dale Turner: Indigenous philosophers and word warriors.[27] Indigenous philosophers "are central to the future survival of indigenous communities as distinct peoples because without indigenous philosophies we lose our languages, our ceremonies, and our unique ways of understanding the world. Without indigenous philosophies, our 'indigeneity' would lose its significance in our relationship with the dominant culture."[28] "Word warriors" are those who will mediate and interpret Indigenous ways to the broader society,[29] and challenge "white supremacist attitudes and white ideals in the minds of native students."[30]

An elder once explained to me that the most essential aspect of being Anishinaabe is respect. He then related a familiar Anishinaabe creation story that explains how humans were the last beings to join Creation and thus are the weakest and most dependent upon other beings for our sustenance. Many other Indigenous peoples share this fundamental value of respect for all other beings. This notion of respect is connected to humility and eternal gratitude for the gift of life each of us takes everyday—even when that gift comes at the cost of another's life, whether animal or plant, to sustain us. Seeing ourselves as part of a complex matrix of life is integral to Anishinaabe philosophy, and Anishinaabe stories will remain its original form of expression.

NOTES

1. Devon A. Mihesuah and Angela Cavender Wilson. *Indigenizing the Academy: Transforming Scholarship and Empowering Communities* (Lincoln: University of Nebraska Press, 2004); Michael M'Gonigle and Justine Starke, *Planet U: Sustaining the World, Reinventing the University* (Gabriola Island, BC: New Society Publishers, 2006); Blair Stonechild, *The New Buffalo: The Struggle for First Nations Higher Education* (Winnipeg, MB: University of Manitoba Press, 2006); Dale A. Turner, *This Is Not a Peace Pipe: Towards a Critical Indigenous Philosophy* (Toronto, ON: University of Toronto Press, 2006).

2. Lyons, as cited in Mary Isabelle Young, *Pimatisiwin – Walking in a Good Way: A Narrative Inquiry Into Language as Identity* (Winnipeg, MB: Pemmican Publications, 2005), 151–152.

3. Basil Johnston, *Ojibway Ceremonies* (Toronto, ON: McClelland and Stewart, 1982), vii.

4. Basil Johnston, *Ojibway Heritage* (New York: Columbia University Press, 1976), 127; Johnston, *Ojibway Ceremonies*, 54–55.

5. Devon A. Mihesuah, *Natives and Academics: Researching and Writing about American Indians*, 184.

6. Johnston, *Ojibway Heritage*, 70.

7. Wilfred Pelletier and Ted Poole, *No Foreign Land: The Biography of a North American Indian*, 40.

8. Ibid., 51.

9. Ibid., 41–42.

10. Ibid., 41–42.

11. Ibid., 206–7.

12. Johnston *Ojibway Ceremonies*, vii.

13. Blair Stonechild, *The New Buffalo: The Struggle for First Nations Higher Education* (Winnipeg, MB: University of Manitoba Press, 2006), 134.

14. Howard Adams, *Tortured People – The Politics of Colonization*, rev. ed. (Penticton, BC: Theytus Books, 1999), 53.

15. Adams, *Tortured People*, 54.

16. Basil Johnston, as cited in Roger Spielmann, *'You're So Fat!' Exploring Ojibwe Discourse* (Toronto, ON: University of Toronto Press, 1998), 234.

17. Turner, *This Is Not a Peace Pipe*, 99–100.

18. Tom Holm, J. Diane Pearson, and Ben Chavis, "Peoplehood: A Model for the Extension of Sovereignty in American Indian Studies," *Wicazo Sa Review* (Spring 2003): 8.

19. Ibid., 12.

20. Ibid., 13.

21. Ibid., 17.

22. Ibid., 19.

23. Eric Hobsbawm, *On History* (London: Abacus, 1997), 364–65.

24. David Orr, in M'Gonigle and Starke, *Planet U*, 152.

25. Lee Maracle, *I Am Woman: A Native Perspective on Sociology and Feminism* (Vancouver, BC: Press Gang Publishers, 1996), 97.

26. Ibid., 40.

27. Turner, *This Is Not a Peace Pipe*.

28. Ibid., 119.

29. Ibid., 74.

30. Howard Adams, *Prison of Grass: Canada from a Native Point of View*, rev. ed. (Saskatoon, SK: Fifth House Publishers, 1989), 146.

RESOURCES

Adams, Howard. *Tortured People – The Politics of Colonization.* Revised edition. Penticton, BC: Theytus Books, 1999.

———. *Prison of Grass: Canada from a Native Point of View.* Revised edition. Saskatoon, SK: Fifth House Publishers, 1989.

Hobsbawm, Eric. *On History.* London: Abacus, 1997.

Holm, Tom, J. Diane Pearson, and Ben Chavis. "Peoplehood: A Model for the Extension of Sovereignty in American Indian Studies." *Wicazo Sa Review* (Spring 2003): 7–24.

Johnston, Basil. "How Do We Learn Language? What Do We Learn?" In *Talking on the Page—Editing Aboriginal Oral Texts: Papers Given at the Thirty-second Annual Conference on Editorial Problems, University of Toronto, 14–16 November 1996*, ed. Laura J. Murray and Keren Rice, 43–51. Toronto: University of Toronto Press, 1999.

———. *Ojibway Ceremonies.* Toronto, ON: McClelland and Stewart, 1982.

———. *Ojibway Heritage.* New York: Columbia University Press, 1976.

Kipp, Darrell R. *Encouragement, Guidance, Insights, and Lessons Learned from Native Language Activists Developing Their Own Tribal Language Programs.* Browning, MT: Piegan Institute's Cut-Bank Language Immersion School, 2000.

Maracle, Lee. *I Am Woman: A Native Perspective on Sociology and Feminism.* Vancouver, BC: Press Gang Publishers, 1996.

Mihesuah, Devon A. *Natives and Academics: Researching and Writing about American Indians.* Lincoln: University of Nebraska Press, 1998.

Mihesuah, Devon A., and Angela Cavender Wilson. 2004. *Indigenizing the Academy: Transforming Scholarship and Empowering Communities.* Lincoln: University of Nebraska Press, 2004.

M'Gonigle, Michael, and Justine Starke. *Planet U: Sustaining the World, Reinventing the University.* Gabriola Island, BC: New Society Publishers, 2006.

Pelletier, Wilfred, and Ted Poole. *No Foreign Land: The Biography of a North American Indian.* Toronto, ON: McClelland and Stewart, 1973.

Spielmann, Roger. *'You're So Fat!' Exploring Ojibwe Discourse.* Toronto, ON: University of Toronto Press, 1998.

Stonechild, Blair. *The New Buffalo: The Struggle for First Nations Higher Education.* Winnipeg: University of Manitoba Press, 2006.

Turner, Dale A. *This Is Not a Peace Pipe: Towards a Critical Indigenous Philosophy.* Toronto, ON: University of Toronto Press, 2006.

Young, Mary Isabelle. *Pimatisiwin—Walking in a Good Way: A Narrative Inquiry Into Language as Identity.* Winnipeg, MB: Pemmican Publications, 2005.

Telling All of Our Stories
Reorienting the Legal and Political Events of the Anishinaabeg

KEITH RICHOTTE JR.

<h3>WHAT IS A STORY?</h3>

In this essay I seek to establish that the scope of what constitutes the category of Anishinaabeg stories is—or at least could and/or should be—larger than what one might first imagine. It is important to consider the question that opens this essay, because Anishinaabeg, and others, will be better served by conceptualizing aspects of what we now consider tribal "histories" as tribal "stories." More specifically, we would do well to reconceptualize the legal and political histories of Anishinaabeg as stories. It is becoming increasingly imperative that we rethink these events in more tribally cogent ways.

To understand the necessity of reconceptualizing the legal and political histories of Anishinaabeg as stories, we must first briefly explore the ideas of "story" and "history." While linked to a certain extent by the narrative process, the English language and Western thought nonetheless divide the two into separate concepts. Stories are the lesser of the two. While not so ephemeral as to always or completely lack real people, settings, or events, or behavioral directives or moral lessons, the word "story" necessarily implies—if not outright admits—a lack of substance or gravitas. The word "history," on the other hand, carries an air of authority. History, unlike stories, is defined by its claim to accuracy and truthfulness. It is also defined by its relationship with the linear progression of time. The formidable notions of truth and time in Western thought combine to create the heavy verity that is history.[1] Stories, on the other hand, are more flexible than history. They can be funny or sad, they can be entertaining or they can offer a life lesson, they can carry important information or they can be completely filled with fluff. They can even accomplish many of these things at the same time—but they cannot support the mantle of history.

This is a very shallow description of some very deep and complex ideas within Western thought. I do not mean to suggest that "story" and "history" are polar opposites in the West. Nor do I mean to suggest that the common ground between the two is narrow or nonexistent. Story and history clearly are interrelated. The exceptionally broad lines that I have drawn between the two obfuscate not only the messy areas where these concepts blur together but also the contested edges each holds on its own. Nonetheless, "story" and "history" are separate concepts in Western thought. They describe separate categories and spheres of understanding.

Anishinaabemowin, the language of Anishinaabeg, seems to make no such distinction between story and history, or at least makes any such distinction barely visible.[2] Two of the leading dictionaries of Anishinaabemowin each have multiple entries for the English word "story," but neither has an entry for "history."[3] This is not absolutely irrefutable evidence, as both references clearly state that each is somewhat limited in what it is able to accomplish. Yet, it is remarkable for both texts, separated by over a century in their respective publications, to not include a word and a concept as vital as "history" within Western thought. The lack of importance of the Western concept of "history" within Native communities as a whole has been suggested elsewhere as well.[4]

The comparison I make between Western "history" and Anishinaabeg "stories" is not as dichotomous opposites, but as separate methods for understanding the past.[5] Whereas history is expressed as a distinct concept within the Western tradition, it is expressed through the prism of story in Anishinaabe tradition. These disparate conceptualizations are not rare, as other differences of thought and worldviews exist between the Western world and Anishinaabeg. The related concept of time is also illustrative through its expressions within the English language and Anishinaabemowin. In English, "time" exists as an entity unto itself, as does "history." Yet, while the two aforementioned Anishinaabemowin dictionaries do have entries for "time," the concept does not stand alone. "Time" is always conditioned in some way so that it carries some greater specificity: *aabiding*—at one time; *azhigwa*—at this time; *gomaapii*—for some time, etc.[6] Time and history, critically important concepts in the Western world, are less important and regarded with less deference among Anishinaabeg. Other meaningful distinctions are readily apparent as well.[7]

These briefly outlined examples are but a few of the more easily discernable differences between Anishinaabeg and Western worldviews. Yet, they illustrate the growing need to reconceptualize the legal and political "histories" of Anishinaabeg as tribal "stories." Anishinaabeg have come to understand what Western "history" means through hundreds of years of colonial experience, but it is not an idea that fits easily or comfortably within Anishinaabe philosophies or lifeways. Conceptualizing significant moments within Anishinaabe communities as "histories" has the effect of diminishing the importance of those moments. Contemporary tribal events are susceptible to becoming stony, immovable relics of the past when enmeshed in the component parts of history—truth and time. Consequently, they either lose, or more likely never gain, the pliability and vitality of stories.

There is another side to this coin. Whereas "history" threatens to mummify the legal and political events of Anishinaabeg, treating them as stories will allow them to live and breathe, and participate in and contribute to contemporary society. To gain a deeper appreciation of why it is imperative that we begin understanding the legal and political events of Anishinaabeg as stories, we must first reflect upon what stories mean to Anishinaabeg.

Any scholar placing him or herself in the particularized field of Anishinaabeg Studies—and even those in the more general field of Indian or Indigenous Studies—knows, or quickly comes to know, several characteristics about stories and their place within Anishinaabeg and other Indigenous communities.[8] They are not merely diversions to pass the time, or simple parables to entertain and educate the young. Rather, they are fundamental to conceptualizing both Anishinaabeg as a people and Anishinaabe epistemologies and hermeneutics. Knowledge of who Anishinaabeg are, how they think, and how they interpret the world in which they live emerges from stories.

Thus, perhaps the most prominent characteristic of stories is that they are fundamentally critical. To not know or recognize that stories are irrevocably linked to Anishinaabe identities and worldviews is to not know or recognize Anishinaabeg. They are also functional tools. One of the reasons that stories are so critical to Anishinaabe worldviews is that they not only provide an epistemological base for conceptualizing the world in which they exist, but also offer an actionable directive. By using the word "directive," I do not mean to suggest that Anishinaabe stories dictate action through force in the same manner as a mandate or edict. Instead, they invite critical reflection upon themselves and provide a strategy for behavior, attitudes, and beliefs. They also require activity on the part of those who hear (or read) them.[9] Anishinaabe stories are meant to work, and they require work as well.

Another prominent characteristic of Anishinaabe stories is that some are more important and prominent than others. For instance, there are differences between stories and sacred stories.[10] Sacred stories generally involve certain subject matters and are only told during certain times of the year, whereas the non-sacred stories do not carry such proscriptions. Perhaps the best example of their varying levels of authority is that Anishinaabemowin has two different words to denote the different types of stories. Additionally, in Anishinaabemowin, nouns are considered either animate or inanimate (which offers another insight into the epistemological constructs of Anishinaabeg). The noun for sacred stories, *aadizookaan*, is animate (which, of course, carries a certain connotation), whereas the noun for stories, *dibaajimowin*, is inanimate (which does not carry the same connotation). Finally, "[Anishinaabe] stories are flexible in nature and scope."[11] This is important because it acknowledges the adaptability of the story and how that can affect its participation within Anishinaabe life. The teller of a story, the listener(s) of a story, and the story itself exist in a dynamic relationship that responds to its circumstances and environment. Put another way, the connectivity among the parties permits a healthy degree of freedom. The storyteller is not completely bound to a concrete recitation of a story, but is given the freedom to craft the narrative for the audience and the situation. The listener is not completely bound to a concrete interpretation of a story, but is given the freedom to find her or his truth within the telling. The story itself is not completely bound to a concrete telling, but can change and adapt to fulfill its purpose. This is not to suggest that stories retain no corpus, or that any or all details may be changed, swapped around, or disregarded. It is necessary to acknowledge that despite changes to accommodate the context in which stories are told, they have cores that remain through various retellings.[12] Nonetheless, Anishinaabe stories are not primitive credos forever frozen in dusky amber.[13] These stories are alive and remain relevant because Anishinaabeg have allowed them to adapt and change throughout time to their new environments (much like Anishinaabeg themselves).

I have very briefly outlined four prominent characteristics of Anishinaabe stories that should readily come to mind for any scholar of Anishinaabeg Studies: they are critical to Anishinaabe epistemologies and identities, they are functional tools, they have varying levels of importance, and they remain alive and active. This list is not definitive. Others better versed in Anishinaabe stories than myself (including other authors in this collection) could discern other characteristics and/or offer greater clarification. Yet, this list is illustrative of the problems and promise of the question that opened this essay.

Consider that question once again: What is a story? More to the point, what is an Anishinaabe story? What can the answer tell us about the importance of understanding the legal and political events of Anishinaabeg as stories?

A larger question looms: Is it necessary, or even desirable, to craft a determinative answer? In one sense, it is important to know what Anishinaabe stories are, as stories are so fundamentally critical to the people. In another sense, the search for the definitive explication of what constitutes an Anishinaabe story runs the same risk as searching for a definitive explication of a particular story. If one claims that a certain version of a Nanaboozhoo (the Anishinaabe trickster figure) story is the "correct" or the only ideologically proper version of that story, then one necessarily delimits the authority of the active participants: the teller, the listener(s), and the story itself. There no longer remains any flexibility for context or individualized interpretation for any of the involved parties.

If we recognize the threat of dogmatism to Anishinaabe stories, then we must also be willing to accept that an Anishinaabe definition of "story" requires the same level of dynamic interpretative contextualism that the stories themselves require. Consequently, if we free ourselves from the shackles of a determinative definition of "story," then it becomes possible to recognize a greater number of events and ideas as Anishinaabe stories. A more expansive notion of story frees Anishinaabeg and scholars from occasionally helpful, but most often cumbersome and confining, English words like "myth," "spiritual," and the particularly onerous "traditional."

If we were to understand the legal and political histories of Anishinaabeg as stories, we would infuse these events with a much greater range of abilities to aid communities and to function effectively within those communities. Rather than existing as dead, concretized statutes moving progressively further away from present-day concerns along a linear timeline, major moments in the legal and political lives of Anishinaabeg—treaties, constitutions, elections, etc.—would remain relevant, and would allow the personal and communal knowledge of those events to inform and guide the thinking of today's tribal leaders and community members. These new types of "stories" can give us so much more than what they presently give. All we have to do is simply regard them in the way that we as Anishinaabeg used to do so naturally and regularly.

My suggestion—that we begin regarding tribal political and legal events as stories rather than histories—perhaps seems odd or off-putting, if not downright radical. One might argue, even after some contemplation, that there is something distinguishable, if not irreconcilably different about, for example, Nanaboozhoo stories and the enactment of the Minnesota Chippewa Tribe Constitution. One might feel uneasy about lumping together what are often called the "authentic" or "traditional" stories of Anishinaabeg with various communities' difficult and necessary political and legal responses to colonial impositions. With these potential objections in mind, I offer two responses.

The first is that we as Anishinaabeg and Indigenous peoples need to be very careful when we use English words like "authentic" and "traditional" to describe ourselves and our heritage, because such words run the risk of further imposing Western understandings of history and time on Indigenous peoples. English words like "authentic" and "traditional" carry not only particular understandings of history and time, but value judgments as well. The more authority and validity we give to those words, the further we slide down the ever-present slippery slope where the only true Anishinaabe identity only exists somewhere in the past. If our "traditions" can only be regarded as "authentic" if they supposedly emerge from an idealized, uncontaminated past, then we come ever closer to vanishing as a people, as Westerners have been predicting, projecting, hoping for, dreading, working towards, and expecting for centuries.[14]

The English language is an exceptionally powerful tool, yet words that have come to be associated with Indigenous peoples and their lifeways—such as "myth" or "traditional"—fit uncomfortably at best. Those English words diminish the efficacy of Anishinaabe culture by rendering Anishinaabe beliefs obsolete. The twin forces of the Western idea of history—truth and time—cast a negative judgment on words like myth and tradition. What one might describe as the traditional stories of Anishinaabeg are not traditional in the sense that they are limited in relevance to circumstances that existed in the past or that no longer occur. They are traditional because they retain their ability to speak to Anishinaabeg in multiple settings, including modern ones. Traditional stories are traditional because they defy temporal limitations.

By failing to recognize the legal and political events within Anishinaabe communities as stories, as opposed to histories, we run several risks:

1. *Identity*: A limited understanding of Anishinaabe stories threatens to freeze the "authentic" Anishinaabe identity in a long ago, presently inaccessible time. The further we get from our identity and our stories, the more likely we are to play the role of the vanishing Indian.

2. *Availability*: By setting limits on what constitutes a story, and treating stories as only that which is "traditional," we potentially limit their ability to speak to us today. Flexible as they have proven to be, without additional room to grow, our stories could find themselves shrinking in relevance. If we treat our stories as dusty relics instead of contemporary tools, they have the potential to lose their functionality.

3. *Adaptability*: By limiting Anishinaabe stories to a canon of that which is already known and has been already told, we ignore one of the foundational strengths not only of the stories, but of Anishinaabeg. We ignore the capability of the stories and the people to adapt and remain relevant over changing times. The crushing forces of colonialism have not destroyed Anishinaabeg, because Anishinaabeg have managed to change, adapt, and hold onto themselves at the same time. The same should be true of our stories.

4. *Opportunity*: Perhaps most importantly, if we regard the legal and political events of Anishinaabeg merely as history and not as stories, we stand to lose the chance to fully learn from those events. Stories make sense to Anishinaabeg, whereas the idea of history is still relatively new and less appreciated. As such, it is easier to disregard history. But if we disregard these legal and political events by subjugating them to a lesser status than stories, we waste the hard-earned knowledge and lessons that they offer.

The second response that I offer to those concerned about reconceptualizing legal and political events as stories is that my suggestion is not really all that new or radical, but rather a necessary twist on some ideas that have been around and popular within Indian Country for a while. In essence, I am merely reiterating a now familiar refrain—Anishinaabeg need to rely on their own knowledge, experiences, resources, and intelligence to confront the internal and external problems facing communities—in another new and important context. For example, Anishinaabe legal scholar John Borrows eloquently argues that Canadian law and Canadian courts would greatly benefit from learning the stories—Borrows labels the stories "law"—that developed within Indigenous communities, and that it is fundamentally necessary to do so if the Canadian legal system is going to adequately interpret Indigenous rights.[15] Likening tribal stories to common law, Indigenous "law" is far from inaccessible. Borrows states, "The acquisition of First Nations law does not flow from magical rituals or mystical processes. While some may understand it through non-linear processes, this law can be discerned on other bases as well."[16] Borrows is quick to note that certain ceremonial and religious aspects of Indigenous culture should not be open to anybody and everybody, but that much of the law of Native communities "is acquired in the same way other legal education is acquired: through years of study and hard work."[17] Importantly, Borrows also argues that Indigenous law is available to Native and non-Native alike.[18] This is a fundamentally important point because it recognizes the contributions that Indigenous knowledge can make not only to Indigenous communities, but to the larger world as well. Borrows's approach would certainly benefit

Native communities by breathing new life into tribal stories and offering a more tribally centered interpretation of Indigenous rights, but it would also add to the greater good by providing another base of knowledge with which to interpret the world for everybody. Other scholars and philosophers—Anishinaabeg and non-Anishinaabeg alike—concerned with Native peoples and Native North America have made similar overtures toward rediscovering and reinfusing Indigenous concepts in law and politics and elsewhere.[19]

While Anishinaabe scholar and activist Gerald Vizenor's work has found its most receptive audience among literary critics, his detailing of the concept of survivance should be appealing to anyone interested in strengthening Indigenous peoples and nations. According to Vizenor, "Native survivance is an active sense of presence over absence, deracination, and oblivion; survivance is *the continuance of stories*, not a reaction, however pertinent" [emphasis added].[20]

Vizenor seems to discourage essentializing his concept through his densely idiosyncratic language and statements like "Survivance is a practice, not an ideology, dissimulation, or a theory."[21] However, while Vizenor notes that "the theories of survivance are elusive, obscure, and imprecise by definition, translation, comparison, and catchword histories," he also tells us that "survivance is invariably true and just in native practice and company."[22]

Through this description, one begins to understand that survivance is comprised not of ideas, but of actions expressed as ideas and expressed as stories. Vizenor's writings on multiple subjects also makes clear that survivance is not merely an activity of the past, but a method by which tribal peoples actively engage with their contemporary circumstances.[23] Vizenor refers to the present wave of storytellers as "postindians": those who create Native stories in a postmodern world.[24] This establishes a connection between the postindians and the combatants of an earlier age. Vizenor states, "The postindian warriors encounter their enemies with the same courage in literature as their ancestors once evinced on horses, and they create their stories with a new sense of survivance."[25] This is another brief detailing of a complex idea, but it suffices to note that survivance is a method by which Indigenous peoples connect themselves to their past and build their own identities, resistances, and stories in the present despite—and not just in response to—colonial impositions. Others (perhaps including Vizenor himself) have relegated Vizenor to literary theory, but his understanding of survivance should speak to anyone concerned with the legal and political matters of Anishinaabeg and other Indigenous peoples. It is through treaties and constitutions and other similar mechanisms that many stories of survivance are told.

I hope to echo Borrows, Vizenor, and other scholars both in their call for a greater exploration of Anishinaabeg and other communities' tribal knowledge, and in their understanding that this knowledge has a significant contemporary usefulness to which Indigenous peoples need to return, and which they can share with the non-Indigenous world. Where I hope to further contribute to this movement is by asking Anishinaabeg and others to reevaluate what we consider traditional and what we consider ours to share. By reconceptualizing our legal and political events as stories, rather than as histories, we can bring those events into a realm of understanding with which Anishinaabeg have been most familiar. In so doing, Anishinaabeg will better be able to utilize these stories to fully contribute to the greater good of the community and others. These legal and political events are part of who we are and should be regarded as such.

A short example will help to illustrate the potential of these legal and political events when considered as stories:[26]

It was another chilly October day on the Turtle Mountain Band of Chippewa Indians reservation. But this particular day in 1932 wasn't going to be like any other. Our people had to make a tough choice that day. Listen to this and ask yourself how you would have chosen.

Our people were hungry when they met with the new superintendent that day. Surely many of them were hungry because they did not have enough food to go around for themselves and their families. Times were tough for many people back then. But everybody in the community was hungry for change as well. Listen to the decision that they made and ask yourself this: Did they choose with their hearts or their minds or their stomachs? Did they choose out of hope or out of fear?

The new superintendent offered up a constitution and our relatives wanted a constitution. But that's only part of the story. Our relatives wanted a constitution because they thought it would help them get things done. Lots of folks were unhappy about conditions on the reservation for a lot of reasons. Most people felt cheated by the federal government back when the tribe and the feds negotiated an agreement. The federal government had stacked the deck by opening up land to settlers way before they attempted to negotiate with us, and they only offered ten cents an acre for the land that they had already taken. Ten cents an acre was a bad price even for the type of deals that the feds made with Indians. It was another tough situation, but enough of our relatives figured that something was better than nothing and they signed the agreement.

After a short while, folks started calling the agreement with the feds the "Ten Cent Treaty" and it didn't take long to figure out that it wasn't just the price of the deal that made it bad. The Ten Cent Treaty created a reservation of twelve miles by six miles, which was way too small for the number of people that lived there. Many folks were given allotments very far away from the reservation, which caused even more problems. On top of everything else, we have many Métis, or mixed blood, relatives. So lots of people outside of the tribe kept trying to convince the government that the people of Turtle Mountain shouldn't get the "special rights" that Indians got.

Not too long after the Ten Cent Treaty, our relatives decided that the federal government hadn't treated them fairly and that they should do something about it. The traditional leadership had basically dissolved under the pressure of the Ten Cent Treaty negotiations (if you can call them negotiations) and we were looking for something new. Eventually a new idea gained popularity; people started thinking about and talking about and trying to write a constitution.

Most white people didn't think much of Indians at this time, and the super-intendents at Turtle Mountain weren't any exception. The superintendents generally thought that the folks at Turtle Mountain were either ignorant Indi-ans or ignorant white folks trying to pass themselves off as Indians to cheat the government. And you have to remember that the federal government was trying to get people to give up being Indian at this time as well. So, the prospect of the federal government recognizing a new tribal constitution wasn't all that likely.

But that didn't stop us from trying. Many thought that a constitution would be a key to beginning a lawsuit against the feds for the depredations committed under the Ten Cent Treaty. And it's probable that some folks thought that a new tribal government would help to fend off the attacks from those who argued that we shouldn't get the "special rights" that Indians got. Others must have thought a new tribal government would be a good way to take back some control over their own lives and away from the superintendent.

So, the folks at Turtle Mountain wanted a constitution. But they got more than what they bargained for in the meeting with the new superintendent. The new superintendent told them that he had a constitution drawn up for them, which had been written by a white attorney who lived outside of the reservation. He also said that they shouldn't bother discussing it, but that they should just adopt it if they ever wanted to get their claim going against the United States. Well, Nanaboozhoo must have been in the room trying to stir up a little trouble because everybody wanted to talk about it. Lots of folks were unhappy. This con-stitution did not come from the community, and many realized that it was a bad document that had the potential to take away more authority than it gave. One guy even said, "I feel that this constitution invests altogether too much power in the hands of the superintendent. The various articles all seem to be so construed as to give the balance of power to the Agency office, and on these grounds I think the plan is not only unfair, but unjust." None of the discussion moved the new superintendent though.

The folks at the meeting had a decision to make. They had wanted a constitution for a long time, but they didn't like the one that was before them. Was it worth the trouble that this bad constitution might cause to have something to address the other problems facing the community? Or should they hold out the hope that if they rejected this one, they could convince the government to accept one that was more to the community's liking? It must have been a very difficult decision and everybody involved must have known that their actions would have lasting consequences for the tribe for many years to come. The first time they voted, everybody was split on what to do. Later they voted again and they made their choice.

In the end the people in the meeting decided to adopt the constitution. What do you suppose our relatives thought about when they cast their ballots? What do you suppose they thought the future was going to be like because of the decision? I'm sure they did what they thought was best, but why do you suppose they thought it was the best decision to make? What do you suppose you would have done if you had been in their shoes?

This is a very simple telling of a story that is full of details and complexities and nuance. I do not claim that my story of the adoption of the first tribal constitution on the Turtle Mountain Reservation in 1932 is by any means definitive. But I do want to suggest that it can be a first step in contemplating the legal and historical events of Anishinaabeg as stories.

If we reconsider the characteristics of stories that I outlined earlier in this essay, then my version of the adoption of the 1932 Turtle Mountain Constitution makes sense as a story. First, while stories have a central place within Anishinaabe worldviews and understandings of ourselves, so do the statements that we have made, and continue to make, about ourselves as political entities. One of the dominant characteristics that separates tribal peoples from other minorities in North America is our political status. Treaties have helped to establish a variety of statuses, and further political expressions, such as constitutions and tribal codes, continue to refine them. For better or for worse, part of understanding contemporary Anishinaabe (and other Indigenous) identities is understanding our unique political relationship to others. Since our distinct political statuses are part of who we are, why would we not recognize them through story? Why would we not use the events that helped form ourselves and our identity in a manner that makes sense to us?

Second, the stories about legal and political events are available for use as functional tools. Merely knowing the facts about the first Turtle Mountain Constitution, for instance that it was enacted in 1932, makes it easy to throw those facts away as outdated relics from a much different time. Contemplating the story of the adoption of the Constitution forces one to confront the issues that confronted community members at the time. Additionally, by using questions to frame the story—a common rhetorical device in Indian Country—one is guided down a path whereby reflecting on what happened at one time might shed a new perspective on what is happening today.

Third, it can fit comfortably within the structure of Anishinaabe stories. One would never confuse the adoption of the 1932 Turtle Mountain Constitution with an *aadizookaan*, a sacred story. Yet, it should also be clear that the story of the Constitution is important in its own right and should be told within the community. The 1932 Constitution began Turtle Mountain's often contentious history with constitutionalism. Understanding those origins and understanding how they might continue to affect the community today is not sacred, but is certainly important enough to inspire deep reflection, and be remembered as one of the events that shapes who we are and how we might think about ourselves in the future.

Finally, this story has the capability to remain alive and active because it is dynamic and flexible. How to interpret the story will depend on the teller, listener(s), the story itself, and the circumstances in which it was told. For example, one could read the story of the adoption of the Turtle Mountain Constitution as an example of overreaching ambition. One might conclude that the community's willingness to adopt a constitution to begin a claim against the federal government, despite the flaws in the document, displayed a lack of patience and reasonableness. The subsequent difficulties with constitutionalism that the community has faced since then might attest to this reading. Conversely, one could read the adoption of the Turtle Mountain Constitution as an example of tribal agency and resistance. Despite its flaws, the people of Turtle Mountain were able to adopt a constitution, and not under the Indian Reorganization Act of 1934, which had yet to even be written as a bill, but during the end of the disastrous Allotment Era. This remarkable achievement shows that the spirit and determination of a tribal people can succeed in shaping the community's future even during the darkest of times. Other interpretations are available as well.

By recognizing the legal and political events of Anishinaabe communities as stories rather than as histories, we stand to garner new ways of understanding and passing down more recent tribal knowledge that we are continuing to accumulate on a daily basis. We need not radically alter our understanding of the world, but rather merely reorient ourselves to the ways Anishinaabeg have understood their environments from the beginning. Doing so will have several positive consequences, not the least of which will be to loosen the Western world's grip on authority, authenticity, history, and time, particularly as it concerns who we are and how we define ourselves. At a time when tribal communities are becoming more and more intertwined with the non-Native world and are facing ever greater pressures in an increasingly complex global society, we would do well to look within ourselves for answers by simply doing what we do and being who we are. We must tell all of our stories.

NOTES

1. For a general discussion of the importance of time and history in the Western worldview, and how that corresponds with Native worldviews, see chapters "Thinking in Time and Space" and "The Concept of History," in Vine Deloria Jr., *God Is Red: A Native View of Religion* (Golden, CO: Fulcrum Publishing, 1994). This work is primarily concerned with the fundamental differences between Christianity and tribal religions, but nonetheless offers some broad insights into how religious understandings and practices are informed by the large categories of time, space, and history, among others.

2. Before I continue, I must disclose that I do not and cannot claim fluency in Anishinaabemowin. Unfortunately, I, like many other Anishinaabeg, have suffered one of the most dastardly effects of colonialism: I was not given Anishinaabemowin as a primary or even secondary language. My greatest exposure to my tribal language was through the four semesters' worth of Anishinaabemowin classes that I took as an undergraduate at the University of Minnesota. As such, I am limited in what I can definitively claim about Anishinaabemowin. Nonetheless, my experience (limited as it may be), coupled with other, more useful and tangible evidence, strongly suggests that there is little to no division between the concepts of "story" and "history" in Anishinaabeg worldviews.

3. Frederic Baraga, *A Dictionary of the Ojibway Language* (1878; repr., St. Paul: Minnesota Historical Society Press, 1992); and John D. Nichols and Earl Nyholm, *Concise Dictionary of Minnesota Ojibwe* (Minneapolis: University of Minnesota Press, 1995).

4. For example, highly respected Indigenous scholar Vine Deloria Jr. noted, "Even the closest approach to the Western idea of history by an Indian tribe

was yet a goodly distance from Western historical conceptions." Deloria Jr., *God Is Red*, 102.

5. Having noted that the understandings of history in Western and Anishinaabeg cultures are fundamentally different, I want to be as clear as possible as I navigate these big ideas in a small space with relatively few words. I do not mean to state, or even imply, that the Anishinaabeg, or any Indigenous peoples for that matter, did not understand or have any conception of history. The ahistorical Indian—formerly popular (and perhaps still so) in ethnohistorical and popular-culture depictions of Indigenous peoples—is a regrettably durable symbol. Yet, the ahistorical Indian is also a fallacy. For a useful discussion of tribal conceptions of history, see Peter Nabokov, *A Forest of Time: American Indian Ways of History* (Cambridge: Cambridge University Press, 2002). Even simple forays into the literature on Anishinaabeg make this clear. For example, William Warren's *History of the Ojibway People,* perhaps the most famous and useful text written about Anishinaabeg in the nineteenth century, is constructed entirely from oral histories. William W. Warren, *History of the Ojibway People* (St. Paul: Minnesota Historical Society, 1885; repr., St. Paul: Minnesota Historical Society Press, 1984). Citations are to the 1984 edition. Warren made note of this in describing his evidence. "In this volume, the writer has confined himself altogether to history; giving an account of the principal events which have occurred to the Ojibways within the past five centuries, as obtained from the lips of their old men and chiefs who are the repositories of the traditions of the tribe"; ibid., 26. It should be recognized that Warren was a product of his times and did disclaim the evidence to some extent, apologizing "for any discrepancies in time or date which may occur in the oral information of the Indians, and the more authentic records of the whites"; ibid. Nonetheless, Warren recognized the necessity of privileging tribal sources when writing tribal histories, noting that while "much has been written concerning the red race," what has been written "is mainly superficial"; ibid., 24. The important work of Frances Densmore is instructive in this regard as well. Densmore noted various ways that Anishinaabeg remembered and passed down important personal and societal events, including alterations to feathers worn in the hair, notches in sticks, and pictographic writings, among others. Frances Densmore, *Chippewa Customs* (Washington, DC: Smithsonian Institution, 1929; St. Paul: Minnesota Historical Society Press, 1979), 173–83. Citations are to the Minnesota Historical Society Press edition.

6. Nichols and Nyhom, *Concise Dictionary*, 270.

7. To briefly illustrate another example, dreams and visions hold a much greater significance for Anishinaabeg than for their colonial counterparts. In her excellent study of relationship between two prominent *manidoog*, or spirit

beings, and their relationship with Anishinaabeg, Theresa S. Smith details the importance of the dream world to Anishinaabeg. Smith uses the word "myth" to denote tribal stories. "The memories of myth, born in the worlds of waking experience and dream, are true because they are meaningfully real to their owners. . . . We should first clarify the character of myths as reflecting the content of dreams. In the traditional [Anishinaabeg] world-view, sleep is not a withdrawal from life but a distinct personal experience that both requires the engagement of the self and is understood as an arena in which important and even formative life events occur. . . . The occurrences are, in fact, often considered to be 'of more vital importance than the events of daily waking life.' This is because it is in the realm of dreams that [*Manidoog*], other-than-human visitors, most often appear to human beings." Theresa S. Smith, *The Island of the Anishnaabeg: Thunderers and Water Monsters in the Traditional Ojibwe Life-World* (Moscow, ID: University of Idaho Press, 1995), 20–21. That Smith finds it necessary to explain (in English) for her audience the importance of dreams and dreaming to Anishinaabeg makes clear that dreams and dreaming hold differing emphasis and significance. Even foundational precepts of what is and is not real are matters of contestation between Anishinaabeg and the Western world.

8. One of the most prominent chroniclers of Anishinaabeg philosophy and lifeways in the last four decades, Basil Johnston, has made note of the importance of these gifts. "It is in story, fable, legend, and myth that fundamental understandings, insights, and attitudes toward life and human conduct, character, and quality in their diverse forms are embodied and passed on." Basil Johnston, *Ojibway Heritage* (1976; repr., Lincoln: University of Nebraska Press, 1990), 7.

9. Johnston is again instructive. "It is not enough to listen to or to read or to understand the truths contained in stories; according to the elders the truths must be lived out and become part of the being of a person." Johnston, *Ojibway Heritage*, 7.

10. Smith, *The Island of the Anishnaabeg*, 52–55.

11. Johnston, *Ojibway Heritage*, 8.

12. For example, in discussing one particular Anishinaabeg story, Smith notes that "There is no definitive version of the story, but among the many tellings there does exist . . . a basic or core narrative. In other words, there are certain events and actors that always appear, and the general movement of the narrative includes specific actions that produce unvarying results." Smith, *The Island of the Anishnaabeg*, 158.

13. As noted by Smith, "[Anishinaabeg] tradition is not a 'religion of the book.' It has no canon, just as it has no dogma." Ibid., 18.

14. For a recent study on the trope of the "vanishing Indian" by an Anishinaabe historian, see Jean M. O'Brien, *Firsting and Lasting: Writing Indians out of Existence in New England* (Minneapolis: University of Minnesota Press, 2010).

15. Borrows writes, "By inquiring into the First Nations legal viewpoint which gives meaning to particular Aboriginal rights, courts can approach these cases on a more principled and global basis, while retaining their fact- and site-specific context. When courts incorporate Indigenous laws into Canadian Aboriginal rights law they give fuller meaning to them as sui generis interests." John Borrows, *Recovering Canada: The Resurgence of Indigenous Law* (Toronto: University of Toronto Press, 2002), 12.

16. Ibid., 25.

17. Ibid.

18. Borrows states, "The fact that First Nations law can be learned in a manner familiar to most people means that the interpretation of this law for the benefit of Canadian courts is not the exclusive domain of Aboriginal people, though caution should always be exercised in this regard. Cultural knowledge should remain under community control, and to educate non-Aboriginal people in the details of Indigenous law poses a risk of unjust appropriation of this knowledge. However, it is conceivable that a non-Native person who received the training, confidence, and certification of a First Nations community may be able to provide the bridge by which First Nations law is communicated to Canadian courts." Ibid., 25–26.

19. For example, in his scathing critique on the Western concept of sovereignty, Rotinohshonni scholar and activist Taiaiake Alfred offered a salvo of hope. "In recent years, indigenous leaders from around the world have had some success in undermining the intellectual credibility of state sovereignty as the only legitimate form of political organization. Scholars in international law are now beginning to see the vast potential for peace in indigenous political philosophies." Taiaiake Alfred, *Peace, Power, Righteousness: An Indigenous Manifesto* (Don Mills, ON: Oxford University Press, 1999), 63. In a recent work, Osage scholar Robert Warrior read a range of Native nonfiction writings from different eras—including the 1881 Osage Constitution—in an effort to maximize their present-day utility. "Here, I am not reestablishing the existence of this intellectual tradition so much as I am further exploring some of the specific historical and theoretical ways that the Native nonfiction writing tradition challenges contemporary Native intellectuals." Robert Warrior, *The People and the Word: Reading Native Nonfiction* (Minneapolis: University of Minnesota Press, 2005), xiii. Anishinaabe scholar Wendy Makoons Geniusz, in her recent book on the botanical teachings of Anishinaabeg, contrasts the purposes of such research for non-Natives (as a form of

salvaging a dying culture) and for Natives (as a way to continue to provide for future generations). Wendy Makoons Geniusz, *Our Knowledge Is Not Primitive: Decolonizing Botanical Anishinaabe Teachings* (Syracuse, NY: Syracuse University Press, 2009), 8. Geniusz notes, "For indigenous people, an important step in decolonization is taking control of research"; ibid., 10. This slight sampling only barely reflects the many calls to reclaim Indigenous knowledge, values, and experience, and to utilize them in a contemporary context.

20. Gerald Vizenor, "Aesthetics of Survivance: Literary Theory and Practice," in *Survivance: Narratives of Native Presence,* ed. Gerald Vizenor (Lincoln: University of Nebraska Press, 2008), 1.

21. Ibid., 11. It should be noted that this hardly prevents scholars from theorizing about Vizenor's work. See A. Robert Lee, ed., *Loosening the Seams: Interpretations of Gerald Vizenor* (Bowling Green, OH: Bowling Green State University Popular Press, 2000).

22. Vizenor, "Aesthetics of Survivance," 1.

23. For example, see Gerald Vizenor, *Manifest Manners: Narratives on Postindian Survivance* (1994; repr., Lincoln: University of Nebraska Press, 1999).

24. Ibid., viii.

25. Ibid., 4.

26. My dissertation concerned the history of constitutionalism at the Turtle Mountain Band of Chippewa Indians reservation. I focused on four main events: the agreement between the tribal nation and the federal government in the late nineteenth century, the enactment of the first constitution in 1932, the enactment of the second constitution in 1959, and the efforts at constitutional reform in the early twenty-first century. This story will focus primarily on the first constitution, with reference to the agreement between Turtle Mountain and the United States. Keith Richotte Jr., "'We the Indians of the Turtle Mountain Reservation . . .': Rethinking Tribal Constitutionalism beyond the Colonialist/Revolutionary Dialectic" (Ph.D. diss., University of Minnesota, 2009).

RESOURCES

Alfred, Taiaiake. *Peace, Power, Righteousness: An Indigenous Manifesto.* Don Mills, ON: Oxford University Press, 1999.

Baraga, Frederic. *A Dictionary of the Ojibway Language.* 1878; repr., St. Paul: Minnesota Historical Society Press, 1992.

Borrows, John. *Recovering Canada: The Resurgence of Indigenous Law.* Toronto: University of Toronto Press, 2002.

Deloria Jr., Vine. *God Is Red: A Native View of Religion.* Golden, CO: Fulcrum Publishing, 1994.

Densmore, Frances. *Chippewa Customs.* Washington, DC: Smithsonian Institution, 1929; St. Paul: Minnesota Historical Society Press, 1979.

Geniusz, Wendy Makoons. *Our Knowledge Is Not Primitive: Decolonizing Botanical Anishinaabe Teachings.* Syracuse, NY: Syracuse University Press, 2009.

Johnston, Basil. *Ojibway Heritage.* 1976; repr., Lincoln: University of Nebraska Press, 1990.

Lee, A. Robert, ed. *Loosening the Seams: Interpretations of Gerald Vizenor.* Bowling Green, OH: Bowling Green State University Popular Press, 2000.

Nabokov, Peter. *A Forest of Time: American Indian Ways of History.* Cambridge: Cambridge University Press, 2002.

Nichols, John D., and Earl Nyholm. *Concise Dictionary of Minnesota Ojibwe.* Minneapolis: University of Minnesota Press, 1995.

O'Brien, Jean M. *Firsting and Lasting: Writing Indians out of Existence in New England.* Minneapolis: University of Minnesota Press, 2010.

Richotte Jr., Keith. "'We the Indians of the Turtle Mountain Reservation . . .': Rethinking Tribal Constitutionalism beyond the Colonialist/Revolutionary Dialectic." Ph.D. diss., University of Minnesota, 2009.

Smith, Theresa S. *The Island of the Anishnaabeg: Thunderers and Water Monsters in the Traditional Ojibwe Life-World.* Moscow, ID: University of Idaho Press, 1995.

Vizenor, Gerald. "Aesthetics of Survivance: Literary Theory and Practice." In *Survivance: Narratives of Native Presence,* ed. Gerald Vizenor. Lincoln: University of Nebraska Press, 2008.

———. *Manifest Manners: Narratives on Postindian Survivance.* 1994; repr., Lincoln: University of Nebraska Press, 1999.

Warren, William W. *History of the Ojibway People.* St. Paul: Minnesota Historical Society, 1885; repr., St. Paul: Minnesota Historical Society Press, 1984.

Warrior, Robert. *The People and the Word: Reading Native Nonfiction.* Minneapolis: University of Minnesota Press, 2005.

On the Road Home

Stories and Reflections from Neyaashiinigiming

LINDSAY KEEGITAH BORROWS

Boozhoo nindinawemaaganidok, niiji-anishinaabeg, niiji-bimaadiziig.
Nigig indodem.
Keegitah nindizhinikaaz.
Neyaashiinigiming indonjibaa.
Indabinoojiiwaadiz geyaabi. Niizhtana ashi niswi.
Gaawiinoon igo aapiji gegoo inkendanziin.
Bangii eta go gegoo ningikendaan.

[Greetings to all my relations. I am from the otter clan. My name
is Keegitah. I am from the place where there is a point of land, a
peninsula. I am still a child in learning about our ways. I am twenty-
two. I don't know very much. I only know a little.]

ANISHINAABEG STORIES TAKE ME HOME. STORIES ARE THE CENTER,
the periphery, and the negative spaces within and beyond our circle of
dreams. There is value in searching for a center in a field of studies, but
the trickster doesn't know boundaries. As we rest in our perceived centers,
blindly comfortable, Nanabush is active throughout our field.[1] We live his
stories, and they place, displace, and replace us. Nanabush teaches and teases
us as we live and learn his ways. In so doing, we seemingly lose our center—
who we thought we were as Anishinaabeg: "the good people." Thus, when
we come home, we realize we are also leaving home. Old centers are lost and

new ones re-form. We feel comfortable for a while, and then another story comes along and the cycle begins again. This is the balance we live within. Our stories talk of balance.[2] There is a balance in centering and de-centering Anishinaabeg Studies.

Balance requires being aware of the healing and harm found within stories. It is true that Anishinaabeg stories can communicate boundless creativity. They can convey adaptability in the face of change. Yet stories can also become obstacles to growth. If we hold onto them too tightly we can squeeze the life out of them. They must be given room to live and grow. Without this space to breathe, stories could disconnect us from those we (should) love. They have great power, and they can help us learn how to live ethically and sustainably with all our relations. In this spirit, I will discuss their positive dimensions; but we must never forget that stories can also cause great harm. Stories are what we make of them; they live in and through us, and our trickster-inflected lives. This knowledge makes stories both sacred and scary because this is basically who we are as people, including Anishinaabeg people. They reflect who we are and who we would like to become. In this light, stories are symbols. Language is a symbol. We use language to tell our stories. Our stories talk of everything, even in their silence, in their negative spaces. Again, this is part of their balance, and our balance. This is why stories can focus our attention and provide a methodology for Anishinaabeg Studies—we are stories. We can't speak without them. In fact, we can't live without them. This is how I understand Anishinaabeg stories. They are embedded in our lives, and our lives are embedded in stories.

My family history teaches me ways to articulate the legal, ceremonial, and intellectual stories of my community, Neyaashiinigiming.[3] My grandmother is a great storyteller. The early life of my Nokomis, Jean Arlene Jones Borrows, tells a story of our home and people, the Chippewa of Nawash.[4] One day I asked her to tell me her life story. She thought for a few moments and said, "To tell you all of my story would take me until my journey home because I'd be crying so much." With an ever-present twinkle in her eye, and excitement about the world, she gains strength from all her experiences, both good and bad. While it is sometimes hard for her, she loves to share stories, and I love what she tells me. Her stories teach me of a past that is my own, although I did not live through those earlier times. Her stories give me strength when I recognize the strength they give her too. As Nokomis often reminds me, each of our stories begin in a world not forgotten, but largely unremembered, as I will recount below. She says we gain glimpses of that world through listening to the sounds of the animals, trees, and water. It is usually during the hardest times that premonitions and visions come from this other-world, teaching, warning, and guiding. Nokomis was introduced to the other-world at a young age because of the many trials and dangers she faced. Her stories are imbued with messages from these spirits.[5] Despite our connections to the spirits, who know our beginnings, our stories can never be told in their fullness. They can, however, be partially recalled, interpreted, and woven into and through our earthly experiences.

I learned a similar teaching from another elder on our reserve. One bright winter's day, while home at Cape Croker, I walked around the lake and down the pot-holed road to visit Basil Johnston. He told me stories. I was entranced. In time, I asked where he learned so many stories. He quietly stood and retrieved a large book from his shelf. It was a 1917 collection of stories translated by William Jones, called *Ojibwe Texts*.[6] He opened the book and opened my understanding. Pages of notes and markings were bright on the old paper. He said that book was like his Bible. These stories helped remind him how to live well. Then he told me some of the oral stories of my great-grandpa Josh. Basil heard them when he was a younger man. These experiences also had a significant impact on his life. Then he told me of his own personal life experiences and stories he learned and lived over the years. He also taught me about silence and how "positive" those so-called "negative spaces" can be. These various sources and more have fueled his writing. They are at the center and edge of his storytelling. They helped structure a method for viewing life; they teach about our adaptability and inertia, and they show our struggle between sustainable and destructive ways. Thus, as we neared the end of our visit, Basil cautioned me: "It's one thing to know a story, or to hear a concept and learn a word; it's quite another to act on it." He said that we can talk of humility, but until we can look at the squirrel sitting on the branch and know we are no greater and no less than her, it is only then that we have walked with humility. Stories grow when they are lived; at their best, they are a call to act in harmony with the world around us. As we visited together, my center was displaced and another one re-formed. I felt the balance of life in the stories he shared that day.

All these experiences were in my mind as I thought about my potential contribution to this anthology. I reread the question posed in the editors' call for abstracts: "In the current climate of globalization, what are the roles of "story" in moderating multi-dimensional struggles for tribal sovereignty, 'traditionalism,' and cultural innovation?" I struggled to understand what was being asked. This question sounded so unlike Nanabush that I was reminded of Nanabush. I could also hear Basil in my mind, chiding academics for their foolish phraseology. He might even laugh, or scowl, at our "multi-global-dimensional sovereign-traditional innovative" thingies.

So, in thinking about the question of centers, I returned to where I began, my Nokomis. In her stories, I see how Anishinaabeg narratives speak through the ages because they teach us important themes. Their details can paint beautiful or troubling images, but it is their thematic messages that most nourish our hearts. Our timeless stories have changed over time and thus remain constant. They are continuously in a settled state of static flux. They have global implications for local, practical, day-to-day events. Louise Erdrich concluded her book *Four Souls* by writing: "Even our bones nourish change, and even a people who lived so close to the bone and were saved for thousands of generations by a practical philosophy, even such people as we, the Anishinaabeg, can sometimes die, or change, or change and become." I think Louise[7] is saying that without change we would die, and by changing we die. That's so Nanabush of her. In seeing her work in this way, I find that another center is displaced and another one is re-formed. Stories help us live and die, create and destroy; they connect and separate us from our world. Whether this happens in a positive or negative way is completely dependent on how we live them.

Louise's words remind me of another experience I had at Cape Croker this past fall. Donald Keeshig, an elder at home, looked me in the eye one evening and said, "If there is one thing I'm not scared of, it's dying. I'm going to another beginning." I think he was referring to physical death, and I took an important lesson from his teaching. However, I think another lesson can be drawn from his words. It relates to cultural change. Anishinaabeg culture doesn't die by changing, it brings a new beginning. We don't ever really die as a people, but we do experience new beginnings that build on earlier foundations. Our past histories can never be separated from our present stories; we wouldn't be here without them.

This brings me to my contribution to this anthology. I want to tell a story of centers, edges, balance, change, and decay. In doing so, I will speak directly to their theme in an indirect way. In other words, I will write about what I have learned about being Anishinaabekwe from Nanabush, Nokomis, Basil, Donald, Louise, and my family. I will do this through a short piece of creative writing. The setting is a young woman at her grandma's home at Neyaashiinigiming. She will see she is a story, and that many people have a role in centering and de-centering Anishinaabeg Studies.

"BOTH SIDES NOW"

Arlene Mitig's beaded earrings danced to the pothole bumps as she drove her white Cadillac down the old dirt reservation road. Her two preteen granddaughters—Jane and Anne—sang Joni Mitchell loudly in the backseat, swaying their heads and waving sticks like lighters at a concert. It was a treat for Arlene to have them with her. They had traveled four hours north from Toronto to visit for the weekend. In response to their fervent pleas, she took them to her brother Eddy's house. Every year, Arlene grew more distant from him as he became more creative with his drug use: gasoline, glues, and aerosol whipped cream—all that do-it-yourself stuff. Her granddaughters loved him though. He often hosted bearded, shoeless, unwashed, "back-to-the-land" folk. Jane and Anne would rate his guests on a hippie scale from one to ten. They especially loved the story of how he got his hook hand. Every time, the story was different. Every time, they believed him.

"Girls, do you know what those are?" Arlene pulled over to the side of the road where a group of spindly red twigs grew in a bush formation.

"Nanabush intestines!"

"That's right. The trickster is in these plants. You should sing to them so their medicines know we're the good spirits, and they shouldn't harm us." Arlene, Jane, and Anne got out of the car and stood in front of the red plants. The girls continued their rousing rendition of "Both Sides Now": *"Rows and floes of angel hair / and ice cream castles in the air / and feather canyons everywhere / I've looked at clouds that way."*

As they sang, Arlene saw the willows weep and aspens quake as she breathed in the fresh hardwood air. Since she turned seventy-five, her conversations with the land have been increasingly frequent. She often walks to the edges of the wood behind her cabin and pushes through the curtain of green. Inside the forest, the veil thins, and she hears the next world whisper, preparing her for the journey home. She's not scared of death. Her people, the Ojibwe, confront death daily. This is what happens in a hunting and fishing community. Two of her brothers died when their boat capsized one late autumn evening. They had been fishing for whitefish on Lake Huron when the wind, or maybe the water lynx, Mishi Bizheu, suddenly tossed the tranquil sea into frenzy.[8]

"Nokomis! Let's go. We're done singing," Jane called as she ran back into the car.

"Oh, okay. Off we go then."

They were only a few minutes from Eddy's house. She hoped he was home. It had been a while since she'd last seen him. The drive followed along the top of a limestone escarpment dotted with caves. It was majestic. Tourists thought it was beautiful too. The Canadian government had turned the land just north of them into a National Park about twenty years ago. Now she never knew who was going to appear when she went fishing, swimming, or walking. Arlene parked the car next to the cave that bordered her brother's property. Many years ago she had been walking through the cave system and found herself on Eddy's land. She had stumbled upon his marijuana patch.

"Uncle Eddy!" Anne called as she ran out of the car. "Where are you?"

Jane and Anne ran to the side of the house, where they found his rocking chair and fossil-covered picnic table. Arlene felt the stillness of Eddy's cabin. He wasn't home. She could feel someone was close by, though. When she rounded the corner, a man was sitting in Eddy's marijuana patch.

"Nokomis, who is that?" Jane said, running to her grandmother's side.

The man stood up quickly, gray-blue eyes surprised, staring like a deer in the headlights. He had long white hair flowing from his head and chin. His skin was like leather; she guessed it was from years spent dancing under the sun with choreographing drugs.

"I rate him an eleven," Anne whispered to Jane.

"Boozhoo! You a friend of Eddy's? I've never seen you around here," Arlene said.

Despite his startled face and mature age, he raised his skinny frame quickly, though with the aid of a wooden walking stick. Arlene noticed the sleek eagle carving on the head of the cane. She wondered if he was from one of the surrounding reserves. When he spoke, his accent gave him away as a visitor.

"Are you one of the Indigenous Natives of America?" he asked carefully and skeptically, perhaps because of Arlene's lighter skin tone and honey-brown eyes. Her Ojibwe father had married a white woman from Utah when he was a Hollywood stunt-Indian back in the '30s. Her mother made the costumes for the Indian men, and he fell in love, first with a headdress, then with its maker.

"Yeah, I'm an Indian," Arlene said. I guess I forgot my feather at home today though, eh?" She paused for a moment, and then laughed. The man relaxed, although initially taken aback at her humor. Arlene sensed he hadn't spoken with anyone for a while. His speech was slow and careful. She surmised that he must have read a lot from the way he phrased his question. Only a white author would succeed at making the phrase "Indigenous Natives of America" that complicated, and redundant.

Jane skipped forward and asked, "Do you know where Uncle Eddy is?"

"Uncle Eddy? No, I don't know him. But if these are his plants, I'd like to meet him."

"He'd be happy to sell you this stuff. But if you think it'll help you get over your loss"—the man stiffened at this, but Arlene continued without noticing—"you've got it all wrong. The real medicines are in the woods and earth all around you. Just last month, a medicine woman from northern Ontario came here. She said the plants growing between the cracks in my gravel driveway would fight off depression. The real medicines are everywhere, and usually where we don't expect it."

The man stood silently, reminiscent of a scarecrow in loose patched pants, brown with dirt, with a red plaid button-up shirt.

Arlene asked, "Your name is?"

He shook his head, as if to return to consciousness. "I'm Hiram Berry."

"Hiram," she said pensively. "That's from the Bible. We have a lot of Christian names around here too. It's from the missionaries who came in the 1600s; they passed a lot down."

"I'm, uh, actually named after my great-great-great-grandfather. He fought with the Union in the Civil War. I'm from New York City, but I moved to northern Vermont in 1969 with my late wife, Griselda. It was always the two of us together, doing everything. Now it's just me." He seemed confused by himself for telling her all this, but continued: "I've read a lot about Native Americans and I know you have vision quests. I want to be in touch with the spiritual world you know."

Something in his searching eyes reminded her of Eddy. Arlene looked again at his walking stick with its carved eagle head. "Well, Hiram, you're in luck. I'm headed over to a sweat right now with my granddaughters. It's at the powwow grounds. I'll take you there, but every good Indian has an Indian name. You can be Migizimaanose—Walking Eagle." Jane stifled a snicker. She too saw that he wasn't quite able to take off. A grin crept across Hiram's face. He was pleased, honored even. The four of them walked out of the marijuana patch towards her Cadillac.

After summer, the only activity on the powwow grounds was the occasional moonlit truth-or-dare games played by teenagers, or the wandering animals crossing the field, who simply wanted to get to the other side. However, every three months a sweat was held on-site by the Minwendam—one of many Ojibwe spiritual societies at Neyaashiinigiming.

Arlene, Jane, Anne, and Hiram pulled into the parking lot, which was really just an open circular grass field, surrounded by trees. The sweat lodge was in the middle of the field, where the drums usually sat during the powwow. Hiram stepped from the car with wet eyes and a blotchy face. When he had entered the car, the girls resumed singing "Both Sides Now." Hiram had burst into tears and told Arlene this song was special to his late wife, Griselda. She had been an aspiring folksinger who worked in the underground New York City music scene. When Joni Mitchell arrived in New York in the mid '60s, Griselda helped her make it big. She even inspired the lyrics: *I've looked at clouds from both sides now / from up and down and still somehow / it's cloud illusions I recall / I really don't know clouds at all.* He told Arlene about their life together in Vermont living off the land, their isolated bliss, their love and his recent dismay with a cancer diagnosis, failing dental health, drug and alcohol addictions, and a general lack of will to live. Arlene had listened in silence as they drove and assured him the sweat would help heal and answer his questions. She wished Eddy could meet him. They could help pull each other out of their slumps. Jane and Anne ran off to play with kids in the park, so Arlene could begin to prepare herself for the sweat.

"*Boozhoo kwe! Aaniish ezhi-ayaayan?*" Chief Anangokaa greeted Arlene in his low voice. He always made an effort to speak the language to everyone, even though most people only know a few greetings and words these days.

Arlene's Ojibwemowin laid suppressed deep inside her. Whenever she heard it, images from residential school rose in her mind. Every time it was spoken, she had flashbacks of friends with needles poked through their tongues. It traumatized her, but she worked hard to not let it beat her. She replied, "*Boozhoo* Chief! This is Hiram; he's visiting us from Vermont."

Chief Anangokaa looked at the leather-skinned man knowingly. "Hiram! Hmm, that's a Christian name, eh? From the Bible, I think. Have you ever done a sweat before?"

Arlene noticed Hiram bow down a little. "Chief, thank you for accepting me onto your land. No, I haven't done a sweat before, but I've read about them in *The Church of Native North America.*'"

Chief Anangokaa and Arlene exchanged playful looks. She said, "Ahh yes, I've heard of that one. I know that author, in fact—Ima T. Rickster."

Arlene smiled before continuing:

"The lodge is sacred and its wisdom is old. Some men in the community build the domed structure from saplings of the willow tree and cover it in canvas several weeks before the sweat. There's lots of intricate symbolism; I learn something new every time I participate. Tobacco is always offered in thanksgiving. Medicine plants line the pathway into the lodge. Within the lodge it's pitch dark. Cedar and sage hang from the low ceiling, conjuring healing powers. There are four doorways so that spirits can enter from each of the four sacred directions. Only the eastern doorway is to be used by humans. It's a cleansing ceremony performed entirely in Ojibwemowin. Don't worry if you don't understand the words; you'll understand the Manidoos."

Hiram looked like he was being fed cake—every word was rich to him. He didn't want to miss a bite.

By this point about ten other people from the community had arrived. They were all sitting around talking. Hiram asked, "How hot is it in there?"

Arlene never thinks of such dangers. She trusts the sweat leaders and spirits, but she tells him some of what she knows anyways. "If you have any metal on you it will melt to your skin, so you should take that off. Rarely do people die from overexposure to heat, dehydration, smoke inhalation, or improper lodge construction, though it can sometimes lead to suffocation. But I suppose rarely is more than never, eh?" Hiram raised his eyebrows and Arlene added, "Oh yes, and if the rocks heating the lodge aren't completely dry before being put in the fire, they'll crack and explode when water is poured on them. The rock-shrapnel will hit you like a bullet."

Before Hiram could respond, Chief Anangokaa, the sweat leader, invited everyone onto the path of life leading into the lodge.

"*Nindinawemaaganidog*, before we enter the sweat today, remember you are being reborn. You entered this world from the darkness and heat of your mother's womb. You enter the womb again today, leading to a new life. I will now open the eastern doorway and you can crawl humbly into the other world. If you bring any bad thoughts into the sacred space, you will harm everyone."

Arlene and the participants bowed their heads as they prepared their minds for the cleansing powers of the sweat. Arlene didn't notice Hiram was first in line to enter the lodge. By the time she looked up all she saw was a bare bottom crawling through the door. Next to the chair where they had been sitting was a pair of neatly folded brown pants and a red plaid button-up shirt. He had gone in naked. This was not what her people did.

Inside, the intense heat of the lodge never ceased to surprise Arlene. Every time she was inside, she let her mind go loose. Her spirit seemed to travel from her body and connect to stronger forces. Adjusting to the heat, songs, and sounds, she saw something move among them, though it was mostly dark inside. The only light came from sparks when water hit the grandfather rocks in the center. They leapt and swirled, forming pictures in the air.

As Arlene peered through the dark, Chief Anangokaa began singing his prayer to the beat of the water drum. *Gizhe Manidoo, wiidokowishin, zhi-wenemishin, chigoyakow bimoseyaan omaa akiing.* Arlene felt the pulse of the drum pull the water from within her body, drawing sweat from every pore. Her cotton clothes stuck to her, but she was unaware of her skin as she focused her mind on the spirits. She couldn't help but glance over at Hiram. All she could see was his body, naked, momentarily illuminated as a spark danced across a rock.

The chief poured some more water over the stones. Suddenly, a thunderous crack burst from the stone pile. A slivered shard flew from the rocks, followed by a terrible thud, which came from Hiram's chest. Arlene saw Hiram's eyes go wide in the dark. His body tensed, then slumped to the ground. Then she smelled burning flesh. It overpowered the cedar, sage, and sweat. It entered her body. She felt it prick her heart. It twisted deep inside. As her mind caught the change, Arlene saw a woman rise from the clouds of smoke hanging over them. From the steamy rocks in the dark lodge, a woman's long blond hair swept over the room. The woman went to Hiram, who emerged from his limp frame. He suddenly looked forty years younger. The moments slowed. The couple embraced before the scene slowly dissipated. Peace settled over the lodge. Arlene then felt someone warm hold her hand. Her brother Eddy was sitting next to her. His presence kindled a new light. Interconnected images of flowers, leaves, lines, and berries swirled through the air, storied patterns woven through time. This led her to think of the girls playing outside. She thought of the dead porcupine she picked up off the road last night, still sitting in the trunk of her Caddy. She had much to teach her granddaughters. She couldn't wait to do some quill work with them later tonight.[9]

Mii ih, miigwech bizindawiyeg.

NOTES

1. Nanabush is active throughout Anishinaabeg territories; for one example, see A. F. Chamberlain, "Nanibozhu amongst the Otchipwe, Mississagas, and Other Algonkian Tribes," *Journal of American Folklore* 4 (1891): 193–213.

2. Karla Sanders, "A Healthy Balance: Religion, Identity and Community in Louise Erdrich's *Love Medicine*," Buena Vista University, available at: http://www.jstor.org/pss/468016.

3. My father, John Borrows (Kegedonce) has written about our family history; see John Borrows, "A Genealogy of Law: Inherent Sovereignty and First Nations Self-Government," *Osgoode Hall Law School* 30 (1992): 291.

4. Our reserve, *nindishkoniganim*, is located on the Georgian Bay side of Lake Huron at Neyaashiinigmiing, or Cape Croker, Ontario. *Ishkonigan* is the Ojibway word for reservation—it literally means "the leftover thing." Our land traditionally extended much farther, but after allotments and illegal cessions, this beautiful part of the land is all we have left.

5. For a discussion of Ojibwa spiritual beliefs and the importance of stories from the perspective of an Ojibway elder from Neyaashiinigmiing, see Basil Johnston, *Manitous: The Spiritual World of the Ojibway* (St. Paul: Minnesota Historical Society Press, 1995).

6. William Jones, *Ojibwa Texts*, vol. 7, collected by William Jones, edited by Truman Michelson (Leyden: E.J. Brill Ltd.; New York: G.E. Stechert & Co., 1917–19), at http://www.archive.org/details/ojibwatextscoll07jonerich.

7. You will note that I use first names at times in this article. I do this because I have a relationship with those who I am citing, and it would feel disrespectful to call a friend, family member, or elder by their last names.

8. See John Borrows, *Drawing Out Law: A Spirit's Guide* (Toronto: University of Toronto Press, 2010), 199.

9. I'm not exactly sure who will read this book, and I don't have any great desire to control my story's meaning beyond what I've written. I don't want to steal the story from you. It wouldn't be right to be too explicit when, in my view, Anishinaabeg stories are meant to encourage the listener's imagination and interpretive participation. At the same time, I hope what I wrote earlier gives you some context to better understand my theme and story. Plus, you have a whole book in your hands to further work out its details; throughout these pages, people far wiser than me have provided guidance about how to approach Anishinaabeg stories. Besides, if you can't figure it out, the trickster is always nearby, providing alternative interpretive pathways.

About the Authors

Kimberly Blaeser, a Professor at the University of Wisconsin–Milwaukee, teaches creative writing, Native American literature, and American nature writing. Her publications include three books of poetry: *Trailing You,* winner of the first book award from the Native Writers' Circle of the Americas, *Absentee Indians and Other Poems,* and *Apprenticed to Justice.* Her scholarly study *Gerald Vizenor: Writing in the Oral Tradition* (1996) was the first Native-authored book-length study of an Indigenous author. Of Anishinaabe ancestry, and an enrolled member of the Minnesota Chippewa Tribe who grew up on the White Earth Reservation, Blaeser is also the editor of *Stories Migrating Home: A Collection of Anishinaabe Prose* and *Traces in Blood, Bone, and Stone: Contemporary Ojibwe Poetry.* Blaeser's current mixed-genre project, which includes her nature and wildlife photography as well as poetry and creative nonfiction, explores intersecting ideas about Native place, nature, preservation, and spiritual sustenance.

John Borrows is a Professor of Law, Public Policy and Society at the University of Minnesota Law School. He is Anishinabe/Ojibway and a member of the Chippewas of the Nawash First Nation. His publications include *Recovering Canada: The Resurgence of Indigenous Law* (Donald Smiley Award for the best book in Canadian Political Science, 2002), *Canada's Indigenous Constitution* (Canadian Law and Society Best Book Award 2011), and *Drawing Out Law: A Spirit's Guide.* Professor Borrows is a recipient of the Aboriginal Achievement Award in Law and Justice, a Fellow of the Trudeau Foundation, and a Fellow of the Academy of Arts, Humanities and Sciences of Canada (RSC), Canada's highest academic honor.

Lindsay Keegitah Borrows is Anishinaabekwe, and her family is Nigig dodem from the Chippewas of Nawash from Cape Croker, Ontario. She received her B.A. from Dartmouth College in Native American Studies.

During her four undergraduate years, she studied the Maori language at the University of Auckland, New Zealand, and Anishinaabemowin in Bemidji, Minnesota, and at home in Cape Croker. She graduated from Dartmouth with an honors thesis and a Presidential Scholar distinction. Her undergraduate thesis is a creative writing piece on the interactions of Indigenous language and law with nation-states. She spent time when she was younger in Iqaluit, Australia, Arizona, British Columbia, and Ontario, where she was involved with Indigenous peoples of each area. She worked as a coastal naturalist on B.C. Ferries for two summers, educating locals and visitors to Vancouver Island about Coast Salish land.

Jill Doerfler (White Earth Anishinaabe) is an Assistant Professor of American Indian Studies at the University of Minnesota-Duluth. She is interested in the diverse ways in which Anishinaabeg have resisted pseudoscientific measures of blood (race/blood quantum) as a means to define identity. Her article "An Anishinaabe Tribalography: Investigating and Interweaving Conceptions of Identity during the 1910s on the White Earth Reservation" was published in *American Indian Quarterly* (33.3) and won the 2010 Beatrice Medicine Award for Scholarship in Native American Studies. She was a member of the Constitutional Proposal Team of the White Earth Nation (2009) and co-authored *The White Earth Nation: Ratification of a Native Democratic Constitution* with Gerald Vizenor. She looks forward to a referendum vote on the now ratified constitution.

Heid E. Erdrich is an independent scholar, curator, playwright, and founding publisher of Wiigwaas Press, which specializes in Ojibwe-language publications. She grew up in Wahpeton, North Dakota, and is Ojibwe enrolled at Turtle Mountain. Heid attended Dartmouth College and Johns Hopkins University. She taught college writing for two decades, including many years as a tenured professor. Heid now teaches as a visiting author and she works with Native American visual artists. She has won awards from the Minnesota State Arts Board, Bush Foundation, and The Loft Literary Center, and she received the 2009 Minnesota Book Award for poetry. Her most recent book is *Cell Traffic: New and Selected Poems*.

Matthew L. M. Fletcher is Professor of Law at Michigan State University College of Law, and Director of the Indigenous Law and Policy Center. He is the Chief Justice of the Poarch Band of Creek Indians Supreme Court, and also sits as an appellate judge for the Pokagon Band of Potawatomi Indians, the Hoopa Valley Tribe, the Nottawaseppi Huron Band of Potawatomi Indians, and the Lower Elwha Tribe. He is a member of the Grand Traverse Band of Ottawa and Chippewa Indians, located in Peshawbestown, Michigan. In 2010, Professor Fletcher was elected to the American Law Institute. Professor Fletcher graduated from the University of Michigan Law School in 1997 and the University of Michigan in 1994. He recently published *American Indian Tribal Law* (2011) and *Cases and Materials on Federal Indian Law* (2011) with Getches, Wilkinson, and Williams.

Eva Marie Garroutte is a citizen of the Cherokee Nation and a tenured Associate Professor of sociology at Boston College. She maintains a faculty affiliation with the Research Center for Minority Aging Research/Native Elder Resource Center at the University of Colorado Denver, a nationally known center dedicated to the study of Native American health. Her publications include a book, *Real Indians: Identity and the Survival of Native America,* and various articles in sociological and health-related journals. Her current work examines the medical communication needs of Native American elders.

Basil H. Johnston was born on the Parry Island Indian Reserve and is a member of the Cape Croker First Nation (Neyaashiinigmiing), where he currently resides. Educated in reserve schools at Cape Croker and Spanish, Ontario, Johnston earned a B.A. with Honours from Loyola College in Montreal, and completed a secondary-school teaching certificate at the Ontario College of Education. He taught high school in North York, Ontario, from 1962 to 1969, before taking a position in the Ethnology Department of the Royal Ontario Museum (ROM) in Toronto. He remained at the ROM until 1994 to initiate a Native approach to teaching at the museum, and to record and celebrate Anishinaubae heritage, especially language and mythology. He has lectured at a number of universities and is a highly respected author, storyteller, and preserver of the Anishinaubae language. He has written fifteen books in English and five in Anishinaubaemowin, including such notable titles as *Anishinaubae Thesaurus, The Manitous: The Spiritual World of the Ojibwe, Ojibway Heritage, Ojibway Ceremonies, Ojibway Tales, Indian School Days,* and *Honour Earth Mother.* In addition to numerous awards and honorary doctorates, he is the recipient of the Order of Ontario.

James Mackay is a Lecturer in Comparative Literatures at European University Cyprus. He is the editor of the *Salt Companion to Diane Glancy* (2010), and has also edited a special issue of the journal *SAIL* on the subject of "constitutional criticism." He has previously published articles on the works of, among others, Jim Barnes, Diane Glancy, E. Pauline Johnson, and Gerald Vizenor, and is currently working on a monograph on writers who adopt a spurious or exaggerated Native American persona. Other projects include *Tribal Fantasies,* a collection dealing with modern European depictions of Native subjects, and a special edition of *EJAC* looking at older manifestations of the same (both projects co-created with David Stirrup).

Edna Manitowabi is Odawa/Ojibway from Wiiwemikong, Mnidoo Minising, and is head woman for the Eastern Doorway of the Midewewin Lodge. She is a Professor Emeritus at Trent University in Peterborough, Ontario. Edna is well-known nationally as a Traditional teacher, ceremonialist, drum keeper, and grandmother. She has been instrumental in the reintroduction of Traditional teachings and ceremonies and is an active researcher of Traditional medicines. Edna is the founder of the annual Indigenous women's symposium at Trent. It was through her vision that Indigenous Studies and Trent started Nozhem Theatre: First Peoples Performance Space, which is developing an international reputation in Indigenous theatre and dance performance.

Molly McGlennen was born and raised in Minneapolis, Minnesota, and is of Anishinaabe and European descent. Currently, she is an Assistant Professor of English and Native American Studies at Vassar College. She holds a Ph.D. in Native American Studies from the University of California, Davis and an M.F.A. in Creative Writing from Mills College. Her scholarship and creative writing have been widely published in journals and anthologies. Most recently, her first collection of poetry, *Fried Fish and Flour Biscuits,* was released by Salt's award-winning Earthworks Series.

Cary Miller is a descendent of the St. Croix and Leech Lake Bands and is an Associate Professor in the History Department at the University of Wisconsin–Milwaukee. Her research interests include Anishinaabe history and culture, Native American women's history, and Indigenous forms of leadership. Her articles have appeared in *American Indian Quarterly*, and her book *Ogimaag:* Anishinaabeg Leadership, 1760–1845, was published in 2010.

Dylan A. T. Miner (Michif) is an artist, activist, historian, and curator. Miner holds a Ph.D. in art history from the University of New Mexico. He has published and lectured extensively, with two forthcoming books on art and indigenous politics. To date, he has published more than forty journal articles, book chapters, review essays, and encyclopedia entries. In 2010, he was an Artist Leadership Fellow at the National Museum of the American Indian (Smithsonian) for his project *Anishinaabensag Biimskowebshkigewag (Native Kids Ride Bikes)*. Since then, he has hung a dozen solo exhibitions in the Americas and Europe. As a founding member of the artists' collective Justseeds, he was awarded the Grand Prix at the 28th Biennial of Graphic Arts in Slovenia, and installed a solo Justseeds exhibition at the 29th Biennial. Recently, he had a solo exhibition in Norway, collaborating with the Sami people, as well as another at an artist-run centre in Ottawa. He has also toured Australia, exhibiting his work and lecturing, as part of an Indigenous cultural delegation to Queensland. Currently, Miner teaches in the Residential College in the Arts and Humanities at Michigan State University and coordinates the Michigan Native Arts Initiative.

Melissa K. Nelson is Anishinaabeg/Métis/Norwegian, a citizen of the Anishinaabeg Nation (Turtle Mountain Band of Chippewa Indians). She is an Associate Professor of American Indian Studies at San Francisco State University and the president of the Cultural Conservancy, an indigenous-rights Native organization. She is the editor of *Original Instructions: Indigenous Teachings for a Sustainable Future* (2008), and producer of the award-winning documentary short film *The Salt Song Trail: Bringing Creation Back Together* (2005).

Margaret Noori/Giiwedinoodin (Anishinaabe heritage, waabzheshiinh doodem) received an M.F.A. in Creative Writing and a Ph.D. in English and Linguistics from the University of Minnesota. She is Director of the Comprehensive Studies Program and teaches American Indian Literature at the University of Michigan. Her work focuses on the recovery and maintenance of Anishinaabe language and literature. Current research includes language proficiency and assessment, and the study of Indigenous literary aesthetics. To see and hear current projects, visit www.ojibwe.net, where she and her colleague, Howard Kimewon, have created a space for language shared by academics and the Native community.

Thomas Peacock (Fond du Lac Band of Lake Superior Ojibwe) is an Associate Professor of educational leadership at Winona State University and of counseling psychology at Troy University Tampa Bay (Florida). His M.Ed. and Ed.D. are from Harvard University. He has authored or coauthored seven books on Ojibwe history, Native education, and racism, including *A Forever Story, Collected Wisdom, The Seventh Generation, The Good Path, The Four Hills of Life, Ojibwe Waasa Inaabida: We Look in All Directions,* and *To Be Free.* He is currently working on a book on hope.

Julie Pelletier is Chair and Associate Professor of the Department of Indigenous Studies, and Director of the CN Indigenous Resource Centre at the University of Winnipeg. She is a descendant of the Wesget Sipu Fish River Tribe of northern Maine. Julie earned her Ph.D. and M.A. in Cultural Anthropology at Michigan State University and was the first graduate student at MSU whose doctoral research was funded by a tribe, the Sault Ste. Marie Tribe of Chippewa Indians. She has conducted fieldwork in the Upper Peninsula of Michigan with the Anishinaabeg, and in Aotearoa/New Zealand, with the Maori. Her research interests include decolonization, identity issues, representation, and ritualization. Most recently her research has focused on American Indian casino gaming as site of contestation.

Brock Pitawanakwat (Anishinaabe, Whitefish River First Nation) researches the intergenerational legacy of Indian Residential Schools on Indigenous childcare, ecologies, economies, education systems, and languages for the Truth and Reconciliation Commission of Canada (TRC). He is a recent graduate of the University of Victoria's Indigenous Governance Program, with a dissertation that explores how and why Anishinaabeg maintain and revitalize their ancestral language of Anishinaabemowin. Brock's chapter contribution does not represent the views of the Truth and Reconciliation Commission.

Keith Richotte Jr. is an enrolled member of the Turtle Mountain Band of Chippewa Indians and an Associate Justice on the Turtle Mountain Court of Appeals. Richotte is also an Assistant Professor at the University of North Dakota School of Law and is currently serving as a postdoctoral fellow at the University of North Carolina. Richotte earned his J.D. from the University of Minnesota Law School in 2004, his LL.M. from the University of Arizona College of Law in 2007, and his Ph.D. from the University of Minnesota in 2009.

Leanne Betasamosake Simpson is a writer, activist, storyteller, and scholar. She is a citizen of Kina Gchi Nishnaabeg-ogaming and is a member of Alderville First Nation. Leanne holds a Ph.D. from the University of Manitoba and has published three edited volumes, including *Lighting the Eighth Fire: The Liberation, Resurgence and Protection of Indigenous Nations* (2008) and *This is an Honour Song: Twenty Years since the Barricades* (with Kiera Ladner, 2010). Her third book, *Dancing on Our Turtle's Back: Stories of Nishnaabeg Re-Creation, Resurgence and a New Emergence* was published in May 2011 and turns to Nishnaabeg theory and philosophy for guidance in building and maintaining resurgence movements. During her career, Leanne has published over thirty scholarly articles, and has written fiction and nonfiction pieces for *Now* magazine, *Spirit* magazine, the *Globe and Mail, Anishinabek News,* the *Link,* and *Canadian Art Magazine.* Leanne is also an oral storyteller and language-learner. She lives in Nogojiwanong, the inspiration for much of her work, where she homeschools her two children.

Niigaanwewidam James Sinclair is Anishinaabe and originally from St. Peter's (Little Peguis) Indian Reserve. He is an Assistant Professor in the Department of Native Studies at the University of Manitoba, where he researches, writes, and instructs in the fields of Anishinaabeg narrative, narrative theory, and Indigenous Studies. In 2009, he coedited (with Renate Eigenbrod) a double issue of the *Canadian Journal of Native Studies* (29.1–2) focusing on "Responsible, Ethical, and Indigenous-Centred Literary Criticisms of Indigenous Literatures," and was a featured author in *The Exile Book of Native Canadian Fiction and Drama,* edited by Daniel David Moses (2011). He is also the coeditor (with Warren Cariou) of *Manitowapow: Aboriginal Writings from the Land of Water,* an anthology of Manitoba Aboriginal writing over three centuries (2012).

Heidi Kiiwetinepinesiik Stark (Turtle Mountain Ojibwe) is an Assistant Professor of Political Science at the University of Victoria. She received her Ph.D. in American Studies from the University of Minnesota, Twin Cities, in 2008. Her doctoral research focused on Anishinaabe treaty-making with the United States and Canada. Her primary area of research and teaching is in the field of Indigenous comparative politics, Native diplomacy and treaty, and Aboriginal rights. She is the coauthor of the third edition of *American Indian Politics and the American Political System* (2010) with David E. Wilkins.

David Stirrup is a Senior Lecturer in American Literature at the University of Kent (UK), where he is also Director of the Centre for American Studies. He works on Native North American literatures, Indigenous and postcolonial theory, and contemporary U.S. and Canadian literature more broadly. His publications to date include *Louise Erdrich* (2010) and essays on a range of nineteenth, twentieth, and twenty-first century Native North American writers, installation art, and indigeneity at the Canada-U.S. border, and Indigenous rights discourse and the European Far Right. He is currently working on a monograph project on ethics and aesthetics in contemporary Anishinaabeg writing.

Gerald Vizenor is Distinguished Professor of American Studies at the University of New Mexico, and Professor Emeritus at the University of California, Berkeley. He has published more than thirty books. *Native Liberty: Natural Reason and Cultural Survivance, Survivance: Narratives of Native Presence, Native Storiers, Father Meme, Fugitive Poses: Native American Indian Scenes of Absence and Presence, Hiroshima Bugi: Atomu 57,* and *Shrouds of White Earth* are his most recent books. Vizenor has received an American Book Award for *Griever: An American Monkey King in China,* the Western Literature Association Distinguished Achievement Award, and the Lifetime Literary Achievement Award from the Native Writer's Circle of the Americas. He is the series editor with Diane Glancy of *Native Storiers: A Series of American Narratives* at the University of Nebraska Press. He is also series editor with Deborah Madsen of *Native Traces* at the State University of New York Press.

Kathleen Delores Westcott was born in 1946 into the Turtle Clan of the Anishinaabe people and is enrolled at the White Earth Reservation, Mississippi Band. She is Anishinaabe/Cree and French Canadian on her mother's side, and Scotch-Irish on her father's side. She received a master's degree in art therapy from the University of Wisconsin, Superior. She describes her occupation as healer, teacher, and creator of handwork. Kathleen lives in Brimson, Minnesota, on several acres of heavily logged boreal forest. Her vision is to restore this land, thus providing for the return of plants that have played a key role in maintaining physical, mental, and spiritual health among the Anishinaabe people for many generations. Kathleen's two children have given her two grandchildren, one of whom resides with her.

Proceeds from the sale of this collection have been donated to The Enweyang ("Our Voice") Language Nest, an Ojibwe language immersion lab school housed at the University of Minnesota Duluth. All subjects are taught using the Ojibwe language in an environment that is supportive of Indigenous culture, perspective, and learning traditions. Young children and teacher candidates are mentored by master speaker/teachers throughout the instructional day. The program strives to create both speakers and teachers for the future.

A language nest program requires the creation of curriculum and resources to support the rich linguistic and cultural environment. Storytelling is a favorite activity, and traditional Indigenous stories are used as a means of preserving culture. An Ojibwe language literacy project is just one of the important initiatives that proceeds from this anthology will be used to support.

More information about the Enweyang Language Nest may be found at http://www.d.umn.edu/enigikendaasoyang/enweyang/index.html.